REAL ESTATE OFFICE MANAGEMENT

Third Edition

Real Estate Brokerage
Managers Council

Real Estate
Education Company
a division of Dearborn Financial Publishing, Inc.

This publication is designed to provide accurate and authoritative information in regard to the subject matter covered. It is sold with the understanding that the publisher is not engaged in rendering legal, accounting or other professional service. If legal advice or other expert assistance is required, the services of a competent professional person should be sought.

Acquisitions Editor: Christine E. Litavsky
Managing Editor: Jack Kiburz
Interior Design: Lucy Jenkins
Cover Design: Rattray Design

Published by Real Estate Education Company®,
a division of Dearborn Financial Publishing, Inc.®

Printed in the United States of America

96 97 98 10 9 8 7 6 5 4 3 2 1

Library of Congress Cataloging-in-Publication Data

Real estate office management / Real Estate Brokerage Managers
    Council. — 3rd ed.
        p.   cm.
    Includes bibliographical references and index.
    ISBN 0-7931-1530-2
        1. Real estate business—Management.   2. Office management.
    I. Real Estate Brokerage Managers Council (Chicago, Ill.)
    HD1375.R3928   1996   96-8781
    333.33'068—dc20   CIP

Real Estate Education Company books are available at special quantity discounts to use as premiums and sales promotions, or for use in corporate training programs. For more information, please call the Special Sales Manager at 800-621-9621, ext. 4384, or write to Dearborn Financial Publishing, Inc., 155 N. Wacker Drive, Chicago, IL 60606-1719.

Contents

Acknowledgments

Back in the early 1970s, the office administration courses of the REALTORS National Marketing Institute® achieved prominence in the field of management education for REALTORS®. As the number of brokers attending the courses increased, it became apparent that a book was needed to assist students in their studies and to aid brokers in managing their real estate businesses successfully.

Real Estate Office Management: People, Functions, Systems was originally planned by the Editorial Book Development Subcommittee of RNMI under the chairmanship of REALTOR® Albert J. Mayer III, CRB, CRS, GRI, RM, who served as technical adviser. The book rolled off the press for the first time in 1975.

The structure of RNMI has changed since those days. The Institute is no longer a single entity, but is comprised of two distinct Councils: the Real Estate Brokerage Managers Council™ and the Residential Sales Council™. The primary function of these councils is to provide real estate education for industry members. As such, each council offers its own educational designation to its members who meet the respective council's professional and course-related requirements. The Managers Council awards the Certified Real Estate Brokerage Manager (CRB) designation and the RS Council awards the Certified Residential Specialist (CRS) designation.

Real Estate Office Management is now in its third edition and is published by the Managers Council as part of its commitment to educating real estate brokerage managers. The Council offers a variety of other books and products as well, including educational programs on audiotape and videotape.

Many RNMI members and office administration course instructors shared their knowledge and expertise to produce the original version of *Real Estate Office Management*. Their names are listed here with grateful acknowledgment for their time and effort.

Contributors

Edward J. Boleman
F. C. Tucker Company
Indianapolis, Indiana

Fred E. Case
University of California
Los Angeles, California

Joseph B. Carnahan
Paul-White-Carnahan
Realty Co., Inc.
Mission Hills, California

Arthur R. Close
Portland, Oregon

Richard M. Caruso
Rich Port REALTOR®
LaGrange, Illinois

H. Harland Crowell
Crowell & Co., Inc.
McLean, Virginia

Carl Deremo
Real Estate One, Inc.
Farmington, Michigan

Albert J. Mayer, III
Theodore Mayer & Bro.,
REALTOR®
Cincinnati, Ohio

David B. Doeleman
Gibson Bowles, Inc., REALTORS®
Portland, Oregon

Bruce T. Mulhearn
Bruce Mulhearn, Inc.
Bellflower, California

William M. Ellis
Shannon & Luchs Company
McLean, Virginia

Ross C. Munro
React Realty
Cherry Hills, New Jersey

Richard C. Farrer
Hayward Realty Investment Co.
Hayward, California

Robert H. Murray, Jr.
Schindler-Cummins
Houston, Texas

Gary Fugere
Real Estate 10, Inc., REALTORS®
Minneapolis, Minnesota

George A. Nash
Bermel-Smaby, REALTORS®
Burnsville, Minnesota

Art Godi
Art Godi Associates
Stockton, California

William D. North
Kirkland & Ellis
Chicago, Illinois

Larry E. Greiner
University of Southern California
Los Angeles, California

Roger Pettiford
Columbia Realty Co.
Colorado Springs, Colorado

Joseph F. Hanauer
Thorsen, REALTORS®
Oak Brook, Illinois

Henry S. Harrison
Harrison-Durocher Incorporated
New Haven, Connecticut

Darrel Johnson
Real Estate 10 Inc., REALTORS®
Minneapolis, Minnesota

Earl J. Keim, Jr.
Earl Keim Realty
Dearborn, Michigan

Joseph P. Klock
The Klock Co.
Miami, Florida

Henry A. Leist
Henry A. Leist, Inc.
Cincinnati, Ohio

Bernard J. MacElhenny, Jr.
MacElhenny, Levy & Co., Inc.
Santa Barbara, California

Ronald A. Schmaedick
Rams Realty Inc.
Eugene, Oregon

Warren H. Schmidt
University of California
Los Angeles, California

Norman B. Sigband
University of Southern California
Los Angeles, California

Edward L. Sowards
Sowards Inc.
Rockford, Illinois

Rich Port
Rich Port, REALTOR®
La Grange, Illinois

Barry G. Posner
University of Massachusetts
Amherst, Massachusetts

Ralph W. Pritchard, Jr.
Thorsen, REALTORS®
Oak Brook, Illinois

Kenneth J. Reyhons
Ken Reyhons, REALTORS®
Colorado Springs, Colorado

Clifford A. Robedeaux
Robedeaux, Inc.
Milwaukee, Wisconsin

Don C. Roberts
Don C. Roberts, Inc.
Whittier, California

Richard Ryan
Shannon & Luchs Company
McLean, Virginia

John W. Steffey
Chas. H. Steffey, Inc.
Baltimore, Maryland

Wayne R. Weld
Indian Hills Realty
Columbus, Ohio

Leonard L. Westdale
Westdale Company
Holland, Michigan

Florence Willess
Ebby Halliday
Dallas, Texas

Original Reviewers

Joseph B. Carnahan
Paul-White-Carnahan
Realty Co., Inc.
Mission Hills, California

Albert J. Mayer, III
Theodore Mayer & Bro.,
REALTORS®
Cincinnati, Ohio

William M. Ellis
Shannon & Luchs
McLean, Virginia

Ralph A. Pritchard
Thorsen, REALTORS®
Oak Brook, Illinois

Lydia Franz
Century 21-Country Squire,
REALTORS®
Barrington, Illinois

Clifford A. Robedeaux
Robedeaux, Inc.
Milwaukee, Wisconsin

Joseph F. Hanauer
Thorsen, REALTORS®
Oak Brook, Illinois

RNMI members who reviewed single chapters of the book include Robert A. Doyle, Amery Dunn, Helen Hirt, Dorothy J. Peterson and George R. Winters.

Reviewers for 2nd Edition

Drexanne Evers, CRB
Drexsells Real Estate
Clarksville, Ohio

Neil D. Lyon, CRB, GRl
Hunneman & Company
Boston, Massachusetts

John W. Lane, CRB, CRS, GRI
Spectrum Marketing Group of
America, Inc.
St. Charles, Illinois

Albert J. Mayer, III
CRB, CRS, GRI, RM
Theodore Mayer & Bro.,
REALTOR®
Cincinnati, Ohio

Henry A. Leist,
CRB, CRS, GRI
Henry A. Leist, Inc.
Cincinnati, Ohio

Ronald P. Noyes, CRB, GRl
Ron Noyes and Assoc.
Swarthmore, Pennsylvania

Contributing Reviewers for the 3rd Edition

Alan Bigelow, CRB, CRS
Baird and Warner
Chicago, Illinois

Tom Martin, CRB, CRS
Tom Martin and Associates
Greensboro, Georgia

Drexanne Evers, CRB
Drexsells Real Estate
Clarksville, Ohio

Ron Schmaedick, CRB
Realty Executives
Eugene, Oregon

Harold Kahn, CRB, CRS
Kahn REALTORS®, Inc.
Newburgh, New York

Bonnie Sparks, CRB, CRS
Ruhl & Ruhl, Inc.
REALTORS®
Bettendorf, Iowa

Foreword

I am overwhelmed and very excited by this latest revision of *Real Estate Office Management: People, Functions, Systems*. The management of people and all the responsibilities that come with it have changed dramatically over the past several years. Whereas the manager used to be responsible for planning and budgeting, as a leader today the manager is responsible for setting the direction of the organization. The manager was responsible for organizing and staffing, and today must align people to move efficiently and effectively in the established direction. Controlling and problem solving are overwhelming today. The manager can't be everywhere. *Motivation* and *empowerment* are now the operative words enabling people to make their own decisions.

Today's brokerage manager-leader is faced with unprecedented challenges in a continual whirlwind of change. The manager-leader needs to "future-think," to anticipate, to prepare and to empower. This text provides a basis for the manager to do just that. Chapter after chapter complements the updated Real Estate Brokerage Managers Council CRB Management Series courses. The text does not by any means replace the courses, but focuses on the same four basics of effective management: planning, capital (financial management), marketing and people.

Each chapter is filled with contemporary theories and practical real estate business applications from some of the best real estate minds in the country, each of whom gave their time and talents to assist you in leading a competitive brokerage firm to the greatest success.

You may be overwhelmed by the rapid changes in the real estate industry as evidenced between the covers of this book. But you will also be challenged by the suggestions herein and excited by the creative possibilities. This book will give today's manager-leader a sound basis for achieving the ultimate goal of being an outstanding real estate brokerage leader.

—Bonnie Sparks, CRB, CRS
Contributing Editor
Ruhl & Ruhl Inc. REALTORS®

Chapter 1

Dimensions of Management:

The 7-S Model

Knowledge and understanding of the principles and background of any field are basic to effective functioning within that field. Management is an area in general; real estate office management is a field in particular. Managers of all types of organizations, ranging from government to business to the military, perform essentially the same functions. Successful managers have two different sets of knowledge and understanding. They know management and they know the business that they are managing.

Just as selling real estate requires a knowledge of the principles of selling, so does managing a real estate business require an understanding of the essentials of managing an organization. This chapter introduces the 7-S model of organizational management. This model provides a valuable framework for organizational analysis and decision making for all types and sizes of organizations. As we discuss the elements of managing a real estate business throughout this book, we will examine how the 7-S model can be applied.

TRADITIONAL MANAGEMENT THEORIES

Few real estate managers have been trained specifically for positions in management. Most likely they rose to their present management position by being especially good specialists in sales. Now they must manage the activities of others. Management requires very different kinds of sensitivities, judgments and skills. Often managers look to the literature on management theory for strategies and techniques to help them be more effective in providing leadership to their organization. Although management theory does not provide answers, it can provide a framework for understanding and a systematic guide for action.

Four traditional theories of management are:

1. *Bureaucratic process:* This is the traditional school of management that is concerned primarily with the structure and functioning of the formal organization.
2. *Behavioral:* This school is concerned with the essentially human character of the business organization. Its focus includes motivation, perception, learning, personality, group dynamics, leadership, satisfaction, morale and organizational change.
3. *Quantitative:* The primary emphasis of this school is on the development of structured decision making and control models using mathematical models and processes.
4. *Systems:* According to this school, the organization is a highly complex system in which management acts as the force that integrates, coordinates and directs the enterprise toward the achievement of organizational objectives.

Each of these theories is based on the concept that one aspect of management is the most important one to focus on, whether it is the organization's strategic objectives, its formal organizational structure or the behavior of the people who get the work done.

WHERE THE 7-S MODEL CAME FROM

In early 1977, the business consulting firm of McKinsey & Company began to question this concept. The firm began to realize that changing the structure of an organization was only a small part of the total problem of management effectiveness. It was clear that much more goes on in restructuring a business than can be accomplished by merely changing the boxes and dotted lines on an organization chart.

Looking at the relationship between an organization's strategy and its structure added a useful dimension to management thinking, but it was still not enough. The crucial problems in strategy most often were those of execution and adaptation—getting the job done and staying flexible, goals that involve people as well as structure. But the techniques of the behavioral sciences that focused on the human character of the business organization— motivation, perception, learning, personality, group dynamics, leadership, satisfaction and morale—were also not enough.

McKinsey assembled a team to review the firm's thinking on organizational effectiveness. Leading the project were management gurus Tom Peters and Robert Waterman, authors of the 1982 management classic *In Search of Excellence.*

When McKinsey's researchers interviewed senior executives in the top performing companies, they found that:

> They were concerned that the inherent limitations of structural approaches could render their companies insensitive to an unstable business environment marked by rapidly changing threats and opportunities from every quarter. . . . Their organizations, they said, had to learn how to build capabilities for rapid and flexible response. Their favored tactic was to choose a temporary focus, facing perhaps one major issue this year and another next year or the year after. Yet at the same time, they were acutely aware of their peoples' need for a stable, unifying value system—a foundation for long-term continuity. Their task, as they saw it, was largely one of preserving internal stability while adroitly guiding the organization's response to fast-paced external change.[1]

In other words, McKinsey found that in a fast-paced and unstable business environment innovative companies must not only be good at producing a superior product. They must also be skillful at continually responding to changes in their environment. They have a bias toward action, they value and support initiative and improvisation, and they encourage questioning and creativity rather than blind obedience on the part of their staff.

As a result of its research, McKinsey formulated the 7-S framework for organizational thought. This model recognizes the complexity of organizations by encompassing seven interdependent variables: structure, strategy, systems, style, skills, staff and shared values. It is the relationship between all of these variables that influences an organization's ability to change. It is difficult, if not impossible, to make significant progress in one area without making progress in the others as well.[2]

According to Peters and Waterman, the 7-S framework helps to force explicit thought about not only the "hardware"—strategy and structure—but also about the "software" of organization—style, systems, staff, skills and shared values. It says, in effect, that the things managers used to dismiss as intuitive, irrational and informal—people, style, values—can and must be managed. They have as much to do with how things work (or don't work) in a company as the formal structures and strategies do.[3]

The most brilliant strategies and tactics are of little use if the organization does not support or cannot execute them. The 7-S model can be used to assess how organizations align behind specific strategies. *Alignment* is defined as the proper positioning in relation to each other. The organization's people and processes must be in alignment with its strategy. For example, if your market strategy has always been to focus on a particular target market and you change your strategy to include other markets, this is likely to affect your staffing needs, organizational skills and the systems you employ.

The 7-S model also provides a useful tool to evaluate possible causes of problems in an organization. For example, if two agents are fighting over leads, the manager, believing they have a personality conflict, might reprimand them and tell them to behave like adults. But using the 7-S model could cause the manager to consider the referral system as a possible source of the problem. Perhaps the referral system is unfair and should be revised. If you don't correctly identify the cause of the problem, your "solution" won't solve it. The 7-S model helps managers think through all aspects of an issue they are facing or a change they are considering making.

Figure 1.1 depicts the 7-S model graphically. The shape of the diagram is important. It suggests at least four things:

1. A multiplicity of factors influence an organization's ability to change.
2. The variables are interconnected. It is difficult, if not impossible, to make significant progress in one area without making progress in the others as well. Similarly, if there is anything wrong in one of these areas, it will affect the entire organization.
3. The corollary to number two is that to successfully execute a change in one area requires that attention be paid to the other S's. For example, inadequate systems or staff can stymie the best-laid plans for clobbering competitors.
4. There is no starting point or implied hierarchy among the seven factors. Even though shared values is in the center, it is no more important than any of the other factors. It takes all seven to have a well-functioning organization. And any of them may be the driving force in changing a particular organization at a particular time.[4]

In the remainder of this chapter we'll examine each of the variables of the 7-S model.

STRUCTURE

Most organizational discussions begin with structure. There is both a formal and an informal structure within a firm. The formal structure is reflected in the organization chart showing who reports to whom. However, there are also informal relationships within the organization. The sales associates report to the sales manager is an example of a formal reporting structure. The training manager reports to the owner but works closely with the sales managers is an example of an informal structural relationship.

Structure also deals with how tasks are divided and coordinated. Are they centralized or decentralized, specialized or integrated?

An important key to structure is the organization chart. Small real estate firms typically are highly centralized. There may be no need for an organization chart, as all lines lead to the owner or manager. Carefully written job descriptions may be sufficient as long as staff know to whom they should look for information and guidance.

**FIGURE 1.1   The McKinsey 7-S Framework© for
                Organization Analysis**

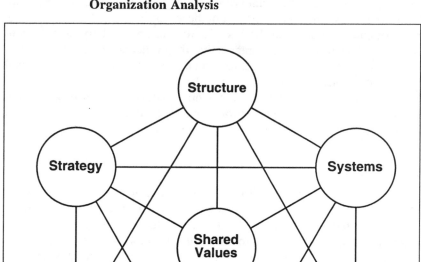

A larger real estate firm, particularly one with branch offices, will have a more decentralized organization chart, with the managers of the branch offices reporting directly to the firm's president. Finally, a large diversified firm is likely to be organized functionally, with specialized departments handling such functions as sales, accounting, insurance and property management. Residential sales offices would then report to a sales manager who is a senior officer reporting directly to top management. The organizational structure of a real estate firm is discussed in greater detail in Chapter 4.

You need a structure that is flexible and that keeps people in mind. As Fletcher Byrom, chairman and chief executive of Koppers, put it: "I think an inflexible organization chart which assumes that anyone in a given position will perform exactly the same way his predecessor did is ridiculous. He won't. Therefore, the organization ought to shift and adjust and adapt to the fact that there's a new person in the spot."[5]

Structure is related to the S's of staff and style. Many management layers may encourage bureaucracy rather than independence. Moreover, if people are tightly categorized into certain job functions, cross-functional teamwork is discouraged.

The challenge of structure is not in how to design the perfect structure. Rather, it is about the organization's ability to use structural change to respond to changes in the external environment.

STRATEGY

Strategy is a coherent set of actions aimed at gaining a sustainable advantage in the marketplace. Strategy deals with the external environment—customers and competitors. Its goal is to achieve dominance in its marketplace, for example, by providing customers with better service or by becoming the technology leader in that market area. Strategy is how the organization creates unique value.

Firms can have different types of strategies, such as a financial strategy, a marketing strategy or a recruiting strategy. For example, a company's goal might be to recruit wives of doctors as salespeople because it is not reaching that target market. The company would develop a specific strategy for whom it wants to recruit and how it will go about doing so. If the company wants to increase its inventory of new construction, it might have a strategy for prospecting for and winning over homebuilders.

Some experts think that 90 percent of all strategies don't work because managers fail to consider the implications for all elements of the organization when they attempt to implement a new strategy. The organization must be aligned around the strategy. Do the reward systems, recruiting practices, values and skills of the firm support the strategy? The strategy must be communicated to the firm's staff. New standards of performance must be established. Reward and recognition systems must support the strategy, and desired behavior should be recognized. In short, it is necessary to manage the intangibles of style, values, culture and so on. They must be turned into tangibles—numbers, trends, graphs—and concrete measures of progress must be established.

SYSTEMS

Systems are the processes and workflows, both formal and informal, that determine how things get done from day to day. These include budgeting systems, accounting procedures, compensation systems, training systems and communication systems.

If there is a dominant variable in the 7-S model, say Peters and Waterman, it could well be systems. To understand how an organization really does (or doesn't) get things done, look at its systems. To change an organization without disruptive restructuring, they advise, try changing the systems.[6] Systems may sound dull, but their impact is felt throughout the organization, particularly if there is a problem. One real estate firm found this out when it implemented a new computerized billing system on its computer. Under the firm's compensation system, its salespeople are charged back for different things, depending on their compensation plan. Each month, the salespeople receive a billing from the accounting department. But with the new billing system, some of these chargebacks weren't correct. Suddenly the sales staff was upset. There were problems with shared values and with strategy. Management style can also come into play if the manager doesn't have an appropriate style to handle the problem. Everything is interrelated. Superior systems are needed in order to avoid those kinds of problems.

Key systems must support the organization's business strategy. Peters gives the example of a manufacturing company whose stated goal was to make its firm more market oriented. But in the company's planning meetings, very little time was spent on issues having to do with customers, marketing, market share or other issues having to do with market orientation. Without a change in this key system, this goal will remain unattainable.

If the company has a goal of fostering teamwork, all of its systems should support that goal. A compensation system in which individual commission split plans are negotiated for top performers would be extremely detrimental to a team building effort. Under such a plan, salespeople are motivated by their personal productivity and have no reason to be concerned with the success or failure of colleagues. On the other hand, a profit-sharing plan would help to strengthen team efforts by encouraging everyone to take an active financial interest in the firm.

Training systems should also foster teamwork. Sales associates could be rewarded for helping to train each other. A mentoring program fosters teamwork by bringing together the experienced team members with members who have less experience, further ensuring that all salespeople interact and work together for a common goal.

Recruiting systems should focus on recruiting sales associates who are team-oriented. A referral system that rewards agents for successfully recruiting other agents would help to better align recruiting efforts with team building.

If the company's systems don't support its strategies, they need to be changed to be brought into alignment.

STYLE

Style is the way management behaves, thereby indicating what it considers important. "It is important to distinguish between the basic personality of a top-management team and the way the team comes across to the organization," says Peters. "Organizations may listen to what managers say, but they believe what managers do. Not words, but patterns of action are decisive. The power of style, then, is essentially manageable."[7]

A manager may tell salespeople that they are very important to the firm. But is the door open so the salespeople can talk with management any time there is a problem or is the manager only available one afternoon a month? What message is really being given to the salespeople?

One element of a manager's style is how he or she chooses to spend time. What a manager devotes his or her attention to can reinforce the company's message and nudge people's thinking in a desired direction. Another aspect of style is symbolic behavior. By constantly talking about and advancing what it thinks is important, management can change the orientation of the organization.

Management style is the key to creating a learning environment that encourages and supports ongoing learning. In a learning organization, management pushes decision making down, fosters open communication, rewards innovation and does not punish risk taking. Management style can empower people.

A manager's style should not be rigid. Because staff at different stages of development require a different level of support and direction, effective managers learn to be flexible in their style, adapting it to meet each individual's specific needs. Here is an example of how two managers with very different styles might deal with the same problem.

> Frank has been with the company for five years and has had a slow but steady increase in productivity. Frank's goal for the year is $2 million in sales, or approximately 5 sales per quarter at $100,000 each. The first quarter went poorly. Frank sold only two homes for $75,000 each. He has developed a bad attitude. Now it's time for his quarterly review meeting.

These managers each take a different approach based on their style.

> Alice takes Frank out to lunch and says: "Your sales are down slightly this quarter, but I have confidence that you will be able to make this up over the remainder of the year. If you're having any personal or business problems, feel free to drop in."

Alice has a "Country Club Management" style which reflects a low concern for productivity and a high concern for people. She focuses on meeting subordinates' personal and social needs. She concentrated on making Frank feel good about her and about himself, but barely mentioned the productivity issue.

Charlie invites Frank into his office and says: "You did not reach your first-quarter goals. In order to catch up, you will need to sell eight houses this quarter, take _x_ listings, conduct _x_ open houses, and make _x_ cold calls.

"You will need to come in early and work late, because the more hours you put in, the better your chances of meeting the goal. I'm glad we had this discussion. I believe we will be able to rectify this situation."

Charlie's style is called "Authority/Obedience Management" because it reflects a high concern for productivity and a low concern for people. Charlie is a strong taskmaster, highly controlling and intolerant of people who don't produce. He wants results, believes he knows the best way to get them and wants people to do as they are told. There was nothing personal in Charlie's approach; he simply dictated what Frank must do next.

A manager with a more participative, empowering style would acknowledge that Frank has had a bad quarter and work with him to find solutions for improvement. This approach is more likely to be effective with an experienced salesperson like Frank. Managerial style is discussed in more detail in Chapter 2.

Style is not confined to management. It flows through an organization and is reflected in its culture. Peters believes that an organization's culture has a lot to do with its performance. He gives the example of a company that was considering a certain business opportunity. The opportunity was a winner from a strategic standpoint, but two years after making the acquisition, the company backed out at a loss. The acquisition failed because it wasn't consistent with the parent company's established corporate culture. Consequently, the will to make it work was absent.

Strategic moves frequently are frustrated by cultural constraints. This is most evident in mergers. No matter how closely related their businesses are, the two companies that are merging will do almost everything differently. The two cultures must be integrated for the merger to succeed, but this is not an easy task. It's necessary to make changes slowly. To uproot tradition too quickly can create morale problems and cause salespeople to leave, taking with them the vital skills that were the reason for the merger in the first place.

STAFF

The 7-S of *staff* refers to the people in the firm; the company demographics. Demographics includes such things as the ratio of men to women in the firm, the average age of salespeople, their experience level (the number of experienced agents versus new recruits), the level of diversity, the ratio of superstars to solid performers to low producers. A company's demographics affects how well people work together. For example, a successful real estate firm in a major city consists of a middle-aged male manager who has 24 saleswomen working for him. Most of these women are also middle-aged and have been in the business for many years. If this manager were to hire a 23-year-old male who is new to real estate sales, it's not difficult to imagine the havoc that might result.

Again, hiring a recruit based solely on that person's productivity potential could be disastrous if the recruit doesn't fit into the firm's culture. A salesperson who prefers to work independently is less likely to fit in an organization that values teamwork than someone who gets satisfaction from building teams and motivating other people. In such an environment, a top performer who insists on working solo will not be as strong an asset as an equally productive team player. Similarly, a person who thrives in a bureaucratic environment is unlikely to do well in a firm that emphasizes independence and creativity. Firms need to pay attention to their management style in recruiting sales associates and select people who will be comfortable—and productive—under that style.

The characteristics of a firm's ideal recruit should also be driven by the firm's overall objectives and strategies. If the firm's strategy is to increase its share of the high-end home market, it would target recruits who have experience in this market. If its strategy is to become a technology leader, it makes sense to hire sales associates who are comfortable using technology to increase their effectiveness.

In the 7-S framework, the element of staff is also concerned with what companies do to foster the development of their people. McKinsey's consultants observed that top-performing companies pay extraordinary attention to the socialization process in their companies. They pay particular attention to how they introduce new recruits into the organization and how they develop them and manage their careers through such support devices as assigning them mentors. They consider people "as a pool of resources to be nurtured, developed, guarded and allocated." This view makes the 7-S dimension of staff worthy of practical control by management.[8]

SKILLS

Skills are the capabilities that are possessed by the firm as a whole, as opposed to the skills of the individuals within the firm. Another term for a company's skills that will be used in this book is "core competencies." *Core competencies* are the collective learning of an organization. They are the skills a company is good at and upon which it wants to build its business. They are the skills which develop organizational capability.

A particular salesperson may be good at prospecting "for sale by owner" properties and spend all of his or her time doing that. This is an individual, not a company, skill. If selling new construction properties is a company skill, or core competency, everyone in the company is well trained regarding new construction: how to list it, how to market it and what markets to target.

A company's core competency may be serving a particular market, anticipating market changes or implementing change quickly and effectively. Some examples of core competencies in real estate are training new sales associates; marketing to first-time buyers; relocating corporate transfers; appraising large commercial properties; attracting and retaining strong salespeople.

Organizations facing major shifts in business conditions need to do more than shift strategic focus or change their structure. Frequently they need to add a new skill, or new capability. For example, when the Bell Telephone System was deregulated, the resulting companies needed to develop a marketing capability in order to survive. Managers must constantly be scanning the external environment to keep abreast of changes that will affect their businesses. Different scenarios will require different core competencies. Moreover, sometimes developing a new capability means "weeding out old skills—and their supporting systems, structures, etc.,— to ensure that important new skills can take root and grow."[9]

Real estate firms need to have at least one viable core competency to enable them to adjust to a changing market. For example, a firm that specializes in selling high-end residential property could exploit this core competency and sell high-end commercial property in case the high-end residential market dropped in the future. By leveraging its knowledge of the high-end market, the firm would remain focused on its core competency, but it would be better protected against future market shifts.

Core competencies should drive numerous business decisions and practices. For example, if your core competency is selling high-end homes, you would want to put your marketing dollars in high-end magazines. In addition, you would not want to acquire a business that specializes in low-end condos, even if it is a money-maker, because it would divert resources from the firm's core competency.

Core competencies should also drive recruiting, hiring and rewarding sales associates. For example, if a firm's core competency is building relationships that increase its referrals, the firm will seek to recruit new sales associates who have a proven ability to build ongoing relationships with customers. The company will further support this core competency by paying a higher commission split for repeat business, thereby encouraging sales associates to spend time building relationships with their customers.

To maintain a competitive advantage, companies must be able to sense shifts in the environment early, learn new skills quickly, and embrace and adapt to change. To achieve any of these a firm needs to build organizational capability.

SHARED VALUES

These are the values that the top management team wants to diffuse throughout the organization. Shared values go beyond the formal statement of corporate objectives. They are the fundamental ideas around which a business is built and help determine its direction and ultimate goals. *Shared values* are not morals or ethics, but business values, guidelines or codes that help shape behaviors and attitudes. For example, General Electric's slogan "Progress is our most important product" is a shared value that encourages the firm's engineers to tinker and innovate. The drive to accomplish these values pulls an organization together and provides stability.[10]

Here are examples of shared values in a real estate firm.

- Customer service is our #1 priority.
- We are good neighbors (community service).
- Getting along with coworkers is important.
- Making lots of money is nice, but enjoying your work is more important.
- We value superior ethical behavior.

A firm may value an interdependent structure where everyone is supportive of everyone else so that they become successful together. Or it may value independence: "I'm here to do my job; you do your job, and let's stay out of each other's way." The problem arises when one person is an independent, insisting on working alone, and everybody else was hired under an interdependent structure. The lack of shared values affects the other elements of the organization. It points to a problem with management style because the manager hired that salesperson knowing they didn't have the same values as the rest of the company. That salesperson probably isn't going to abide by the systems the firm has established or by the strategies it has adopted. There is a ripple effect throughout the organization.

Because shared values shape behavior, it is better to ensure that the company's values are helpful ones. "We avoid firing people at all costs" is not a helpful value. It may make people feel secure and feel that they can trust management, but it can send the message that people can get away with anything.

There are two kinds of values: what one says and what one does. These can conflict with one another. For example, the manager may say people are the firm's most important asset but then cancel the training budget without consulting anyone. Or the manager may state that teamwork is important and then institute a contest that rewards an individual. As actions speak louder than words, people will realize that what the manager does is representative of his or her true values. Since top management sets the tone in an organization, people will begin to share the values the manager acts on, rather than those the manager states.

CONCLUSION

Management has become an ever more complex task in today's rapidly changing business environment. In order to survive and thrive in this environment, managers must constantly reevaluate their organizations and build the capabilities for rapid and flexible response to external change. The 7-S model provides a useful framework for managers to understand the complexity of their organizations by recognizing the seven interdependent variables of structure, strategy, systems, style, skills, staff and shared values. The 7-S model can assist managers in thinking through all the aspects of any issue they face and can help them to successfully guide their organization's response to changes in the external environment.

ENDNOTES

1. Tom Peters, Julien Phillips and Robert Waterman, "Structure is Not Organization," in *Business Horizons,* June 1980, p. 16.
2. "Structure Is Not Organization," p. 17.
3. Tom Peters and Robert Waterman, *In Search of Excellence,* p. 9.
4. "Structure Is Not Organization," p. 18–19.
5. *In Search of Excellence,* p. 9
6. "Structure Is Not Organization," p. 21.
7. "Structure Is Not Organization," p. 22.
8. "Structure Is Not Organization," p. 24.
9. "Structure Is Not Organization," p. 24.
10. "Structure Is Not Organization," p. 25.

Chapter 2

Characteristics and Leadership Qualities Essential to Success

There exists neither a formula to follow nor a set of questions to ask that will assure a person's being qualified to manage a real estate business. But experience and a study of many people who have succeeded reveal some of the skills and practices essential to success in this field and some of the questions to be asked as a self-examination of one's general qualification for management.

The information in this chapter can serve as a guide to measuring people and their skills and aptitudes for management positions. It is information that can be helpful to people already in management positions, who are interested in analyzing their skills and methods and improving them; and it will interest salespeople and other staff members who want to know more about management techniques and challenges. It can help the latter group decide whether or not to work toward a management position.

This chapter also examines the elusive quality called leadership. Leadership involves not only the operation of a real estate business today but what will happen to it in the future. What today's leaders do to meet today's problems will be a factor in their survival to meet and beat tomorrow's difficulties. It's a credit to the vision and spirit of today's leaders in real estate that tomorrow's standards are being thought about and formulated now. Problems change greatly over time. The concepts of leadership are little altered over the years.

ESSENTIAL CHARACTERISTICS OF
SUCCESSFUL MANAGERS

What are the characteristics of a successful real estate broker? What traits are essential to generating the best efforts of others?

The general brokerage operation, no matter what its size, has three managerial components: corporate, office, and sales or line management. The person operating a small brokerage firm will be involved in all three; the larger the firm the more likely a manager's responsibilities will be limited to just one of the components. But large or small, certain characteristics are essential to successful management, to generating the best efforts of all subordinates. What are they?

The list of desirable characteristics will invariably include:

- Stability
- Knowledge
- Dedication
- Integrity
- Flexibility
- Ability to make decisions
- Desire
- Ability to manage oneself

People at the management level in real estate have a specific purpose: to provide the direction by which an organization functions continuously and successfully. They know how to work with and through other people to attain reasonable goals. They are able to recognize problems and know how to attack and solve them. As experienced business people, they know the positive value of making mistakes, admitting them and correcting them. These abilities enable them to achieve the purposes to which the real estate business is dedicated: service and profit for all.

Without effective management, even the best trained, most enthusiastic salespeople will fall short of their goals. Strong, continuous management is the glue that holds a business together. Good managers know that well-made plans are worthless without an enthusiastic, well-trained team to carry them out.

STABILITY

Stability of mind and purpose is essential to successful management practices. Strong managers will focus on the goal to be achieved and not allow themselves to be diverted from it by anything less than a better idea for ways to achieve the goal. In this sense, stability does not imply rigidity. There always exists the possibility of a better way of doing things. The talent to recognize and act on plausible suggestions is a mark of stability.

There are three facets to stability in management:

1. Physical
2. Emotional
3. Financial

Physical Stability

Good health is essential. Real estate business managers must be equal to the same demanding work schedule salespeople follow plus be ready to extend themselves and go that extra mile. Physical stability is an essential quality to successful leadership.

There's a saying that "when you've got your health, you've got just about everything." Whether or not this is fact, it is a fair reminder that good health is essential to doing a job well. History has examples of people who overcame health handicaps to go on to great achievements. But most people require a sturdy constitution to meet the onslaughts of the day whether they're in management or some other position.

This book is not a primer on how to stay healthy. But the mention of health as one of the essential elements of successful management is germane. Without good health, any manager will soon weaken under the stresses and strains of his or her responsibilities.

Increasingly, people are questioning the old Puritan work ethic, an ethic that wore people out by the time they reached retirement age. Today's smart managers, in fact most working Americans, are not ready to accept such oppressive work habits. They believe in and practice a balance of work and play. They seek recreation that is completely free of work relationships.

According to management guru Peter F. Drucker, "More and more of the people, especially most of the highly educated ones, can expect to work sometime during their lives as managers or as professionals in an organization and to participate actively in managerial work." ("Op-Ed," *New York Times,* May 5, 1974). He concluded that this group had increasingly become the central leadership group in our society and collectively its decision makers.

Drucker believes that because so much of managers' time and effort is devoted to their "public" (organization) life, they need a private life with wholly different concerns, different values and above all different personal ties and different friendships. They need not just a hobby but a serious outside interest in which they can excel and be recognized as accomplished performers.

Why are such pleasures necessary for management people? Precisely because they form the armor against the gossiping, the inevitable defeats and the setbacks sure to be encountered in managerial life. They provide the needed, refreshing breakaway from the pressures and responsibilities of leadership.

Emotional Stability

The manager's emotional stability needs to be at its best when those he or she supervises are in the throes of emotional turmoil. When other tempers flare, when arguments assume the tensions of a pitched battle and when "team effort" threatens to go up in a cloud of smoke, it's the manager's emotional stability that is needed to calm things down.

It's a mark of emotional stability to understand there is more than one way to attack a problem and to know how to employ the better way. It's the talent to fight the fight in the manner of a healthy debate and not let it turn into a name-calling, finger-pointing free-for-all. In another time emotional stability might have been labeled a serene spirit. Today it is called being "unflappable."

At times management is called upon to listen calmly to both sides of a heated argument. A classic example common to real estate offices is the competing claim for a sales commission between two sales associates when the situation is not covered by the operations manual.

Whatever the controversy, try to avoid making judgments. There is seldom a single, right answer to any problem. Your role as manager will be more effective if it consists of asking the right questions and leading those engaged in the controversy to find a reasonable solution.

Whether there are major or minor differences, wise handling of emotional situations will result in fewer such incidents in the future. Effective managers learn how to handle differences fairly and amicably and teach staff people to do the same. When a problem is solved on the basis of what is right rather than who is right, you've not only solved a problem, you've strengthened the organization and its people.

Busy or unheeding managers who don't make the time to listen to associates' difficulties compound problems.

Good managers make it look like they're doing nothing at all. They find time to sit down and talk to people about their problems. They do it not by dropping the matter but by making an appointment if they can't handle it at the moment.

Emotional stability is needed to bolster sagging spirits. When, for example, a salesperson fails to get the listing he or she is working on diligently or when sustained effort to make a sale fails, it's the manager's role to sit down and *listen*. Listen as that salesperson tells you what happened. Ask a few relevant questions. You don't have all the information you need. Then help analyze how he or she might have done it differently. Finally, give the salesperson the fortitude and heart to go out and give the next opportunity all he or she has got.

Emotional stability relating to the job is also needed at home. When a manager's spouse and family are relentlessly reminded of the burdens of the job, it inevitably leads to stresses and strains that have a bad effect on both business and home life. If, for example, you dwell endlessly on your office problems and ignore your spouse's frustrations, you're heading for trouble.

Marriage counselors tell us that it's *healthy* to communicate frustrations. You are, in effect, sharing your burdens with your spouse. But it's *unhealthy* to so concentrate on those burdens that they close out all other interests and diversions. Soon your spouse will resent your job, the firm and the bad effect it's having on family life.

The other side of this coin of emotional stability is the problem of coping with home difficulties so they do not have a negative effect on business life. Some people have a unique ability to seal off personal problems from business hours. In fact, there have been people who have achieved success by burying themselves in their work to escape an unpleasant home situation.

Wise managers sustain open communications with their staff so they are aware of the existence of personal problems. Helping sales associates keep things in perspective, being understanding and supportive when they're going through difficult phases, not only cements personal relationships between managers and their staff but also strengthens loyalties to the firm.

Financial Stability

Financial stability is a necessity to good management of a real estate office. It is difficult to succeed when hounded by creditors, whether for personal or company indebtedness. A poor personal credit reputation in the community can have a direct, negative bearing on the credit rating of the firm as well.

Tardiness in paying other brokers their share of commissions will quickly cripple the operation of a real estate business in the eyes of competitors. This careless practice is likely to result in losing top salespeople to a more reliable firm. It is easier to be financially stable if you apply your sense of fairness to designing a procedure that insures prompt payment.

Companies set up on a proper financial basis plan to plow back into the business a reasonable percentage of profit dollars. Financial stability demands that the manager not overspend profit dollars merely to keep salespeople happy. Many real estate office managers have given away their businesses through overspending on things like unreasonably high commissions and top-of-the-line equipment and facilities to attract or hold salespeople. This practice is self-defeating because there is nothing left to manage.

Market fluctuations in the real estate business are as inevitable as in any other field. Whatever the reason for a down market, firms that are prepared to cope with severe market slumps maintain adequate cash reserves. They can weather the vicissitudes of market downswings while other less provident firms surrender to the first wave of reverses. Unprepared firms are the first to merge, sell out or simply close down.

Salespeople respect managers who budget the finances of a company carefully. They want to know why a certain number of dollars are being spent in certain ways and how they are likely to profit from it. People are happier when working for a financially stable organization. It helps assure their personal financial security.

As an example of how sharing budget information with a staff pays off, consider the following experience of a successful, medium-sized real estate firm.

The manager shares his budget plan with his staff each year. This is done before the budget is finalized. He shares it with his salespeople so they know it's a realistic plan, based on what he expects the firm to produce. He goes over the general classifications, telling the salespeople what is planned and why. Then he asks for their opinions as to whether or not it's practical. Let's say they "buy" it (though he has remained open to their suggestions for possible revisions).

Three months later one of the salespeople comes to the manager and says, "We're not spending enough on advertising." The manager then responds, "But Julia, this is exactly what we budgeted to spend. Remember the day we went over the whole budget together? You thought then—three months ago—it would be enough."

KNOWLEDGE

No newcomers to real estate office management can possibly bring to the job all the knowledge they'll need. But what they don't bring with them they can surely get.

Three specific kinds of knowledge will be needed:

1. Knowledge of the real estate business
2. Knowledge of people
3. Knowledge of sound management practices

Plan your program to continually add to your knowledge in all three areas.

Knowledge of the Real Estate Business

This includes everything from how to get listings, write ads that attract prospects and find customers to buy the properties listed, to sales psychology and financing. While actual experience in all of these areas is not essential, it does add to the manager's credibility with sales associates. One manager of a real estate office of 46 agents in a large midwestern community had been in the business of real estate sales for two years before becoming a manager. Although coaching and managing newer associates worked well for both manager and sales associates, and recruiting new sales associates was a successful endeavor for this manager, getting the respect of the seasoned associates and achieving credibility in hiring experienced agents was definitely a difficult process.

It is essential to be knowledgeable about the community in which you do business. Information should include schools, industries, churches, parks, libraries, shopping, banking, zoning restrictions, tax rates, history, civic and cultural opportunities and socioeconomic data.

New information should be shared with staff. It is the kind of knowledge needed by the salespeople as they pursue their daily work. It's important that you be a fount of information for them. But you should carry it a step beyond that. When a manager stops teaching, that manager stops leading and can soon lose credibility. As the leader, it is your duty to show staff where to get information and how to develop their own contacts. If you do this, you'll not only help them grow, but you'll also strengthen the firm's image in the community.

Knowledge of People

You'll need to have and to keep on acquiring knowledge of people, how to motivate them and how to establish empathy with them. The people in this case are those associated with you in business as well as the customers, clients and all other people you deal with including bankers, mortgage company personnel, city officials, builders, lawyers and business, civic and cultural leaders in your community.

A manager with empathy listens to a salesperson's problem and helps him or her analyze it. But the manager remains objective and helps the salesperson find a workable solution. Salespeople are often involved with the emotions of a transaction. When a manager shares these emotions he or she is unable to give salespeople the help they really need. The manager who empathizes understands, but stops short of becoming involved emotionally. When you feel yourself getting emotionally involved in a salesperson's problem, it is a good practice to defer answering his or her call for help. Don't rush into suggesting a solution. Wait several hours (or even several days if necessary and if possible) before you make a judgment or suggest a course of action. Taking this necessary time will make it more likely you will come up with a truly objective decision.

Knowledge of Sound Management Practices

A manager also needs as much knowledge as possible on sound management practices. This includes knowing how to recruit a good sales and office staff, understanding financial systems and records, developing budgets, setting up marketing and statistical controls, developing a policy and procedures manual, planning, organizing and supervising the work toward the overall survival, growth and profit goals of the firm. Beyond such basics as knowing how to rent office space, developing a floor plan for it, equipping and furnishing it, a well-informed manager knows how to keep up to date on what's going on in the real estate profession locally and nationally.

Training and information on good real estate marketing management practices are available from a variety of sources.

Management development courses are scheduled regularly by the Real Estate Brokerage Managers Council™. Instructors are professional REALTORS® with a wealth of management knowledge and experience to share. Role-playing sessions offer training in actual real estate office problems. After-hours informal sessions enable students to talk with their peers.

Other kinds of personal development sessions are available in many communities. While they may not be programmed to fill your particular needs, you are likely to find them a profitable investment of your time. Wherever you find it, whatever form it takes, additional learning will help expand your horizons and enable you to become a better manager. Individual study is important, too.

The greatest collection of real estate books outside the Library of Congress is located in the National Association of REALTORS® library in Chicago. Any REALTOR® member may borrow from this collection at any time. A letter or phone call will elicit prompt service.

Your local public library can be a valuable source of business reference materials. Even the smallest public library has access to a wealth of material from its state library. And in heavily populated areas most public libraries are now part of a unit system offering reciprocal use of all nearby collections. If you cannot conveniently go there, your librarian can have their books sent.

Remember to build your own business library too. Encourage those on your staff to use it and to suggest titles and publications they'd like to have available. Learning of this kind soon becomes contagious and leads to profitable discussions and exchanges of ideas.

DEDICATION

Real estate is a service business where, with dedication, a manager can enjoy the satisfactions known only to people who help others solve their problems and realize their ambitions.

Managers who are dedicated to their job can find satisfaction from three sources: their own accomplishments, their staff's accomplishments and the satisfaction of the customers and/or clients they all serve.

Total dedication to the real estate business starts with being there.

In his tersely written book on management, *Up the Organization,* Robert Townsend draws the analogy between managers and playing coaches. He believes managers should be first on the field in the morning and last to leave at night. They should be ready to help their salespeople at any time. If they're not, they're not good managers in Townsend's opinion.

People who have other people reporting to them should be on hand to reassure the hesitant, give a green light at the proper moment, be calm in a time of crises and do whatever else is necessary to help the "players" advance toward their objectives.

A good manager makes being there a two-way street. Just as he or she is available for them at all hours for important action, they understand the manager may call on them on the same terms. Neither, it is understood, abuses this right.

Anything short of this, according to Townsend, and a manager's people will lose satisfaction, then interest and zeal.[1]

Dedication to the success of the business does not have to be at the sacrifice of dedication to one's family. People's work habits vary as much as their thumbprints. What takes one person only eight hours to accomplish may require an additional two or four hours of effort for another. The job may be everything to a single person, whose lifestyle can accommodate lengthy work hours. Another person, whose dedication to family comes first, may plan his or her working time to allow large blocks of time with family. A good manager will understand these differences, help each set realistic goals and respect varying work habits so long as they do not interfere with job performance.

What of managers' and salespeople's dedication to the public they serve? Certainly any marked degree of indifference to the public will soon be reflected in a downward sales curve. Missed appointments, tardy arrivals, inaccurate handling of records and details all indicate indifference. They soon result in a poor reputation for performance and loss of referrals and repeat business.

INTEGRITY

One of the most important traits salespeople observe about the manager is whether he or she has integrity.

What is integrity? "Integrity" is perhaps too solemn a word for the characteristic we're talking about. The old-fashioned phrase "all of a piece" is more like it. H. L. Mencken, who in his time was regarded as an outrageous man, was a person of unquestioned integrity. Like many other writers of great talent he was offered huge sums to do some other person's bidding. But he turned down the big money and never wrote a piece he didn't want to write. He was impervious to the seductions of wealth because he liked his life; he enjoyed what he was doing. He lived by his code of values.

People may forgive a manager's lack of some other important traits of good leadership but they will not overlook a lack of integrity. And they will fault top management for having placed such a person in a position of authority.

FLEXIBILITY

Flexibility is the fine art of maintaining a healthy balance between being firm and bending to every suggested change. When written goals are established and communicated effectively to a sales staff, a flexible manager will be willing to adapt to changing situations and make reasonable compromises when it seems sensible. This does not imply surrendering to every pressure that comes along, for to do so is to become known as a wishy-washy manager.

In describing the pace of business in the 1990s, Tom Peters quotes David Vice of Northern Telecom, "The 1990s will be a decade in a hurry, a nanosecond culture. There'll be only two kinds of managers—the quick and the dead."[2] Leaders who do not respond quickly to changing business patterns are soon left behind.

But there's a fine line between knowing what changes are taking place and participating in them. This is where a combination of knowledge and flexibility can be most productive.

Do you know the best sources or can you develop new methods for mortgage financing? Are you aware of vacant land that may be coming on the market and how that land might be developed to fit into the growth pattern in your community? Have you investigated how television might be serving your market better than print media? Have you made the acquaintance of top management people for the new factory that's being built near your town? What new marketing techniques might you develop to attract these company workers to buy your listings? If your salespeople suggest a rearrangement of the office and present it to you with logical reasons, do you sit down and discuss it with them or are you likely to reject it out of hand?

Develop friendships with the better minds in the business. A number of groups exist today that are made up of successful brokers from different markets. They are not competing with each other at their meetings. They are simply people who like to get together from time to time to exchange new ideas and techniques in the real estate marketing business.

Continuing education is an essential part of being flexible. This not only implies fact-finding knowledge but also a better understanding of behavioral sciences and decision-making skills. As these are developed, a good manager learns how to really listen and how to respond in a positive manner. He or she encourages subordinates to continue to bring in ideas even though a great many of them will prove unworkable. Differences of opinion need not be a negative part of the day's management work if a manager knows how to communicate the difference between what's right and who's right, between opinion and fact.

As managers incorporate new ideas and change into their daily thinking, they naturally begin to consider change in their own business position. The can't promote themselves until they train their successor.

Some managers shun this facet of flexibility because of a fear that the successor may do a better job! When a manager stays on in the same position year after year, stagnation of the organization is a predictable result. An important facet of flexibility is to have as many people as possible know how to perform all the duties within to the office. Encourage everyone to flex their business muscles, to try new ideas and to work in creative ways to help the organization grow.

ABILITY TO MAKE DECISIONS

People look to a manager for answers. Unless he or she can provide them, they will start looking elsewhere. Although some decisions will have to be made more quickly than the following might indicate, it is a useful guide to the mental process.

First, be sure you understand the problem and the ramifications of any solution.

Review the problem in terms of existing policy. Ask if it is similar to past problems or if it is completely new or if former solutions apply.

What would be an ideal solution? List all you can think of.

Gather all the data, get the facts and interview every person involved.

Separate fact from opinion. Weigh the information to determine what is true and can be substantiated and what is opinion. Discard the latter.

Determine the objective you want to reach. Review exactly what you want to accomplish in solving this problem. Is it simply a matter of settling an argument between salespeople or will it have ramifications throughout the entire organization?

List the possible solutions and their results. In a previous suggestion you listed all the ideal solutions. Now list only those that comply with the policy of the firm.

Determine the course of action most likely to succeed. You must now decide how you are going to present the solution to the staff. A management decision is always limited by two factors: the sophistication of the people who will carry out the decision and your ability to convince others that it is the best solution.

If you come up with a decision that is beyond the understanding or capabilities of the staff, they will not respond. Though it may have looked good on paper, it will be of no practical use

Also, if you may come up with a wonderful solution but cannot show others how it will help them, they will not respond. Therefore, you must be sure how you will convince others of the benefits involved.

Put the solution into action. Don't wait until tomorrow or next week. Implement the action today. A good manager goes through the decision-making process constantly and is never reticent to put the solution into action.

Remember that people make decisions work. Therefore, they are always considered limiting factors in whatever area, human or material, your decision may affect. You must tell the people the reasons for a particular decision. Make sure everyone understands.

Don't worry about a decision after it is made. You cannot always be right. A poor decision is usually better than no decision at all. One who never makes a decision loses the ability to lead others and therefore is not effective as a manager.

Finally, follow up on the decision. Evaluate it. If necessary, revise it. Talk to the people involved to see if the decision is solving the problem. If, in fact, it is not, then it is necessary to revise the decision.

DESIRE

Desire plays a major role in successful management. Good managers want to solve problems. They enjoy people and like to see them succeed. And they certainly want to succeed themselves.

Good managers actually seek problems that need to be solved. They relish analyzing them and working out solutions. They also enjoy sharing their knowledge. They want to teach salespeople where to find answers. And they are able to communicate it all in a direct, understandable way.

Desire can be the means of making poor salespeople great. It's what enables people to commit themselves to others and to their success. Managers know that if their staff succeeds it is a direct result of their leadership; if they do not, the failure is at the manager's doorstep and they have failed, too.

LEADERSHIP QUALITIES ESSENTIAL TO SUCCESS

In addition to the characteristics discussed so far, successful managers possess the quality we call leadership. There is no all-encompassing definition of leadership. Ask a group of people to define leadership and you'll get as many different answers as there are people. But, however you define it, there is a never-ending need for men and women who possess the skills and that special inner drive that propels them into positions of leadership.

What is this elusive, exclusive quality called leadership? There are many definitions. Whether wholly new or reflecting some change from past concepts, all are germane to the job to be done in the real estate business today.

Leadership has been called the ability of a person to influence other people to create, perform and actuate results. This is done through reasoning, integrity, compassion, understanding, credibility and confidence of direction and not through fear of change.

Batten says, in *Tough-Minded Management,* "Positive leadership, simply defined, means the kind of direction which assumes a job can be done, the problem solved and the negative attitudes overcome until proven otherwise."[3]

The authors of *Leadership and Organization* define it as "interpersonal influence, exercised in situations and directed through the communications process toward the attainment of a specified goal or goals."[4]

All these indicate the art of leading requires creativity, positivism, problem solving, goal setting and achieving, communication, confidence, integrity and empathy.

MANAGING ONESELF

Finally, good managers/leaders can manage themselves. It has been implied throughout this chapter in a variety of ways. Too frequently the last person we study is ourself. Here is a list of 20 questions to examine to see if you have some basic management characteristics.

1. Am I sensitive to people, their desires, their fears? Do I have empathy?
2. Am I able to motivate, direct and lead others? Do I manage my time effectively?
3. Can I give full attention to people when problems are discussed?
4. Can I create an atmosphere where others can express themselves?
5. Do I listen only to what I want to hear?
6. Do I practice two-way communication?
7. Am I creative? Can I bring new ideas to the sales staff?
8. Can I encourage ideas from the sales staff?
9. Can I make decisions?
10. Do I realize that any program will not work without complete and eager participation of the salespeople?
11. Do I recognize that people are my real strength?
12. Do I treat everyone fairly or do I tend to have favorites?
13. Do I really want to see other people succeed?
14. Do I have the courage to carry out company policy even though it may not benefit some?
15. Do I lose my temper when my decisions are questioned?
16. How much criticism can I take from the salespeople?
17. Do I know how to make a profit and develop my business?
18. Do I really want the responsibility of managing others?
19. Am I willing to pay the price to be a manager?
20. Do I understand when I have to be the boss in control of my people?

If the foregoing kind of self-examination does not appeal to you, there's another way to have a good look at yourself and your management talents.

Take a piece of paper and draw a line down the center. Put a plus sign at the top of the left column, a minus sign at the top of the right column.

For the next few hours, or even a couple days, list in the plus column all the areas in which you believe you control situations that confront you. Under the minus sign list those areas you feel you do not control or which you know can be improved.

When you've listed everything you can think of, ask yourself: "Am I a manager or am I being managed by others?"

If the minus column outweighs the plus column, you may want to review this chapter to see if you have the basic characteristics for a management position. You may conclude that you are fighting yourself to accomplish something you honestly do not want. As the philosopher Seneca put it, "Do not ask for what you will wish you had not got."

If the plus column outweighs the minus column, you have the promise of being a successful manager.

Leadership is what you hope you provide. It is what people expect from you. But the definition of what you provide and what they expect you to provide can be quite different.

Most people in business today are managed, not led. They are treated as staff or personnel and not as persons. Management cannot create leaders. It can create conditions that encourage people with the potential to become leaders. Or, it can stifle them.

Leadership, says Peter Drucker, "is the lifting of a person's vision to higher sights, the raising of a person's performance to a higher standard, the building of his personality beyond its normal limitations."

Leadership is not a chevron on the sleeve or a title on a door. It is a functional process.

TRANSITION FROM MANAGING TO LEADING

Management by dictate has become a less effective way of managing people. Sales associates today are more concerned with the quality of their lives and want a larger voice in determining their jobs. To manage effectively, managers must become leaders who can motivate people to do their best. As Walter B. Wriston put it in the *Harvard Business Review*, "Talent is the number one commodity in short supply. You can't have enough good people in your organization. . . . So the job of the manager today is very simple and very difficult: to find the best people, motivate them to do the job, and allow them to do it their own way."

An important element of leadership is the variable of style in McKinsey's 7-S model. In making the transition to leadership, the manager moves from a style of managing others to a style of leading them. The leadership style is collaborative, with an emphasis on teamwork. The manager guides and develops his staff, but people manage themselves. People use their judgment to make decisions quickly without having to wait for permission, and taking risks is encouraged. Instead of controlling and solving problems, the leader motivates people to find solutions to problems.

A leadership style gives management and staff the capability to be flexible, make fast decisions and take risks in order to respond to rapidly changing opportunities and threats in the external environment.

Management Style	Leadership Style
Directing others	Guiding/developing
Competing	Collaborating
Using hierarchy	Using network
Consistency/sameness	Diversity/flexibility
"Slow" decision making	"Fast" decision making
Requiring permission	Using judgment
Risk-averse	Risk-taking
Individual contributor	Team player
Being managed	Self-managing
People as expense	People as asset[5]

The manager as leader sets the firm's direction. In the 7-S model, one of the manager's main functions is to articulate the firm's superordinate goals: the fundamental ideas around which the business is built. If they are well-articulated, superordinate goals provide meaning for people. And making meanings is one of the main functions of leadership.[6]

LEADERSHIP STYLES

There are many ways of defining leadership styles. The most effective leaders are those whose style incorporates a high concern for both people and production.

Impoverished Management Style

Managers with this style have low concern for both people and production. They exert the minimum effort needed to get required work done. They are unlikely to care about building an effective team. Their behavioral characteristics include: apathetic, a bystander, delays, gives up easily, indifferent, noncommittal, resigned, withdrawn.

Organization Management Style

This style is characterized by a reliance on compromise and rules. Managers with this style are uncomfortable with the idea of teams unless they are governed by rules. Characteristics of organization men and women include: accommodating, cautious, conformist, likes the tried and true, prefers the middle ground. This style is unlikely to be successful in a competitive, rapidly changing business environment.

Country Club Style

This manager focuses on meeting subordinates' personal needs and is likely to create a comfortable, friendly organizational atmosphere. Teams are likely to appeal to this type of manager. But the country club style manager's inability to say no and to make hard or unpopular decisions is likely to have a negative effect on productivity. Behavioral characteristics include: agreeable, can't say no, avoids negatives, thrives on harmony, unlikely to probe, sensitive, easily hurt.

Authority/Obedience Style

Managers with this style are strongly task-oriented, controlling, and intolerant of subordinates who are nonproducers. They may want the benefits of teams but are unable to give up control. Behavioral characteristics include: controlling, decisions are final, expects compliance, impatient, has all the answers.

Team Management Style

Team managers have a leadership style in which work is accomplished by committed people. These managers assume productivity goals will be met and promote participation. They create interdependence through a common stake in the organizational purpose (superordinate goals), leading to relationships of trust and respect. Behavioral characteristics include: candid, confident, fact-finding, follows through, open-minded, positive. Managers with this style are the most likely to achieve Wriston's goal of utilizing the talents of staff by motivating people to do the job and allowing them to do it their own way.

People's basic instinct for self-preservation is very strong; their need for self-esteem is normal. A good leader understands this and finds ways to make maximum use of each person's style in a creative way.

SELF-INSIGHT AND ANALYSIS OF OUR SUBORDINATES

If leaders are to understand other people, they must first have a thorough understanding of themselves. That is, they must understand their own personality, goals, motivations, wants and needs, prejudices, attitudes, knowledge, concepts of ethical behavior and their reactions when they are in a subordinate position.

True leaders must understand the people they manage. They have to be empathetic and able to put themselves in the other person's shoes. Why are they motivated? Why do they resist? Why do two people respond differently and sometimes oppositely to the same situation?

When a leader wants to motivate his or her subordinates, Abraham Maslow's "Hierarchy of Needs" provides an excellent key to people's needs. According to Maslow, the pyramid of individual needs ranges from the base physiological needs (food, shelter and air), then security (no harm, continued earnings), social (sense of belonging) to ego (self-worth and confidence, recognitions). At the top of the pyramid is the greatest need of all—that of self-actualization (a sense of accomplishment).

Maslow's hierarchy can guide leaders in their thinking as they ask themselves the following questions, found in Paul G. Buchanan's *The Leader and Individual Motivation.*[7]

- Why do people behave as they do?
- How can I get people to respond the way I want them to?
- Why don't people understand things that to me are simple and clear?
- Why do they sometimes act against their own interests, resisting changes that may benefit them?
- Why do they sometimes react one way in a given situation and very differently in the same situation at another time?

Forming impressions of others is part of our daily experience. What do I think my salespeople think of me as a person, a leader, a helper? Positive leaders trust their motives and actions, have confidence in their ability to understand themselves and others and exude self-discipline in controlling their personal feelings so as not to blind their perceptions. They will check their impressions against facts before reaching a conclusion. They will be open-minded and willing to listen to suggestions of others.

Leaders' knowledge of themselves and their empathetic understanding of the people they manage work inseparably in dealing with situations and problems faced by management and salespeople.

NEED FOR PERSONAL OR HUMAN DIRECTION

Once managerial leaders recognize the differences (sometimes small, sometimes immense) in the individuals under their direction, they must develop an ability to diagnose and fully understand each person's unique behavior. They must be able to sense when individual egos are threatened, personal relationships between salespeople are on the threshold of a breaking point, or feelings appear to overwhelm sensible objectivity.

It is sometimes suggested that a well-organized and implemented policy and procedure manual will preclude any major occurrence of management-personnel breakdown. It is true that such a manual sets forth the firm's modus operandi and thus prevents many disputes. But this dispassionately written document of company goals and policies can never replace a strong leader. This individual's leadership talent can transform potential conflict into the more manageable form of a problem to be solved. Here again, a leader guides people into determining what is right, not who is right.

If leaders are to accomplish their role as a coordinator and not a manipulator of human behavior toward a common goal, they must determine the abilities and attitudes of their people in a given situation. They get the complete facts of why, where and what through proper communication. The leaders are good listeners who draw on past and present experiences with the salesperson and determine the self image of that person. Then they develop that person's abilities, and alter or enhance their behavioral attitudes to rectify the situation. In consequence, the salesperson is led toward fulfilling his or her needs.

The ancient Chinese philosopher, Lao-tzu, said, "To lead the people, walk behind them." A modern use of the exhortation is found in the example of how one leader helped "coach" his subordinates.

When Benjamin F. Fairless was chairman of U.S. Steel Corporation, he coached his subordinates by responding with searching questions when they came to him for an answer to a pressing problem. Said Fairless, "When one of my vice-presidents or the head of one of our operating companies comes to me for instructions, I generally counter by asking him questions. First thing I know, he has told me how to solve the problem himself."

Fairless knew how to lead his people from a possibly self-destructive encounter with the boss to a positive, creative exchange that resulted in the growth of the person's self-esteem.

NEED FOR POSITIVE DIRECTION

We are brought up to find out why an idea won't work rather than how to make it work. What a negative concept on which to base our lives! Yet we've done it traditionally.

Leaders know how to organize situations so that people do not have to defend either themselves or their ideas. Relieved of the burden of self-protection, people can be taught how to expend their energies on positive action.

Those who learn to bypass the traditional, negative approach and attack problems and possibilities in a positive way are our real leaders. They are our time and money savers. They are the people who move America and its businesses off dead center and onto the mainstream of progress.

If you have a person on your staff whose standard response is negative (not infrequently, those who consider themselves experts are especially prone to this), call on this individual in the next staff or sales meeting with a restricting lead-in: "Tell us what you like about the suggestion just made." You'll accomplish two things with this approach. First, you'll show the whole group you are alert to this person's negativism and can manage the situation. Second, you teach them one of the ways to keep what might be a weak idea alive until it gains some strength.

People are conditioned to think and act critically and accept criticism for bad ideas, as long as it is done with a minimum of personal reference.

They tend to suppress their hostile reactions by covering them with humor or by withdrawing from the conversation unless, of course, they come out and shout another person down. Neither of these reactions produces the result you seek: ideas and how to make them work.

Positive leadership need not be clothed in complex terms or abstract concepts. Simply defined, positive leadership means the kind of management that sees what needs to be done, assumes the job can be done, explores the possibilities and decides how to accomplish it.

The best leadership motivates people to work by telling them how essential they are to the success of the business and what's in it for them, the personal benefit. By relating job processes to company, department and personal goals, good leaders stretch the imagination of their people and send them out to meet the challenge of today, alert to the potential of tomorrow.

Positive leaders ask aloud and often the questions that seek out problems. Then they ask those involved to concentrate on what solutions are possible. They are receptive to every solution suggested, no matter how improbable it may at first appear. Having strengthened their staff's self-confidence by sharing the problems with them and asking their help in finding solutions, they demonstrate their courage and self-confidence. People have a right to expect this of their leaders.

THE LISTENING LEADER

A good leader listens. It is said that a person ceases being a supervisor and becomes a leader when he or she stops talking and starts to listen.

Leaders listen as problems are conveyed to them. They listen with eyes as well as ears. They see tension. They see anger building. They see indifference. And everything they see converges into the total knowledge they accumulate as they listen.

One of the most important ways a leader listens is to ask mirror type questions that lead a subordinate to understand why a problem exists. Feeding the question back to the salesperson often results in that person supplying their own answer.

Good leaders also listen to themselves. They ask: Why am I doing this? What will it accomplish? For whom? Do others understand both the questions and my answers?

As good leaders listen to themselves with both eyes and ears, they learn to their surprise that many of the things being done may be unnecessary, unproductive or even downright harmful to morale. For example, is all the data you ask your people to assemble really useful? If not, you can eliminate the procedure, remembering to tell everyone involved why it's being dropped and how they'll benefit.

Another point most people fail to recognize or admit is the degree of destructiveness in each of us. We each think of ourselves as the exception to the rule, the one who behaves decently. And we are shocked when someone has the temerity to point out how damaging are some of our most common actions.

This enters the leadership picture when the staff meets competition from their leader. A leader is sure to have ideas, too. And he or she may feel they should be put forth for the simple reason that the firm can't afford to lose any idea that could prove useful. So what does a leader do?

If the leader contributes ideas throughout the meeting, he or she will unconsciously favor them. Subordinates are hypersensitive to this and it reduces their commitment and the probability of success. The leader is destroying their creativity.

According to George M. Prince, author of *The Practice of Creativity,* there are specific times when leaders may contribute their ideas.[8] They are welcome during the discussion of early possible solutions and when pressing for ideas later in the meeting; but the leader should offer them when there is no other action. If a member voices an idea, the leader should support it, restating it to make certain he or she understands what the member had in mind. The leader can then add to, build on or strengthen the idea. After every member's ideas have been explored thoroughly, the leader may introduce his or her own. However, the general rule is that the leader always gives precedence to the ideas of others.

Assume there is value in any idea a member offers. Search out that value no matter how wild the statement may sound. Humor and laughter are often used as a before-the-fact defense against attack. You can easily retreat to "I wasn't really serious about this idea." A good leader probes laughter not only for the above reason but also because the elegance of an emerging idea may be intuitively pleasing before anyone is consciously aware of what the idea really is. The value of such intuitive urgings must not be underestimated.

HOW A LEADER LOOKS TO OTHERS

If one were to ask, "What is your opinion of your manager?" one could get answers like: "Willing to listen," "Do not always agree with but respected," "Firm but fair," "Lets us know he or she cares," "Rules with an iron hand," "Doesn't get along with the group as a whole" or "Never bends, even when wrong."

Good leaders know they cannot please all their people all the time. They understand that their greatest challenge as a leader is to make work so interesting that their employees will go at it with real motivation to succeed. The techniques of good management, handled with skill, can help leaders guide their people to achieve personal goals as well as the firm's goals.

Listed below and on the pages that follow are some proven techniques that real estate business leaders have found effective in recent years.

Twenty-One Suggestions for People Who Want to Lead[9]

1. Let each person know where he or she stands; do not fail to discuss their performance with them periodically.
2. Give credit where credit is due, commensurate with accomplishments.
3. Inform people of changes in advance; informed people are more effective.
4. Let people participate in plans and decisions affecting them.
5. Gain your people's confidence; earn their loyalty and trust.
6. Know all your people personally. Find out their interests, habits and touchy points and capitalize on your knowledge of them.
7. Listen to your subordinates' proposals. They have good ideas too.
8. If a person's behavior is unusual for him or her, find out why. There's always a reason.
9. Try to make your wishes known by suggestion or request whenever possible. People generally don't like to be pushed.
10. Explain the why of things that are to be done. People do a better job then.
11. When you make a mistake, admit it and apologize. Others will resent your blaming someone else.
12. Show people the importance of every job. It will satisfy their need for security.
13. Criticize constructively; give reasons for your criticism and suggest ways in which performance can be improved.
14. Precede criticisms with mention of a person's good points; show you are trying to help.
15. Do as you would have your people do. The leader sets the style.
16. Be consistent in your actions; let your people be in no doubt as to what is expected to them.
17. Take every opportunity to demonstrate pride in the group. This will bring out the best in them.
18. If one person gripes, find out what the grievance is. One person's gripe may be the gripe of many.
19. Settle every grievance if at all possible; otherwise the whole group will be affected.
20. Set short- and long-range goals by which people can measure their progress.
21. Back up your people. Responsibility must accompany authority.

LEADERSHIP IN THE FUTURE

It has often been said that to achieve our goal through others, we smile at some, swear at others, counsel most. But we should never forget to treat each person as an individual.

Frank Nunlist, Chairman of the Board of Worthington Corporation, was quoted in *Tough-Minded Management* on considering the future. As

Nunlist looked toward the year 2000 he said, "I believe the characteristics of our society will be far more varied than they are today and that Big Brother and Big Father will not be wanted or accepted.

"What will be wanted will be thoughtful, creative, imaginative, understanding, intelligent leadership—leadership that will be effective because its reasoning toward the common goal is valid, sound and thoughtfully conceived; leadership that shuns the use of power, manipulation and fear. There is no doubt in my mind that leadership by thought will replace leadership gained through the power of money, the power of politics, the power of military might or the power of personality."

Nunlist continued, "[Tomorrow's leader] will realize the great strengths that lie in the point and counterpoint of individualism. He [or she] will spend more time in creating satisfactions for people as individuals and will tend to destroy some of our present concepts of mass management."[10]

Today's smart leaders will keep uppermost in mind that they need all the help they can get. This can be one of their most important discoveries in establishing their leadership. And they will remember that they are not permanent. No one is. One day they will be succeeded or replaced. The best leaders will have prepared their successors for a very exciting, rewarding role.

CONCLUSION

There is no formula that guarantees an individual will be an effective manager of a real estate business. But successful managers have been found to possess certain characteristics that enable them to manage effectively and to obtain the best efforts from their subordinates. These include physical, emotional and financial stability; knowledge of the real estate business, of people, and of sound management practices; dedication to the success of the business; integrity; flexibility; the ability to make decisions; and the desire to be a successful manager.

However, these management characteristics are not enough. Today managers must also be leaders. It's not enough to focus on the operation of your real estate business today. You must also develop a vision of the future and communicate that vision to your sales associates. You must create an atmosphere of trust in which people can be creative and take risks. In his seminars, Tom Peters asks if anyone there knows how to manage the human imagination. So far, he says, no hand has gone up, including his. But, says Peters, we'd better learn how to manage the human imagination—and quickly—because "imagination is the main source of value in the new economy."[11]

ENDNOTES

1.   Peter Townsend, *Up the Organization,* p. 84.
2.   "Crazy Times Call for Crazy Organizations," from *The Tom Peters Seminar,* in *Working Women,* August 1994.
3.   J. D. Batten, *Tough-Minded Management,* p. 36.
4.   Robert Tannebaum, Irving Weschler and Fred Massarik, *Leadership and Organization.*
5.   Dana Gains Robinson, *Supervisory Management.*
6.   Tom Peters, Julien Phillips and Robert Waterman, "Structure is Not Organization," in *Business Horizons,* June 1980, p. 25.
7.   Paul G. Buchanan, *The Leader and Individual Motivation.*
8.   George M. Prince, *The Practice of Creativity.*
9.   J. D. Batten, *Tough-Minded Management,* p. 75.
10.   J. D. Batten, *Tough-Minded Management.*
11.   "Crazy Times Call for Crazy Organizations."

Chapter 3

Transition to Management

People moving into management in the real estate business usually have had experience in selling real estate. They are likely to be individuals whose advice and counsel is sought by fellow salespeople. In other words, they have demonstrated the ability to acquire knowledge, use it themselves and share it with others. Their plan of action and thought processes, at least to a degree, agree with those in top management. They not only give their best to "this sale" but also plan ahead to next week, next month, even next year and what they want to achieve then.

As new managers begin their work, they understand that an effective, efficient, high quality real estate business operation is their primary function. They want their salespeople to succeed. Their growth and recognition come first in the managers' thinking and actions. Managers know the success of others helps assure their own.

Managers are practical and know that the transition from sales to management cannot happen overnight. The time required to make a successful transition will vary with the individual and the firm. Depending on the manager's prior role in the firm and whether or not he or she has any management experience and/or formal training, a number of personal adjustments have to be made and training acquired. The new manager will likely develop a job description outlining his or her new role and expectations for personal growth.

One of the most important personal considerations for new managers is to make certain that in learning new skills, they are careful not to change their personal style and way of doing things and relating to others—the qualities that brought them to management positions.

Perhaps the greatest challenge to the new person in management is making the transition from being "one of the bunch" to becoming their leader. This is a major psychological transition. When attacked a step at a time, it's not the traumatic experience some people expect or fear.

TRANSITION CAN BE DIFFICULT OR EASY

Transition can be tough. Ask anyone who's been through it. It's tough to change from doing things to directing others to do them. It's tough to move from being one of the bunch to being the boss and being accepted in your new role. It's tough to learn where to turn to find out many of the things you'll need to know. Tough as it all is, it isn't impossible. People do it every day. Many make the transition from doing to directing with only a minimum of trauma.

How you make the transition to management will depend on the needs of your firm and what you bring to the position. Write out a position description for your new position. It should cover both the needs of the business and your personal needs. Put this in print before you start the new position. What will you be doing now that you did not do before? How many functions from your old position will still be required of you? Will your needs be satisfied more fully in the new position? Do your needs fit the company's plans for the future? How will your time organization differ in the new position? If it looks like you will be doing more of the same old thing or doing it faster or doing it for the salespeople, you have not described a true management position.

Your personal job description will vary according to the set-up of your firm. You may be a selling broker, a sales manager/broker or a full-time administrator. The principles of management apply in all these roles. How you fulfill your management role will depend on your skills, traits and needs. The way you do it should be very authentically your own. The big challenge is to get organized and get going.

Professor Theodore Levitt of the Harvard Business School, discussing the crucial factors that affect managerial success or failure, once made the point that there is no such thing as the right way for a manager to behave or to accomplish a task.

Each person brings to a management position unique traits and talents. A manager may share with his or her peers some skills and the desire to succeed; but in the end it is the manager who will do the job and do it in whatever way he or she sees fit, working within the established structure.

Levitt asserted that one can be taught *about* management but cannot be taught management.

He further said that it is altogether proper to try to learn better, more practical technologies of management, including planning, budgeting, control systems, communication, manpower development and the like. But it is not desirable to try to change the personality of the manager. An individual's interpersonal skills in dealing with people and situations, the most important aspect of that person's basic working method, are not appropriate subjects for arbitrary manipulation. They are, however, subjects to be studied to increase understanding of people.

Once the owner of a real estate business adds a salesperson on any basis other than that of equal and codeterminer of the firm's policy and procedure, the functions of that broker change to a management role. He or she is no longer free to engage in total self-determination and a program of personal action. That broker becomes a manager of the behavior of at least one other person. The manager immediately takes on a new role which includes planning things the firm must undertake, organizing his or her own energies and those of the salesperson, directing and motivating the salesperson, and controlling or reviewing the results of the action of the salesperson. The manager decides in which areas the salesperson is free to work, sets the standards by which actions may be taken, reviews the results of the salesperson's performance, and coaches the salesperson toward accountability.

The reluctance or inability of brokers to manage their business is considered by many the greatest single force suppressing prestige and status for the real estate industry.

In precise management terms, a manager decides upon goals, quotas, deadlines, standards and budgets. He or she uses the management process, which is planning, organizing, directing, motivating and controlling work effort, to organize people, money and time. The legal relationship of the independent contractor or employee has no bearing on the need for good management or the need for individuals associated with the firm to fit into the managed program.

Real estate sales and management are quite different worlds. Your situation may require you to move back and forth from one to the other, or you may move wholly into the field of management. Your management role will depend on the size of your firm and whether you continue to sell. Whatever your role, remember that real estate salespeople need management and that without real estate sales there is nothing to manage.

THREE MANAGEMENT POSITIONS

Three basic types of management positions are generally found in real estate offices:

1. Selling brokers
2. Sales managers/brokers
3. Administrative brokers

Selling Brokers

Selling brokers are usually found in relatively small offices of three to ten people. Selling brokers continue to depend on their own sales production as their primary source of income. They sell in competition with their own salespeople. Learning how to do this in the fairest way possible is extremely important.

It is estimated that approximately 75 percent of all real estate firms in the United States are in the small office category just described. Thus, the selling broker is by far the most common type of real estate business manager.

When salespeople understand how a selling broker operates and know he or she makes every effort to be fair with them, the broker's competitive selling role will be accepted. For example, selling brokers who are fair do not take all company leads but work primarily on listing property and representing buyers from their own personal referrals. They do not take and service the best company leads nor do they allocate all the undesirable leads to their salespeople.

One of the advantages of a selling broker is that he or she is constantly aware of every aspect of the market being encountered by the salespeople. Consequently, the selling broker doesn't have to rely on the salespeople's reports on the changing situations and new problems they encounter day by day. Whether it's a softening of the market, difficulties developing in mortgage funding or rumors of a proposed zoning change, the selling broker has those problems too. The broker has given them thought and is often prepared to act by the time the salespeople pass along the information.

Another advantage is that the selling broker is alongside the salespeople as they work and can spot bad habits as soon as they begin to develop. Such an early warning system can save time and dollars in taking corrective action quickly. Such counseling can be on a one-to-one basis or may be incorporated in the firm's continuing training program. In the latter case, such training can also prevent the same bad habits in other salespeople.

A marked disadvantage of a selling broker is that he or she must bother with details of their own sales rather than manage.

Sales Managers/Brokers

Sales manager/broker management situations are usually found in firms with a staff of 15 to 20 people. In this type of operation the manager spends most of his or her time bringing good people into the business, training them and helping them achieve their goals. Although a portion of this manager's income continues to come from his or her own sales production, the major part is derived from the bottom line.

The dual role enables the manager to do a thorough job of in-house training as well as provide leadership in selling. It is a delicate balance, calling for a keen sense of fairness. But the total effort is aimed toward the ultimate achievement of the firm's sales goals.

In a larger firm, the manager can often delegate more nonselling responsibilities to others than might be possible in a smaller operation. Even part-time sales work restricts the amount of time such a manager can devote to planning growth, setting objectives, planning and controlling the budget and measuring results on a regular basis. This manager's skillful use of the talents of several staff people in helping with these tasks or even having staff take on some can add measurably to his or her success as a manager. Such help need not come from salespeople. Secretaries, accountants, clerks or receptionists are a few of the sources for such help.

Administrative Brokers

Administrative brokers are usually found in large firms, often those having multiple offices. Their primary management responsibilities are to plan the firm's operations and supervise a sales manager or managers who in turn direct the salespeople. Administrative brokers do little or no listing or selling. On occasion they may assist in bringing in account type sales.

These managers spend a great deal of their time planning the overall destiny of the firm, both short-term and long-range. They work with sales managers rather than salespeople. Their income derives almost entirely from the bottom line of individual offices and the whole company.

The owner of a modest size real estate business sometimes plays a similar role as he or she administers everything that goes on in the business. The smaller the firm, the higher the production per person needed to make it all fit together into a successful operation.

THREE LEVELS OF MANAGEMENT

No matter which of the three foregoing types of real estate business management positions you hold, you will find yourself managing people at two, and in some cases three levels:

1. You manage yourself
2. You manage others
3. You manage others who manage others

With such diverse combinations of business styles it is important to keep your thinking free of restricting rules that limit how any one owner or firm operates. Each was described briefly above to enable you to identify in a general way how your firm and your job fit the most common types of brokerage firms.

Certain generalizations can show the ways a real estate business can be organized. Whatever the size of your firm, whichever type of management you choose as being best suited to your needs, all share the goal of a successful, profitable operation. Each also shares the problem of keeping abreast of how things are going with salespeople and being alert to those who need help or closer direction or supervision. Everyone in management shares the challenge of being a continuing source of encouragement and enthusiasm.

SOME COMMON TRANSITION PROBLEMS

Management training courses conducted by the Real Estate Brokerage Managers Council™ of the REALTORS® National Marketing Institute® each year serve thousands of members and offer them an opportunity to share ideas and problems. In addition to discovering that their problems are shared by many, real estate managers learn how to overcome the difficulties of a period of transition as they move from selling positions to management.

Four problems seem to be shared by most new managers:

1. The tendency to do it yourself
2. The belief that you not only know how to do it but that you can get it done a lot faster
3. The fear of losing a listing or a sale
4. The tendency to motivate the way you like to be motivated

The "I Can Do It Myself" Syndrome

Ego contributes a lot to this problem. Wanting to "do it yourself" is really lacking confidence in your salespeople. You don't want to believe they will ever be quite as good as you are because you have both the knowledge and the experience needed.

At this point it's a good idea to remind yourself that you've been appointed, not annointed. Let go of your own ego a little and build up the salesperson's. Give salespeople the knowledge and confidence to go out and do it themselves. Be sure to encourage them to do it their own way.

As long as you continue to do it yourself there's no arguing with you when things go wrong. If you fail, you can come back and say you failed because of the "dumb seller," "tight buyer" or because somebody "didn't understand the market." Whatever reason you've chosen to hide your failure, there's no arguing with you when you're the boss. No one is likely to have the temerity to sit you down and review, step by step, the course of events.

And the salesperson hasn't learned a thing except, perhaps, that you're not the leader he or she thought you would be. Until a person fails, he or she really hasn't learned. If the salesperson tries something and fails, a skilled manager encourages thorough feedback. Careful, relevant questioning can tell the manager what happened and help the salesperson understand what went wrong, why and how to try to correct it this time and prevent its recurrence.

A good manager maximizes reward situations and minimizes anxiety situations. When a salesperson succeeds, be prompt and generous with your praise. Spread the good news. This soon results in people coming to you with their successes as well as their problems. You'll be better informed on all counts. Your salespeople's successes will stroke your ego, too.

Still another facet of the "do it yourself" syndrome is a natural reluctance to give up doing what you enjoyed. Everyone who likes selling likes the competition, relishes the contacts with buyers and sellers and enjoys helping them realize their dreams and ambitions.

As a successful salesperson you enjoyed the one-to-one confrontation of selling. Learn to transmit this sense of competition to your salespeople in a selling sense, not a managerial sense. Successful salespeople have a habit of feeling they've got to win. When you send them out to do that, that's good management. But if you use that same one-to-one confrontation in a management encounter and you win, you've lost! If salespeople are put down because of your competitive spirit, which is really ego acting, and you tell them in an abrasive way that they're doing it all wrong, the very determination that made you a success in selling will defeat you in management.

Enjoyment of direct contact with people was perhaps one of your major reasons for going into real estate sales in the first place. You like people, like dealing with people and like to be with people. Now your challenge is to move away from that particular set of people, buyers and sellers, and develop new contacts. These new people will be important to your success as a manager: bankers, builders, civic leaders, developers, local government and other management people. Soon this new mix of people will replace the buyers and sellers of the past who now become part of your management routine only occasionally.

The "I Can Do It Faster" Syndrome

The belief that you not only know how to do it but you can do it faster is similar to the "do it yourself" syndrome.

Lack of confidence in salespeople is rooted in failure to give them adequate training. If you succeed as a teacher, you'll set them free to go out and use your teaching, knowing you'll both benefit, personally and financially. Teach them, trust them and turn them loose to do the job in their own way. Your way worked for you. Somebody let you do it your way and didn't force you to follow theirs. Steer clear of trying to force people to do things your way. It might not work for them. Give them the necessary guidelines and train them to develop their own techniques.

As you learn to do this, you will be developing your management skills and you will win the respect of the people you've trained. Be there to answer their questions and make suggestions when asked but let them do the job themselves.

The "I'm Afraid of Losing Money for the Company" Syndrome

Fear of losing a listing or a sale is the third most common problem. Every listing and sale may be extremely important to your immediate income needs. That's understandable. But it's equally important to let salespeople do their jobs. It affects your immediate relationship with them and the long-range success of both the salespeople and your firm. Put in that perspective, it becomes easier to keep hands off. It's important that you do.

If the salesperson gets the listing or makes the sale, you'll both have reason to celebrate. But if you take over the transaction and you succeed, your salesperson will never be convinced that he or she wouldn't have done as well. And if you fail, you've failed both the salesperson and yourself, and you've weakened your relationship in the bargain.

Let salespeople do their jobs. If they succeed, celebrate. If they fail, sit down with them quietly and get the thorough feedback mentioned earlier in this chapter, letting them tell you what they think went wrong. They may ask you how you'd have done it. They may suggest ways in which they will do it differently next time around. In either case, they've learned through their failure, which is a growing process available to each of us in no other way.

The "I Always Liked This Motivation Technique" Syndrome

Managers often stand in the way of good management because they tend to motivate others the way they would like to be motivated.

Gil comes to me with a problem. I listen and, after pondering for a few minutes, turn to him and say: "Well, Gil, if I were in your shoes I guess this is what I would like to have happen." Unfortunately, I'm not in Gil's shoes and, in any case, the motivation I give him is completely unsuited to his personality. However, Gil will seemingly accept my answer but never use it and probably never ask my advice again. I tried to motivate him the way I would like to be motivated instead of the way he should have been motivated.

Fear Motivation

There are three basic types of motivation. The first is known as fear motivation and it has been around for many years. It's not unusual for a manager to address a sales meeting and threaten a salesperson by saying, "If you don't have three more listings next month, you're out." Or, "If you don't have four sales next month, you're out."

Obviously, if the threat is carried out, pretty soon there won't be anyone left on the sales force to motivate, because somewhere along the line they will not meet the demands put upon them and it will be necessary to dismiss them. If the threat isn't carried out, it doesn't take long for the salespeople to find out that the manager is just blowing off steam. When this happens, there's no motivating factor at all. If one individual is terminated because he or she doesn't perform and another one who didn't perform isn't, it doesn't take long before the manager is accused of favoring one person over another.

About the only time fear motivation should be used is when the manager and the salesperson have agreed on what is expected and the salesperson hasn't performed. Then the manager has to give him or her one last try. For example: When Gil joined the company, he was told that the company required salespeople to earn at least $8,000 in their first year to cover minimum desk costs. Gil has been with the company six months and has generated only $2,500. The manager has a counseling session with Gil and says, "Gil, for the last six months you've sold only $2,500. You know we need approximately $8,000 to cover our minimum expenses. Therefore, Gil, in the next 90 days it is important for you to meet the following goals: We would like to see x-amount of listing activity and x-amount of sales activity. If you're not able to make that particular goal then I'm afraid it will be necessary for you to take your license elsewhere." This is a form of fear motivation, but it's directed to an individual who was aware from the outset that a certain level of performance would be expected of him. The manager didn't call Gil into the office and say, "You're out because you didn't do what I expected," and Gil could not reply, "We never discussed expectations." In this case, the salesperson and manager agreed in advance what was expected, the salesperson had not performed and was given one more try through a type of fear motivation.

Incentive Motivation

This is commonly used in the real estate business. It usually employs sliding scales of commission, bonus plans or sales contests. Incentive motivation is frequently used because it's easy and requires very little thought. If the salesperson who wins the contest gets a color television; if he or she makes $10,000, the reward is a bonus and so on. Incentive motivation is a type of motivation in which a manager finds love instead of respect. "I'll give you a trip to Florida if you'll love me." "I'll give you a bonus if you'll love me." Basically, the manager is trying to buy people's affection rather than setting up respect that will stand the test of time. If a manager depends exclusively on incentive motivation, whenever difficult decisions are made that are not agreeable to the salesperson, he or she will simply leave the firm. Salespeople may also leave when another company offers a better incentive plan.

Incentive motivation can have a positive effect when used for morale reasons or to accomplish a specific goal. It is seldom successful when management is trying to increase volume. Real estate does not lend itself to this type of reaction. A salesperson can't stay out an extra two hours and work in the evening and be sure to come home with a listing or make a sale.

Sales contest incentive plans are good to raise morale in general or to get specific duties done by stating, "If you make five calls a day for the entire week we will give you a small incentive." Giving a small incentive to someone who makes five calls a day for a week or whatever may serve to get specific projects started. But incentive motivation has limited capabilities. It doesn't take long before salespeople feel that incentives are their right and are no longer motivated by the incentive itself. This is seen in comments such as, "You owe me the trip to Florida because I won the contest," or "You owe me that $500 bonus because I made $15,000."

Personal Motivation

The only true form of motivation that can be used day in and day out in the real estate business is personal motivation, where the manager gets inside the salesperson's head and finds out what turns that individual on and off. When this occurs, the manager can truly stimulate and motivate the salesperson the way the salesperson thinks instead of the way the manager thinks. The reason this technique is not used frequently in real estate is that it takes a tremendous amount of time to get into somebody else's head and find out what their action and reaction to certain situations will be.

Selling sales managers in real estate find their own sales work requires so much time they are not free to devote the time and effort necessary to be personally aware of each one of their salespeople.

When Gil or Susan has a specific problem, the selling sales manager is present. But when Gil's and Susan's problems are solved, the sales manager goes into the field to do his or her own listing and sales work; this manager does not find time to sit down with the salespeople and chat with them on a casual basis to really discover what kind of people they are.

Specialists in the field of personal awareness say there are also three modes of subliminal motivation managers should be aware of.

Negative Motivation

The manager who employs negative motivation gets things done through a negative reaction. This is well typified in fear motivation. Constantly saying "If you don't do this" and "If you don't do that" is a negative motivator. Generally, the success pattern of a negative motivator covers a short period of time, giving people 14 days or 30 days at the most, to accomplish something. But once it's accomplished, that negative motivator cannot continue to be used because its negative style can give only short-term positive results.

Neutral Motivation   Neutral motivation does not necessarily mean that the recipient is satisfied. But if it is not present it will very likely cause stress. An example of this could be a real estate company in a ten-year-old office that has never been decorated or painted inside or outside and has huge chuckholes in the parking lot. Some of the salespeople may leave the firm because they're embarrassed to bring their clients into a shabby office. They leave and go to other offices that are better kept. However, if that broker filled the chuckholes and repaved the lot and painted the property inside and out today, it does not guarantee the salespeople will stay. The broker has simply done what is expected. Therefore, it is known as a neutral motivator.

Time after time it has been shown that certain incentives are basically neutral motivators. Though salespeople may experience a short burst of enthusiasm when they win an incentive, it won't be long before they take that incentive for granted and wonder when they will be given another.

Experiments in industry have shown that raises may stimulate the recipients for one to two weeks. But the recipients soon take the raise for granted and wonder when the bosses are going to give them another raise that, of course, they well deserve, at least in their own minds. Therefore, incentive motivation many times becomes an unending circle of giving and giving for only short-term responses.

Positive Motivation   The final mode of subliminal motivation is called positive motivation. This type of motivation creates and maintains positive results. Positive motivation can best be exemplified by the personal motivation mentioned earlier. Understanding why people act the way they do and being able to motivate them as they would like to be motivated is certainly positive in nature and can have good long-term results. In addition to building successful friendships, it also provides a level for dynamic leadership because it builds respect.

It is true that at any one time a manager may employ all three forms of motivation (fear, incentive and personal), as well as all three modes of subliminal motivation (negative, neutral and positive). However, managers should be conscious of how they use these techniques and what they are trying to accomplish each time they're confronted by a people problem.

MOVING FROM THE SALES FORCE TO A LEADERSHIP ROLE

An almost universal plea from people moving into management positions that require them to supervise their former peers is: "Tell us how we become boss after we've been a buddy."

Two short sentences may sound like a pat answer to this important query, but they are a guide:

1.   Know yourself.
2.   Be yourself.

Neither is easy. Achievement of each comes more easily to some than to others. But it is important to do both to the best of your ability.

Know Yourself

As you move into management to supervise people with whom you once worked side by side, accept the premise that they already know a great deal about you. They may even know some things about you better than you do yourself. They are likely to know which parts of your old job you enjoyed most, which things you did because they had to be done, and what you put off until the last moment or maybe never got around to at all. Recognize and admit to yourself what others may know about you that you don't like to face up to yourself.

Were you great on getting listings and sales but reluctant to keep a daily time sheet? Don't be surprised if this work/procrastination pattern emerges in those you supervise. As you discipline yourself to get more things done on time so will those who report to you.

There is no definitive study of the business of upward perception and performance (how you look to your subordinates and how they react to how you look to them). Informal observations in the general field of management suggest that appraisals of the boss by subordinates are most accurate; appraisals by the boss of subordinates are less accurate, and self-appraisal is least accurate. Such perception applies in real estate management just as it does in any other business.

If you listen sensitively to what others try to tell you about yourself, you can learn a great deal. Observe which of your communications elicit fast action by the group and which have to be pushed. They may reflect your own strengths and weaknesses. The best practice is to seek upward appraisal from sales associates closest to you whose judgment you trust and who will not substitute praise for appraisal.

Be Yourself

You were chosen for or chose a management role because of your skills and what you are. Don't try to be somebody or something else. And if the offer of promotion to management is conditioned on a remake of your personality, turn the position down. It is better to continue what you're doing in your own way. Let no one turn your whole world topsy-turvy as they try to fit you into their mold.

This doesn't mean you should not sometimes and in some ways adjust to changing conditions or adapt to new ways of doing things. To do this is a management strength. But adjust and adapt in your own way. Don't try to change yourself. Your sales associates know how to react and work with the real you. To be other than your authentic self will throw them into a state of confusion and will weaken your efforts in your new position.

If your company does not offer a training program, take advantage of courses and publications that are available. They will help you achieve a management frame of mind, add to your skills and strengthen your self-confidence and enthusiasm for the job.

Only as you train for management and gain experience in the daily operation of a business can you hope to rise to a position of leadership in your field. If you become a truly successful leader you will carry along those whose success depends upon you and upon whom your future success depends.

OTHER TRANSITION CHANGES

Following are some frequently asked questions from people new to management and one possible answer for each.

Q. How can I organize my time so routine work and personal things can be handled after spending necessary time with salespeople?
A. By learning to delegate routine chores, reserving only the most difficult, sensitive problems for your attention.

Q. How can I overcome resentment of men who are managed by a woman?
A. Forget your gender and focus on your job.

Q. How can I remove myself from competition with other salespeople?
A. Go into another area of selling such as commercial-industrial or concentrate on referral business only. Don't seek out new clients.

Q. How can I learn to assume responsibility in management when my previous responsibility was only to my customers?
A. Involve your salespeople more; you'll have to make some decisions but let them make some of their own.

Q. How do I learn to handle disputes or terminate salespeople without tearing myself up emotionally?
A. Look at these responsibilities in a positive way. You're working for everyone's benefit. Above all, be consistent.

Q. How can I motivate salespeople so they are as goal-oriented as management?
A. It's your job to constantly remind salespeople of the company goals as well as their own and how they are interdependent. Be sure they have the whole picture and know how they will benefit.

Q. How do I establish guidelines that will constitute success for the company? As a salesperson they were my own goals. Now others are involved.
A. You've got to know what you are trying to achieve. Establish overall goals for the company; then decide on primary objectives for the next three to six months. Keep the sales staff informed.

Q. How do I assume responsibility for administering policies I had no part in making, particularly in a branch office where all decisions are made in the main office?

A. You can't motivate others to do something you don't believe in yourself. There will always be minor differences. Some of these can be resolved by discussing them with top management. If a firm's policy is wholly negative to you, you ought to consider going elsewhere.

Q. How can I show leadership over friendship?

A. Friendship involves two factors: leadership or respect and loving or caring about the other person. If you are consistent in your decisions and as fair as you can be, you'll gain the respect of your staff. Then the quality of caring about each other is a natural result.

CONCLUSION

Making the transition from a sales position into management takes time and requires a change in your thinking. If you are a sales manager or administrative broker, you will need to take satisfaction in the success of the salespeople you manage rather than in your own sales. If you are a selling broker, you will need to find ways to manage the competition with your salespeople as fairly as possible.

During the transition period, it is important to be aware of, and try to avoid, the common problems shared by most new managers. Your role has changed. Your new focus must be to manage your business. Have confidence in your salespeople. Give them the tools and training they need and allow them to do the job in their own way. If they fail, use it as a learning opportunity. In doing this, you will be developing your own management skills.

One of your major functions as a manager is to motivate your sales staff. But what would motivate you may not be what motivates them. You need to take the time to learn what motivates each individual, bearing in mind that some types of motivation are short-term or create a cycle of perceived entitlement. Positive motivation has good long-term results and builds respect.

Finally, there may be a rocky period when you begin to supervise people who were previously your peers. These people know you and know your weaknesses, probably better than you do. Get training. If your company doesn't have a training program, read publications on management and take courses such as those offered by the Real Estate Brokerage Managers Council™. As you gain skills and experience, you will strengthen your self-confidence and gain the respect of those you manage.

Chapter 4

Strategic Planning

There's an old saying: "If you don't know where you're going, any road will get you there." But in today's competitive real estate environment, that is a recipe for disaster. One of the real estate broker's primary responsibilities is to formulate the vision of where the firm is going and to develop the strategic plan that will take it there.

It's not enough to look only a few months ahead. Long-range planning is essential. Brokers must try to anticipate the future and develop creative alternatives that will enable their firms to achieve their goals.

It is not enough merely to set goals. A set of activities must be outlined to achieve those goals. The company's efforts must be organized to achieve those goals, and systems of feedback must measure its success in achieving them. Strategic planning is a dynamic process that involves continually revising the plan in light of changes in the company's situation or the external environment.

This chapter discusses the steps involved in developing a strategic plan for the firm. It then looks at how sales associates can develop their own personal business plan and how their plans tie in with the company's plan.*

---

* Information in this chapter is abstracted and adapted from *Strategic Planning for the Real Estate Manager,* 3rd Edition, by Ken Reyhons, CRB, CRS, published by the Real Estate Brokerage Managers Council™, 1993; and from "How to Run a Business Within a Business," a presentation by Bonnie J. Sparks, CRB, CRS, DREI.

SURVIVAL DEPENDS ON STRATEGIC PLANNING

The real estate brokerage business has become extremely competitive. Factors that have contributed to this increased competition include the entry into the marketplace of non-real estate corporations such as Merrill Lynch, the proliferation of real estate franchises, and stricter underwriting requirements for mortgage loans as a result of the problems in the savings and loan industry in the 1980s. Moreover, changes in social patterns and new technology are changing how and where people live and work. In this risky, competitive and rapidly changing environment, strategic planning is no longer an option for the real estate manager. It is a necessity if a firm is to survive and prosper.

Strategic planning is a structured process of planning activities directed toward achieving a firm's goals. There are many ways to write a strategic plan. A commonly used process involves these five steps:

1. Situation analysis, internal and external
2. Mission statement
3. Objectives
4. Strategies
5. Tactics

Each of these steps in the strategic planning process is discussed in detail in this chapter.

STRATEGIC INTENT

Before a firm can begin strategic planning, it must define its strategic intent. Another term for strategic intent is vision. The concept of strategic intent is relatively new. It was identified by two academics who were doing research on why some small international firms grew to dominate world markets in specific industries. For example, in 1970, Honda was much smaller than General Motors and had not yet begun exporting cars to the United States. Yet in 1987, Honda made almost as many cars as Chrysler. Instead of trying to imitate what General Motors was doing, Honda set out in a new direction that focused on its own people and capabilities. The Japanese automaker's emphasis was on creativity, commitment and an obsession to dominate the field. Honda's strategic intent was to become "The Second Ford," i.e., to become the automotive pioneer of its era. Although Honda began with ambitions that were far greater than its resources and capabilities at that time, it was able to create an obsession with winning at all levels of its organization and to sustain this obsession for as long as it took to overtake General Motors, its top competitor. Academics have termed this obsession *strategic intent*. It is a broad, long-term goal that drives the firm's decisions about which strategies to pursue.

As the example of Honda illustrates, strategic intent has three characteristics:

1. *It remains stable over time.* It took Honda many years to become a major competitor in the United States automobile market.
2. *It captures the essence of winning.* There was a feeling that there was a risk of losing and an identifiable enemy (General Motors) to conquer.
3. *It sets a target that requires personal effort and commitment.* Managers and employees at every level were motivated to do their best to advance the cause.

In the real estate industry, many real estate franchise companies have made it their goal to overtake the industry's largest, Century 21®. The goal of some companies is to be the leader in discount brokerage while others want to be the leader in brokerage technology. A Denver brokerage with only 11 sales associates achieved its vision of dominating the condominium and townhome market in its area because the thought of doing so dominated the associates' professional lives.

When writing a company's strategic plan, brokers should consider including a "strategic intent statement." Such a statement could motivate the sales force and support staff to greater performance and give the company a new sense of direction, or at least a clearly defined direction.

If the company already has a clearly defined direction and mission, its strategic intent statement may be obvious. If not, it may reveal itself during the planning process. But once the company's strategic intent has been defined, it will drive the entire strategic plan. The clear direction it provides will affect the firm's marketing, recruiting, training and allocation of resources. The vision of the firm's strategic intent can mobilize the entire organization.

SITUATION ANALYSIS

The situation analysis is the cornerstone of your strategic plan. You need to take a detailed look at the present state of your company, competition and environment to formulate your plan for the future. In developing your situation analysis, you need to answer at least four questions:

1. Where am I today?
2. How did I get here?
3. What is my competition doing?
4. What kind of environment will we have in the future?

THE INTERNAL SITUATION ANALYSIS

Toward the end of your fiscal year or calendar year, hold a major planning session involving all of your firm's decision makers for the purpose of developing your internal situation analysis. It is important to establish a climate of openness, candor and honesty. All participants should check their egos, special interests and pet peeves at the door and try to be as objective as possible.

The internal analysis can be as comprehensive as you want. Make sure you have all the information you need to have an accurate picture of your company but don't gather so much data that you are drowning in statistics and information.

Using the past as reference and being alert to trends and patterns, go back over the past three years and consider the following factors:

- *Production Trends.* Review the numbers and types of listings you have obtained in the past, paying particular attention to the price ranges or geographic areas that have sold more quickly. Some of the questions you may want to ask are: What percentage of your listings sold? At what percent of the listed price? What is the source of most of your sales? What types of buyers have you served?
- *Trends in Market Share.* How does your market share compare with that of your competition? Have you been gaining or losing market share in certain areas or with certain types of products?
- *Success in Target Markets.* How successful have you been in your target markets?
- *Evaluation of Product/Service Mix.* Have you been working in the right product line? Have you concentrated on expensive executive homes while small condominiums or townhomes have been selling all around you? During the recession of the early 1980s, many brokers diversified and offered property management services for owners who had to leave unsold homes behind. Look for trendlines like these.
- *Sales Associate Longevity.* How long do your good producers stay with your company? What is your fallout ratio with new sales associates? Excessive turnover may indicate problems with recruiting, training or other areas.
- *Financial History.* Examine trends in your profit and loss statements in light of past production. Is the same amount of production resulting in less or more income? What impact have changes in your compensation program or commission split had on financial statements? Examine financial reserves and debt structure as well as cash flow.

Company Strengths and Weaknesses

Each participant in the planning session should list all the strengths they perceive the company to have. Try to identify the unique competencies in your firm that give you advantages over the competition. Building on these strengths may give you new opportunities for growth and new target markets.

Next, look at the problems or potential problems within the firm. Look for patterns or concerns to determine if they are coming from one or two areas of the company. For example, if you have experienced an extraordinary number of customer complaints, you may need to strengthen your training or monitor your agents' activities and contracts more closely.

Some areas you may want to examine in your evaluation of company strengths and weaknesses include the following:

- Your own leadership ability
- Management talent and stability
- Company financial condition
- Marketing programs
- Sales tools and equipment
- Image and reputation
- Office facilities and working conditions
- Support staff
- Internal policies
- Reporting systems and procedures
- Associate compensation program
- Sales associate capability and stability

Core Competencies

Another key assessment that should be part of the internal situation analysis is the identification of the company's core competencies. These are the skills and activities that the company does well. The company can exploit these strengths to gain a sustainable competitive advantage over its competitors. For example, Honda's core competency is its ability to develop a broad spectrum of engines and power trains for everything from lawn mowers to luxury cars. The main characteristics of a core competency are that it

- provides access to a variety of markets,
- benefits people, and
- is difficult to imitate.

A company's core competencies need to be in alignment with its strategic intent. It does no good to have the strategic intent of "dominating the luxury market in your area" unless your sales associates possess the competency of expertise in luxury homes.

THE EXTERNAL SITUATION ANALYSIS

The next step is to look at the factors outside the firm. These include the competition in the marketplace; the local, regional and national economy; and the political, social and technological forces that may affect your company. How to conduct an external market analysis is discussed in detail in Chapter 16.

First identify your competition. Not everyone in the real estate business is your competitor, and some firms that are not in the brokerage business *are* your competition. Your most direct competitors are those who cause you the greatest concern as you formulate your objectives. As you review the brokerage companies in your area, ask yourself these questions:

- Which companies compete with us for sellers/listings?
- Which compete with us for buyers?
- Which compete with us for sales associates?

When you've narrowed down your list of direct competitors, obtain as much information as you can about them. Then evaluate your position in the marketplace relative to them. Look aggressively for "loose bricks" in their corporate structures. Loose bricks are your competitors' unprotected market segments, weaknesses, voids, poor organization or lack of control. These loose bricks create opportunities for your company.

You may even be able to use your competitors' strengths to your advantage. For example, your major competitor may be a national company in which all major policy decisions are made centrally by people who have little knowledge of your local area. You can use their size, typically an advantage, against them in recruiting sales associates by emphasizing that if they join your company, they will be working with local owners who are knowledgeable about their market and who take a personal interest in their sales associates' careers.

In your internal situation analysis, you will identify many conditions that you can correct or change. But there are many factors in the external environment over which you have no control but which will affect your planning. These uncontrollable factors force you to make your best guess as to what will happen in the future. For any size of company, assumptions must be made in four major areas:

1. *The Economy.* What are the general economic conditions nationally, regionally and locally? You also need to consider unemployment and employment trends, the economic base in your market and the national trends in those industries, the availability of mortgage money and the trends in mortgage interest rates.
2. *Social Trends.* What are the demographic trends in your markets and how do these correlate with your company's marketing and strategic plans?
3. *Political Trends.* The "political" includes legislation, regulation and taxation that may be imposed nationally, statewide or locally. What is likely to happen regarding growth limits, zoning restrictions, environmental regulations, mortgage interest rate deductions and other political issues?

4. *Technology.* How will computers, the Internet, cable television and other forms of technology affect the way that real estate is listed and sold?

MISSION STATEMENT

A mission statement is a pronouncement of the company's reason for being in business. Using the information obtained in the situation analysis, the mission statement sets the direction, purpose and tone of the company.

The mission statement should do the following:

- *Identify the products and services you offer or plan to offer to the public.* Do you intend to specialize in residential, commercial or industrial properties? What services will your company provide?
- *Identify your target markets.* What cities, parts of cities or counties do you intend to serve? Whom will you serve—first homebuyers, retirees, transferees, upscale buyers?
- *Describe the methods you might use to deliver services to your customers and clients.* You might want to give the locations of your offices or to mention that you use a computer to deliver your services.
- *Mention the value of your services.* This could allude to your fee structure or the extra services you provide for your fee.
- *Spell out the unique services of the company.* What are the unique benefits you offer your customers? Mention the qualities and core competencies that make your firm special.
- *Define your relationship with your competitors.* Are you the premium company or the discount broker?

The mission statement should include a statement of function and scope that sets the parameters within which you will operate. Functions, programs, services and markets not included in this statement should generally be avoided.

The key is to make your mission statement support and amplify your strategic intent. It should reinforce the business you are in and define the arenas in which you will operate.

Writing your mission statement is an excellent opportunity for you to evaluate whether you should continue to do things as you've always done them. The planner should always be able to answer the question: Are we in the right business or should we change our business?

The statement of mission, function and scope is a clear signal to sales and administrative staff of the company's direction. It should be displayed in your offices and distributed to your sales associates for their presentation manuals so their customers will better understand what your company and your sales associates are all about.

OBJECTIVES

Determining objectives is the beginning of the actual strategic planning process. The situation analysis has helped you identify market opportunities, areas within your organization that you need to improve and where your competitors are most vulnerable. Setting objectives is where the company determines what it will do to take advantage of these opportunities. The objectives should be consistent with the company's mission statement as well as with its strategic intent. They should address much more than production. They should speak to growth, diversification and other desired outcomes. Your objectives should also exploit your company's core competencies or skills.

A helpful technique in writing objectives is to write your strategic intent and mission statement on a large piece of paper and hang it on the wall. Refer to these as you determine what you need to accomplish at various points in your planning period in order to achieve your goals.

Be careful not to set too many objectives. You should be familiar with your resources and your market as a result of your situation analysis. Prioritize and select those objectives that are most important to you.

Objectives should be specific and measurable. They should be set high enough to be a challenge, but low enough to be attainable.

Everyone who has a responsibility to make the plan work should be involved in setting objectives. Top management has the responsibility to ultimately set the firm's course and strategic intent. Office or department managers are responsible for setting objectives for their branches or departments. Sales associates aid in the situation analysis and also set their own objectives and personal production goals which are evaluated and considered in setting office and company objectives. Support staff also can make valuable contributions to formulating objectives. Many times they have a much clearer picture of what is needed to make the office work than upper management does.

STRATEGIES

Objectives define what has to be done; strategies define the activities necessary to get the job done and to achieve strategic intent. Strategies are broad courses of action selected from among many alternatives to achieve an objective. Each strategy supports a specific objective, although sometimes an objective may have several strategies supporting it. Strategies consider both current and future resources. People become an integral part of the plan as responsibility for each activity is assigned and accountability systems are established. Strategies should answer four questions:

1. How will we get where we want to go?
2. When will each step of the plan be completed?
3. Who is responsible for accomplishing each phase?

4.   What resources need to be committed today and in the future?

To be workable, strategies must be measurable. They must be written in specific terms so it can be determined whether the strategic activity was successfully carried out. Strategies must include a time frame. The time frame can be expressed in deadline form ("The sales staff will be expanded to 10 by October 1."); on a continuing basis ("Career nights will be held monthly."); or conditional ("The new accounting systems will be installed within 60 days after delivery of the new computer and software system."). Resources must be in place or available or a strategy is not workable. In the real estate business, resources include people, finances and facilities. Finally, responsibility must be assigned. A strategy must name the players who will make it work and who will answer if the plan doesn't work.

TACTICS

In the tactic phase the strategic planning process moves to the routine of everyday work. Tactics are short-range activities that are directed to achieve a specific strategy. Tactics are focused on present activities. Just as there may be several strategies to support each objective, there may be several tactics developed to carry out each strategy.

Real estate managers are usually quite comfortable making tactical plans because they deal with everyday jobs and tasks. Tactics should be developed to answer four questions:

1.   What needs to be done today, this week, this month?
2.   Who will complete which tasks?
3.   How will this activity be measured for effectiveness?
4.   What resources need to be committed now?

There is often confusion about which activities are strategies and which are tactics because there are several similarities between them. Here are some of the differences between the two:

- Each tactic is usually a single activity; strategies usually involve a series of activities.
- Tactics are usually carried out by one or two people; strategies typically involve several people.
- Tactics use current resources; strategies may involve resources not yet available.
- Tactics are usually measured in simple terms by a supervisor; the work is either done or not done. Strategies are usually measured by a series of reports and accumulated data and are supervised by top management.
- Tactics typically are completed within a short time span; strategies may take several months to several years to complete.

To summarize, the company's vision, or statement of strategic intent, sets the tone for the strategic plan. The situation analysis tells you how your company looks, both internally and in relation to the competition. The mission statement provides an overall view of where the company is going. The objectives spell out specifically what the company wants to achieve. The strategies are the broad courses of activities that you believe will cause the objectives to be accomplished. Finally, the tactics are the specific, day-to-day activities that will make the strategies a reality.

STRATEGIC PLANNING AND McKINSEY'S 7-S MODEL

McKinsey's 7-S model of organization analysis, introduced in Chapter 1, is an excellent tool to assist brokers and managers in strategic planning. This model recognizes the complexity of organizations by encompassing seven interdependent variables: strategy, structure, systems, skills, staff, style and shared values.

Strategy is by definition the key element in strategic planning. But strategy is useless unless the organization can execute it. To accomplish the strategic plan, all of the other elements of the firm must be aligned behind it and support it. The 7-S model can help the firm to accomplish this alignment.

The firm's structure should be based on its mission as identified in the planning process. A firm that has decided to specialize in residential real estate will have one kind of structure, while a firm that has chosen to diversify into related fields will be set up very differently. Structure also deals with how tasks are divided and coordinated. It places responsibility by indicating who is responsible for accomplishing what tasks.

As part of its situation analysis at the beginning of the planning process, the firm will identify its skills, or core competencies. The firm's skills must support its objectives if they are to be achieved. For example, if the firm's goal is to dominate high-end sales in its market, then it needs to develop and build upon its organizational capability in serving the high-end residential market.

Staff are a critical component in the company's plan. To accomplish its strategy of dominating the high-end home market, the firm would recruit sales associates who have experience in this market. Training, compensation and award systems would then support the plan's objectives. Systems must also be set up to provide feedback as to whether a plan is succeeding.

Changes in organizational strategy may be frustrated by the firm's style, or cultural constraints. It is important to make changes slowly and carefully to avoid morale problems and an exodus of valued sales and support staff.

Shared values are closely related to the firm's mission statement. They are the fundamental ideas around which the business is built and help to determine its direction and goals. The firm's shared values must support its strategic plan and must be clearly communicated to staff to help shape their behaviors.

STRATEGIC PLANNING FOR SALES ASSOCIATES

In order for the company's strategic plan to succeed, the sales associates who are responsible for making it work must understand and concur with it. Salespeople are more likely to do this if you help them formulate their personal goals and then translate their combined goals into the goals of the company. In this way, their personal business plan ties in with the company's strategic plan.

Sales associates can use the same planning process used by the company. They can do their personal situation analysis by examining where they are in terms of their family life, what values are important to them and where they are in their career life cycle and on Abraham Maslow's hierarchy of needs. These provide a look at people's motivation for doing things.

Sales associates may be in the introductory and learning stage of their career, the highly productive and highly competitive growth stage, the more stable maturity stage or the decline stage. Their needs for money, time to pursue personal and family goals, and social interaction and recognition by others will be different depending on which of these stages they are in.

Maslow's hierarchy begins with survival—making enough money to pay the bills, and security—putting away money for the future. This frequently corresponds with the introductory stage of the career life cycle. Maslow's levels three and four are affection—a sense of belonging, and recognition—the need to be respected by others. These levels often correspond with the growth stage of the career cycle. The highest level in the hierarchy is self-actualization. Those at the maturity stage are often at this level. Finally, those whose careers are in decline are likely to need affection and security. (Further discussion of career life cycles and Maslow's hierarchy of needs can be found in Chapter 11.)

Sales associates' business development plans will look different depending on where they are in their career life cycle and on Maslow's hierarchy of needs. When they reach the maturity stage, it is important that they create and constantly adjust their business development plan to provide continual challenges.

As part of their situation analysis, associates should also identify their basic skills, the things they are good at and on which they want to build their business. Like the firm's core competencies, these personal skills should provide access to a wide variety of markets, benefit the customer and be difficult to imitate. Examples of these are negotiating skills, customer service skills or skills at productively using new technology. As they develop their personal business plan, sales associates should work to achieve a sustainable competitive advantage, something that provides them with an edge over their competitors.

Next, they should examine their own sales history. What have been their best sources of income? Where did most of their buyers and sellers come from? What are their best and worst sources for sold listings or sold buyers?

Sales associates can also evaluate the competition in their target market and make assumptions regarding the external environment.

The next step in creating the business development plan is to create a strategic intent that captures the essence of winning for the sales associate. This should set a target that deserves personal effort and commitment. An example of a strategic intent is to be the top producer in the salesperson's market area. The associate should then write a mission statement that strives toward this strategic intent. This could be in the form of a statement of why their job exists. For example:

> My job exists to represent ABC Realty in providing superior listing and selling services to clients and customers in the anytown area. Capitalizing on existing residential properties using knowledge and skills to maintain superior performance and ethical standards, I will meet or exceed my career goals and assist the company in meeting or exceeding its goals.

The associate should then determine the objectives needed to implement the intent. These should certainly include earning objectives, but they may also include personal objectives, such as earning a designation, spending more quality time with family or becoming more involved in community activities. The objectives must contain criteria, conditions and performance standards, be well-defined, specific, measurable and within a set time frame. An example of an objective is: "I will increase income by 25 percent by the end of this year."

The next step is to determine the strategies or broad approaches used to achieve the objectives. A strategy might be to create in the customers' and clients' minds an image of personal success in listings and sales of higher priced properties in the sales associate's marketplace.

Action plans are the specific steps taken to implement the strategies. An action plan might be to establish membership in key local business and service organizations. Then the activities that must be accomplished in order to achieve each action plan must be listed. These might include the following:

- Meeting with manager to brainstorm appropriate farm area
- Calling Homebuilders Association to get information on joining
- Researching organizations whose members own higher priced properties and find one to join

Figure 4.1 illustrates a sales associate's personal business plan.

Once they have developed their strategic business plan, sales associates should consider the personal barriers to accomplishing their objectives.

FIGURE 4.1   Example of a Sales Associate's Personal Business Plan

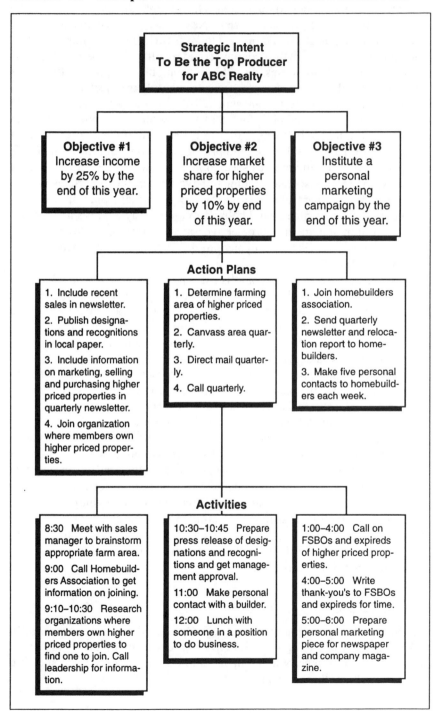

Barriers could include too many commitments, poor time management or lack of experience in a particular area. They should develop a plan to help them overcome these personal barriers. Next, they should consider internal or external changes that could prevent them from accomplishing their plan. For example, a change in the economy could result in there being no market for higher priced properties. For this reason, it is important that sales associates develop alternative strategies to meet their objectives.

The sales associate's plan should be aligned with the company's strategic plan, values and philosophy. In other words, the company and the sales associate should be going in the same direction. If the sales associate's strategy is to list and sell more high priced properties, but the company is perceived by the community as specializing in low and moderately priced property, the sales associate is going to have an uphill battle. Sales associates need to ask themselves: How does my business plan fit with my company's business plan? Am I helping my company achieve its strategic intent, mission statement and objectives at the same time I'm achieving mine? What services is my company providing to assist me in accomplishing my objectives?

Resources needed to accomplish the plan must be allocated. These resources are money, time and people. Money must be budgeted for organization membership, time must be allowed for participation in these organizations, and secretarial or clerical support must be available.

The sales associate must monitor performance to determine whether objectives and strategies are being accomplished. Has the action plan resulted in a higher priced inventory and customer base? If not, it may be necessary to revise the plan. It is also important to keep abreast of what is happening in the external environment and how that might affect a strategy. External events may also call for alternative courses of action.

Chapter 11 contains a detailed discussion of how real estate managers can help their sales associates set realistic goals and coach them to meet those goals. Understanding sales associates' personal and business goals also helps managers to motivate and retain their best performers.

By following the steps outlined in this chapter to develop a personal strategic plan, the sales associate has created a business within a business. When salespeople use their plan to focus on the strategies and activities that are most productive for them, they will improve not only their own performance but that of the entire firm.

CONCLUSION

Strategic planning is important regardless of the size of your firm. In today's rapidly changing business environment, it is important to have a strategic vision of what your company should be and a roadmap showing how you will get there. This is the strategic plan.

There is another benefit of a well-written strategic plan in real estate brokerage. Because so much emphasis has been placed on the independent contractor relationship, real estate has been slow to hold people—sales associates and managers—accountable for results. A strategic plan establishes workable standards of performance for everyone involved. Because all strategies include timing and determine responsibility, they provide a standard against which performance can be measured.

Chapter 5

Recruiting Salespeople for Retention

Recruiting sales and office personnel in real estate today reflects the challenges that face every industry in the United States: rapidly developing technology, the requirement to avoid discrimination and the changing average age of the population. Changing demographics affect not only the product most real estate firms have to sell—housing—but also bring a whole new work force into their selling market.

How well your firm responds and reacts to these changes will depend to a large degree on how well you plan and organize your staffing program. Starting with the first considerations—the jobs to be filled, the lead time desired, the kind of people you want, where you'll recruit them and the compensation you'll offer them—to the final and continuing challenge to keep the best people with your firm, a carefully structured program promises a good return for the time spent on it.

Management's challenge is to plan its personnel and program thoroughly, recruit the needed staff skillfully and present the opportunities the firm offers with such enthusiasm that applicants will not only be drawn to the firm, but newcomers will be drawn to the field as well.

MANAGEMENT'S FOREMOST CHALLENGE: RECRUITING

The foremost challenge that faces a broker is that of recruiting and selecting the right salespeople and an effective, efficient ancillary staff. If the broker does this well, a strange phenomenon occurs: he or she will be forced to run a better company. High-caliber salespeople expect and demand high-caliber management. The benefits that derive from this phenomenon are many. The broker makes more money, has fewer problems, gets more sleep and, in general, is happier. The broker's reputation, the company and the industry all benefit. When these benefits are compared to the alternative, it becomes readily apparent that staffing a brokerage office is an area that demands the broker's serious attention.

Wendell French explains the staffing process as "A flow of events which results in the continuous manning of organizational positions at all levels. . . . In a sense, this process is the flow of human resources into, within and out of the enterprise, although these activities are highly interdependent and all can be occurring within an enterprise at any one time."[1]

Just as real estate has adopted sophisticated, modern methods in selling, it is acquiring equal sophistication and technical know-how in personnel practices.

In McKinsey's 7-S model of organizational development, staff is one of the seven elements that must be paid attention to in a successful organization. McKinsey's consultants found that the top-performing companies consider people as resources to be nurtured and developed. This has led to the concept of performance management.

PERFORMANCE MANAGEMENT

Performance management is the process of hiring the right people and helping them develop into superior performers. The performance management process consists of the following three steps:

1. Recruiting, interviewing and hiring
2. Developing salespeople
3. Retaining, promoting or terminating them (retention begins in the recruitment process)

INDUSTRY CONSIDERATIONS

The real estate industry of the 21st Century will be more complex and technical than at any other point in its history. Before brokers choose their first salesperson, replace normal turnover or expand their sales force, it is important that they employ the strategic planning process, taking into account the state of the industry and the direction in which it is moving.

Broker/managers will be keenly aware of the changed attitude of the courts from the time-honored "let the buyer beware" policy to one of consumerism. Agency relationships have become all-important and all-encompassing. They will recognize the steadily increasing role government is playing in areas such as environment and pollution control, redevelopment, financing, equal rights and, in general, managing the economy. They will consider the increased level of competition developing through large multioffice firms, franchise operations, national referral networks, equity purchase companies and guaranteed sales plans. Alternative types of housing such as townhouses, condominiums, cluster homes and second homes must be recognized. Furthermore, they will develop a keen feeling for their local market area, its trends, special situations and brokerage competition. Only after analyzing these and other factors and evaluating their resultant costs and complexities can brokers begin to assess whether they should remain small, specialize or expand. Also, it is at this point that brokers begin to develop a feeling for the type of operation they will run and the kind and caliber of salespeople they will need.

THE COMPANY'S STRATEGIC INTENT, GOALS AND OBJECTIVES

In recruiting salespeople, your goal is not just to fill desks and hold down turnover. As in all the strategies your firm pursues, your goal in recruiting should be to help move the firm toward its long-term strategic intent. As pointed out in Chapter 4, strategic intent is not the same thing as strategic planning. Instead, it is a short phrase that clearly describes what the company wants to achieve in the long term.

The following are some examples of strategic intent in other industries:

- Canon: Beat Xerox.
- Honda: Become a second Ford—an automotive pioneer.
- Coca-Cola: Put a Coke within arm's reach of every consumer in the world.

Each intent describes a target that is difficult to achieve, that was probably beyond the company's resources when it was conceived and will not change every year or two. A company's strategic intent is easy for people to relate to and therefore to commit to. Strategic intent mobilizes the organization.

However, strategic intent alone is not sufficient to guide hiring decisions. You also need to know the specific objectives and strategies that will be used to achieve your firm's strategic intent in order to create an effective recruiting plan. The company's objectives deal with what will be achieved, by when, along the way to achieving the strategic intent. Strategies then are broad approaches to achieve each of the firm's objectives. Finally, action plans are specific steps to achieve the strategies. One of these action plans is the recruiting plan.

Before you can plan a recruitment program, you will need to answer such questions as the following:

- What are the firm's long-range and short-range objectives in terms of size, services, markets, profit and image?
- What will the company provide salespeople in terms of facilities, advertising, commissions, draws, fringe benefits, management professional services, investment opportunities and personal growth opportunities?

The recruiting plan has its own objectives, strategies and action plan that support the firm's strategic intent. For example, an objective may be to hire three new sales agents in the next six months. Possible strategies include holding career nights, using direct mail and buying advertising. The action plan then details the allocation of resources and the specific steps to be taken. For example, for the strategy of holding a career night, the action plan might include deciding on the date and time, mailing out invitations, having staff available for call-in reservations, arranging for refreshments and so on.

PERSONNEL INVENTORY

After you analyze the firm's strategic intent, goals and objectives as they relate to staff needs and have incorporated them into your company plan, you can begin to develop a timetable and budget for whatever money it will require.

A personnel inventory includes the following:

- *Analyze the skills in the organization.* Who does what and why?
- *Determine current and anticipated vacancies in the staff.* What staff positions are now open? Are any staff people planning to leave? When? Will you want to replace them?
- *Determine current and expected expansion or curtailment of departments.* How many people will you need to add if the firm is to strive toward the strategic intent and achieve its goals and objectives? Can any of these positions be filled by present personnel or will they all have to be recruited? If you plan to curtail any part of your present operation, can people so displaced be moved to another department? If expansion is planned, what are the personnel needs to get the new department or office underway? Are there people now on the staff who could be moved into any of these positions?
- *Predict internal shifts or cutbacks in personnel.* Even if you plan to keep the firm at its present size, adding no new services, should you be thinking about shifting some of your staff into new positions or cutting back where work production has proved inefficient and ineffective?

One good way to double-check the completeness of your inventory and begin to think about additions, shifts or possible deletions is to use your company organizational chart as a worksheet. It will give you a quick picture of who is responsible for what is being done and it can suggest possible changes and special strengths or potential weaknesses in the organization.

PERSONNEL PLAN

A personnel plan includes developing the following:

- Job analysis
- Job evaluation
- Job description
- Job specifications

Job Analysis

Firms with well-developed personnel practices use job analyses to develop job descriptions. A good job analysis includes such data as:

- What is the fundamental purpose of the job?
- Is the person an employee or independent contractor?
- What are the job's specific tasks and responsibilities?
- What does the job accomplish toward company goals?
- What are the working relationships of this job, including supervision given and review of accomplishment?

Job Evaluation

Job evaluation is the process of determining the relative worth of the various jobs in your firm and where each job will fit in the hierarchy of your firm. Job evaluation assumes that it is logical to pay the most for jobs contributing the most to the firm's goals; that people feel more fairly treated if compensation is based on the relative worth of jobs; and that the company goals are furthered by maintaining a job structure based on relative job worth. Some of the variables examined in a job evaluation are responsibility, skill, working conditions, effort and compensation scale.

Job Description

Writing in *The Practice of Creativity,* George M. Prince expresses the belief that top management that rethinks work assignments from manager to salesperson will reap enormous rewards. It will need the active help of those involved and much creative behavior to design into each job the maximum in personal achievement and satisfaction.

Job descriptions are summaries of the basic tasks performed on a job. See Figure 5.1. They have several important uses. They are useful in personnel planning, recruiting and counseling. Management can plan more intelligently if it knows the basic duties of a job as well as the qualifications required of the worker. Management can recruit more effectively if it is able to describe the job activities and responsibilities to applicants.

Job descriptions should be flexible as well as accurate. Rigidity destroys their value because if a person is to grow and contribute to a firm's growth, his or her job should be dynamic, not static. Both the supervisor and the staff individual should agree on the content of the description and that it fairly reflects the job. Some of the points to include in a real estate

FIGURE 5.1   Sample Job Description

---

1. **Develop and Implement Business Plan**
   - Find potential customers and clients by identifying target markets.
   - Identify your personal strengths and create programs using those strengths to reach those markets.
   - Execute those programs daily.

2. **Sales Activities Generated as a Result of Business Plan**
   - Prospect for listings.
   - List properties to sell in normal market time.
   - Develop marketing plan for listed properties.
   - Hold open houses on weekends.
   - Answer customer inquiries during floor time.
   - Structure finance programs.
   - Show properties to prospective buyers.
   - Give orientation tours for relocating families.

3. **Preparation and Support Activities**
   - Preview properties.
   - Follow-up on paperwork/sales.
   - Continue education.
   - Attend important meetings.
   - Participate in career nights.
   - Help train less experienced agents.

Source: Carla Cross Seminars, Issaquah, Wash., and *Recruiting Sales Associates,* published by the Real Estate Brokerage Managers Council, Chicago.

brokerage job description are: what salespeople do in your firm; hours of work each week, including nights and weekends; floor time; cold canvassing and similar duties; office employee working hours and duties (inclusion depends on whether salespeople are employees or independent contractors); who the staff person reports to; any staff position reporting to that person.

A growing number of firms prepare two descriptions for each job. One is written by the manager, based on personal knowledge and the operations manual; the second is written by the staff person, based on his or her experience and perception of the job. As the manager sits down with the staff person to review the two descriptions, lines of communication are often strengthened as each learns how the other views what is being done and why. The two then develop a single job description which details duties, time schedule and how the job coordinates with the work of others in the firm.

Job Specifications

Job specifications translate job descriptions into terms of human qualifications. Specifications are written by management based on job descriptions and the qualifications appropriate and reasonable to expect in the person who will do the work.

The job description outlines the duties involved. The job specification details the education, experience, resourcefulness, responsibility, contacts, and mental and physical effort involved in performing those duties. The specifications also cover the supervision and the general job conditions in performing the job.

Depending on the needs of your particular firm, your job qualifications might include such things as fluency in a foreign language, excellent calculator skills, experience in advertising or promotion, or experience in specific types of real estate, such as marketing new homes.

Although each broker has different requirements and needs, there are some common characteristics that brokers look for in the ideal sales agent. One of these is the individual's ability to relate to other people. A genuine liking for people and a high degree of empathy are desirable qualities because sales associates must be sensitive to other people and able to see things from their clients' perspective. Related to this, sales associates should have good communication skills. Not only should they be able to express themselves clearly and simply; they also must be good listeners.

Sales production depends on the individual's personal motivation and ability to keep going regardless of the difficulties he or she encounters. Sales associates need to be self-motivated and goal oriented. In addition, they need to have high self esteem. They must believe in themselves and their self worth. It also helps to have a positive outlook, to be enthusiastic about their career in real estate and the value of the service they provide.

Another important characteristic of successful sales associates is persistence. People who try once or twice and give up have little chance of success. The recruitment process should identify and eliminate individuals who will be easily discouraged.

Successful agents also are flexible and able to work as part of a team without insisting that everything be done their way. Other important characteristics most managers look for are intelligence and knowledge of the real estate business.*

---

* Material on this section was adapted from Ken Reyhons, *Recruiting Sales Associates,* 2d ed., Chicago: Real Estate Brokerage Managers Council, 1990.

Because job specifications usually result from a combination of management planning and job descriptions, they are subject to most of the same influences. The validity of job specifications is proven by the success of the person hired for the job and the degree to which the required characteristics are predictive of performance.

Some candidates who would do well in other firms might not be right for yours. To save time and dollars, focus your efforts on the candidates most likely to fit your company's needs. Strategic intent and company goals and objectives are all important in determining the type of person you are looking for. Another consideration is the fit between the company's and the candidate's style. A candidate who prefers working independently is unlikely to thrive in a firm that values teamwork. Firms need to recruit sales associates who will be comfortable with their management style.

YOUR WORKING PLAN

Now you can begin to get your recruiting plan organized on paper. Start by asking some important questions:

- What kind of people do we want?
- Must we expand present staff?
- Shall we initiate new services?
- Need we replace associates lost by normal attrition?
- Where will we find them—internal recruitment, external sources?
- How will we compensate them—commission, special bonuses, straight salary, fringe benefits (insurance, car, travel expense), incentive programs?
- How much should we budget to cover recruiting costs?
- How much can we spend on advertising—radio, television, newsletters, magazines?
- Should we use direct mail, personal letters, calling programs, career nights?
- Do we need printed forms, records, recruiting brochures?
- What is the target date for the program?
- When can we begin recruitment?
- Do we need a job performance evaluation analysis?
- How do we structure selection interviews?
- What is the starting date for going on staff?

Short-Range Personnel Planning

With short-range planning, major emphasis is placed on filling an immediate need, whether for a salesperson, clerk, secretary or accountant. This stopgap method of planning works for small organizations that intend to remain small. It is an approach that gives little thought to company objectives, expansion, whether horizontal or vertical, competitive influences and the like. It is concerned with filling positions that have been or soon will be vacant, whether through resignation, death or retirement.

Small real estate firms can survive on short-range personnel programs. But they are dependent on stability and may be unable to respond quickly to changing market conditions. They focus on getting maximum production from existing staff.

Long-Range Personnel Planning

Long-range planning in the real estate field places more emphasis on population trends, market projections and possible expansion (vertical or horizontal) as they affect the growth of the market being served or one that may be included in a general expansion program.

The numbers and qualifications of persons presently with the firm are a matter of concern and study by top management. The success of various departments and special projects, if any, becomes an important consideration in any long-range plan. Long-range planning may focus on the growth of the present organization or on designs to change the business character of the firm in the future.

Lead time is an important factor in any personnel program. What are the pressures to get the job filled? If you have a particular person in mind for a job, will he or she need extra time to sever their present ties? How will factors like your location, commission or salary structure, or the general economy affect the time needed to find people you want?

Here is where long-range planning pays off. The better it is, the more likely you will have enough lead time to find the best people. Good long-range planning often prompts management to add a person they really want before he or she is actually needed to avoid losing that person to a competitor.

Bear in mind that you don't recruit experienced agents; you attract them. But don't assume that top performers will come looking for you. You have to seek them out. One way to do that is through cold calls. Cold calls give you an opportunity to emphasize the benefits your company has to offer. These could include your firm's outstanding image in the community, an excellent compensation and benefits package, comprehensive training opportunities, access to up-to-date technology or whatever makes your firm an attractive place to work.

WHERE TO LOOK FOR SALESPEOPLE

There are two sources for salespeople: internal and external. Descriptions of the two follow.

Internal

Sales staff referrals are one of the best sources. Salespeople are often more selective about who they work with than is management. Also, top producers attract other top producers. To be effective, this source must be cultivated continually.

Most companies have built a substantial list of satisfied customers over the years. Many well-qualified prospects may be found from this source.

An outstanding basic and/or advanced training program is hard to keep quiet. Develop one and many well-qualified applicants will find their way to your firm because of it.

Office walk-ins are a source of applicants from a broad cross-section of people. Some are standouts but many are not qualified.

Individuals within your company with access to a specific personnel market such as universities, medical centers, schools or local industries could provide a vital link in locating potential recruits who fit the needs of your company perfectly.

External

Salespeople from other industries are another excellent source. Proven salespeople from other industries are often trained well in the fundamentals of selling, are fast starters and are often really excited about real estate sales.

Sales and motivational courses are an outstanding source of applicants already interested in sales and making an extra effort in that direction.

Career seminars can be effective if they have not been overused in your area.

Prelicensing schools are an excellent source for applicants already oriented to real estate. As with career seminars, local usage greatly affects results.

College and university placement bureaus are often concerned with placing both current graduates and alumni. Financial assistance plans may be necessary to compete for new graduates.

Advertisements provide a source of applicants from a broad cross-section of people.

If you have a sizeable group to recruit (such as when staffing a new department, division or office) consider the services of an ad agency or an employment agency. The former can help you develop display ads for newspapers or text for radio ads; the latter often prove a good investment of the dollar cost in recruiting and doing some preliminary screening of applicants, using your criteria.

Direct mail and cold calling is a final source for when you really need sales help.

HOW TO LOOK

Recruiting is more effective if done on a continuing basis. Hiring decisions made in a crisis result in poor decisions that you will have to deal with later. Even when you have a full staff, it is wise to encourage a continuous stream of inquiries. The lead time between selecting a new salesperson and getting him or her into production is long enough without having to take more time to get your recruiting machinery going again. It is a rare office that can't find space for an especially promising recruit. If you don't, you'll find that promising recruit working for your competition. Therefore, the manager should keep in constant contact with sources through personal visits, mail and the telephone. The image and program of the company as well as the benefits of selling real estate should be emphasized.

Recruiting is as much a daily task for the manager as prospecting is for the sales associate. Just as prospecting is imperative to the success of the sales associate, continual recruiting is imperative to the success of your organization.*

Recruiting Brochures

An attractively designed, well-written brochure can be a valuable aid to a recruiting program. Most real estate firms spend thousands of dollars advertising properties to bring prospects to the point of inquiry; yet many fail to develop even an inexpensive brochure to highlight the advantages of selling real estate and affiliating with their firm.

Brochures can be a valuable tool to leave with applicants; they can be used as a mailer or stuffer or handed to applicants to help them and their spouse make the job decision.

Key elements of a good brochure include discussion of career benefits (high income potential, limited financial investment, high degree of independence, personal growth, investment opportunities, challenge and prestige, it's fun and a people business) and company benefits (training program, experienced management leadership, high caliber sales staff, good company image and reputation, potential income, fringe benefits, personal growth possibilities, facilities, exceptional history and growth record, member of Multiple Listing Service, member of Board of REALTORS®, member of referral and relocation network, closing department, commercial department, insurance department and professional services).

---

* Much of the material here on recruiting is taken from *Recruiting Sales Associates.*

Television and Radio

Television advertising is costly, but it reaches a large audience quickly. Radio advertising reaches a similar audience at lower cost. But with both, you are paying a premium to communicate your message to a great many people who are not interested in or qualified for your openings.

Advertising

If you are always looking for people, you should always be advertising for new people. You could run a regular classified advertisement inviting people to inquire about a career in real estate. Your ads can be general, or they can be directed at a target market, for example, sales associates who have had experience in marketing new homes. You can also run display ads that challenge people to find out more about real estate sales. Figure 5.2 gives some examples of recruiting ads. Newspaper advertising has the advantage of generating quick responses, but you may have to sift through hundreds of applicants. Selecting the best candidates can be time-consuming.

Direct Mail

You could blanket an area with recruiting brochures or postcards, or you could target more specific groups of people through direct mail. A targeted mailing can be more detailed because you know whom you are reaching. Direct mail can also be useful in reaching qualified people who have been referred to you by your sources. It is particularly effective when followed up with a telephone call.

Calling Programs

Telephone calls enable you to sell the benefits of your firm to potential recruits who might not otherwise come to you.

Real Estate Schools

Real estate schools can be an excellent source of new licensees. The owners of the schools are interested in placing their graduates in a good firm. Get to know these owners. Let them know what you are looking for and what you have to offer new associates. You may also want to volunteer to come in and speak to each new class to answer students' questions about a career in real estate. This is a good way to familiarize them with your firm.

Don't forget about your own teaching activities. Teaching courses at your local community college, university, state association or local board is an excellent way to identify potential prospects. Good instructors have great credibility with students and can attract good people to their

FIGURE 5.2   Examples of Recruiting Classified Ads

Opportunities Unlimited

Are you an active member of your community? Do you like people? Involvement? If so, these characteristics can be rewarding to you in the real estate field helping people obtain the homes and lifestyles they desire. That's what real estate is all about!

YOU BENEFIT

by ensuring your own financial and personal growth. Explore a great opportunity for yourself today. For a confidential interview, call Charles R. Butler, 555-4567.

CRB REALTY

Wanted!

Real estate salespeople who have a strong background in MARKETING or corporate and military RELOCATION. Experience preferred but not necessary. Contact Charles R. Butler, 555-4567.
CRB REALTY

Source: Ken Reyhons, *Recruiting Sales Associates,* 2d ed. (Chicago: Real Estate Brokerage Managers Council, 1990).

companies. But don't teach only for recruiting purposes or blatantly pitch your company in class. Make contacts for your company outside of class hours.

Career Nights

Career nights have become one of the most popular methods of recruiting sales associates. They expose your company to many people in a short period of time and give you a chance to demonstrate to potential recruits that your company has high standards and high expectations.

Career nights are most effective if they focus on the future careers of the prospects rather than focusing on your company. Make sure your program covers what attendees want to know. Some of the questions they typically ask are:

- How do I get into the real estate field?
- How difficult is the test?
- What does it cost to get started?
- How do I get paid?
- How many hours do I have to work?
- How will I be trained? Who does the training?
- What do I do in a typical day?
- What kind of people succeed or fail?

When you talk about your company, you should talk in terms of how your company, your people, your tools and your programs can help them become successful.

Who conducts the career night program varies. However, someone should be there who represents top management of the company to give the event credibility. The sales managers looking for new people must be there. In addition, a talk by a sales associate or two can give prospects a good feel for what it's like to work at your firm. Regardless of who is there, be sure you have enough people there to cover the number of possible recruits you expect to attend.

A variation on the career night is a breakfast program with an interesting program related to the real estate business. Another is a Friday afternoon (around 5:00 PM) wine and cheese party to which experienced associates in your firm can invite associates from other companies in your area.

WHAT TO BUDGET

The largest cost of recruiting is the manager's personal time. However, there are some items that require a budget.

- *Brochures.* You can create a well-written brochure produced with desktop publishing and print it on colored stock in one color of ink for just a few dollars per hundred. Or you can produce an elaborate brochure with photographs requiring expensive four-color separations. The largest expenses will probably be for artwork, layout, design and copywriting, especially if they are handled by professionals.

- *Career nights.* Costs can include renting a hotel seminar room, coffee and refreshments, and the invitations or newspaper or radio advertising.
- *Advertisements.* If you consistently run a small recruiting ad in your local newspaper, you should include that cost as part of your regular classified ad budget. Institutional ads in newspapers or magazines can be costly.
- *Direct mail.* A large cost of direct mail is postage. If you prepare frequent large mailings, a bulk mailing permit will greatly reduce your postage costs. A postage paid return card will cost considerably more than normal postage, but you only pay for cards that are returned. If you send letters to targeted prospects, stationery and printing costs will be added to postage costs.
- *Entertainment.* Many interviews with new recruits take place over breakfast or lunch. In addition, some firms reimburse a sales associate who takes a prospective associate to lunch. This can add up to a major expense.

Avoid letting ego drive you to create very expensive ads or brochures. Low-cost ads and brochures that are written well can do a more effective recruiting job than expensive pieces that miss the target. Some sound advice is: Don't spend the money unless you are willing to spend the time. If the manager doesn't commit the time to contact prospective associates, the other tools are a waste of money.

KEEP RECRUITING RECORDS

Whether you use just one or a combination of recruiting sources available, keep accurate, meaningful records of the results. They will be useful in the future as you continue to add to your sales staff. Good records will reflect the effectiveness of the source. What you're after is not a record of the number of applicants any one source generated but which source brought you the best people.

Such records can also suggest what recruiting techniques worked best and any changes or improvements that occur to you as you go through the process. Figure 5.3 and Figure 5.4 show examples of records of recruiting sources and communication methods. Note that Figure 5.4 has a section to keep track of whether the individuals hired by that method succeeded or failed.

SALARIED OFFICE PERSONNEL

Much of the broker's success results from the efforts of the office staff. It is the broker who determines whether the office staff will be an asset or a liability. If they feel that the broker cannot be bothered with them because

FIGURE 5.3   Recordkeeping, Recruiting Sources

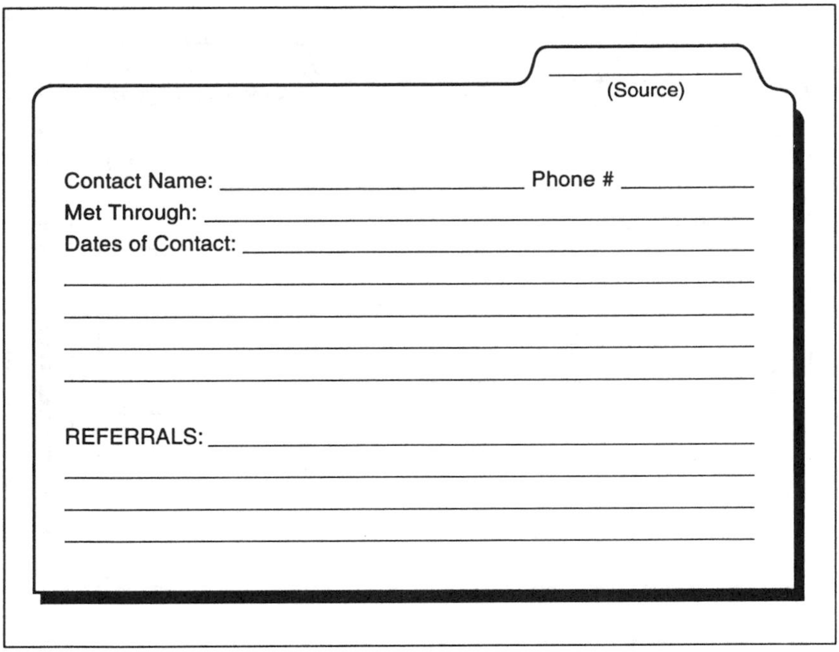

```
                                        ┌───────────────┐
                                        │   (Source)    │
 ┌──────────────────────────────────────┘               └──

  Contact Name: _____  Phone # _____
  Met Through: _____
  Dates of Contact: _____
  _____
  _____
  _____
  _____

  REFERRALS: _____
  _____
  _____
  _____
```

he or she has more important problems—such as the broker's own listings, sales or salespeople's problems—they will reflect this indifference, and disorganization and chaos are likely to prevail in the office.

When office personnel are efficient, responsible and well-organized, they give salespeople confidence, knowing that they can rely on the office staff to back them up while they are out in the field. Your office staff can play a leading role in maintaining friendliness and goodwill and keeping office morale high.

OFFICE PERSONNEL NEEDS

In planning office personnel needs, a broker should carefully spend time determining the type of people needed and what training and experience they should have to maintain the quality and integrity of the organization.

A carefully thought out job analysis for each office position is just as important as it is for the selling staff.

Job analysis can be handled in three ways: by observation, by interview and by questionnaire. Many companies use a combination of all three. One common practice is to have each employee describe his or her job as they see it, including duties, responsibilities, and the lines of authority. When

FIGURE 5.4 Recordkeeping, Communication Methods

	Communication Method		
Contact: _____	Individuals Hired	Succeeded	Failed
Cost Incurred: _____			
# of Inquiries: _____			
# of Interviews: _____			
# Hired: _____			
Notes: _____			
_____			
_____			
_____			
_____			

this course is followed, one should provide guideline questions. Some suggested questions are:

- What is the title of your job?
- Who are your immediate supervisors?
- What experience or education qualified you for your present job?
- Who do you work with inside the company?
- Who do you work with in outside firms on company business?
- What other persons tell you what to do?
- What duties do you perform without supervision?
- What machines are used in your job?
- A person in your job would normally be promoted from what job?
- A person in your job would be promoted to what jobs?
- Do you clearly understand the extent to which you have authority to make decisions?
- Do you have access to confidential information—why—how do you use it?
- What duties do you perform that you feel should not be part of your job?
- Will you please list as many items as you can which you feel are part of your position and how often you perform them?

Once employees have written their job analyses, the broker has a clearer picture of how the employees view their roles. The results are often

FIGURE 5.5   Typical Career Night Agenda

1. Welcome and introduction of participants
2. Have attendees complete registration questionnaires
3. Education and licensing requirements
4. Real estate sales as a career:
   - Advantages of real estate sales
   - Current market conditions
   - Skills necessary for success in real estate sales
5. Characteristics of successful salespeople:
   - Willing to work hard
   - Willing to learn
   - Willing to try
   - Persistent
   - Goal-oriented
   - Dependable, reliable, honest, ethical
   - Personally accountable and responsible
   - Enthusiastic and committed
6. Basic and advanced training needed
7. Financial commitment
   - Start-up costs
   - Ability to stick it out until the income begins
   - Irregular income
8. Tools and programs needed
9. How to develop a personal business plan that works
10. Getting off to a quick start
11. Why do the top producers make so many sales and commissions?
12. How to select a broker:
    - Compare philosophies
    - Compare training programs, both basic and continual
    - Compare management support, experience, designations
    - Compare quality of present staff
    - Determine market segments and market share of those segments
    - Compare marketing programs
    - Analyze total compensation and support package
13. Why salespeople fail
14. Outline your company's training, marketing, philosophy, history, tools, programs and compensation package

FIGURE 5.5   Typical Career Night Agenda *(Continued)*

15. General questions and answers
16. Break into small groups for questions and appointments for interviews

Source: This information was excerpted from Ken Reyhons, *Recruiting Sales Associates,* 2d ed. (Chicago Real Estate Brokerage Managers Council, 1990).

surprising. The broker often has a far different perspective of the employee's roles within the organization than the view the employees hold.

The completion of this job analysis form provides an excellent source of material for an in-depth interview. During the job analysis interview it's easy to review those areas where the employee and the broker are not on the same wavelength. Here is where upward communication can be of great value. Listen well. Repeat back to them what they've said so they know you're listening. This interview can result in a very effective job description, a better understanding and a vastly improved working relationship between office employee and broker.

DEVELOPING A SOURCE OF OFFICE PERSONNEL

An important internal source for filling positions is by promoting staff. People within your own organization may be capable of meeting the challenges of more responsible positions. Many brokers have adopted a philosophy of first trying to promote from within, rather than seeking outside talent. Thus the only openings that must be filled from outside are the job classifications in the lower strata of the organizational structure, which normally require the least amount of skill. Promotion within the office staff is an important means of building and/or maintaining morale.

Another source for recruiting office personnel is through your employees. Many times your own employees know qualified people who are seeking positions. Brokers who take the attitude that people are their most important asset will develop a sense of pride among their employees. Employees will be proud to recommend applicants who want to work with other highly competent people. But it should always be stressed that your firm is not interested in pirating employees from other companies.

In seeking employees from outside sources, the most commonly used medium is newspaper classified advertising. This can be a very effective source because it usually elicits the largest volume of inquiries but demands a lot of time to screen and interview them. Office personnel do not always seek a change in employment for money alone. When writing copy for classified advertising, stress that you have an exciting work atmosphere. Stress the opportunities for advancement.

Some experts in the field of office personnel recruiting feel newspaper classified advertising is not always the best source for recruiting office personnel. Some local junior colleges and business schools have placement offices that will work with a broker to help give guidance about job descriptions and salary ranges in addition to providing qualified applicants. In some areas they prescreen applicants for the employer. Also do not forget employment agencies for office personnel needs.

ENDNOTES

1.   Wendell L. French, *The Personnel Management Process.*

Chapter 6

Selecting Salespeople and Office Personnel

The most critical financial investment that real estate brokers make is in their sales staff because they are almost totally dependent on direct sales for revenue and profit. Effective managers recognize this fact in selecting the best salespeople to be found.

The selection process works best when it is carefully organized. When management understands the logical steps to follow, what is involved at each step and how the applicant either moves to the next step or is disqualified (or disqualifies himself or herself) and is dropped, the entire selection process operates more smoothly. Because the human element is ever present, mistakes will be made; but errors can be minimized by following a step-by-step selection procedure.

SALESPEOPLE ARE A BIG FINANCIAL INVESTMENT

A number of managers cling to the fallacy that when salespeople operate on a straight commission there is no financial investment involved. These managers are not yet aware of the desk costs of supporting the sales organization. Desk costs are the total expense of operating an office divided by the number of salespeople being supported, both producers and nonproducers. If, for example, the desk cost is $1,000 per month per salesperson, in a three-month training and start-up period, a nonproducing salesperson would in six months represent an investment of $6,000. This economic reality is called the "lost revenue rule." The lost revenue rule involves an estimate of dollar sales lost over a period of time by a nonproducer occupying the space that could have been used by a producer. It is activated each time a potential nonproducer is recruited.

CHANGE

Besides the reality of the sales staff investment, another fact must be recognized: We live in a world of accelerating change. Business norms and standards of 20 or even 5 years ago do not apply today.

Change can occur internally through growth, maturity and enlightened management. For example, X Company began business 20 years ago with two people. It has grown to a force of more than 100 salespeople operating out of ten offices. There is a general sales manager, branch office managers, a director of recruiting and training and an administrative staff. X Company has diversified into commercial properties, investments, insurance, leasing, farm and ranch brokerage, all calling for people with special abilities, experience and training. The selection standards X Company used even less than 10 years ago could not possibly serve today.

At the same time, Y Company is struggling to get started. Operating with a limited budget in a highly competitive market (not only competing in sales but also in finding and keeping capable people), Y Company's selection standards will differ significantly from those used by X Company.

But X Company and Y Company have something in common if both have alert, progressive leadership and management, aware of the impact of change in the real estate industry and the necessity of adjusting to it.

The forces of external change, often beyond the control of management, call for adaptations and modifications in the way things are done. This is especially true in the development and utilization of human resources and in the standards and procedures used to acquire on-the-job producers.

External changes affecting the goals and decisions of management can occur in the marketplace as new psychological, social and economic factors influence the attitudes and needs of buyers. Changes brought about by increased government regulation of real estate licensing and laws covering employment practices have a marked effect on screening and selection procedures. The labor market could undergo a radical change with the trend to offer financial assistance to new salespeople. The increased presence of corporate giants in real estate sales could intensify competition for both revenue and labor. The real estate franchise organizations with their mass advertising techniques, extensive communications systems, supportive services and pooling of effort and information continue to bring about significant change in management perspectives and methods among their members.

Some of the most important changes, at least with reference to human resources development, are a result of the wealth of information coming from management and behavioral sciences. These include the following:

- New approaches in determining company staffing needs
- Guidelines for establishing realistic performance standards

- Techniques for appraising and predicting on-the-job potential through more effective interviewing and selecting
- Improved learning and skill development training systems
- Increased personal motivation and improved performance by implementing behavior modification methods through coaching

These techniques and procedures are being used by many real estate firms with remarkable results. Measurable changes include higher levels of individual and group performance, reduction in turnover and increased sales and profits.

WHY PEOPLE FAIL

The principal reason people fail on the job is because management has failed to do its job.

Some failures are beyond the control of management. Even then, it is likely that the reasons for failure are also beyond the control of the person who failed, if management has done its job.

In the real estate industry, the turnover rate of salespeople coming into and then leaving the business has been estimated to range from a conservative 30 percent to as high as 70 percent. There is a saying among real estate managers that, "There is one-third coming, one-third staying and one-third leaving." If this is true, staff turnover is closer to the 60 percent to 70 percent range since two-thirds of the salespeople are in a state of flux, either coming into or going out of the business, all the time.

Many industry leaders agree that the largest volume of turnover occurs within the first six months. This period is not much more than a minimum start-up time in any career. In the life insurance and financial securities industries, sales agents are considered neophytes until they've passed the two-year mark.

During the first six months a great deal of the energy and attention of a new salesperson is directed toward training, gaining working knowledge and experience. This is especially true today with the rapidly increasing technical and legal complexities in real estate. Six months is not enough time to develop the momentum, motivation, self-confidence and professional skills vital to a successful career in selling real estate.

In other words, if industry estimates of turnover are even reasonably accurate, the vast majority of people who enter real estate sales as a career either quit or are phased out before they really get started. This turnover can be kept to a minimum by employing a sound selection strategy. It begins with the job description.

JOB DESCRIPTION

The job description should include both tasks and responsibilities. Tasks are the activities that the sales associate will be expected to perform, such as prospecting, conducting open houses, writing ads, writing letters, preparing and delivering competitive market analyses, presenting offers and so on. Responsibilities could include such things as acquiring additional training and education, following up with lenders and attorneys, making sure the office is secure—lights are off and doors are locked, keeping files in order and making sure they are given to the corporation secretary as the real estate transaction goes into closing. A detailed job description lets applicants know exactly what will be expected of them if they are hired by your firm. Figure 6.1 illustrates a job description for an agent who is new to the industry.

JOB SPECIFICATION

During the fall of 1987, the Real Estate Brokerage Managers Council™, in conjunction with the Life Insurance Marketing and Research Association (LIMRA International), conducted a study to investigate the life experiences that real estate recruiters feel facilitate success. Three hundred recruiters and sales associates identified the following life history (biodata) dimensions as critical to sales success: work ethic, sales temperament, maturity and responsibility, sales prospects, vitality, investment in career, organizational ability and establishment in the community.

Other studies have found that people who have a potential to succeed in sales share certain, basic personal qualities: interest in people, good mental ability, dominance, enthusiasm, aggressiveness, self-confidence, self-discipline and ego.

These life experiences and characteristics vary in degree from person to person, but they are considered essential to success. You should develop a written job specification based on the desired qualities and have potential recruits read this. Only after they understand the expectations and determine they can meet them should they fill out an application form.

MANAGEMENT ANALYSIS

The management analysis describes the climate surrounding and strongly influencing ultimate job performance. What if, for example, management selects salespeople on the basis of job specification calling for, among other things, "dominance, enthusiasm and self-confidence," then by its very nature fails to encourage or perhaps even restrains these characteristics in the selling job itself? The net result will probably be that a number of qualified people will come into the organization only to leave shortly because of their inability to adjust to the management style. From this, it is easy to see that it is important to match people to management style as well as to the job.

FIGURE 6.1 **Job Description for an Agent New to the Industry**

Initial Responsibilities:

1. Meet minimum standards for sales volume.
   a. Represent sellers in listing property.
   b. Represent buyers in obtaining property.
   c. Make a minimum income of $18,000 annually in total listings and sales closed.

2. Attend training.
   a. Begin GRI coursework within one year of associating with the company.
   b. Meet with and begin in field training program with mentor the first day of association with the company.
   c. Attend sales meetings when possible and take advantage of all learning opportunities.

3. Provide Quality Customer/Client Service.
   a. Provide timely, quality service to customers and clients making regular informational and timely follow-up calls.
   b. Use selected tools and services of the company in providing quality service.

4. Exhibit Superior Communication Skills.
   a. Listen effectively to needs and wants of clients and customers.
   b. Allow clients and customers to be influential in any and all decision making.
   c. Be understanding of people with different behavioral styles and communicate from their perspective.

5. Establish a marketing program.
   a. Create a personal contact list.
   b. Create a personal marketing brochure.
   c. Determine with manager a farming area.
   d. Initiate a direct mail campaign.

6. Know and understand the State Real Estate Licensing Laws, the state administrative rules, and the Code of Ethics of the National Association of REALTORS® and be willing to abide by them.

7. Follow up after offer acceptance.
   a. Follow company procedure for accepted offer, earnest money check and disclosures.

FIGURE 6.1   *(Continued)*

---

    b. Stay on top of closing process by making calls and providing material to appropriate parties at appropriate times.
    c. Schedule the closing.
    d. Attend the closing.

Initial Tasks:

1. Prospecting
    a. Maintain a "farm area" of no less than 150 homes in which a monthly contract is made by personal visit, telephone call or direct mail.
    b. Maintain a personal contact list from your sphere of influence in which a monthly contact is made.
    c. Choose from warm canvassing, for sale by owners and expireds for additional contacts monthly.

2. Listing presentations
    a. Make them well-prepared, detailed, organized.
    b. Research similar properties recently sold, currently available, expired; find the most conforming; compare and contrast.
    c. Be prepared to discuss pricing problems.
    d. Be prepared to discuss marketing plan.
    e. Include all appropriate disclosures.
    f. Prepare a Seller's Net Return.
    g. Practice any presentation until confident and comfortable.
    h. Present to potential seller.
    i. Work to get seller's signature on a listing contract.

3. Marketing the property
    a. Classified ads
    b. Flyers to cooperative agents
    c. Flyers to surrounding properties
    d. Calls to cooperative agents
    e. Open houses
    f. Info line
    g. Brochure tube
    h. TV home show participation
    i. Other

FIGURE 6.1   *(Continued)*

4. Buyer qualifications
   a. Know the basic process of qualification and figuring closing costs and how to share the information with the buyer.
   b. Share with the buyer the steps in the purchase from beginning to close.
   c. Share with the buyer the showing process and seek their cooperation for confidentiality and their commitment to view all scheduled appointments.
   d. Include all appropriate disclosures.
   e. Work to get the buyer's signature on a Buyer Agency Agreement.

5. Property showings
   a. Know the process of showing.
      1) Disclosures
      2) Gaining entry
      3) Timing
      4) Keeping buyers together and letting them discover

6. Preparing the offer
   a. Know the alternative terms, conditions, contingencies.
   b. Encourage calculated risks only.
   c. Include all appropriate disclosures.
   d. Secure earnest money check from buyer.
   e. Prepare a Seller's Net Return.

7. Presenting the offer
   a. Humanize the buyer.
   b. Include all appropriate disclosures.
   c. Present entire offer.
   d. Be prepared to handle any objection.
   e. Remain objective.
   f. Review the prepared Seller's Net Return.

SELECTION RATIO

The real objective of the screening and selection process can be summarized in one sentence: You must find a very special person to do a very special job under very special conditions.

Only a small percentage of the applicants for real estate sales work will have the personal qualifications to meet the specific demands of the job within the management framework of a real estate sales organization.

This relationship between the small number of people who qualify and all others who fail to qualify is called the *selection ratio.*

It has been estimated that in all types of businesses involving all types of occupations, the average selection ratio runs about four or five applicants for every person selected. When the ratio drops below this level, the qualifying standards for selection are probably less than desirable. In real estate sales work the selection ratio will be much higher than this across the board average; it will be more like one out of ten or greater.

A high but reasonable selection ratio is almost always joined by a low turnover rate. This leads to a fundamental rule applied to the screening and selection process: Within practical limits, the higher the selection ratio, the higher both the retention rate and the level of production.

A high selection ratio is an effect, not a cause. It happens when skilled management chooses only the people who have acceptable qualifications.

To find the selection ratio for past and present recruiting operations, go back through the past two years and pull the application forms of persons who got through at least the initial interview phase of the screening process. Separate the applications of those who were selected from those who were not, even though some of those chosen may have left. The numerical relationship between those who were selected and those turned down is the selection ratio.

If the ratio is one out of twenty or greater, there is a chance that past and current selection standards have been too rigid. If the ratio is less than one out of five, no doubt the standards have been lax, undefined or non-existent.

VALIDATION OF THE SCREENING PROCESS

Accuracy in decision making calls for a close relationship between information from the various steps in the screening process (application form, interviewing and testing) and the job specifications and job description. The degree or extent of this relationship is called *validity.*

A valid screening process, or any of its subparts, will provide only that information having predictive value about future performance. Information that does not bear directly on anticipated performance is surplus and not valid for selection purposes. Surplus information may have value in helping a manager develop a keener insight into an applicant's potential; and it may have significance later on in training, supervising and counseling a person to higher levels of performance.

Information has predictive validity when it can show some relationship with future performance. Education, work history, financial responsibility, physical health and certain observable or measurable traits and characteristics (mental perception, temperament, enthusiasm, self-confidence and self-discipline) are some of the valid indicators of potential performance. Information about hobbies and pastimes, political preferences or favorite colors rarely bears valid relationship to the ability to do a specific job. Indeed, some inquiries of this nature are no longer legally permissible.

Because of the complexity of human behavior and other variables affecting performance, the accuracy of information from the screening process is almost entirely dependent on probability. The more extensive and valid the information obtained, the greater the probability of making the right decision. No screening and selection procedure will predict with absolute certainty that an applicant will succeed or fail. This is especially true for sales work. Whenever someone claims to have a method, whether it be some special interview technique or some type of test that will measure sales potential with absolute accuracy, they are either ignorant of the facts or devious in their intent. Such claims are usually made to influence gullible, indecisive, uninformed management.

SCREENING PROCESS

All decision making is the result of some form of information feedback. Whether a decision turns out to be right or wrong depends largely on the amount, relevance and accuracy of the information and how well it zeros in on the desired goal or standard.

In the screening process for selecting salespeople, information can be obtained from six basic sources:

1. Prescreening
2. The application form
3. The screening interview
4. Testing
5. The background investigation
6. The evaluative interview

Each of these sources of information can be viewed as consecutive steps leading toward a final decision.

How these six steps can be organized into an information feedback system is shown in Figure 6.2. In this illustration, the first information from an applicant is screened for its valuable parts during Step I, prescreening. This data is fed back and compared to the job specifications and job description. At that point a decision is made to reject or proceed. If the decision is to proceed, further information from the applicant is processed through Step II and looped back through the comparison procedure. This process continues with either rejection or continued acceptance by either party during each succeeding step until all possible information has been processed and compared with the ideal. In the meantime, each step serves to verify, amplify and refine the information coming from the preceding steps.

If this approach, in its basic form, is used, errors in decision making can be greatly reduced, resulting in much higher selection efficiency.

FIGURE 6.2   Decision Making by Information Feedback

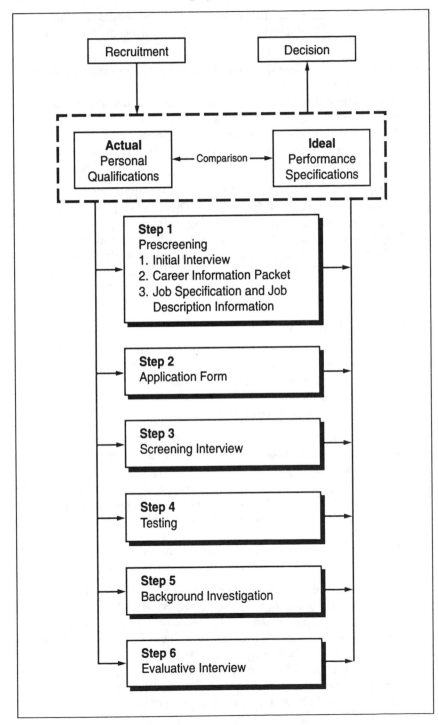

Prescreening

In Step I the vast majority of applicants who would ultimately fail are eliminated or eliminate themselves. They can be grouped into four categories:

1. Those unable to meet basic requirements of the job specification and job description
2. Those with only a passive interest or idle curiosity about a career in real estate
3. Those with misconceptions about the business
4. Those who lack the desire, courage and self-confidence essential to succeed in real estate sales

If Step I is followed consistently, most of the applicants who survive have at least some potential for success. This first step in the screening process requires only a minimum of management time.

Step I involves the use of three sources of information, part of which includes information for applicants to use in making their decisions about real estate sales work. These are the job specification and job description information, the initial interview and the career information packet.

The Initial Interview

Many applicants contact a company in response to recruitment advertising or referral. In fact, when advertising for salespeople, applicants should be encouraged to make their first contact by telephone and schedule an interview appointment.

The initial interview serves four purposes:

1. Conserves time for both the applicant and the manager.
2. Avoids the risk of making impulsive judgments caused by the "halo effect" and "stereotyping," discussed in Step III.
3. Gives management an opportunity to evaluate the applicant's telephone personality: his or her forcefulness, tone and skill in communicating with a stranger, that will be important in telephone listing and sales prospecting.
4. Enables management to quickly gather some personal data and history to use in qualifying the applicant for further screening.

A uniform information checklist or outline should be used in the initial interview. It serves as a guide in obtaining pertinent data and keeps the interview from straying into areas not related to performance qualifications. A number of telephone interview checklists are available in standard forms or managers can create their own.

An adequate checklist will include information such as: name, address, telephone number, present employment status, education and any other information that could have a direct bearing on performance. Space should be provided for making brief notes on how the applicant responds and reacts in the telephone interview.

This part of Step I enables the manager to make the method of compensation clear. Applicants with little or no knowledge of the business may not realize that most salespeople operate on a straight commission basis.

Ordinarily, the interview should not take more than 30 minutes and should always be conducted by the manager or the personnel department.

There will be times when an initial interview will be possible and even practical, such as with walk-in applicants, as a result of career night presentations, or during telephone interviews. Then the manager can implement the second part of Step I, the career information packet.

The Career Information Packet

As the initial interview ends, applicants, even if disqualified at this early point, are told that they will be provided some information to help them understand more about the job. Whether they choose to take it with them or to have it mailed to them can be evidence of their motivation and interest.

The career information packet consists of four pieces.

The first is a brief discussion of the real estate industry. It can include a description of the various divisions and related careers, types and levels of certification, and legal and ethical requirements. This information is available in printed form from a number of sources. The National Association of REALTORS®, most state associations and many boards of REALTORS® provide such material for use in recruiting. A resourceful manager can create material tailored to his or her own firm at very little cost.

The second is a brief history of your company, its growth, competitive position, types of markets and future plans. This information can be arranged under an attractive heading, typed and reproduced in quantity at moderate cost.

The third is a brief statement of company policy and procedures which must be observed in the event an applicant is selected.

The fourth piece is a personal cover letter for the packet. It can be typed and reproduced on quality company letterhead, leaving room for the applicant's name and date. Each letter is signed individually by the broker. Because it will help less-than-desirable applicants disqualify themselves by putting the onus of making the next step on them, it can represent enormous savings in time.

A cover letter for the career information packet might read like the letter reproduced in Figure 6.3. Notice how this letter pulls no punches in making perfectly clear what is expected of the recruit, and what the recruit can expect from a career in real estate sales.

FIGURE 6.3   Cover Letter for Career Information Packet

Date _____

Dear_____

Thank you for your interest in our company.

Because I want you to give serious consideration to a career in real estate sales, I am enclosing some information to assist you in understanding our business. I will appreciate the time you take to review this material and feel sure it will help you make a positive decision.

A career in real estate can be both financially rewarding and personally satisfying. It is sales professionalism at its best. At the same time it demands hard work, long hours and the capacity to deal with frustration and disappointment. In short, it calls for the highest degree of personal courage, determination and stamina.

We are fiercely proud of the people who represent our company. In order to qualify they had to meet the toughest standards possible. They had to undergo a thorough background investigation, intensive interview sessions and take penetrating tests to determine their qualifications for selling real estate. They spent countless hours in training in order to meet rigid licensing requirements. They are truly exceptional people. We need more like them!

If after reading the enclosed information you are interested in discussing a real estate sales career with our company, I would consider it a personal favor if you will contact our sales manager, _____. He/she will be happy to arrange an appointment with you. This may be the rare opportunity both of us have been looking for.

Cordially,

President

This approach, as an initial step in screening salespeople, is not unique or new. It has been practiced in top sales organizations for years with great effectiveness.

Management scientists have verified that individuals with high personal standards are attracted to and look for situations with the same standards. People with a clear self-image prefer to work with people who share their attributes. Company management with a clear self-image and high standards has a natural appeal for success-oriented people. In addition, the more difficult the qualifying standards, the greater the esprit de corps, dedication, loyalty and cooperation of the staff. All this adds up to high individual and group productivity and greatly reduced turnover.

For the same reasons, people who lack the characteristics for success will shy away. Lacking adequate self-confidence and an intense desire for personal achievement, they will go where less is expected of them. Thus, prescreening not only acts as an effective recruiting technique but also allows those who cannot survive to eliminate themselves gracefully.

The time and costs involved in Step I appear insignificant when compared to what is at stake.

The Application Form

The application form, Step II, should include all legally permissible biographical data that relates to future performance. It is the first official document to go into the personnel files. This form is also the only source of information other than testing that can be validated.

There are two ways to handle an application form. It can be included in the career information packet, giving applicants time to fill it out at their leisure, or it can be given to them to fill out at an appointed time prior to scheduling a screening interview (Step III). This enables the manager to review the application form and evaluate whether the candidate should be called for a screening interview. If a screening interview is warranted, the form will help the manager prepare appropriate questions in advance of the interview.

Application forms can be purchased or the manager can create one. Be sure the application form you use satisfies the requirements of applicable equal employment statutes and regulations.

A good application form will ask for detailed personal data including name, address, Social Security number, education and training, as well as employment history.

Other information that may be sought in an application form includes character references, hobbies and pastimes, organizational affiliations and so on. This information may have little relevance to job ability but is useful in helping the manager gain a better overall view of the applicant and in preparing for the personal interview by identifying common interests.

Since the application form serves as the best guide for conducting interviews, it should also provide open space for notes by the interviewer.

Information contained in an application form can be a reliable indicator of an applicant's character and stability. Frequent job changes and transience or lack of credit references should be cause for concern and explored carefully in the screening interview. Personnel specialists say that strong signs of instability in a person's background almost always correlate with unpredictable or unstable performance on the job. Many managers do not take negative information at face value and proceed to select a candidate simply because he or she looks good. When this happens, management has failed and not the sales associate.

One caution: Only questions can be asked and data collected that deal specifically with job performance. Questions about sex, marital status, children and their ages, or specific mental or physical problems are not allowed. Always check with your local equal employment agency prior to preparing forms in order to manage your risk.

The Screening Interview

When Step II is complete, an enormous amount of vital information regarding an applicant has become a matter of record. Before proceeding to Step III, the manager should review both the telephone interview checklist and the application form, paying special attention to chronological gaps, contradictions or inconsistencies in the data and appropriate notations made. If possible the review and note taking should be done without the applicant being present. Before the screening interview begins, the manager should have all previous information well-organized and highlighted. This will help keep the interview structured and on track, save valuable time and provide a businesslike climate to the proceedings.

There are two basic interview techniques: structured and casual. The structured interview is designed to elicit specific information about the applicant, generally following a printed outline or list of questions. Structured interview forms can be purchased. Probably the best is the application form itself, provided there is a space for making notes. The casual interview, although guided or patterned, is intended to help the applicant speak freely and volunteer information about himself or herself. Step III, the screening interview, is usually structured; Step VI, the evaluative interview, is casual.

The screening interview serves two purposes. First, using a structured approach, the manager can quickly verify or clarify existing information on the application form.

The second purpose is observation. This may be the first time the manager has met the applicant. All information accumulated up to this point has been objective in content. Now the applicant sits before the manager displaying physical characteristics and personal mannerisms. This is where the element of personality enters the picture. It is historically the weakest point in the screening process because it is at this point that all prior information feedback, positive or negative, is likely to be dismissed.

First impressions have a dynamic and often misleading effect on one person's judgment of another. Skilled interviewers recognize this pitfall and go to great pains to avoid being trapped into forming impulsive, subjective opinions on the first meeting. The adage that beauty or truth is in the eye of the beholder has no place in the screening and selection process. Poise, charm, charisma or physical attractiveness have little bearing on self-confidence, self-discipline or how hard a person will work. In this regard there are two psychological effects the manager should keep in mind during the initial interview. They are the "halo effect" and "stereotyping."

Halo effect is present when some single facet in a candidate's outward physical appearance or personality tends to overshadow all other considerations. A prominent nose may turn off an interviewer. A winning smile may have the opposite effect.

Stereotyping occurs when the interviewer classifies people on some notion that physical characteristics determine personality and behavior. For example, red-haired persons are quick tempered, fat people are easygoing, a sloping forehead means stupidity, and a receding chin signifies lack of character.

Some traits or mannerisms can provide clues to general behavior and should be carefully noted in the screening interview. Positive attributes to look for include personal neatness, good-natured responsiveness, interest and enthusiasm, communicative skill and self-assertiveness. Negatives to watch for are lack of good grooming, evasiveness, undue restlessness, an unusually subdued or timid manner or excessive bravado.

The screening interview should be conducted in privacy if possible. If it is readily apparent after 15 or 20 minutes that the candidate does not fit the company's criteria, the manager should thank the applicant politely for coming in. If the manager is interested in the candidate, the interview should be continued for no longer than 60 minutes in total. Remember, the purpose of this interview is to get to know the candidate and determine whether the candidate meets the company's criteria.

Inexperienced managers often use the interviewing time to sell the company's benefits to the candidate, but you may be selling your advantages to the wrong person. You haven't yet asked the appropriate questions to determine that.

During this first interview, focus on the candidate. If, as a result of what you have learned, you are interested in this person, set up a second interview to sell the benefits of your company and to further evaluate the applicant.

Here are some questions you may wish to ask in the initial interview.* Because different companies have different responsibilities and desire different characteristics in their sales associates, some of these questions may not apply to your company.

- What is the reason you have decided to enter the real estate business?
- What skills do you have that will make you a successful sales agent?
- Tell me why I should hire you. What do you have to offer a brokerage firm?
- What is your previous experience?
- What is your understanding of how agents get paid in a transaction? Do you know anyone who makes a living selling on a commission-only basis? How much money do you think they earn?
- What do you think separates a top real estate agent from a mediocre one?
- If you were putting your home on the market and were evaluating potential listing agents, for what would you be looking?
- From your vantage point, where do you think our company is particularly strong?
- How many hours per day will you invest in real estate? How many weekends per month?
- Where do you see yourself five years from now?
- Who do you know that you will do business with? Are you willing to farm?
- Do you have a suitable automobile?
- Are you willing to make cold calls?
- How do you feel about education and training programs?

Certain topics may not be brought up in the interview. The following are some questions which are prohibited under federal guidelines. You should also be aware of local and state regulations.

- Marital status or future marriage plans
- Spouse's or parents' occupations or job titles
- Number of children, their ages, or plans for having children
- Babysitting arrangements
- Whether a spouse would agree to overtime work or business travel
- Age or date of birth
- Feelings about working for someone younger
- Place of birth
- Race or national origin
- The origin of a surname
- Religion or what religious holidays are observed
- Political views or political party preference

---

* The following section is based on Title VII of the Civil Rights Act of 1964 and Executive Order 11246, cited in *Reader's Digest Legal Questions and Answers Book.*

- With whom a person lives
- Home ownership or rental status
- Debts and names of creditors

According to the *ADA Compliance Guide* (Thompson Publishing, Washington, D.C., 1991), additional questions that are not allowed include: inquiries that do not relate to the applicant's ability to perform essential job-related functions; inquiries about particular disabilities, disabling conditions, the severity of a disability, or workers' compensation history; and inquiries about the health or disability of family members or other persons with whom the applicant is associated.

Inappropriate behavior on the part of the interviewer can have a negative effect on the applicant's behavior or impression of the company. For example, if the interviewer has a habit of looking at his or her watch continually, the candidate could hurry through answers and skip over important information.

Don't appear to be rushed or abrupt. Make sure you have scheduled an adequate amount of time to meet with the applicant and thoroughly review his or her qualifications.

Don't allow other responsibilities, pressures or problems to intrude on the interview. Have your secretary hold your calls. Interruptions can cause both you and the candidate to lose focus. Stay focused; this is your only opportunity to objectively evaluate the candidate.

Don't allow note taking to interfere with maintaining eye contact with the applicant. If the applicant agrees, use a tape recorder so you can focus on the person, not on your note taking.

Don't be impolite. If possible, offer the applicant a beverage, a comfortable chair, and a few minutes to collect himself or herself before the interview begins.

Don't appear disinterested, even if you know the candidate is a poor match for your company. The candidate will leave with a good perception of your firm if you remain engaged and interested in what he or she has to say.

Testing

Step IV, testing, is the most controversial and misunderstood step in the screening and selection process. Much of the confusion and resistance involving testing has been caused by those who publish and market tests. Exaggerated claims of test effectiveness in predicting job performance cause some managers to rely too heavily on test information, often with unpleasant or discouraging results. In addition, many test publishers prefer to shroud their products with an aura of mystery and omniscience in an attempt to justify unreasonable prices or fees. This attitude has obscured the rationale of the test methods and has led to the alienation of many business executives who are concerned with the risks of adverse or discriminatory selection.

In spite of the criticism testing has generated, a well-designed and validated test, used properly, can prove to be a meaningful source of information.

Why Use Selection Tests?

All individuals are not equally suited for all types of jobs. In other words, different individuals have different probabilities of success in different occupations. The great benefit of selection tests is that they can be used to differentiate well-suited applicants from ill-suited applicants *before* they are placed on the job.

In addition, because the results of computer-scored selection tests such as interest inventories and biographical data are tabulated objectively, the bias of the manager is minimized.

If you use tests, you should administer them following Step III, the screening interview, to further cement your hiring decision.

Test Validation

Before using a test to select a sales associate, you should make sure the test is both valid and unbiased. A valid test gives results that are justifiable and sound. A biased test gives results which are unfairly distorted.*

There are many different ways in which tests can be validated, but one of the most important validation procedures in tests used for employment purposes involves determining how closely the test corresponds to actual on-the-job performance. A statistical analysis can be done to evaluate the degree of correlation between an applicant's success on the test and his or her success on the job. The statistic, called a correlation coefficient, can range from –1 to 1, with 1 indicating the highest correlation. A high

---

* This section on testing was extracted from an article by Michelle Mosher Crosby, Ph.D., an associate scientist in the Marketing Resources Research Department of LIMRA International in Hartford, Connecticut. The article initially appeared in Vol. 3, No. 3 of *Management Issues & Trends* newsletter, published by the Real Estate Brokerage Managers Council™. Crosby used the following references in her article:

Hunter, J.E., and R. F. Hunter (1984). Validity and Utility of Alternative Predictors of Job Performance. *Psychological Bulletin,* 96.

Schmitt, N., R. Z. Gooding, R. A. Noe, and M. Kirsch (1984). Metanalysis of validity studies published between 1964 and 1982 and the investigation of study characteristics. *Personnel Psychology,* 37, 407-422.

Additional information in this section was obtained from *The Validity of Testing in Education and Employment,* U.S. Commission on Civil Rights, Washington, D.C., May 1993.

correlation between test scores and performance is desirable because it suggests that the test score predicts performance very well. A coefficient of .2 is considered to be acceptable and .3 or above is very good.

For example, let's say you administer an intelligence test to applicants for the position of sales associate. Some applicants receive a high score, while other applicants receive a low score. Three months later, on-the-job sales performance is measured. If the intelligence test is a valid test, then there would be a high correlation between a high test score and a high score for actual performance.

In reality, most tests are highly imperfect in predicting on-the-job performance. Low correlations between tests and job performance are common. The typical correlations of from .2 to .4 mean that test scores explain from 4 percent to 16 percent of the observed differences in performance. Many experts believe that tests with even a weak measure of validity will give a business an edge in today's highly competitive environment. However, the weak correlation between tests and actual worker success means you should not make hiring decisions solely, or even primarily, based on test scores.

It is also important to make sure that the tests you use are not biased. Tests are biased when different racial or ethnic or gender groups respond to them differently. If a test is biased, scores may overpredict or underpredict performance for the members of a particular subgroup compared with test takers in general. You should select tests that are designed to avoid bias. For example, tests with scores that refer to the ability to do certain tasks (criterion-referenced tests) are less likely to reflect bias than test scores that refer to the abilities of other individuals (norm-referenced tests).

In recent years, many experts have recommended that the test validation process involve doing a job analysis—determining job tasks and ensuring that employment tests for that job include measures of the tasks. So, for example, a test used to hire secretaries would measure typing, filing and phone answering skills. There are many other mechanisms for reducing test bias that may be incorporated in routine test development procedures. These include reviewing test items for insensitivity to particular racial, ethnic or gender groups, and avoiding "culture-loaded" items, i.e., testing information that is specific to a particular culture as opposed to items requiring only universal concepts or knowledge. Ask test publishers to let you see the descriptive and statistical data needed to verify their claims regarding the construction and validity of their tests.

The courts have been moving away from requiring employers to justify the discriminatory impact of employment tests and toward requiring job applicants to prove discriminatory intent. Nevertheless, using biased tests is illegal, unethical and poor business practice.

Types of Selection Tests

There are many different types of tests for selecting sales associates. Let's turn to a brief discussion of some commonly used selection tests.

Interviews   Though not by definition a test, the interview is the most commonly used selection technique. Interviews are universally used because managers want face-to-face interaction with prospective sales associates. However, they are best used in conjunction with other selection methods to tell you how well an applicant will fit into your company's culture.

General Aptitude Tests   The General Aptitude Test Battery (GATB) and other general aptitude tests are widely used as employment tests. They are general tests of cognitive, perceptual and psychomotor skills used to predict job performance. However, the ability of such standardized tests to accurately report knowledge, abilities or skills is limited by assumptions that these attributes can be isolated, placed on a linear scale and reported in the form of a single score.

Work Samples and Situational Tests   With work samples and situational tests, applicants are asked to perform some of the actual tasks a person on the job would do every day. These approaches have been shown to be highly predictive of on-the-job success.

For example, one commonly used situational test is the "In-basket Exercise." Here, an applicant is presented with an "in-basket" of memos, letters, reports, and so on, that require immediate attention. The applicant's ability to prioritize and perform the tasks is then assessed by raters. Situational tests like these have good validity in predicting on-the-job performance because they measure actual tasks required by the job.

Work samples and situational tests, however, can be time-consuming and expensive to administer. In addition, they only give a measure of the ability the applicant brings to the job—not the potential the individual has if given additional training. For this reason, work samples and situational tests are much better suited for hiring experienced rather than inexperienced associates.

Intelligence Tests   Mental abilities (or intelligence) tests have long been used for personnel selection. It is generally believed that the more intelligent a worker is, the higher the individual's productivity will be. Mental abilities tests have been demonstrated to be valid predictors for a wide variety of occupations.

However, these tests suffer from the same flaws as general aptitude tests. They ignore the complexity of human intelligence and ability by attempting to reduce multiple facets of knowledge, learning and thinking to a single score. In addition, these tests may not present the whole story, because there are other important qualities that a good salesperson should have, such as motivation and honesty. As a result, mental abilities tests tend to be less predictive of success in sales than in other occupations.

Personality and Interest Inventories   Unlike mental abilities tests, personality and interest inventories have neither right nor wrong answers. Applicants answer questions about their various likes ("I like to play sports.") or how much they agree with different statements ("People who work hard get ahead."). Scales composed of such items are used to assess the degree of interest in a particular activity or the presence of a certain personality characteristic, such as aggression, extroversion, confidence and so on. The scale scores are then used to predict job success. The basic rationale is that successful workers have certain interests or personality patterns and these patterns become the basis for their selection.

Personality and interest inventories have been demonstrated to have relatively poor validity for predicting success across occupations.

Biographical Data   Using biographical data (also called "biodata") is a popular selection test method that has a long history of successful prediction.

The use of biographical data for the selection of sales associates is based on the assumption that "the best predictor of future performance is past performance." Biodata are used as a means of identifying which life experiences differentiate successful from unsuccessful associates. Biodata measure stable, enduring traits that predict success in a given occupation. Biodata typically take many different forms, including questions about personal history (e.g., education, past employment); present situation (e.g., income, club membership); and self-reports (e.g., attitude toward employers, self-ratings of social skills).

Biodata also can be scored consistently and fairly using computers. If scoring is done at a centralized facility, the scoring key can remain intact because people won't learn the "correct" answers (that is, the answers shown to be predictive of success). Centralized scoring also allows for the creation of large data bases which can be used to update, improve and enhance the scoring procedures over time.

Biodata have proven to be excellent predictors of success in sales. One disadvantage, however, of biodata is that very large numbers of sales associates—typically in the thousands—are necessary for the development and validation of biodata measures. For this reason, biodata inventories cannot typically be validated on a firm-by-firm basis.

In sum, there are a number of tests available for the selection of real estate sales associates. Each technique has its advantages and disadvantages. You must weight the benefits and the costs before choosing the selection method best for your company.

Evaluating Selection Tests

With the many brands of selection tests available on the market, you may feel confused about which tests to incorporate in your selection program. Here are some guidelines for evaluating a potential test.

What Does the Test Cover?   All *good* tests provide extensive information outlining what the test is supposed to measure, how the scores should be interpreted and the research undertaken to support it.

Why Should You Use the Test?   There should be a clear statement of the purpose of the test. What is the test intended to measure? For what types of people is the test intended and in what situations can it properly be used? If you are looking for a test to select real estate sales associates in the United States, then a test designed to select car salespeople in Canada is not appropriate.

Is the Test Valid?   There should be a detailed accounting of the test's development and supporting validity evidence. If the authors of the Canadian car salesperson test claim their test can be used to select American real estate sales associates, they must provide validity evidence supporting this claim. The validity evidence should inform the potential users of appropriate and inappropriate uses of the test. Remember, a correlation coefficient of .2 is considered acceptable and .3 and above is very good.

Is the Test Designed for Real Estate?   It is important to use a selection test that has been designed for use in real estate. A test that is useful for selecting other types of employees (even other sales occupations) may not be valid for selecting real estate salespeople.

How Do You Use the Test?   There should be clear guidelines for the interpretation of the test results and for its use in personnel selection. The appropriate use of the selection test and its placement in the overall selection process varies depending on the design and purpose of the individual test. The authors should provide guidelines for the use of their specific selection test.

Are Instructions Clear?   There should be precise instructions for the administration and scoring of the test. If the test is administered or scored in a fashion that deviates from the instructions, the validity and utility of the test will be jeopardized.

Another point to remember is to be wary of sales pitches that make extravagant claims such as "we'll help you select the right sales associate every time." The chances are that these tests do not provide evidence and information to substantiate the claims.

Also, do not let price influence your decision. An inexpensive test may provide ineffective results. On the other hand, an expensive test may not be the most valid either.

Finally, managers should also note that the relationship between the selection test and on-the-job performance is never perfect, but using a valid selection test can substantially improve the odds of selecting successful salespeople.

The Background Investigation

Step V, checking a candidate's background, accomplishes three things:

1. Verifies or contradicts the details on the application form or elicited in the screening interview.
2. Supplies additional data prior steps have not developed.
3. Helps establish the candidate's credibility or memory for particulars.

The background investigation is usually confined to two essential sources of information: financial status and employment history. There may be times when a manager will want to check the character references offered by an applicant; however, information from these sources usually lacks objectivity. Remember, however, you can only ask questions that relate directly to job performance. Financial status may have no bearing on how the associate might perform. A check of financial references can only be done with the agreement of the candidate. Make sure you get permission in writing to make a financial check.

Probably the single best source of financial information is the local credit bureau. They usually have a detailed analysis of an individual's credit rating for at least seven years. They are also a source of evidence of past lawsuits, bankruptcies or criminal involvements of a serious nature. The manager must receive the candidate's permission to verify financial information through a credit bureau.

Verifying previous employment is often more complicated and less productive than checking a candidate's financial background. Many employers are reluctant to give out information on a former employee, especially when a negative appraisal is involved. Furthermore, when an employer reports negatively on an individual, there is always a chance it is due to a personality conflict or some other less-than-objective opinion of past performance. It is the policy of many companies that all such inquiries are handled by the personnel office. However, most personnel departments will only verify factual data, such as dates of employment and salary. If at all possible, you should talk to the applicant's immediate supervisor to determine his or her personal characteristics and quality of performance.

The main reason for checking an applicant's employment history is to substantiate the information coming from the application form, including dates of employment, wages or salary, job title and responsibilities and reason for leaving. The secondary purpose is to determine as nearly as possible the quality of performance, daily attendance and ability to get along with others.

If convenient, the employment investigation should be conducted by telephone by the manager. At least the last two or three positions should be verified. Use of a telephone checklist is the best approach. See Figure 6.4. Since it is a structured form, it keeps the investigation on track and more businesslike. Background investigations that tend to meander and pry rather than obtain substantive performance-related information waste valuable time and can cause the former employer to be less responsive.

If a candidate is currently employed, permission to contact the present employer must be obtained. To omit this might prove embarrassing and damaging and expose the broker to legal liabilities. Another caution: If you make financial or employment checks on one candidate, you must make them on all candidates. This lessens your risk of liability by demonstrating that you have not shown favoritism or discrimination.

The Evaluative Interview

During the first five steps of the screening process most unqualified applicants have been eliminated. For example, an initial group of fifty applicants may now be reduced to ten. Your ultimate goal might be to select the four or five most qualified.

At the end of Step V, data on each remaining applicant has been assembled. All along the line, well-organized information on the candidates has been consistently compared with the most acceptable standards embodied in the job specification and job description, to be verified and supplemented in succeeding steps. A complete file of critically useful information is now available for reference in Step VI, the evaluative interview. The evaluative interview serves two purposes: It pulls together all the information from the previous steps, so you can offer the candidate a position, and it gives you an opportunity to sell your company benefits to the candidate. These benefits include the characteristics, policies, procedures, and so on, that attract people to work for your firm.

Step III, the screening interview, was, for its own practical purposes, structured. It followed a particular outline, looking for as much specific, detailed information as possible in the shortest period of time, verifying and amplifying the objective data from the application form. The evaluative interview should be far less structured. It should be casual, giving the applicant ample opportunity to speak freely and ask any questions necessary to better understand your business. Only subtle guidance from the manager is needed.

There is no special formula for conducting an effective evaluative interview. It should always be carried out in privacy. The applicant should be helped to feel at ease. The principal objective is to develop open, frank

FIGURE 6.4   Telephone Checklist Form

Applicant _____

Former Supervisor _____ Title _____

Company Where   Telephone
Applicant Worked _____ Number _____

1. I wish to verify some of the information given to us by
    _____, who is a candidate for a position with our
    firm. Do you remember him/her?

2. What were the dates of his/her employment with your com-
    pany? From _____ to_____.

3. What was he/she doing when he/she started?

4. What was he/she doing when he/she left?

5. He/she indicates he/she was earning $____ per ____ when
    he/she left. Is this correct?

6. How much of this was salary? How much was commission?

7. How much customer contact was involved in the job?

8. How did his/her performance compare with others in his/her
    group?

9. Did he/she supervise anyone else?____ If yes, how many?

10. How well did he/she handle people?

11. How did he/she get along with other people?

12. Why did he/she leave your firm?

13. Would you rehire him/her? _____ If not, why not?

14. What did you feel were his/her strong points?

15. What did you feel were his/her weak points?

Additional Comments: _____

_____

_____

_____

_____

Date of Check _____ 19 _____ Made by _____

but always friendly discussion encouraging the applicant to take the initiative.

The personnel file, containing all the information accrued from the preceding five steps, is the best guide in keeping the evaluative interview alive and providing the necessary cues to keep the applicant talking about himself or herself. Every opportunity should be given the candidate to sell himself or herself to management. Close observation and accurate mental note taking is the key to a successful evaluative interview. The manager should constantly analyze and compare what is being seen and heard with the information gathered in the previous steps. The manager should be alert to the smallest fragment of information that may be of significance in the selection decision, developing any topic this might suggest.

A multiple interview in Step VI is suggested. As a rule, the sales manager has initiated and controlled the screening process and no doubt will make the final decision. But observations and opinions from other levels of management, especially top management, can add a critical dimension at this time. Others participating in the evaluative interview should be provided full information gathered on the applicant in advance of such participation. Their presence should be informal, allowing the candidate to feel as comfortable and relaxed as possible. Candidates should not feel they are undergoing an interrogation.

THE SELECTION DECISION

It cannot be stressed enough that the objective of the screening and selection process is to find a very special person to do a very special job under very special conditions. The only way to achieve this objective is by matching organized, factual information about a person with a realistic job description and job specification. Then effective decision making becomes a matter of reducing the probability of error between what is and what is not desired.

Just as there is no single reason why a person is eventually selected, there is no one reason for eliminating someone. Once an individual has been eliminated there is no reason for further personal communication other than the courtesy of a letter thanking him or her for their time. This letter is a courtesy and permits the applicant to feel free to pursue other opportunities.

SELECTING OFFICE PERSONNEL

The primary objective of a real estate sales office is to sell real estate. The primary function of every person employed in that office is to achieve that objective, directly or indirectly. A topflight real estate sales force cannot operate at peak efficiency without a qualified office staff backing it up. This goes far beyond having people with certain skills sitting behind desks answering telephones or processing paperwork. Every member of the office staff should realize that the only justification for every job is optimum sales and profit.

Management can and should apply the same basic screening and selection process to office personnel that it applies to salespeople. In the six steps leading to the selection decision, the only differences would be in the job analysis and performance specification and in testing.

As in the case of salespeople, the job analysis should spell out in detail the required skills and responsibilities which are critical to satisfactory performance. The personal traits and characteristics necessary to job achievement should be defined. Sales support people would in fact possess many of the personality traits looked for in salespeople. A cool, unfriendly receptionist or a tense, high-strung secretary, no matter how skilled in the particular job, can create serious problems. Compatibility among the people in an organization enhances the spirit of mutual concern and cooperation, overall morale and necessary teamwork.

Testing may evaluate skills such as typing, shorthand, clerical, computer and computational abilities, or whatever the job requires. But such tests should be valid and relevant to an applicant's ability to do the work required.

The final proof of effective hiring and selection procedures lies in the performance of the people chosen. Job competence is the final objective. Having chosen well, management's next concern is to train people well and motivate them so they are most likely to succeed and stay with the firm.

Chapter 7

Written Instruments Between Broker and Salesperson

Two major written documents govern the relationship between brokers and their salespeople. One is the operations manual; the other is a contract or agreement between a broker and the individual members of the sales staff.

The operations manual is the written instrument that provides guidance to salespeople who are independent contractors and directives to employee salespeople and other employees.

The written contract between independent contractor salespeople and the broker spells out the salesperson's rights and obligations. It also enables the broker to discuss problems in particularized terms, minimizing the risk that independent contractor status will be lost through inadvertence and misunderstanding. Contracts may also be written to cover the relationship between brokers and salespeople, but these are less common.

This chapter examines the need for and content of both types of written comments, what they can and cannot accomplish and/or control, and the wisdom of having legal counsel in all contractual matters.

MUTUAL RESPONSIBILITIES MUST BE CLEARLY SPELLED OUT

People in real estate sometimes feel that their offices are unlike those of other sales organizations because the relationship between management and staff is different in this business. This is true for the most part. However, to use this as a reason for not having modern management controls and techniques is illogical. On the contrary, the unusual relationships in real estate indicate an even greater need for good management. It seems basic that brokers and salespeople should have a clear understanding of what to expect from each other and the conditions under which each will function for their mutual benefit.

That understanding is usually spelled out best by a contract and implemented by an operations manual.

COMPANY SIZE

Any question about how large a company must be before it should have written policy and procedures can be put to rest because the operations manual is probably more important for the small office than for the large one. This is true because in a small office the broker often also lists and sells. The likelihood of policy and procedures problems increases when the broker is wearing two hats. The broker could conceivably be involved in a disagreement with a salesperson and be expected to judge himself or herself—an almost impossible situation.

PURPOSES OF AN OPERATIONS MANUAL

Just as brokers are charged with winning the approval, respect and good will of many groups outside the company, so they must establish and maintain good public relations among their employees and salespeople. A good operations manual is a great aid in this regard.

Many brokers practice management by crisis and not the wiser method of management by objectives. In the latter, establishing a written policy is necessary to set the pace in a company large or small. It should also reflect the company's strategic plan objectives.

What the Manual Should Be

A properly written manual is not easy to compose and is difficult to make complete enough to cover every situation; further, it is often subject to interpretation on even the items included. These are arguments against having written policy. But the benefits far outweigh the negative factors.

The manual should:

- provide a clear understanding of the relationship between broker and salesperson, management and employees and the relationship of administrative functions and sales functions;
- permit the anticipation of and resolution of controversies before they arise;
- stabilize both management and sales as it builds confidence that management as well as the salespeople know the rules by which the game is to be played;

- prohibit favoritism since all must operate within the framework of the manual's predetermined rules and guidelines; and
- provide stability of organization and permit the staff to function effectively in the absence of management.

The alternative to a written operations manual is to have the policy statement in the broker's head; and when the broker is not there, it's not there. What's more, the broker might forget it.

Uses of the Manual

The operations manual has many uses. Besides setting forth the rules under which the business operates, it serves to back up management decisions. It becomes the uninvolved "third person" that is sought out to give an unbiased opinion on the matter under consideration.

It is a valuable aid in recruiting, interviewing, selecting and/or hiring and retaining good coworkers. In recruiting, the prospective salesperson can be told that the company has a written statement of policy. In interviewing and selecting, the manual can serve to let the prospective salesperson know what he or she can expect and the framework within which work is done in the company. Fear of the unknown is a great obstacle to success in the sales field. A good, clear statement of policy helps to give the prospective salesperson a feeling of security. It is important that these facts are all understood before a contract is signed or a person is employed.

In training new salespeople, the operations manual is an essential tool. A specific period of indoctrination should be spent with each new salesperson covering every aspect of the manual in detail. If no other formal training is given by the broker, the manual at least serves to give new salespeople the orientation they need.

Sales meetings present a particular challenge to the average broker, and the manual becomes a priceless tool in making such meetings meaningful. A review of one item of the manual each week will pay valuable dividends in communication, feedback and understanding between all members of the team.

Parts of some operations manuals are concerned with the salesperson's liability in certain seasonal changes, conditions under which property is shown or the problems of unoccupied properties. It is important to review these matters regularly, and the manual is the reminder to do it.

One thing that should be avoided in the use of the operations manual is getting the public involved. Many of the problems between salespeople involve the public. But while the public is not concerned with a broker's internal policies, they might turn salesperson against salesperson by favoring one salesperson in a dispute. Therefore, brokers should bring in the client to determine the facts only as a last resort and then exercise great discretion.

There are some things an operations manual is and some things it is not. It is a statement or declaration of the company business philosophy, procedures, rules and regulations, and generally it will spell out what is expected of salespeople in their day to day activities as well as what they can expect from the company. It can include an organizational chart and job descriptions. It should be a viable tool, a constitution and a declaration of interdependence.

It should not be a contract and should not be interpreted as being under the law of contracts. For example, the broker-salesperson agreement that is a contract would spell out the commission split. The operations manual would describe the procedure in the event of a dispute between salespeople about commission splits.

CONTENTS OF THE MANUAL

Just as an architect could not build a structure successfully without a plan, the operations manual must have a plan. And all good planning starts with clear objectives. So the author of policy must begin with the company's strategic intent, goals and objectives. These can be stated in general or specific language in the preamble.

Next comes the outline or index of items to be covered. It should be alphabetical and in sufficient detail to allow for ease in finding specific provisions.

No two real estate offices are alike, and it is unwise to copy another's operations manual exactly. However, a manual from another company can provide a good starting point.

A list of possible subjects to consider might include:

Advertising and promotion	Listing procedure
Agency policy	New homes and tracts
Associates' sales kit	Newspapers
Bonuses	Offer procedure
REALTOR® Code of Ethics	Office cooperation
Compensation policies	Open houses
Co-op sales with outside brokers	Other departments
Description of associate's job	Prospects
Escrow	Qualifications
Fair housing laws	Residential sales department
Floor duty	Salesperson-client relations
Growth opportunity	Sales meetings
General	Screening prospects
History of company	Selling policies/procedures
Inquiries	Signs
Interoffice exchange of clients	Termination
Introduction	

Somewhere in its makeup the manual should refer to and incorporate already published statements such as the REALTOR® Code of Ethics, MLS rules, License Authority rules, and federal, state and local fair housing laws and regulations, and a company policy on agency. A simple reference to these is not enough. Copies of these "rules" should be put in the loose-leaf manual, and they should be covered in all discussions of policy.

Brokers must use good judgment in including in policy such matters concerning the day to day practice of their business that have become part of the law. It is not realistic to assume that all members of the staff are aware of and familiar with local, state and federal laws that concern discrimination, signs, business solicitation, lending of money and such items. In addition to this, most license authorities issue bulletin rules and findings that are matters of policy for brokers. They must keep abreast of them and be sure their staff is informed.

This does not mean the manual must be revised every time a city ordinance is passed; but it is good to republish the provision, discuss it and add a copy to the loose-leaf manual. At a later time some added wording may be necessary if it affects policy.

The manual should be limited to matters of policy and procedure such as who pays for long distance phone calls. It should not be a training manual in the sense that it spells out such things as telephone technique, how to list, show and present offers. The danger in including sales training material is that the manual becomes unwieldy, policy statements are lost in the mass of words, and simple variations in sales procedures become violations of policy. None of these is desirable. A bare bones policy statement works best.

The manual cannot be made the total answer to each policy matter. When a decision cannot be made easily about a specific problem, it should clearly state how it is to be interpreted and by whom.

FORMAT

The size of the manual is not important. Usually from 15 to 30 single-spaced typewritten pages will cover everything. However, it is usually wise to limit each page to only a few items, leaving space for changes or additions. If space is allowed for changes, they are made more easily because only one page is affected. For example, a policy statement on the handling of keys to clients' homes might change with the added use of lock boxes, comboxes or keysafes of some type. This might involve adding a paragraph. Space should be available on that page to avoid redoing the entire manual. Incidentally, that page should be signed and dated when reissued.

The index is most conveniently set up in alphabetical form, cross-indexing some items that may come under several categories. For example, "Earnest Money" could be mentioned under contracts, trust accounts, responsibilities of salespeople and cooperative sales.

WRITING THE MANUAL

Other people in the company besides the broker can be helpful in preparing the manual. A partner, manager or salesperson can offer valuable viewpoints in some instances. When asking for help in setting policy or in composing the language, you should not give the impression that you are abandoning your responsibility and privilege of policy making. You can get good ideas from staff, give recognition for their help and still not risk a strained relationship that could arise if such cooperative policy making is not handled with tact and skill.

Before asking for help you should carefully determine which items you will open to staff opinions. It would be inviting disaster to have a sales staff decide such items as commission splits.

The best approach is to prepare the "proposed statement of policy" in each matter and submit it for discussion—not necessarily for approval or change. It could be reworded, clarified or expanded to make it more clear but that is all that should be discussed.

The method of building an operations manual in this manner is going to get much better results than trying to make it letter-perfect. Begin with the obvious requirements, the "must" provisions, and then build it one page at a time.

When the time comes to write, you need not worry that you will not do a good job of composition. You need not be a Hemingway. It is sufficient to set down in plain terms what you think should be said, have it reviewed by someone else, publish it and put it into effect.

Tips on Writing the Manual

In writing policy it is best to use "thou shalt. . ." as much as possible, rather than the "thou shalt not. . ." approach. Positive statements are more persuasive than negative ones. For example, the provision on sales meetings should read that salespeople are "encouraged to attend and to remain for the entire meeting" rather than to state that they "should not miss the weekly sales meeting and are discouraged from leaving early."

Write carefully, then read and reread to determine if it is too vague or too limiting. Some provisions concern matters that require a certain amount of good judgment and must necessarily be left open to reasonable interpretation. One such concern is long distance telephone calls. Most companies allow such calls under certain conditions for business reasons. The broker might err by making the controls so tight that salespeople could lose business in trying to comply. However, it is equally unwise to be too vague. For example, a provision that "long distance calls may be made for a business reason" with no further guidelines or procedures for control could result in misunderstandings and abuses leading to serious budget problems.

Brokers have a responsibility to create policy for their firm that is workable, understandable and as complete as human nature will allow. To be too strict is only going to set up daily violations of policy and the entire project becomes an exercise in futility.

Tips on Revising the Manual

Frequently in a growing company the need arises to add to or to revise policy to keep it meaningful and viable. It is a good habit to put items and articles relating to policy in a file to be considered in future revisions or additions to the book. Thoughts you might have or topics that come up at meetings should be noted and put in the file. Such things are often forgotten when entrusted to memory and they could prove valuable in future revisions.

Publications of local, state and national REALTOR® associations often contain statements, findings, warnings and other good general material that could be made a part of policy or form the basis for new provisions. The decisions made by the broker in current disputes within the company should be duly noted, dated, spelled out and filed for future reference in similar situations. This leads to consistency in management and adds to the sense of continuity and fairness on the part of the staff.

When making major or minor changes or adding provisions to the operations manual, it is always wise to do it with an eye on the relative importance of the change. Lead time, the time to get used to the new provision before it becomes effective, is usually of some reasonable length. For example, a change in policy concerning compensation might require a lead time of several months to allow salespeople to accept the change. The newer the idea, the more people it affects, the longer the lead time required.

A wise broker tries to make any change less traumatic, any transition smoother. Most brokers find it advisable to first draft a "proposed policy change" and at an informal meeting get the agreement of the managers if it is a large company. In a smaller company or a branch office the broker might meet with the leaders of the sales force and explain it to them so that they know what to expect when it is presented to the entire staff. This provides a chance to get direct feedback on the proposal and gives the leaders a feeling of being part of the management team.

DISTRIBUTING THE MANUAL

A loose-leaf binder is usually the best form. The master copy should be kept by the broker with reference copies available to all the staff. When a new manual is to be introduced or a major revision made, it is usually best to get a copy to each of the staff, have it approved and call in the old copies. The larger the company, the more important it is not to have many copies floating around because they are frequently in various stages of completeness and confusion is the result. A small company with tight controls may find it workable to have a copy in the hand of each salesperson and employee. When changes are made, the manuals should all be turned in, amended and reissued. This is usually done at one meeting.

It may seem unnecessary to have every page of the manual initialed by each salesperson, but this is an effective way to achieve evidence of understanding. The "independent contractor agreement" between the broker and salesperson (if he or she is not an employee) should be signed by both parties, but the policy manual need only be signed by the salesperson to indicate that individual's acceptance of it.

CONTRACTS AND AGREEMENTS

The threshold question that must be answered before any consideration can be given to the form and terms of contracts or agreements between a broker and a salesperson is whether the salesperson will be an employee of the broker or will be affiliated with the broker as an independent contractor. The answer to this question will depend on a wide range of considerations:

- The degree of control that the broker desires or needs to exercise over the salesperson
- The type of work in which the salesperson will be engaged
- The personal and professional qualifications of the salesperson
- The nature of the broker's business and the techniques the broker uses to project himself or herself to the public
- The type and terms of the compensation arrangements offered by the broker and by competitors
- The legal liabilities and rights accruing to the broker and salesperson under each status

There is no "right" answer as to whether or not salespeople should be employees or independent contractors. On the contrary, any effort to generalize with respect to the proper status of salespeople can be dangerous, if not disastrous, for the broker.

This is because there is no such relationship as an "independent contractor employee." A salesperson may be an employee or an independent contractor but may not be both simultaneously. When brokers misconceive the true relationship between themselves and their salespeople, they fail to recognize and fulfill the legal obligations which are attributable to that relationship. Every broker must appreciate that the employee relationship is not legally interchangeable with that of independent contractor. Nor is one superior to the other in all cases. Employees enjoy many rights denied by law to independent contractors, and independent contractors have legal rights not available to employees. This gives them greater flexibility when it comes to determining or changing responsibilities or terminating an employee.

It is uncommon for employers to enter into a contractual relationship with employees. Most employers prefer to have an at-will relationship with their employees. By electing a contractual relationship both parties tend to restrict themselves, as duties and responsibilities are included in the contract or are presumed. However, for independent contractors, a contract is indispensable, even though the courts weigh practices and activities more heavily than the language of the contract in determining the relationship.

Employee versus Independent Contractor

How associates are compensated, how they pay and report taxes, and whether the broker has the right to control their activities are the key issues which help establish whether a sales associate is viewed as an independent contractor or as an employee.

Most employees receive wages based on the number of hours they work. In contrast, independent contractors receive compensation based only on their production (i.e., commissions for sales, listings and rentals).

Another factor involves reporting taxes. A broker withholds taxes from an employee's paycheck and forwards those taxes to the government. A broker does not withhold taxes from an independent contractor's income—independent contractors are responsible for paying their own taxes.

The last key issue involves the broker's right to control activities. A broker may exercise control over the activities of an employee or a statutory independent contractor without jeopardizing the salesperson's status. However, a broker may not exercise control over a common law independent contractor's activities, such as attending training seminars or participating in floor duty.

Types of Independent Contractors   There are two types of independent contractors: common law independent contractors and statutory independent contractors.

The statutory independent contractor status was created in 1982, when Congress added to the Internal Revenue Code a three-part test to determine the status of a real estate salesperson. One major difference between common law independent contractors and statutory independent contractors is that brokers can control the business activities of statutory independent contractors but not those of common law independent contractors.

Under federal tax laws, statutory independent contractors must have a current real estate license, and at least 90 percent of their income as a licensee must be based on production. The statutory independent contractor also must have a written contract with the broker. That contract must contain the following clause: "The salesperson will not be treated as an employee with respect to the services performed by such salesperson as a real estate agent for federal tax purposes." These final four words are very important as they can limit the scope of matters for which the salesperson is an independent contractor. For purposes other than federal tax such as unemployment taxes or worker's compensation insurance the salesperson may be considered an employee. Also, unless the state has adopted language similar to that of federal law, the salesperson may be an employee for state tax purposes.

In examining the differences between whether an employee, statutory independent contractor or common law independent contractor relationship exists, there are various indicators that have come to be recognized as relevant considerations. While a comprehensive and all-inclusive enumeration of such considerations is impossible, those that have been recognized by the courts as among the more significant include the following.

Training

No common law independent contractor may be required by the broker to attend sales training, instruction and indoctrination courses. If the broker believes training and indoctrination courses are indispensable for an untrained or inexperienced salesperson, the broker should make this person an employee. This does not mean that the broker may not make available training courses, seminars and other educational opportunities that the independent contractor salesperson is free to attend or not.

Hours of Work

A broker may not control the hours of work of a common law independent contractor salesperson. A requirement that a salesperson accept floor time assignments from the broker is not consistent with independent contractor status. For this reason, assignment of independent contractor salespeople to fixed hours or days of work at a model home site seriously endangers their status. Similarly, a requirement that an independent contractor salesperson participate in weekly open house caravan tours is impermissible.

Priority of Assignments

If the broker has the right to interrupt the work of a salesperson or otherwise set the order of that person's services (by, for example, requiring the salesperson to work on certain listings or clients in preference to others), the salesperson could well be deemed an employee or statutory independent contractor. The broker cannot reserve first call on the time and efforts of the common law independent contractor salesperson.

In addition, quotas related to how an independent contractor does business (number of floor hours, number of prospecting calls) are inconsistent with the status of common law independent contractors. However, an independent contractor may be terminated for failing to achieve a production quota.

Company Identification

A broker may require employee salespeople to wear distinctive articles of clothing, name tags and to otherwise identify the firm name on their personal vehicles. No such requirement is appropriate for independent contractor salespeople. Moreover, it would be inconsistent with the independent contractor status for a salesperson to be given a title commonly recognized as signifying employee status. For this reason, independent contractors should not be designated by such titles as "vice-president," "sales manager" or "sales supervisor."

License Fees and Dues

A broker may not pay the license fees or membership dues of independent contractor salespeople although he or she is free to pay those of employees and statutory independent contractors.

Expenses

Independent contractor salespeople are responsible for paying their own automobile and transportation expenses and other expenses they incur in obtaining and selling clients. The broker may not reimburse such expenses as he or she may do in the case of an employee or statutory independent contractor. The requirement that independent contractor salespeople pay their own expenses does not mean that the broker may not make available space, secretarial and telephone service in the broker's office and business cards, forms and stationery on which the broker's name appears. The broker may not, however, pay or reimburse expenses attributable to an office that the salesperson maintains outside of the broker's premises.

Fringe Benefits

Common law independent contractors are not entitled to sick pay or to participate in the broker's pension and profit sharing plans, wage continuation plans, health and accident insurance plans or qualified group insurance programs unless permitted by the broker to pay premiums to participate in group health insurance. Inclusion of a salesperson in such programs or plans is tantamount to an admission by the broker that the salesperson is an employee because such programs or plans, to the extent they are qualified under the Internal Revenue Code, are limited to employees. To include independent contractor salespersons in such plans and programs is to expose them to disqualification. Similarly, an independent contractor salesperson's vacation schedule may not be subject to the control of the broker. On the other hand, an independent contractor is entitled to establish his or her own retirement plan as a self-employed person. To do so reinforces his or her status as an independent contractor. Statutory independent contractors may receive these benefits, but they may not exceed 10 percent of the salesperson's total income from real estate sales.

Taxes and Social Security

All independent contractors pay estimated federal taxes on a quarterly basis, and they make self-employment compensation payments using form SE in lieu of Social Security payments. Brokers must provide a form and withhold Social Security from any nonproduction income. Brokers also must withhold federal and state taxes for employees, as well as providing W2 forms and contributing Social Security payments for them. State tax treatment of statutory independent contractors varies from state to state.

Reports and Procedures

While a broker may require employees and statutory independent contractors to adhere strictly to the office operations manual, this degree of control is impermissible with common law independent contractor salespeople. The operations manual constitutes mere *guidance* to the independent contractor salesperson, and this fact should be specifically stated in the manual if it is to be distributed to such salespeople. Reports by independent contractor salespeople, except as to listings obtained, sales made and information necessary to permit the broker to record and close transactions and comply with local, state and federal laws, should not be made mandatory. At the same time, the broker is free to provide such cooperation and advice as the independent contractor salesperson requests concerning the efficient and effective conduct of his or her work.

DETERMINING THE PROPER RELATIONSHIP

Only the broker can determine whether it is possible to function effectively with the limited degree of control required to preserve the common law independent contractor relationship. In making this determination, however, the broker must consider the experience and personality of the sales applicant. If the applicant is experienced, it may be unnecessary to require mandatory training or persuade the applicant of the value of floor time and adherence to proper office routine. If the applicant is aggressive and self-motivated, it may be unnecessary for the broker to specify not merely "what" the job is but also "how" to do it.

In addition, the broker must consider the extent to which the applicant will be engaged in activities other than "pure sales." If the applicant will be involved in property management and rental activities, a degree of control will be required that will almost inevitably exceed that allowed in an independent contractor relationship.

At one time, it was thought desirable for brokers to use both the independent contractor and the employee relationship because it enabled the broker to maintain closer control over new or inexperienced salespeople, who could then change to independent contractor status when they gained sufficient experience. It also was believed that having both employees and independent contractors in the same organization enabled the broker to "heighten" the distinction between them, thereby reinforcing the validity of the independent contractor status. However, many attorneys now advise against mixing independent contractors and employees. The broker who does so must be very careful to treat them in a distinct manner. This can be difficult to do, and there is a serious downside for the broker if there is any mistake.

ESTABLISHING THE RELATIONSHIP

Once the broker has determined the type of relationship he or she desires to establish with the sales applicant, the next decision is whether that relationship should be established by oral or written agreement.

In most employer-employee relationships, an oral understanding is usually sufficient and preferable to a written agreement. Any oral employment agreement should be supported by a clear and comprehensive operations manual to which the broker and salesperson may refer for a definition of their respective rights and responsibilities.

A written employment contract has the benefits that it sets forth the terms of the employer-employee relationship more precisely and thereby limits the areas of potential controversy and litigation. In addition, it permits the broker to differentiate between employees in a way that cannot be achieved if the relationship is defined by an operations manual or by custom. However, with a written agreement the broker gives up the at-will employment provisions contained in most state common law. Consequently, any written agreement must be very specific as to when disciplinary actions would be taken against an employee as well as under what circumstances employment can be terminated. In addition, a written agreement can muddy the waters as to whether a salesperson is an employee or an independent contractor.

However, a written agreement becomes advisable for common law independent contractors and is indispensable for statutory independent contractors. A written contract provides a salesperson with a source of ready reference about his or her rights and obligations. It enables the broker to discuss problems in particularized terms, citing chapter and verse. As a consequence it minimizes the risk that independent contractor status will be lost by inadvertence or misunderstanding.

DRAFTING THE AGREEMENT WITH
THE SALESPERSON

No agreement with a salesperson, whether employee or independent contractor, should be drafted without advice of counsel. It may not reasonably be assumed that an agreement which is acceptable in one state will be acceptable in another. Nor may a broker assume that an agreement which is found satisfactory by another broker will be automatically adaptable to his or her operation.

There is grave danger in utilizing model or specimen forms. Such forms are designed basically for use by attorneys to provide them with a format upon which they may build as the laws of the state and the particular needs and desires of the parties require.

This is not to say that an organization may not develop a standard form that may be used in establishing a relationship with a salesperson provided it is understood first that the form will be used only for those salespeople engaged in the same activities and second that any differentiation between salespeople, however slight, will be reflected in changes to the agreement and will be reviewed. See Figure 7.1.

The cost of securing review by counsel of the terms of the employment or independent contractor agreement is a small price to pay to minimize the significant risks created by a defective agreement. Moreover, once counsel is familiar with the broker's business and relationships with salespeople, the legal costs of maintaining the agreements in current form and updating them as changes in the law require will be reduced.

MONITORING ADHERENCE TO THE AGREEMENT

Because employers normally enjoy substantial control over their employees, the monitoring of the adherence of employees to their agreements involves essentially routine personnel administration.

This is not so in the case of the independent contractor salesperson. As indicated elsewhere, the status of a salesperson is determined by that person's relationship with the broker in fact and not by the mere terms of the employment agreement. The most carefully drafted agreement will not preserve the independent contractor relationship if the parties themselves have ignored its terms.

This means that the broker who has independent contractor salespeople must establish a routine or program that will identify and correct any actions or attitudes inconsistent with the written agreement. Such a program may be complex or simple depending on the size of the organization, number of salespeople, range of activities, number of offices, personalities of the salespeople, office procedures, management and other factors. Essentially, however, any program must be able to accomplish the following tasks.

FIGURE 7.1 **Broker-Salesperson Contract—Independent Contractor**

> This Agreement, made this _____ day of _____,
> 19 ___, by and between _____,
> hereinafter referred to as "Broker" and _____,
> hereinafter referred to as "Sales Associate", for and in consider-
> ation of their mutual premises and agreements and for their
> mutual benefits.
>
> ## W I T N E S S E T H:
>
> WHEREAS, said broker is engaged in business as a general
> real estate broker in _____ County, State of
> _____, and is qualified to and does pro-
> cure the listings of real estate for sale, lease or rental and pro-
> spective purchasers, lessees and renters thereof and has and
> does enjoy the good will of, and a reputation for fair dealing with
> the public, and
> WHEREAS, said Broker maintains offices in said
> _____ County property equipped with furnishings,
> and other equipment necessary and incidental to the proper
> operation of said business, and staffed with employees, suitable
> to serving the public as real estate brokers, and
> WHEREAS, said Sales Associate is now, and has been
> engaged in business as a real estate salesperson, and has
> enjoyed and does enjoy a good reputation for fair and honest
> dealing with the public as such, and
> WHEREAS, it is deemed to be to the mutual advantage of
> said Broker and said Sales Associate to form the association
> hereinafter agreed to under the terms and conditions hereinafter
> set out,
> NOW, THEREFORE, for and in consideration of the prem-
> ises and of the mutual covenants hereinafter contained, it is
> mutually agreed as follows:
>
> 1. Broker agrees to make available to the Sales Associate all
>   current listings of the office, except such as the Broker for
>   valid and usual business reasons may place exclusively in
>   the temporary possession of some other Sales Associate,
>   and agrees, upon request, to assist the Sales Associate in
>   his/her work by advice and instruction and agrees to provide
>   full cooperation in every way possible.

FIGURE 7.1   *(Continued)*

2. Broker agrees that the Sales Associate may share with other Sales Associates all the facilities of the offices now operated by said Broker in connection with the subject matter of this contract, which offices are now maintained at _____.

3. Sales Associate agrees to work diligently and with his best efforts to sell, lease or rent any and all real estate listed with the broker, to solicit additional listings and customers of said Broker, and otherwise promote the business of serving the public in real estate transactions to the end that each of the parties hereto may derive the greatest profit possible.

4. Upon entering into the association with _____ the Independent Contractor has promised that he/she will endeavor to obtain the GRI designation within three (3) years from date of contract.

5. Sales Associate agrees to conduct his/her business and regulate his/her habits, so as to maintain and to increase the good will and reputation of the Broker and the Sales Associate, and the parties hereto agree to conform to and abide by all laws, rules and regulations, and codes of ethics that are binding upon or applicable to real estate brokers and real estate Sales Associates.

6. Subject to the foregoing, however, Sales Associate shall be free to control and manage the real estate business which he/she conducts hereunder. To that end, he/she shall select his/her own sales methods, procedures and devises, may employ such assistants or employees as he/she alone shall deem fit, and, except to the extent provided in this Agreement, shall be free from direction or control by Broker.

7. The commission to be charged for any services performed hereunder shall be those determined by the Broker, and the Broker shall advise the Sales Associate of any special contract relating to any particular transaction which he/she undertakes to handle. When the Sales Associate shall perform any service hereunder, whereby a commission is earned, said commission shall, when collected, be divided between the Broker and Sales Associate, in which share as set out in the commission schedule, current at the date of acceptance of the transaction by the owner, and the Broker shall receive the balance. In the event of special arrangements with any client of the Broker or the Sales Associate, a special division of commission may apply, such rate of division to be agreed upon in advance by the Broker and the

FIGURE 7.1 *(Continued)*

Sales Associate. In the event that two or more Sales Associates participate in such a service, or claim to have done so, the amount of the commission over that accruing to the Broker shall be divided between the participating Sales Associates according to agreement between them or by arbitration under the rules and regulations of the American Arbitration Association. In no case shall the Broker be personally liable to the Sales Associate for any commission, nor shall said Sales Associate be personally liable to said Broker for any commission, but when the commission shall have been collected from the party or parties for whom the service was performed, said Broker shall hold the same in trust for said Sales Associate and himself/herself to be divided according to the terms of this agreement.

8. The division and distribution of the earned commissions as set out in paragraph 7 hereof, which may be paid to or collected by either party hereto, shall take place as soon as practicable after collection of such commissions from the party or parties for whom the services may have been performed.

9. The Broker shall not be liable to the Sales Associate for any expenses incurred by him/her or for any of his/her acts, nor shall the Sales Associate be liable to the Broker for office help or expense, and the Sales Associate shall have no authority to bind the Broker by any promise or representation, unless specifically authorized in a particular transaction; but the expense of attorney's fees, costs, revenue stamps, title abstracts and the like which must, by reason of some necessity, be paid from the commission or are incurred in the collection of, or the attempt to collect, the commission, shall be paid by the parties in the same proportion as provided for herein in the division of the commissions. Suits for commission shall, agreeable to the law, be maintained only in the name of the Broker, and the Sales Associate shall be construed to be a subagent only, with respect to the clients and customers for whom services shall be performed, and shall otherwise be deemed to be an independent contractor and not a servant, employee or partner of the Broker.

10. This agreement and the association created hereby, may be terminated by either party hereto, at any time upon written notice given to the other; but the rights of the parties to any commissions which accrued prior to said notice, shall not be

FIGURE 7.1   *(Continued)*

divested by the termination of this agreement. It is specifically agreed, however, that all listings are the property of the Broker. Any listing shall be re-assigned by the Broker and the Sales Associate shall have no continuing interest in a listing if there is not a pending transaction which is successfully closed. The associate will have rights if a pending transaction does close successfully if the transaction was pending prior to his termination.

11. The Sales Associate shall not, after the termination of his/her contract, use to his own advantage, or the advantage of any other person or corporation, any information gained for or from the files or business of the Broker.

12. In keeping with real estate code and regulations; it is understood that an associate with or without the participation of the Broker will not accept gratuities, finder's fees, or rebates from the public in connection with his/her real estate activity without the full knowledge of buyer, seller, and Broker.

13. It is understood that since service is required to the benefit of the owner, that if the Sales Associate shall terminate his/her association with Broker, the Broker has the right to re-assign any listings in the associate's name to other associates within the office and the terminating associate shall have no rights thereto if there is not a transaction in escrow at the date of termination.

14. Sales Associate agrees and accepts this written notice of the Broker that it is the Sales Associate's sole responsibility as an Independent Contractor to make payment in the manner prescribed by the Federal Government for his/her self-employment and federal income taxes.

    It is understood that payments on a timely basis as the Associate's responsibility is a necessary requirement for the maintenance of the Independent Contractor status; and failure to perform would be cause for termination of this contract by the Broker.

15. Ninety percent (90%) or more of the remuneration for services performed by salesperson is directly related to sales or other output rather than to the number of hours worked.

16. For workers' compensation purposes, salesperson understands that he or she is not covered under the worker's compensation law of the State of _____ because of the method of remuneration set forth above.

FIGURE 7.1 *(Continued)*

IN WITNESS WHEREOF, the parties hereby have signed or caused to be signed, these presents this _____ day of _____, 19 ____.

BROKER _____

SALES ASSOCIATE _____

Periodic Review of Terms of Agreement

This review should occur at least annually and preferably more often. The purpose is to fix the terms of the relationship firmly in the minds of the broker and salesperson and to provide an opportunity to make such changes in the contract as are deemed necessary. Of course, too frequent reviews can lead to a question of control, bringing the salesperson's independent contractor status into question.

Review of Plans, Policies, Forms and Procedures

This review is intended to assure that the relationship with the salesperson is consistently recognized by the broker's organization. For example, this review would reveal that the operations manual specifies that adherence to it is mandatory for all salespeople, or that an independent contractor salesperson cannot be assigned to open house duty and so on.

Review of Salesperson's Representation to the Public

This review is intended to assure that the salesperson does not identify himself or herself as an employee of the broker in dealing with the public. In soliciting listings or customers, or in making appearances in the community, the independent contractor must be careful to identify himself or herself as being associated with and not employed by the broker. Further, independent contractors must not, in their dealings, use a title to which they are not entitled or ascribe to their broker a degree of control over their activities inconsistent with their status.

The manner in which the foregoing tasks may be performed is varied. Some will be performed by the broker, some by management and some may involve counsel. Some brokers with large organizations have gone so far as to establish an internal security system whereby the actions of both management and salespeople are tested by persons unknown to either.

Regardless of the complexity of the program or the manner of its execution, its effectiveness depends on systematic and continuing implementation.

SUMMARY AND CONCLUSION

In applying these tests to determine whether an employee, statutory independent contractor or common law independent contractor relationship exists, there are many considerations. Check with an attorney for complete details and to determine the current law in your state.

Chapter 8

Training the New Associate for Success

Having assembled the best staff available, the broker now faces the challenge of providing a thorough orientation and training program for them. A good training program not only enables salespeople and ancillary staff members to do their jobs more effectively but also saves management time in the long run.

Chapters 8, 9 and 10 deal with training salespeople to become not only productive but content, if not happy, in their work.

THE PURPOSE OF TRAINING

Since people are our firm's only sustainable competitive advantage, developing people through learning experiences is good business. Sales associates work best when they are learning and growing.

This and the next two chapters focus on developing salespeople by providing them with the training they need to become top performers—the kind who will give your firm a competitive edge. Development of your salespeople is the second phase of performance management. Using McKinsey's 7-S model, developing staff involves having a management style that encourages learning by setting up training systems to impart the skills that support the company's strategies and communicating the firm's shared values.

Stated in its simplest terms, the purpose of a broker's training program should be to teach the sales staff how to market real estate effectively, ethically and profitably as well as how to perform other supportive services. Listing and selling real estate is what brokers and salespeople are paid to do, and they cannot do it any better than they know how.

Within the broad framework of this goal, the objectives of the training program can be separated as they pertain to the broker and salesperson respectively.

THE BROKER'S OBJECTIVES

A real estate salesperson has time and knowledge to offer. With good time management and training he or she can provide a better service that results in higher sales and profits. Well-trained salespeople produce sooner, produce more and stay with your firm longer. Training also provides many other benefits.

Reduce Staff Turnover

A good initial training program will help prevent early discouragement on the part of new salespeople. A continuing educational program will sell the veteran salesperson on the personal benefits of remaining with the organization. These two factors combine to assure the broker a more stable sales force.

Improve Company Image

Because of the one-on-one nature of real estate selling, a salesperson's performance is often the only way the seller or buyer has to judge an entire firm. The more competent the individual, the better the image of the entire organization. This point should be made early and often. When in the field, the salesperson is not only part of the organization, in many cases he or she *is* the organization. Not only is the salesperson's reputation on the line but so are those of the other salespeople and the firm itself.

Reduce Need for Supervision

Increased competence on the part of salespeople means less need for the broker to spoon-feed and hand-lead them beyond the early days of indoctrination. This frees the broker for more productive and potentially more profitable activities.

Make Recruiting Easier

There is no stronger magnet for attracting good salespeople to a firm than word-of-mouth advertising of its training program and the success of those who have benefited from it. Thorough training is promised frequently in real estate recruitment but often it is not delivered. When the promise does become a reality, it creates a continuing flow of new trainees. If for no other reason than to meet the competition for good salespeople in today's market, the best possible training program should be a top priority item for every broker.

Improve Company Morale

A well-rounded training program motivates the trainee to better efforts, makes for better communication between salesperson and broker and keeps management in touch with what's happening on the firing line, particularly if the broker participates actively.

THE SALESPERSON'S OBJECTIVES

The informed salesperson is confident, and confident salespeople close more transactions and have greater security.

Produce Sooner

Confident, well-trained salespeople become productive more quickly.

Produce More

Trained salespeople also close more transactions, resulting in their earning more income.

Self-Assurance

Salespeople who are sure of themselves and unafraid of what they'll encounter in the field are happier, more poised and more productive.

Personal Satisfaction

The knowledge that they are growing in professionalism and know-how gives salespeople a tremendous ego boost which is not completely provided by even large amounts of monetary compensation.

Greater Income

An effective training program enables salespeople to meet their objective of increasing their income.

SETTING UP A TRAINING PROGRAM FOR NEW ASSOCIATES

Regardless of a firm's size, a well-planned and conscientiously executed training program is not an option; it is an absolute must, both to achieve the benefits mentioned earlier and because a broker has an obligation to train salespeople adequately before they represent the firm in the field. This is not only a moral obligation to the public and others in the real estate business but a practical obligation to protect the broker's reputation and avoid the possible danger of losing his or her brokerage license through the actions of an incompetent salesperson.

Smaller firms have several options for setting up a cost-effective training program. They can combine with friendly competitors to offer training, with each firm taking responsibility for the instruction in its particular specialty.

Educational programs are offered by local boards, state associations and the REALTORS® National Marketing Institute®. The Institute is comprised of the Real Estate Brokerage Managers Council™, which covers the brokerage management profession and the Residential Sales Council™, which covers the sales profession. The books, films and audiovisual programs offered by these Councils and by other organizations can be used in the training program for new salespeople and refresher courses for both the broker and experienced salespeople. If buying or renting all these materials at once proves too costly for a single firm, they can be purchased on a cooperative basis by several friendly competitors, to be loaned back and forth as needed. Many audiovisual programs can be rented at reasonable fees. Publications are also available through the library facilities of the National Association of REALTORS®.

Larger firms may employ an instructor or may divide training responsibility among several people within the organization.

Training skills can be acquired by attending the management courses offered by the Real Estate Brokerage Managers Council™ or a variety of instructor development workshops.

CATEGORIZE THE SUBJECTS

The first step in setting up a training program is to make a list of all the things that salespeople need to know in order to function successfully within your organization. The next step is to group these subjects into categories such as:

A. Introduction and orientation
    1. To the company
    2. To the business

B. Listing practices
    1. Measuring property
    2. Preparing the CMA and the seller's net return
    3. The listing presentation
    4. Contracts and forms

C.   Marketing the listing
  1.   Personal marketing
  2.   Advertising
  3.   Open houses
  4.   Flyers
  5.   Canvassing
  6.   Calling other sales agents
  7.   Telephone techniques
  8.   Follow-up with sellers

D.   Buying practices
  1.   Qualifying buyers
  2.   Showing properties
  3.   Understanding financing
  4.   Preparing the offer
  5.   Presenting the offer
  6.   Handling counteroffers
  7.   Negotiating and closing

E.   Prospecting

F.   Forms and accounting procedures

G.   Personal career planning, time management

The objective is to organize things so the training process follows a logical sequence. This will enable salespeople to relate to what they have learned previously and prepare for the next subject.

Next, fill out the outline by listing the topics to be taught under each of the general categories. The first list of details is now integrated into the category outline. Every element desired in the training program should appear in one of the general categories with everything arranged in logical sequence.

Now decide what visual aids, reading programs, films, tapes, recordings or guest lectures are available and pencil them into the outline. Make note of any costs involved in lecture fees and rental of teaching aids. Finally, decide what teaching techniques will be most effective for the various subjects. These may include lectures, demonstrations, role playing and other exercises.

PLAN TIME

Now estimate the amount of time to be spent on each part of the training program, being careful to budget the hours so the time devoted to a particular topic is consistent with its importance to the firm. Allow time between segments for the salesperson to absorb the material and practice the techniques.

Once the program content and time segments are worked out, break it up into a comfortable, workable schedule so that each training session is long enough to be substantive and short enough to avoid confusing the trainee with more than he or she can absorb and put to use quickly.

CHOOSE LOCATION

Certain environmental elements are critical to choosing a location for a training program. First, there must be reasonable privacy as free from distraction as possible. A training program can be conducted in a real estate office, providing the location and/or time provides for an environment free of distractions. It is better to rent a meeting room in a local hotel if facilities in the broker's office are not conducive to a distraction-free environment.

Provide comfortable seating, adequate light, good acoustics and proper ventilation. A prime objective of any training program is maximum attention. Uncomfortable people simply cannot concentrate.

At this point in planning your training program, estimate the cost. Nothing pays off more handsomely in future profits than the money spent to recruit, train and retain salespeople. If corners must be cut to meet your budget, cut them somewhere else.

WHO DOES THE TRAINING?

One possibility is to hire a full-time training director or instructor to conduct the training, but smaller firms in particular will want to explore other options. Possibly the owner or manager could do the training, or it could be done by other successful sales associates who need and want recognition. Bringing in a retired real estate broker as a trainer is another option. If you team up with friendly competitors to offer training jointly, instructors can be drawn from both firms to teach the subjects in which they have particular expertise. Or you could hire an outside firm that does training, but make sure any firm you consider specializes in training real estate sales associates.

Another option is to draw on outside sources such as lenders, appraisers, city or county assessors, builders or attorneys. Using a combination of all of these demonstrates the team-building process essential in real estate sales and enables sales associates to learn from the "expert" in each topic area.

QUALITIES FOR TEACHING

The trainer must actually want to teach. Still better is compulsive teacher who cannot resist helping others. This characteristic is more important than knowing the job well and certainly more important than the ability to actually do the things the trainer wants to teach others to do. A star salesperson is not necessarily a good teacher, nor is a successful broker.

The teacher must be understanding. Some will say "patient" is the proper word; but good teachers appear to be patient only because they understand that learning takes time and empathy, both essential to the teaching process.

Great teachers do not consider teaching a sacrifice or a chore. They get their reward from the achievements of those whom they have molded and motivated and sent into the field. The person who would rather make a million dollar deal than teach ten people to do the same is not likely to be a great teacher.

None of this should be construed as advocating that the star salesperson be kept out of the training program. On the contrary, nothing could be more stimulating to a group of newcomers than hearing a brief presentation by someone who has succeeded in the field. This is especially true if this individual validates what is being taught, proving that it really works when salespeople get out in the field. The point is that teachers are a breed apart (whether a teacher comes from the top, middle or bottom of the sales force or has never made a sale in his or her life) and the single criterion is the ability to instruct others so they understand and are motivated to put to use in the field what they learned in the training course.

DEVELOPING A FORMAL TRAINING PROGRAM

The success of training relies heavily on how thoroughly the course developer works upfront. Understanding the learners, writing quality objectives and researching delivery methods are all critical steps in creating effective training materials.

Keep in mind that sales associates are adult learners who are learning to further their professional development. They are motivated to attend training to fulfill short-term and long-term goals, so the more directly the training is related to their problems, the happier they will be.

A critical step in developing a training program is to establish the learning objectives. Objectives are the picture of what the learners will be able to do after they've completed the course. They might answer questions such as: In what way will trainees change? or What will trainees be doing differently? Objectives are critical to a course's success. A course without objectives is like a trip without a destination. You can't get there if you don't know where you're going.

There are three kinds of objectives: skills objectives, knowledge objectives (also called understanding objectives) and attitude objectives. All objectives should include a verb that describes performance and measurable criteria. A skills objective might use a verb such as list, demonstrate or identify. A knowledge objective might use compare, evaluate, interpret or comprehend. Verbs that would indicate an attitude objective include believe, enjoy, value and be motivated to.

Attitude objectives are tricky. For one thing, it is very difficult to train someone to have a different attitude. However, through training you can ensure that they have the necessary knowledge and skills and that they understand the consequences of their attitude and behavior. So if your objective is for the sales associate to "feel confident," you can provide the knowledge and skills an individual needs to be successful and hope a feeling of confidence will follow. If you use attitude objectives, it is important to include the behaviors you will observe or measure in order to determine if the desired attitude has been achieved.

EXPLAIN THE BENEFITS OF TRAINING

During the training, be sure to let the learners know what the learning objectives are. Specifically, tell them what they will know how to do after the lesson and how it will benefit them or how it will help them avoid a problem. Give examples of these benefits based either on personal experience or that of other people. Principles acquire meaning when they can be related to people benefits in real life.

It is tempting to write objectives that actually describe goals or desired outcomes, such as increased productivity on the part of the sales associate. But for purposes of creating the course, the desired outcome is of little use to you. It does not help determine what to teach or evaluate how well students have learned the course material. Objectives should describe what students will learn, not what you hope they can or will do as a result of their learning. However, students will have greater interest in the course if you tell them how they can benefit from what they will learn.

TRAINING TECHNIQUES

In developing your course, it is important to assess the style of your learners. Every learner has a preferred learning style, a method by which they learn most effectively. To train adult learners successfully, managers must be sensitive to the different ways in which different people learn. Kenneth Murrell has developed a model to explain how different people learn. Murrell's model describes four different learning styles.

1. *Cognitive learners* learn through thought or other mental activity. They quickly grasp intellectually what they are trying to learn. They prefer rationality and logic and tend to be more oriented toward tasks than people. Effective teaching techniques for cognitive learners include technical or business reading, lectures and video, and self-paced, self-study learning materials.
2. *Affective learners* learn best through feelings or emotions rather than logic. They tend to be intuitive and spontaneous. Because affective

learners desire personal interactions and learn best by experiencing, group exercises and role playing are effective teaching tools for this group. They also tend to learn through interactions with their peers. Many salespeople are affective learners.

3. *Concrete learners* learn by doing. They want to be hands-on and to physically approach or touch what they are working with. Practice exercises and role plays are effective techniques for concrete learners because they can learn by trying or doing.

4. *Abstract learners* are reflective. They learn by relating what they are learning to past experiences and prefer to interact in their heads. When teaching abstract learners, you should allow them to think and analyze before they try to do something. Problem solving is also an effective tool.

Most people combine elements of several learning styles, but may lean more strongly toward one of them. Because people learn in different ways, it is important to build a variety of training techniques into your course.

TRAINING AIDS

Visual aids should be an integral part of a good training program. In their most rudimentary form they will include the use of blackboards, art pads, flash cards, charts, graphs and even enlarged photographs.

The purpose of such aids and other more sophisticated equipment such as video is to add the strong impact of seeing as well as hearing the message. The ancient Chinese proverb "One picture is worth a thousand words" is confirmed by studies that indicate that the attention of the viewer is greatly intensified by focusing eyes as well as ears on a message; comprehension of the materials is also dramatically increased and perhaps most important of all, retention is greater.

Overhead Projector

Once you graduate from the blackboard and flipchart, your first investment might be the purchase or rental of an overhead projector. This relatively inexpensive device has several advantages over a blackboard: Material projected is larger in size; the instructor need not turn his or her back to the group in order to use it; complex diagrams, formulas and the like can be retained for the balance of the class or may be photographed and converted to permanent transparencies. Modern overhead projectors can be used in full room light and will project black and white as well as multicolored images.

The advantage to overhead projection is that the projector will faithfully reproduce on the screen anything written, printed or illustrated on a transparent film placed on its face.

Slide Projectors

The slide projector employs full color or black and white photographic slides usually from either 35mm or "Instamatic" cameras. Despite the difference in format size, the frames on which they are mounted are interchangeable and both types can be used in the same program.

There are a variety of types and makes of slide projectors. The carousel carries slides in a circular "bonnet" which is easily removable so the same slides can be stored permanently in the carriers (which can be interchanged for different programs). Other types mount the slides in a straight column ferris wheel. Activated by either manual control or an automatic advancing mechanism, the projector shows each slide in order on a standard movie screen. Slide film projection is best in a darkened room. One advantage of the slide film presentation is that instructors can, using their own camera equipment and a bit of ingenuity, create their own audiovisual programs. On the other hand, one disadvantage is that the slides must be shown in the order in which they are placed in the carrier. If you decide to skip several slides, you still have to project each one to get to the one you want to show the class.

Projectors which can be controlled automatically by cassette tapes are also available. Once the program has started, the sound is automatically synchronized with the picture on the screen and the slides advance automatically by an inaudible electronic pulse on the tape. Where the automatic advancing ability is not present, a tone, beep or "cricket" can be recorded on the audio tape which gives the monitor of the class a cue to advance the slide.

Television Recording and Videotape

One of the most exciting tools in the audiovisual field is the in-house closed circuit television and videotape recorder system. Although a camera, recorder and monitor set can be purchased for about $1,500, the investment could run to more substantial sums. The simplest system allows trainees to not only hear but also to see themselves in simulated selling situations.

As in the case of the slide projector, videotape recorder programs can be put on tape permanently to be replayed any time a new salesperson is added to the staff or an experienced salesperson wants to brush up on a particular technique.

You don't have to make your own tapes to utilize video, however. Also available are a variety of prerecorded videocassettes that enhance training programs. The Real Estate Brokerage Managers Council™ offers an extensive series of tapes to provide a training program for your new associates, complete with workbooks and supplementary reading, or to provide a visual supplement to your existing training program.

ROLE PLAYING

Whether used theater style in the training center or in conjunction with a tape recorder or videotape recorder, role playing is one of the most effective training methods used in classroom instruction.

The object of role playing is to simulate as closely as possible the selling situations in which salespeople are likely to find themselves. This might include problems as diverse as dealing with an irate seller whose door was left unlocked, a skeptical buyer who wants to be shown why a home is priced at $100,000, a nasty telephone caller inquiring about a classified ad or an intrepid soul who is sure he can sell his property himself and avoid paying a broker's commission.

The situation and the characters involved must be clearly defined before the role playing session begins.

Although it is strictly make-believe, it must be serious to be effective. No laugh breaks or funny remarks will salvage a difficult selling situation in the field, so avoid them in the training session. One of the purposes of role playing is to portray the pressure of a situation so that players can become familiar with handling it before encountering it in the field.

Lessons learned here cost only the training time. The same mistake made in the field may not only destroy a substantial commission but may foul up the plans of buyer and seller as well and do permanent harm to the firm's reputation.

Following the role playing session, there should be an immediate critique. If a tape recorder or videotape system has been used, there can be no question of what was said. It should first be played back for both the participants and those who watched them.

The first critique should be made by the participants themselves who will very likely be keenly aware of their mistakes.

Nonparticipating people in the class might be asked to make comments and criticisms along the same line: "What was done well, or how could it have been done more effectively?" The wrap-up might be a run-through of the same situation with the characters in the drama attempting to take advantage of their own criticisms and the suggestions of their peers and the instructor.

Finally, the instructor should add any suggestions he or she may have for improving the participants' techniques and correcting their errors. This must be done tactfully. The purpose of role playing is definitely not to embarrass the participants. A good starting point for the instructor's critique is to ask what the participant did right. Follow-up questions include: "How can you think of a better solution?" or "If you were in that position what would you have done differently?"

Tips on Role Playing

In the opening situation, it is usually a good idea for the instructor or someone experienced in role playing to take one of the parts. This lends stability to the experiment and keeps the subject matter on target. It also avoids situations where the party playing the customer feels sorry for the salesperson and lets that person off the hook by dropping out of character, giving hints that no real customer would ever volunteer, or simply agreeing with him or her just to ease a tense situation.

For role playing to be effective, the tough customer must remain tough, the silent customer must remain silent and the angry customer must keep on shouting until the salesperson has communicated effectively and the customer is once again ready to listen.

Role playing can be employed to polish telephone techniques, listing solicitations, sales presentations, qualifying inquiries and the like as refresher training for salespeople. It is an excellent idea to mix the veteran performers with novices in role playing situations. Both can benefit, although it may be pretty tough to get star salespeople to submit to the tortures of a live audience and the brutally factual attention of the audio tape or television camera. But a top salesperson who is persuaded to join the role playing sessions has far more to gain from it than a newcomer to whom even the simplest words of wisdom are useful.

Here are three roleplaying situations. They are presented to show you how such situations are used in some training programs. You may use them as they are given here or develop others suited to problems in your market area.

Situation 1

Salesperson	*Client*
Scene: Seller is building a new home. Listing is 60 days old. Salesperson has been told to get the price down to the market. Two showings—eight ads—no offers—listed $10,000 over market.	Mr. & Mrs. Seller's new home is nearing completion. Salesperson has not been in touch. Doors left unlocked—lights on.
	Nearby home sold by competitor recently.
	Salesperson went to high school with Mrs. Owner.
	Husband opens with: "Well, stranger—got our place sold yet?"

Situation 2

Salesperson	*Customer*
Scene: REALTOR®'s office at 9:00 p.m. Second showing is over. All went well.	Mr. and Mrs. "Never-pay-retail" have looked for six months.
	Now rent month to month.
Property on the market four days—eight showings—priced right—good motive.	No money problem—but no decision either.
Your own listing and right for these buyers.	Wife opens with: "We sure like that house, but we think it's much more than we want to pay. We're really in no hurry, you know."

Situation 3

Salesperson	*Client*
Scene: Office of owner who had salesperson check a two-family property for him.	Mr. Owner opens with: "You come recommended—that's why I called you. Now, I'll list with you for 30 days at $90,000. Do a good job and I'll extend it for another 30, and I don't want any sign or nosy neighbors, and the price is firm—I got an appraisal."
He inherited it and now wants to sell it.	
It's a nice $75,000, 20-year-old property—needs work.	

LECTURES AND LECTURETTES

Lectures are useful for communicating quickly to a large group. However, lectures place the burden for promoting learning on the instructor. In addition, there is no way to know if the learners understand or agree with what they are hearing. The learners are essentially passive listeners and have no opportunity for feedback or to put into practice what they are learning. Consequently, lectures should be used sparingly in training new sales associates.

Lecturettes are less formal lectures in which the instructor asks questions throughout the presentation, providing some opportunities for feedback from the learners. But they are still primarily a passive teaching method.

DISCUSSION

Discussion techniques get learners actively involved in the learning process. There are several types of discussion techniques that can be used effectively. A question and answer discussion, the Socratic approach, consists of asking the learners questions and leading them to volunteer the answers. This technique provides immediate feedback and enables the trainer to probe the subject in greater depth. Small group discussions generally are used in a training setting to enable teams of learners to put into practice what they have learned. The trainer divides the class into small groups and gives them a problem to solve. Then each group presents its solution to the class. Small group discussion fosters more communication and a closer working relationship among the team members. It is particularly effective for adult learners because it enables them to learn from their peers.

Another form of discussion is brainstorming. Brainstorming gives participants an opportunity to generate a set of options without fear of censorship and is an effective way of obtaining creative new ideas.

TOWN HALL

The Town Hall teaching technique uses participants as a resource. The trainer asks the learners for their concerns and expectations for the class. The trainer or someone else records all of the participants' contributions, but refrains from giving input. The town hall helps the trainer determine what should be covered in the training session and make decisions based on the input of the class.[1]

CASE STUDIES

Case studies, a technique popularized by the Harvard Business School, has become a popular tool in real estate training. The case can be presented in writing or on videotape. The tasks can be set up in various ways. The learners may be asked such questions as:

- What is the problem?
- What is the solution?
- What errors or mistakes were made?
- How could the procedure presented be done correctly?

Case studies give the trainer an opportunity to test whether the learners have understood the information they've been given and can apply it in a real world situation.

FIELD TRIPS

Field trips allow participants to observe processes that can then become in-class activities or mini case studies. Participants exercise their observation skills and have a hands-on learning experience. For example, on a field trip to the assessor's office in your municipality, associates can be shown how the appraisal formula is arrived at and how come the calculations closely resemble market value. This will give both new and experienced associates a better understanding of how to arrive at market value. This knowledge can then be applied in a classroom exercise.[2]

PUBLICATIONS AND PERIODICALS

Every real estate office should have its own library and a portion of its operating budget set aside for the purchase of new books. A growing number of books is being published by the two Councils of the REALTORS® National Marketing Institute®, including the one you are now reading. Trade publishers also have a number of excellent titles relating to the industry. Many are available on loan from the library of the National Association of REALTORS® and your local public library.

After you have assembled even a modest collection, use it to plan a program of recommended reading for salespeople. Salespeople should be encouraged to continue their education by reading the new titles in your library, reviewing older ones and keeping up with newspapers and trade publications subscribed to by the firm.

AUDIO- AND VIDEOTAPE LIBRARIES

In addition to keeping an up-to-date library of publications and periodicals, consider maintaining a library of audio- and videotapes that sales associates can borrow to continue their education on their own. Many prerecorded tapes are available inexpensively from training companies and professional organizations such as the Real Estate Brokerage Managers Council™. In addition, computerized education programs are available. These not only allow learners to assimilate the material at their own pace, but also provide immediate feedback that reinforces learning.

INTRODUCTIONS ARE IMPORTANT

New salespeople should be introduced to everyone in the firm so they can find out how others' jobs and responsibilities relate to what they will be doing. They should become familiar with the functions and operations of every department. Make sure they have a copy of all the firm's listings. Give them a copy of your company's policies and be sure they understand them.

PRODUCT KNOWLEDGE

It is essential that new salespeople study maps showing church, school, library and park locations and districts. They should be familiar with shopping centers and public transportation in the area. They should review current listings, particularly those that affect the area they will serve. You might assign them a "farm," a specific territory they will work.

See that they know within a reasonable time the number and type of homes, school and church locations, distance from shopping and all other information pertinent to the assigned area. This product knowledge is vital.

SALES TECHNIQUES AND TOOLS

Basics are still basics. A manager can help new salespeople avoid pitfalls but he cannot let them skip the basics. Don't ever assume new salespeople know the basics. They will need pointers on sales techniques, deliveries and canvassing, when to talk and when to listen and all the other knowledge they will learn to use that will enable them to become successful.

Familiarize them with sales bulletins and case studies of different sales problems and their solutions. Have them assemble a listing and selling kit that should include whatever you feel is important to effective selling or listing of properties. Have them prepare a suitcase of everything they will need for an open house.

Explain local methods of cooperating with other brokers and how they work. This is a good time to acquaint new salespeople with the caliber of their competition. Explain interoffice coop relations and company policy for such sales. If they have had an opportunity to study the policy and procedures manual, the training course is an excellent time to make sure they understand it.

PARTICIPATION IS IMPORTANT

When designing your training program, allow for as much participation as possible. For most adults, peer group learning is the most effective training technique. So as you design your training session, maximize the opportunities for learners to share their ideas with others in the group.[3] In addition, adult learners like to apply their learning immediately. Role playing and other practice sessions provide an opportunity to do this.

After the training session is completed, provide opportunities for sales associates to apply what they have learned on the job. The sooner this is done after the course concludes the better. Managers also need to ensure that what the sales associates have learned is reinforced and supported on the job. They should not be learning one thing and seeing others do something different. Learners need a consistent message.

Sense Mood

Be sensitive to the mood of the class. Shuffling, coughing, wandering gazes and side bar conferences are signs they have "pulled the shade" on the instructor. Regain their attention by changing the pace, changing the subject, changing the approach, changing voice level, asking questions or inviting feedback.

Be the center of attention, use the full voice range, dramatic gestures, movement, facial expressions and pauses to liven up the presentation. Do not hesitate to dramatize. The job requires it. There is a risk of occasionally feeling like a fool but restraint fosters a doubt of the instructor's sincerity. Trainees evaluate the message on the basis of everything they hear, see and even feel during the presentation. Anyone who doubts this should try reading the most profound truths from an encyclopedia in a monotone.

In addition to oral quizzes and rap sessions which should be part of regular training sessions, a written examination (preferably fill-in-the-blanks) is a good measuring tool for comprehension. Tests can be used just as effectively after a training film as after a live lecture or discussion session. Success in the examination provides trainees greater satisfaction than they would feel if they merely survive the course by sitting through it.

Measuring the Results

Regardless of the teaching inputs in a training course or the amount of preparation and the skill of the instructor, the fact remains that the most important thing is what happens after the course ends. Only if salespeople use what they learn immediately after they learn the theory can they test its validity and report back to the next class any problems encountered.

MANAGEMENT STYLE

There are many ways to create a learning environment. One way that managers can develop their people is through management style. Management behaviors that support learning include communicating openly, encouraging sales associates to make decisions and come up with their own solutions to problems, rewarding innovation and not punishing risk taking, and providing the level of support and direction that matches each individual's needs.

One of the most powerful ways you can affect your sales associates' growth is by adapting, or flexing, your style to meet their specific needs. Every individual is at a different level of development and thus requires a different level of support and direction from you. This is known as situational leadership.*

Sales associates generally fall into four developmental categories based on their varying levels of competence and commitment. For each developmental level there exists a corresponding management style, as

---

* The information on situational leadership and management style is adapted from Kenneth Blanchard and Patricia and Drea Zigarmi, *Leadership and the One-Minute Manager,* New York: Morrow, 1985.

FIGURE 8.1   Four Developmental Categories

Developmental Level	Leadership Style
Low Competence Low Commitment	Directing
Low Competence High Commitment	Coaching
High Competence Variable Commitment	Supporting
High Competence High Commitment	Delegating

shown in Figure 8.1. These four management styles vary in the amount of support and direction they provide:

1. *Directing:* low support, high direction
2. *Coaching:* high support, high direction
3. *Supporting:* high support, low direction
4. *Delegating:* low support, low direction

An enthusiastic beginner is most likely to respond positively to a coaching style that provides a great deal of both support and direction. Delegating is called for in the case of a peak performer, as these individuals typically require little direction or support. On the other hand, you may need to use a supportive style for an experienced, but disillusioned sales associate, while a directive style is needed for one who is both inexperienced and has a low commitment to your firm or to real estate sales in general. (However, if a sales associate has a low level of commitment and this attitude does not eventually improve with your support, you should probably consider termination.)

Using one management style for all can lead to sales associates who are frustrated because they are being overmanaged or undermanaged. By diagnosing each individual's developmental level and using the appropriate management style for each, you can eliminate overmanagement and undersupervision. However, this is not as easy as it sounds because an individual may be at different developmental levels for different tasks. For one task an individual may be a peak performer while for another he or she may be a disillusioned learner.

One way to reach a common understanding of how you will support and direct an individual so that performance goals are met is through contracting. In contracting, the manager and sales associate discuss and negotiate the associate's goals and performance standards. They also discuss which management style(s) would best fit the associate's needs in which situations. This involves analyzing the sales associate's developmental level together for each major task. In this way, they reach agreement regarding how the manager will support and direct the associate.

Situational leadership helps people develop more quickly because they get the support and direction they need for their individual developmental levels. And as they become ready, they are learning to support and direct themselves.

MENTORING

A mentoring program often moves the new sales associate from the classroom to the streets for field training where they can meet the buying and selling public. Classroom training is not enough. Sales work is a skill that requires practice. A mentoring program gives the new associate the opportunity to practice his or her sales skills under the watchful eye of an experienced sales agent. The mentor guides the trainee and monitors the trainee's performance, correcting errors until the trainee has mastered the skills necessary to succeed in real estate sales.

In a small firm, the broker may function as the mentor. In a large firm, this task may fall to a successful sales associate. The important thing is that the mentor be a good teacher and make a serious time commitment because mentoring is very time consuming. In the case of a successful sales associate, this is time that person may have spent closing transactions. But unless the mentor puts the proper effort into the mentoring program, it will fail. As a result, one characteristic of successful mentoring programs is that the mentor is compensated for his or her time. In most cases, the mentor's compensation is paid out of the company's share of the commissions generated by the new agent. Taking the commission out of the agent's share has a negative impact on the firm's recruiting efforts.

For how long should a new agent be mentored? Mentoring should be a process, not an event. The best approach is to structure a program that is more intensive at the beginning, then tapers off. However, it should be sufficiently open to allow adequate attention to individual problems. Some skills take longer to develop than others. A successful program continues until the trainee gets it right.

One company has set up the following three criteria for mentors.

1. To be a mentor, one must
    - have listed and marketed 8 residential properties;
    - have closed on 12 transactions (8 sales, 4 listings);
    - be a full-time associate with the firm;
    - be recommended by his/her sales manager;
    - be committed to assisting the new sales associate in field training and in giving the new associate time in handling his/her questions and concerns for a period of 10 weeks;

- agree to meet every two weeks with your sales manager for a brief report regarding the new associate's activity and emerging strengths and weaknesses; and
- agree to be compensated $100 from the company (after associate's compensation) for each of the new associate's first two closings.

2. The mentor program will begin during or immediately following postlicense training and will continue for a full 10 weeks.
3. The mentor may work with only one associate at a time.

The same company has developed a list of nine activities to be accomplished by the mentor and the new sales associate as part of the mentoring program:

1. Mentor should take the new associate on calls to measure properties, give listing presentations, qualify buyers, hold open houses, demonstrate properties, prepare and present purchase agreements and close transactions.
2. Mentor should assist sales associate in setting up desk.
3. Associate should practice the following for critique by the mentor:
   - Measure a house and prepare a comparative market analysis.
   - Present a complete listing presentation.
   - Qualify a buyer using the Buyer Analysis Form.
   - Select and show a property.
   - Prepare and present purchase agreement.
3. Associate should work with mentor on open house preparation:
   - Advertising
   - Canvassing
   - Set-up
4. Associate should begin prospecting, with mentor assisting if necessary.
5. Mentor should assist associate in practicing telephone technique.
6. Mentor should assist associate in goal setting and time management if needed.
7. Associate may assist mentor in writing ads, preparing CMAs, holding open houses, and so on. This should be a learning experience. The mentor is not to take advantage of the associate's time.
8. Mentor should keep associate on a steady, regular track, moving through the daily check list.

ENDNOTES

1. Ed Hall, *It's Showtime*.
2. Ed Hall, *It's Showtime*.
3. Steven K. Ellis, *How to Survive a Training Assignment*.
4. Kenneth Blanchard and Patricia and Drea Zigarmi, *Leadership and the One-Minute Manager* (New York: Morrow, 1985).

Chapter 9

Continual Training

Continual, structured training is one of the strengthening forces of an aggressive real estate firm. The frequency of the training sessions, the time devoted to each and the locale may vary with the size of the firm and the facilities and teaching staff available. Whether it consists of a review of the basics, refresher courses on a specific part of the original training program or is strongly oriented to motivation, continual training is needed by both new and experienced salespeople. It is the way firms keep the sales and office staff up to the minute on current and financial conditions, company plans, policy and procedures and maintain open communication between management and staff and among staff people themselves.

Training induces behavioral changes in trainees, stimulates them to greater achievement, reduces staff turnover, improves the broker's image in the business community and attracts new salespeople to the firm. Finally, it frees the broker to spend more time on other work. Underachievers or marginal achievers eliminate themselves through continued training, and good salespeople are motivated to keep on their toes and do a more effective job.

CULTIVATE TRUE COMPETITIVE ADVANTAGE

Performance management consists of hiring the right people and then providing them with the training they need to become superior performers. Developing people is good business because your sales associates are the only true source of competitive advantage. Your firm's competitive advantage may be that it has the most offices in a market, or it may have the latest computerized listing system. But these advantages are not sustainable because other firms can copy them. In the long term, the only true source of sustainable competitive advantage is a firm's people. They are behind new ideas, new processes, new systems, new marketing plans. People create new competitive advantages. And best of all, people can't be copied. But people need to be motivated and developed through learning experiences, and this should be a constant, ongoing process.

Ongoing training incorporates the following six elements of the 7-S model of organizational effectiveness:

1. *Staff:* Ongoing training helps to develop your staff into superior performers who will give your firm a competitive edge in the marketplace.
2. *Skills:* Training can strengthen the firm's capabilities in particular areas, such as strong customer service.
3. *Style:* Continual training lets sales associates know what management considers important.
4. *Systems:* Associates learn the systems and procedures for how things should be done. In addition, training itself is one of the firm's systems.
5. *Strategy:* Training is an important part of a company's strategic plan to improve its position in the marketplace.
6. *Shared values:* Ongoing training enables management to continually reinforce the firm's values and make sure that everyone is moving in the same direction.

After new salespeople have completed their orientation training, what next? Now they join other salespeople in regular workshops. These may be special training sessions or regular sales meetings. They may be round table meetings, panel sessions with a moderator or perhaps a panel of speakers discussing important topics, followed by a question and answer period. Whatever type of training program is planned, allocate as much time as possible for a discussion period that involves salespeople.

Some firms schedule occasional five-day seminars but many salespeople are reluctant to take this much time away from their selling efforts. Unless your salespeople are employees, their attendance at all training and sales meetings is voluntary. One company closes its offices one full day each year and invites everyone in the company to attend a seminar. The program covers every aspect of residential selling, including condominiums. Outside speakers are featured and a substantial share of the day is devoted to question and answer sessions.

The policy and procedures manual should be reviewed on a regular basis, at least once a year, but its role in continual training has a minimal day-to-day effect.

IDEA MANUAL

One successful firm has developed a work manual to serve its sales department on a day-to-day basis. Each salesperson receives a 3-ring binder that is divided into two main parts.

The first part covers current policies of lenders, selling techniques that are updated weekly, current tax information and a host of formulas to help get the selling job done effectively. As new ideas are heard of or tried they are shared with others and added to each person's idea manual.

The second part deals with administrative functions as they relate to sales procedures. This part is critical in sustaining a positive, identifiable and supportive relationship between the salesperson and the firm every day. It is updated weekly. Salespeople bring work manuals to weekly sales meetings for purposes of review and the input of new ideas from the sales staff and management. The quality and usefulness of this manual rely heavily on the sales staff, but its basic content is the result of management's accumulating information gleaned from years of experience of successful real estate brokers all over the country.

The work manual's importance lies in the way it deals with current situations and supplies salespeople with solutions to problems likely to be encountered; but it frees them from committing the information to memory. They carry it with them everywhere on the job. The firm that recommends the work manual reports it has helped create new concepts in selling real estate because salespeople use it as a foundation on which to build.

SALES MEETINGS

Sales meetings accomplish a variety of purposes including motivation, communication of information and training. More than one purpose can be met at any one meeting.

To avoid duplication, the content of both continual training sessions and sales meetings will be dealt with jointly. Almost every subject suggested for continual training could also be incorporated in a sales meeting agenda sometime during the year. It becomes a management decision whether to schedule training sessions apart from sales meetings or whether time and money pressures dictate combining them.

The sales meeting is one of the most important continual training programs available in real estate. Over the period of a year, ten to thirty minutes in weekly sales meetings devoted to some facet of training can strengthen both management and staff.

Sales meetings, according to the most successful firms, are held at the same time and same hour every week so they become an integral part of the salespeople's schedule. Some firms hold sales meetings in a coffee-and-donut session in the early morning and schedule them to end just as office hours begin. A regular time, a stimulating agenda and a prompt closing will attract a strong attendance. Give your salespeople something to use that week and they'll be there.

Be certain every training or sales meeting has a primary objective and an agenda and that whoever teaches or conducts the meeting has a detailed outline of the training to be included, knows what is to be said and how it will be presented. Give everyone in attendance a chance to participate. What is said by staff to management is as important as what management says to staff.

Use participative techniques so your sales associates become doers instead of passive students. Incorporate a variety of techniques because people have different learning styles and will respond differently to the trainer's teaching style. For example, concrete learners learn by doing in a structured setting; hands-on learning such as practice exercises or role playing work best for them. Affective learners learn through feelings or emotions; they learn best through experiencing and group interactions, so group exercises and role plays are effective techniques to use with them. Abstract learners learn by observing or reflecting back on past experience; observation and problem solving are effective techniques. Cognitive learners grasp a concept intellectually; they learn from reading or hearing about something. Using a variety of techniques will help you reach everyone in the meeting.

Motivational Sales Meetings

Theories abound about the art of motivation and the science of what motivates people. The sales technique portion of training emphasizes how to and skills; the rest of training is to assist in the self development of people who happen to sell real estate.

While some motivation problems are best handled in a one-on-one session, a carefully structured meeting designed to fill human needs can strengthen team spirit. Discussion of common problems by the salespeople promotes empathy and a sharing of ideas.

A motivational sales meeting is structured separately and has different results from a general sales meeting. While the latter covers general business considerations and may feature a speaker on a particular topic, it usually includes an attempt by the manager to induce enthusiasm to perform a general sales function.

This type of meeting is critical to an organization that is dynamic and expanding because it ties both new and experienced staff people together in a feeling of common purpose. It is motivational in the sense that it focuses on general market opportunities and strives to inspire the staff to achieve short-term goals.

The motivational sales meeting is more critical in its structuring, participation and the results it should generate. Motivational meetings are based on the assumption that those in attendance are a more close-knit group and know one another's strengths and weaknesses. The problem is that these meetings have a tendency to become repetitious and challenge management to keep them well-structured and inspirational.

Careful planning of the agenda of every motivational sales meeting is of great importance. Selection of materials is also critical to success. Participation by everyone in attendance is high on the list of factors critical to good motivational sales meetings. Participation can take at least two forms in these situations.

One of the most common types is an award presentation. The competition can range from naming a "winner" who put up the first "For Sale" sign following the last sales meeting to announcing a prize for the salesperson closing the first escrow after the present meeting or perhaps an annual customer service award. Size of the prize is not important when management is motivating well-trained salespeople. What is important is the recognition of the peer group and the satisfaction of one element in the person's hierarchy of needs. Make sure awards are not always presented solely for individual effort. Team effort should also be rewarded.

Another purpose is to motivate everyone to produce at top capacity in all aspects of sales and service. A clear discussion of company goals can form the background of a motivational meeting. When the sales staff knows where the company is going and why, they are motivated to be a part of it and do their share to reach the goal.

Motivational meetings need not always be conducted by the firm. Think about holding meetings outside the company. Qualified speakers are often scheduled to appear before business and community groups. What they say can inspire and inform real estate salespeople as well as others in the community. Management that keeps its eyes open to such opportunities and suggests that salespeople will gain some useful knowledge from hearing these speakers will also benefit. Local real estate boards are another good source of outside speakers and offer individual firms the benefit of banding together to hear someone with a message germane to the industry.

MEETING AGENDA

A strong agenda for sales meetings will repay every minute spent to develop it. Once the purpose of the meeting is decided, an agenda exploring the best ways to achieve that purpose is prepared. Experienced managers know there will always be people around to tell why an idea won't work or a goal can't be achieved. Management's job is to set an affirmative tone for the meeting, provide opportunities for all to participate and then guide the participation toward positive discussion. Problems should be discussed in a constructive manner and meetings should end on a positive note.

Successful firms report that a continuing, regular review of telephone techniques, listing and market analysis ideas, and reminders of how the firm services listings can be handled in sales meetings in a variety of ways that are helpful to salespeople. Straight talk from the manager, moderated discussion panels, or role playing sessions vary the presentation and provide ways to motivate the different types of people in a sales organization, giving them something to use the moment the meeting ends.

How To Prepare an Agenda

A small spiral notebook is an excellent place to collect ideas for sales meetings. Choose a size that can slip into a pocket or purse and keep it ready to record every idea for topics to cover in sales/training sessions. Loose bits of paper too often become lost bits of paper, resulting in the loss of good ideas. Back at the desk, transcribe the ideas in the notebook into the sales meeting agenda.

Keep both the source notebook and the agenda for every meeting on file. Both are valuable references of topics that have been covered. The source book, reviewed from time to time, will enable the manager to spot emerging patterns. The agenda file serves as a record of what has been covered in sales meetings and can be used to convince salespeople that a certain problem or topic was discussed and on what date.

Policy and Procedures Manual   Firms that use their policy and procedures manual as a resource for sales meeting agendas find this also helps them keep the manual up to date. It enables them to make quick changes when conditions call for speedy action and to plan long-range changes under more ordinary circumstances. Discuss any change under consideration and the problem or reason that instigated it. Ask for additional suggestions from the staff. Often the greatest input for a needed change originates with an alert salesperson.

Listings   A review of current listings is important to every sales meeting. Where is the firm weak in listings? What can be done to maintain listings in a particular area? Let the salespeople present the new listings they have. Speaking about them to their peers enables everyone to do a better selling job.

Review changes in old listings. Use sales meetings to generate ideas for what can be said or done to help a particular hard listing to sell.

A caution: Based on office policy on agency, only certain information can legally be shared.

Marketing/Advertising   Are you getting lots of calls on certain kinds of advertising? Is your advertising weak in some area? Where should you be pushing advertising?

Goals/Objectives   The beginning of the firm's fiscal year is the time to discuss goals and establish new objectives in selling. Then review them quarterly so everyone knows where the firm stands in relation to its annual goals. Discuss privately with each salesperson his or her individual goals. But if someone has done a great job in achieving or surpassing their goal be sure to compliment them in the training or sales meeting. It's a great morale builder for the individual and can motivate others to catch up with the leader.

"Want" Problems   "Want" problems presented by a salesperson have been known to create a sale right in the sales meeting. Someone may say "I have a client who needs such and such" and another might know exactly where to find it. Again, office policy on agency will determine what can legally be shared.

Brainstorming/Creativity Sessions   Brainstorm in a positive way. Seek salespeople's ideas in areas where the firm has problems. Ask what they think could be done. Use a blackboard to list every solution offered, no matter how impossible some may appear. Then try to narrow the list down to a reasonable number of choices that seem practical. If a solution does not emerge, ask that the problem be thought about until the next meeting. Get it on the agenda to be dealt with then.

Deal with Problems   Never make a sales meeting into a chewing-out session. Bring things out but never spotlight the salesperson who has a problem. If the problem is a general one and you believe it concerns the entire organization, present it at a sales meeting. Give the exact facts but never use names. Dealing with problems in this fashion can squelch rumors too. If management explains problems to the sales staff openly, sticks to the facts and presents the solution, the problem seems to fade away. If management fails to do this, the rumor grinds on, creating potential harm to both the staff and the firm.

Review the Company Plan   If the firm plans to expand, be sure the staff hears it from management first. When the staff is part of long-range planning, both employees and independent contractors are more likely to make all-out efforts to help those plans materialize.

Referral Service   Because referrals are the backbone of the real estate business, some firms pay a small special bonus in addition to the referral check to salespeople who bring them in. Sales meetings are a good time to pass out these bonuses and referral checks. When a salesperson has had a particularly good period of referrals, it looks like a fine incentive to the others when that person is handed $50 in five dollar bills as a bonus for five referrals in a single week.

Repeat Performances   When sudden changes in the market occur, some large firms schedule a series of sales meetings to be sure every salesperson is aware of how the firm is geared to meet the new situation. That way, a salesperson who misses the session in his or her office can catch it at one of the company's other branches. In this fashion, everyone in the organization eventually attends some class and in a matter of a few weeks the whole organization is attuned to the change.

ATTENDANCE PROBLEMS

Sales meetings that are held at a regularly scheduled time work best for many successful brokers. When the meeting time is firm, management's major concern is to develop the agenda and coordinate the participation of everyone involved. Companies whose salespeople are all independent contractors report that attendance of 75 percent to 80 percent is considered good. If the sales staff is employed and if the ancillary staff is included in sales and training meetings, their attendance can be mandatory. If the meetings are stimulating and have a record of providing useful information and strong motivation, independent contractor attendance will be high.

One motivator for salespeople's attendance at these meetings is the knowledge that they will be given time to present their new listings. This has promise of immediate monetary value to the individual salesperson.

Understanding Abraham Maslow's hierarchy of needs can be helpful in motivating associates to attend the sales meeting. At the most basic survival level on Maslow's pyramid, associates may attend to pick up hints to improve production. Those motivated by the need for security may want to avoid missing changes in company policy. Those who have a need to belong will attend because the meeting is a social event. Sales associates motivated by ego needs for status or self-esteem will attend if they think they will be singled out for recognition. Finally, self-actualized salespeople will attend if they believe the meeting will be a productive use of their time.

Strong leadership in sales meetings also helps attendance. The leader's ability to stay close to the agenda, keep the meeting moving along and close on schedule are positive factors in attendance. The ability to let everyone participate but no one dominate a meeting is also important. Encouraging the participation of individual salespeople often leads to their preparing for the meeting too, knowing their performance will be measured against that of their peers.

All these facets of the meeting have to be handled skillfully by the person responsible. Many situations will need to be dealt with before the meeting occurs to avoid any unpleasant confrontations within the small working group. Handling specific personal problems and any matters of a negative nature in advance of the general meetings will allow management to devote more of everyone's time to positive thinking and working. After all, the goal of any sales meeting is to achieve results through group participation and effort to solve individual real estate situations. The success of the meeting depends on management's ability to draw the best from each person who attends.

DEVELOPING PEOPLE

To adapt an old cliche to the real estate business, no brokerage firm is stronger than its weakest member. Management, whether content with the firm's present size or intent on growth, wants its organization to be strong. It can achieve this by developing people. There are at least three ways to accomplish it:

1. Expanding present positions
2. Training for higher level positions
3. Retraining older members

Expanding Present Positions

Training new salespeople and expanding the positions of those already affiliated with the firm can only be achieved through continual training. New salespeople need on-the-job training where a mentor goes out with them and works with them to obtain listings and sell a property or canvass a farm area. They also need continual on-the-job training through meetings and training, discussed earlier in this chapter, if they are to keep up to date on what is happening in the business.

Salespeople require different amounts of time to reach the stage where they know how best to use their time. Managers who make sure their people get the best on-the-job training, prompt and full answers to questions and a full understanding of the firm's objectives will develop their sales staff most quickly.

There are other sources of development for individual salespeople. Local college and adult education courses offer salespeople educational opportunities they can pursue in their free time, usually at low cost. The real estate industry, both locally and nationally, offers courses of value to salespeople in the industry. The Residential Sales Council™ offers eight sales courses that aid in development of personal selling and human relations skills and that lead to the coveted CRS designation. Management should do everything possible to encourage attendance at these sessions.

Audiovisuals are employed by some firms for unsupervised learning sessions. Good audiotapes and videotapes can be run as one-person training sessions. A salesperson can sit down and watch a good listing and selling videotape, pick up some new ideas and go right out and put them to work. When viewed by more than one person, these tapes can generate lively discussions. A manager or salesperson leading the discussion can make it even more valuable.

Whatever training is offered to help salespeople expand their present positions should be followed with careful evaluation. Management needs to know what the person has learned, how he or she is using it and what the next potential learning or working situation might be.

Training for Other Positions in Real Estate

Every salesperson has to spend a certain amount of time in the ups and downs and frustrations of listing, selling and performing all the other services germane to the real estate business. They must learn to learn from their failures, put them behind them, and start over again.

It is possible to accelerate the learning process for an exceptionally good salesperson or a person who shows promise of having management talent. They are not necessarily one and the same person. But in either case, the person is going to have to work longer hours or know how to use his or her time most productively. This person is going to get involved in more transactions and spend more time with the manager or with other strong salespeople to acquire a wealth of experience and knowledge.

Experience, in the opinion of many successful managers, is really the only solid way salespeople develop the ability to make decisions necessary in the real estate business. Individuals who are aiming at management positions must know how to follow the money market and changing real estate values and trends and must see a great deal of real estate to be able to judge market values accurately. One good way to help such people develop is to begin to include them in the decision-making process of the firm. Invite such people to sit in on discussions of problems. Encourage them to ask any question that comes to mind. Find out what their decision would be and why. Explain what the firm's decision is and why. The two decisions often prove to be quite similar.

All this leads up to the person's growing awareness of problems, how they develop, what can be done to avoid them or how to correct them if they cannot be avoided. A good manager is not one who is always running around solving problems. A good manager is a person who sees problems before they happen and is able to help salespeople avoid danger areas by preventing problems.

The emphasis again is on experience. If you are looking for someone for a management position, look for an individual who has had previous success in management responsibilities or who has owned a successful business or who comes into real estate from some other responsible job. Such a person will bring a knowledge of the complexities of the decision-making process, will have a fairly accurate idea of how to evaluate right from wrong and will be better prepared to step into a management role once he or she becomes well acquainted with the real estate industry.

Retraining Experienced Sales Associates

Real estate management sometimes devotes time and effort to their experienced salespeople only to later lose them to a competitor or have them open their own firm in competition. This can be a difficult and discouraging fact to accept. But more frequently than not, such training and attention results in the experienced salespeople deciding to remain where they are.

If your firm is large enough, conduct quarterly round table discussions for your experienced associates. These could include such topics as holding a successful open house, marketing new construction, turning cold calls into dollars, prospecting for results or personal marketing success. You can provide recognition for individuals by having a sales associate who is successful in a particular area lead the round table on that topic.

In addition, devote an hour or so each week to a training topic of interest to your developing sales associates to fine-tune their skills. Topics might include the following:

- Prospecting
- Cold calling
- Pricing
- Qualifying
- Negotiating
- Handling objections
- Servicing the seller

One way this can be done is through satellite television sessions. Sales associates can attend when a session is being transmitted, or the sessions can be videotaped for viewing later at a more convenient time. Real Estate Television Network and RealNet Direct TV are examples of the televised training that is available. Some of the large franchise organizations have their own television networks.

Once a year, bring in an outside trainer for a full day or half day a week for six to eight weeks to "retrain" developing salespeople. This will instill new life into their daily routine. You might also bring in an outside marketing consultant to remind associates of the value and how-to of personal marketing and get them started on preparing personal marketing programs.

When outside speakers appear before the entire staff, both new and experienced members benefit. Occasionally, having a private session with an outside speaker for a small number of the staff, particularly the experienced members and top salespeople, results in their feeling they are getting special attention. This serves to fulfill an element in their hierarchy of needs. They also learn more by being in an intimate group where their questions are answered personally and they participate in a lively exchange.

Experienced members often like to be asked to help train newer salespeople or to contribute their know-how to a special sales meeting for new salespeople. They will prepare for such a session by reviewing the basics they have so long taken for granted and relish the teaching experience that elicits the enthusiasm of their audience. Everyone gains from such a session.

TRAINING GOALS

Management that instills in every staff member the belief that they have to be their very best in order to achieve self-respect and the respect of their clients and peers will help its salespeople prosper. It is management's role to involve everyone in the continual training that builds a professional image for both the staff and the firm. Salespeople prosper in an organization that fosters learning.

Chapter 10

Coaching the Salesperson

It is commonly said that real estate is a people business. Consequently, one of the most important skills of a real estate brokerage manager is the ability to communicate. The manager's communication style and skills are particularly important in managing the performance of the sales staff. Managers must direct their salespeople, communicate information and decisions to them, and assess their performance. A term used for this is coaching. Coaching involves motivating, teaching, mentoring, and helping salespeople to solve problems. The manager's effectiveness in coaching salespeople is critical to the success of both the manager and the firm.

WHAT COACHING MEANS

The previous two chapters addressed managing sales associates' performance through initial and ongoing training. This chapter examines another aspect of staff development called coaching.* Elements of the 7-S model that will be discussed in this chapter as they relate to the coaching process are staff, style, skills and shared values.

Coaching includes counseling, mentoring, tutoring and confronting/challenging in one-to-one conversations with subordinates intended to solve problems or improve performance. These conversations are critical

* Much of the information in this chapter is adapted from *Social Style/Management Style* by Bolton and Bolton and from Dennis Kinlaw's book *Coaching For Commitment: Managerial Strategies for Obtaining Superior Performance.*

to the manager's success in obtaining ongoing, superior performance from employees. According to Kinlaw, "There are no controls that can force employees to produce superior performance. No policies or systems can make employees take the initiative to identify and solve problems on their own. No rewards or punishments can stimulate an unremitting concern for quality. Sustained, superior performance can be obtained only through commitment, and coaching is a primary means by which managers can build commitment."

In order to coach successfully, managers first need a basic understanding of the process of communication.

THE PROCESS OF COMMUNICATION

Perhaps the first step in becoming a better communicator is to understand the process. Is it simply that one person talks and another listens? Or is it more complex than that?

In the highly emotional areas of interpersonal work relationships and real estate sales, it is imperative that we keep in mind that a speaker transmits more than words. Of course the words carry the speaker's ideas. But the vocal inflection, the intonation of the words and the nonverbal body language also transmit feelings and attitudes. And it is in the nonverbal area that both speaker and listener communicate constantly.

Thus we can define *communication* as "the transmission and reception of ideas, feelings and attitudes, verbally and nonverbally, which produce a response."[2] It is this feedback (or response), both verbal and nonverbal, that permits both parties to evaluate the effectiveness of their communication. However, feedback must be interpreted with care. Often it is unreliable as in the case where the broker explains for five minutes to the new office secretary that "whenever a sales associate secures a listing, he or she will submit to you a Form 42 which you should record in the office log as well as the salesperson's record book and then complete one of these Form 65's for the main office. The next step is to complete a sales breakdown to include commission percentages according to our Schedule 4 unless the salesperson is in either category 2 or 3, and if that is so, use Schedule 5. However. . ."

And at the conclusion of this peroration, the broker says to the secretary, "Of course you see how all this works?"

And the secretary, who was lost after the first reference to "Form 42" calmly, clearly and confidently answers, "Yes, of course I see," and doesn't understand the explanation at all.

Why do people "feed back" to the sender, "Yes, I understand" when actually they do not?

Perhaps there are three reasons: They often think they understand and do not; do not wish to appear stupid; or they are fearful of your response if they tell you honestly that they don't understand. In any event, the expert communicator learns to interpret verbal and nonverbal feedback very carefully.

NONVERBAL COMMUNICATION

The science called body language deals with behavioral patterns of nonverbal communication. What we do with our bodies is frequently in disagreement with what we are saying. A classic example, according to Julius Fast, writing in *Body Language,* is the young woman who told her psychiatrist that "she loved her boyfriend very much all the while shaking her head from side to side in subconscious denial."[3]

Body language can enable business people to shed new light on the dynamics of interpersonal relationships. Those who study it carefully learn to observe the mixture of body movements ranging from the deliberate to the completely unconscious, what each conveys and how to put this knowledge to good use in their daily working relationships.

It is probably no exaggeration to say that we communicate as many ideas nonverbally as we do verbally. The way we stand, the way we walk, the manner in which we shrug our shoulders, furrow our brows and shake our heads all convey ideas to others. But we need not always perform an action for nonverbal communication to take place. We also communicate by the clothes we wear, the car we drive or the office we occupy. It is true that what is communicated may not be accurate, but ideas are communicated.

Real estate professionals must be especially sensitive to nonverbal signals: the pained or delighted look on the prospect's face as soon as the first step is taken into the home; the nervous tapping of the fingers on the table top; the voice inflection of confidence or insecurity when price is discussed and the physical tension in the individual's posture as he or she walks around the property or sits in a chair reading an offer, listing or legal papers.

The same is also true when the broker and salesperson hold a critical interview on compensation, promotion or company strategy. The broker must be sensitive to the crossed arms, tapping heel on the floor, voice level and perhaps the perspiration on the salesperson's forehead.

Where the broker sits during the interview announces the formality or informality of a situation. To treat someone in an informal manner, the broker could come around from the desk and guide the visitor to the couch, then sit in an easy chair. If the interview is to be extremely formal, the broker will remain seated behind the desk.

All these nonverbal signals communicate a message, and we must attempt to decode them.

CONFLICT BETWEEN VERBAL AND NONVERBAL COMMUNICATION

One of the interesting aspects of communication is the task of decoding two messages transmitted simultaneously. This happens often in both verbal and nonverbal communication situations. We have all been in a situation in which an individual has greeted us with "How are you? Good to see you. Come into my office and let's visit for a while." But the nonverbal communication, consisting of a surreptitious but pained glance at the clock, says something else. Or the guest who says, "Of course we want to see your slides of Europe," while stifling a yawn and sprawling in the chair.

Then there is the employee who tries to sound relaxed and comfortable when talking to the boss, but the toe tapping on the floor or fingers drumming on the end table tell a different story.

Interestingly enough, whenever the meaning of the nonverbal message conflicts with that of the verbal, the receiver is most likely to find the nonverbal message more believable.

Does this mean that we should bend every effort to communicate the same message both verbally and nonverbally? Generally, if we are transmitting an untruth verbally, it will conflict with the nonverbal communication. And the alert receiver will almost always be able to determine that a problem exists. Most of us can quickly see the fearful person who exists behind the good-humored, back-slapping, joke-telling facade that is displayed. The nonverbal message is usually obvious; and if it does not agree with the verbal one, the receiver quickly and almost invariably recognizes the one that is true.

THE SOCIAL STYLE CONCEPT AND COACHING

Every person has one dominant style that influences the way he or she works. Often problems between people occur because they have different styles. When we attempt to work with someone who has a different style, the result can be tension or disagreements. The same thing can also happen when you attempt to coach a salesperson whose style differs from yours. However, understanding your own social style and recognizing other people's dominant style will help you coach sales associates more effectively.

Social style is based on observable behavior and how other people perceive that behavior. It has nothing to do with personality or character. People try different ways of relating to others and getting what they want. They continue to behave in the ways that are most efficient for them, and over time these become their dominant style of relating to others. No style is better than any other, and the social style a person has is right for them.

In *Social Style/Management Style,* the authors have identified four social styles that reflect an individual's degrees of assertiveness and responsiveness.

ASSERTIVENESS AND RESPONSIVENESS

Assertiveness is defined as the degree to which a person is perceived as trying to influence the thoughts and actions of others. There are degrees of assertiveness. Those who are "ask assertive" tend to be more tentative and less forceful in expressing opinions, making requests and giving directions than those who are "tell assertive." People who are "ask assertive" also have more of a tendency to be less confrontive, to let others take the interpersonal initiative and to exert less pressure for decisions than their more assertive colleagues.

Responsiveness is the degree to which a person is perceived as expressing feelings when relating to others. Again, individuals manifest different degrees of reliance on feelings. People who are "control responsive" generally are more controlled in their expression of feelings, focus more on facts, appear more task-oriented than people-oriented, and make decisions based more on facts than emotions. Those who are "emote responsive" tend to be freer in their expression of feelings, to be more people-oriented, and to allow feelings to have a greater influence on decision making.

The four social styles discussed below—analytic, driver, expressive and amiable—can be composed of these two dimensions: assertiveness and responsiveness.

Analytical Style

The analytical style is perceived as ask-assertive/control-responsive. Analytical persons are task-oriented, precise and thorough. Analyticals like to deal in facts, work methodically and use "standard operating procedures."

Verbal indicators include: Speak slowly and softly; tentative in expressing themselves; ask rather than tell; controlled in their expression of feelings; focus on facts; not very interested in small talk and jokes.

Nonverbal indicators include: Move slowly and deliberately, often rigidly; lean backward; have less eye contact; limit their use of gestures; have less facial expressiveness; seem serious and reserved; dress formally.

Analyticals' strengths include being logical, thorough, serious, systematic and prudent. On the other hand, analyticals tend not to be spontaneous. Overextended strengths can also become weaknesses. If their style is extended to extremes, analyticals may become nitpicky.

Driver Style

The driver style is perceived as tell-assertive/control-responsive. Drivers are goal oriented. They are disciplined, determined "bottom line" thinkers who push for results and accomplishments.

Verbal indicators include: Speak quickly, intensely, often loudly; are emphatic in expressing themselves; are tell-oriented; are controlled in their expression of feelings; focus on facts; not very interested in small talk.

Nonverbal indicators include: Move rapidly, but rigidly; sit upright or lean forward; have more intense and consistent eye contact; limit their use of gestures; have less facial expressiveness; appear serious and reserved, dress more formally.

Drivers' strengths include being independent, candid, decisive, pragmatic and efficient. However, they may not be supportive and can become domineering.

Expressive Style

The expressive style is perceived as tell-assertive/emote-responsive. Expressives are idea-oriented. They are vigorous, enthusiastic, spontaneous. They like to initiate relationships and motivate others toward goals.

Verbal indicators include: Speak quickly and intensely; are emphatic in expressing themselves; are tell-oriented; are freer in expressing feelings; are more interested in small talk and jokes.

Nonverbal indicators include: Move rapidly; sit upright or lean forward; move and gesture freely; seem more playful; dress less formally; have more intense and consistent eye contact.

Expressives' strengths include being outgoing, persuasive, fun-loving and spontaneous. Their weaknesses include the fact that they may not be precise, and they can become overbearing.

Amiable Style

The amiable style is perceived as ask-assertive/emote-responsive. Amiables are people-oriented. They are friendly, accepting and cooperative, and they like to be liked. People with this style are motivated to help others in a team effort.

Verbal indicators include: Speak slowly and softly; are more tentative and less forceful in expressing themselves; are ask-oriented; are freer in their expression of feelings and focus more on feelings; enjoy small talk.

Nonverbal indicators include: Move more slowly and deliberately; lean backward; have less consistent eye contact; gesture frequently; have more facial expressiveness; seem more playful and friendly; dress less formally.

Amiables' strengths include being cooperative, supportive, diplomatic, patient and loyal. However, they may be indecisive and conforming.

The weaknesses and overextensions of a style may result in managers being ineffective. Good managers develop strategies to minimize their weaknesses and prevent overextending their style. To do this, however, you first need to be aware of what your style is. You can do this by thinking about your degrees of assertiveness and responsiveness and locating yourself on the grid. But it is generally more effective to pinpoint your style through other people's feedback.

It is also important to understand the styles of your associates and subordinates, because many of the problems and misunderstandings that arise at work are style-based. Awareness of your style and the styles of the people around you helps you understand why problems in interpersonal relationships arise. Once you understand why these problems occur, you can style flex to help eliminate them.

STYLE FLEXING

According to Bolton and Bolton: "A person who uses style flex reads situations accurately and responds in ways that are fitting. . . [he/she] is communicating in a way more readily understood by and more agreeable to persons of another social style."[4] When you style flex, you don't need to radically change your style, but you use some body language and wording that matches the preference of the other person. For example, if you are a driver and the other person is an amiable, you might speak more slowly and allow more silence, ask the other person's opinion and state your own opinions less forcefully.

When should you flex your style? If you do it all the time, you are sacrificing your style to that of other people. You should flex your style when something important is at stake, when the other person is under stress or when you want to start off a conversation on the right note.

When you style flex, most of the time you should focus on behaviors you have in common with the other person. You may also need to increase or decrease your assertiveness or responsiveness, depending on your style and that of the other person. For example, drivers and expressives may need to decrease their assertiveness when dealing with analyticals and amiables, in order not to overwhelm them.

In order to flex to a specific social style, you need to understand what drives and motivates each style.

Analyticals are motivated by a need for respect. They value hard work and attention to detail. Things for them must be logical and carefully worked out. When dealing with analyticals, you should stick to business, use action words and provide solid evidence. Don't be casual, loud or informal, don't be vague or disorganized and don't use opinions as evidence.

Drivers are motivated by power. They like to know they are in charge. They need information that allows them to make decisions quickly and get tangible results. When you deal with drivers, you should be clear, specific, to the point and deal with the facts. Don't try to build personal relations or waste their time.

Expressives thrive on recognition. You should ask for their opinions and ideas, support their dreams and intentions, talk about people and their goals. Don't deal with details and don't be dogmatic or cold.

Amiables deal in approval and seek warmth, understanding, friendship and trust. Start with a personal comment to break the ice and be casual and nonthreatening. Don't rush into the business agenda or force them to respond quickly.

THE MANAGER AS COACH

In their 7-S model, Peters and Waterman point out that the quality of its people is a company's only sustainable advantage. Satisfactory performance is not enough. To achieve and maintain its competitive advantage, a company needs superior performance and commitment from its staff. Commitment is evidenced by single-minded, focused behavior and the willingness to sacrifice personal time to meet the commitment. People feel commitment if their work has meaning, if they feel they are contributing to the success of the organization. To feel committed, a person must have clarity about the organization's goals and values and an understanding of how their goals are linked to those of the organization. In other words, they must understand and share the firm's values.

In addition, people do not become committed unless they feel they can do the job well. A manager who wants committed people must make sure that people have the required knowledge, skills and experience, and feel confident about their ability to do the job.

Commitment also requires that people feel they have influence. There are three areas in which managers can and should allow people to have influence: innovation (new ideas), planning (new programs) and problem solving. Finally, to feel committed to a task or job, an individual needs to believe that his or her work is appreciated.

The key to sales associates' commitment is coaching. Coaching provides the main means for people to exert influence on their jobs because of its emphasis on finding ways to improve their jobs. Coaching is face-to-face leadership that facilitates people and enables them to do their best. Coaching focuses on training and empowering people instead of scolding or disciplining them. Managers who have mastered coaching use it to develop rapport with their staff and to create a spirit that can manage dissent and achieve consensus.[5]

Coaching has three major benefits:

1. *Coaching uses people's maximum potential.* Successful coaches know what resources their people represent and make the best use of them. Coaching managers facilitate learning, encourage sales associates to solve problems and make it easy for them to obtain help when they need it.

2. *Coaching is timely management.* It keeps managers aware of events and conditions that affect performance and permits managers to respond to problems and opportunities as they occur. It also develops sales associates who can and will respond creatively to problems and opportunities.

3. *Good coaching builds confidence and the expectation of success.* It clarifies schedules, procedures, and expectations, as well as the organization's priorities and values. It helps people to do things in the right order or to approach them in the right way. It conveys the manager's interest and appreciation and enables the manager to provide support when needed. Sales associates who perceive themselves to be important contributors to the success of the organization are more likely to anticipate problems, take appropriate risks, offer positive suggestions and ask for help when they need it.

Kinlaw describes coaching as eyeball-to-eyeball management. Put another way, it is management by personal contact. Sales associates know that a manager's time is a valuable commodity. The personal contact involved in coaching communicates to them that they are the organization's most important resource.

According to Kinlaw, successful coaching has the following seven criteria:

1. *It is mutual.* Coaching involves the needs and feelings of both parties. It involves listening and showing that you are listening; checking out assumptions; and sharing and clarifying information.
2. *It communicates respect.* Showing respect may mean being supportive and encouraging the other person to come up with the answer, with no negative consequences from what is said in the discussion.
3. *It is problem-focused.* This means focusing on the behavior that needs to be changed instead of trying to change the person.
4. *It is change-oriented.* It results in a positive change in performance and new or renewed commitment to the organization's goals and values.
5. *It is disciplined.* The manager uses the process consistently and is aware of what he or she is doing and of what is and is not working.
6. *It uses specific skills.* Successful coaching requires the disciplined use by the manager of specific communication skills.
7. *It follows a process.* It proceeds through a series of predictable, interdependent stages.

Coaching that meets these criteria and is successful results in a positive change in performance and a positive work relationship.

When it is done correctly, sales associates experience the coaching process as logically and psychologically satisfying. It is satisfying logically because it is objective, with an orderly progression and focus. In other words, it makes sense. It is psychologically satisfying because people's feelings are acknowledged and understood, they perceive they can influence the outcome of the process, and there is closure to the communication.

Coaching has four functions: counseling, mentoring, tutoring and confronting. Counseling produces the resolution of problems affecting performance. Mentoring provides a better understanding of the organization's culture and of the individual's career development opportunities. Tutoring results in learning, particularly of technical skills. However, the aim of all three is to solve problems, and the process is basically the same. Confronting, on the other hand, is intended to improve performance. Confronting brings into the open a specific performance deficiency or challenges a sales associate to take advantage of his or her full potential. However, all forms of coaching have two things in common: They are one-to-one conversations, and they focus on performance or on performance-related topics. Here we will focus on counseling for problem solving and confronting for changes in performance.

All successful coaching conversations are directed toward improving performance and ensuring a commitment to sustained, superior performance. All coaching conversations result in the maintenance of a positive work relationship between the manager and sales associate. To achieve this, these conversations must be disciplined and must follow a process. As Kinlaw puts it, conversations that are random produce random results.

COUNSELING

The goal of counseling is to solve problems that affect an employee's work performance or work relationships. These problems may be nonpersonal, such as the need for additional training (tutoring) or they may be personal. Personal problems could be a problem with drugs or alcohol, excessive gambling, or problems at home (marital conflicts, a death in the family). Handling personal problems can be difficult for the manager. But when a personal problem is affecting a sales associate's work performance, the problem affects the firm and must be dealt with. The focus is on job performance. Problems in job performance that may signal a personal problem include tardiness, excessive absences, changes in work relationships and a decrease in the quality and/or quantity of the sales associate's work. It is important to distinguish between a less serious personal problem that will soon be resolved and a more serious problem that requires professional treatment.

The coaching process for counseling, tutoring and mentoring is essentially the same. It consists of three stages: involving, developing and resolving. Each stage has a set of goals and uses a specific set of communication skills.

Involving

The goals of involving are to clarify the purpose of the conversation, to create a comfortable atmosphere and to build trust. In this stage, the manager needs the following skills.

Clarifying   The manager begins the conversation with a clarifying statement that establishes the objectives for the coaching session. An example of a clarifying statement is: "I gather you are having some problems with the new agent who's been hired. Tell me what the problem is."

Attending   The manager must communicate that he or she is paying attention to the sales associate. This is done through nonverbal behavior. Actions that signify a person is paying attention include being animated, not allowing interruptions, facing the person, using positive body language and maintaining good eye contact.

Acknowledging   The manager must also give verbal signs of being involved in the conversation. Acknowledging statements include: "Right" or "I see" or "I can understand how you feel."

Probing   As the conversation proceeds, managers must ask questions or direct the conversation to gather more information. Probes may be either open or closed. Open probes encourage the sales associate to elaborate and should be used when trying to gather information. An example is: "Tell me what happened." Closed probes are answered with a "yes" or "no" and should be used when focusing on one issue and trying to eliminate alternatives. An example is: "Have you discussed this with your buyer?"

Reflecting   In order to indicate understanding and encourage more involvement, the manager needs to briefly restate what the sales associate has said or is feeling. This is also known as mirroring or paraphrasing.

Indicating Respect   Throughout this stage, the manager must indicate respect for the sales associate by refraining from making statements that ridicule, generalize or judge.

Developing

In a counseling conversation, the goal of stage two is to develop information that defines and gives the sales associate insight into the problem. The manager helps the sales associate develop information and gain insight by using three key skills: self-disclosure, immediacy and summarizing.

Self-Disclosure   A manager uses self-disclosure so that the sales associate feels the manager can identify with the problem. This involves indicating that the manager has had a similar experience. Statements that indicate self-disclosure include: "A similar thing happened to me when I first started" or "I've felt like that too."

Immediacy   In a coaching conversation, a number of things can happen that prevent the conversation from moving forward. For example, the sales associate may become hostile, upset or withdrawn. The manager must be able to focus attention on what is happening in the conversation that is blocking progress. The manager may then postpone the conversation, allow time for the person to collect his or her thoughts or recommend an alternative. For example, the manager may say: "You clearly are very upset right now. Maybe we should talk about that before we go any further."

Summarizing   This is one of the most useful coaching techniques. By stopping the conversation every now and then to review what has been said, the manager ensures that both the sales associate and the manager understand the facts.

Resolving

The goal of the third stage—resolving—is to provide closure to the conversation and a plan for the next steps to be taken, as well as to reinforce positive relationships and commitment. The skills needed by the manager include reviewing, planning and affirming.

Reviewing   The manager should go over the key points of the session to ensure a common understanding. Reviewing also emphasizes the sales associate's achievement and builds closure. An example of reviewing is: "I think you've done a good job identifying the main reasons you feel you don't have time to prospect. You are training two of our newest agents. You have not finished the course on prospecting. And you are very concerned about losing current clients."

Planning   Plans should contain concrete action steps, not just promises to make a better effort. They should also include a way to measure progress and success in the future. It is important that plans be developed with the sales associate and that the sales associate assume responsibility for the plan.

Affirming   A manager affirms by commenting on the sales associate's strengths and positive prospects. For example: "You've done a great job of digging into why prospecting is difficult. I don't think I had that much insight when I was new to the job."

EFFECTIVE LISTENING

In order to successfully conduct a coaching conversation, a manager needs effective listening skills. Listeners receive two types of messages: content and feelings. Feelings often are not stated explicitly, requiring the listener to work harder to identify what is being expressed. The PPF model provides a three-step process for effective listening. It consists of Paraphrasing, Perception check, and Feelings.

Step 1 is to paraphrase what you've heard, repeating the speaker's ideas in your own words, but making the statement more specific. This enables you to check your understanding of the ideas or information being communicated. It also allows the other person to address any misunderstandings and clarify them.

Step 2 is to check your perception of the other person's feelings and to demonstrate your understanding of them. You do this by stating what you perceive the other person to be feeling, without expressing approval or disapproval.

Step 3 is to report how you would feel in the situation and to share information that has influenced your feelings and viewpoint. This increases the sense of equality between you and the sales associate and helps the sales associate understand you as a person.

It's important for managers to be aware of habits that are impediments to effective listening. These include the following:

- Getting emotionally involved or alienated
- Listening for facts only (A good listener hears feelings as well.)
- Preparing to answer (When you're preparing to answer, you stop listening and can easily miss an important point or feeling.)
- Anticipating. (When you anticipate what the other person will say or feel next, you stop listening. Attention must be focused on the present if you are truly going to hear what the other person is saying.)
- Taking notes on everything. (If you are furiously taking notes, you may miss significant nonverbal cues. In addition, your note taking can distract the other person or make them uncomfortable and inhibit discussion.)

CONFRONTING

Confronting is coaching for positive change in performance. The goal of confronting is to encourage an individual to start performing a new task, to move from satisfactory to superior performance, to take on new challenges or to change from unsatisfactory to satisfactory performance. Of these goals, confrontations about unsatisfactory performance are likely to be the most difficult.

Confronting is not the same as criticizing. Confronting is objective; criticizing is subjective. Confronting focuses on a performance problem rather than on the attitudes or personality traits of the person. It describes specific problems rather than general issues. Confronting is concerned with changing the future rather than with placing blame. Finally, confrontation is concerned with improving the work relationship, not with releasing emotions.

The confronting process has three stages.

Confronting/Presenting

The first stage is the manager's description of the performance problem and expectations for improvement. The goals of this stage are to limit resistance and negative emotions, define the topic and focus on change. The manager should be specific about how the sales associate's performance does not meet the company's standards. It is important to stick to one problem so as not to confuse the agent. This is known as "scoping" the problem. It is also important to include a future-oriented statement. For example, you want all sales associates to attend the monthly sales meetings. Instead of asking, "Why haven't you been at the last two meetings?" make your comment future oriented by asking, "What can you do to make sure you're at the next meeting?"

Use Reactions To Develop Information

The goals of the second stage are to diffuse resistance, develop information about the problem and agree on the problem and its causes.

When people are confronted, they are likely to react in one of the following ways: make excuses, rationalize their performance, become defensive, claim the problem doesn't exist or become withdrawn. To respond to one of these reactions, the manager must learn to drop the agenda. In other words, the manager needs to forget about what he or she wants to say and focus entirely on what the sales associate is saying. Only after the manager has listened to and understood the associate's reaction can he or she proceed to the next step.

Here is an example of dropping the agenda and focusing on what the sales associate is saying.

> *Manager:* You wanted to be in the million dollar club by the end of the year. We're into the second quarter and according to my records, you've closed one $75,000 sale to date this year and you have a $90,000 listing that is set to close. How can we get you back on track?
>
> *Sales Associate:* I was counting on my friends to buy, but they're not interested.
>
> *Manager* (dropping agenda): Why don't we start with the problem you've mentioned, list any other problems you can think of and then see what we can do?
>
> *Sales Associate:* I'm really sorry, but I've had so many crises this quarter. I know I need to concentrate on my production.
>
> *Manager:* So some things have been happening that became higher priorities for you than production?

Next the manager must develop information to decide what the problem is and how to solve it. To do this the manager uses the skills of attending, acknowledging, probing, reflecting and summarizing described earlier.

It is important for the manager and sales associate to agree on the problem and its causes. To accomplish this, the manager uses the confirming skill. One method to confirm is to have the sales associate restate what the manager has said.

Manager: So it seems the major problem in meeting your goals is that you've had a number of crises this quarter. Based on what you've said, I can see how you got behind. How about summarizing what you now see as the major issues?

RESOLVING

At the third stage, the manager's goals are to encourage the sales associate to take ownership of the problem, determine the next steps, develop a positive relationship and gain commitment. The skills used to accomplish these objectives are planning, reviewing and affirming, discussed earlier.

In deciding how to resolve the problem, the associate should assume responsibility for the plan, including specific action steps and a way to measure progress. Reviewing the primary information provides a method for confirming understanding, creating closure and affirming the associate's commitment. Finally, affirming is designed to reinforce the associate's confidence and competence.

COACHING FOR ACCOUNTABILITY

Performance management begins in the recruiting and selection process. When you choose the right people in the first place, the time and energy you put into developing them will yield higher returns for both you and them.

Following counseling, the second phase of the performance management process is development. (The third phase—retaining—is covered in Chapter 11.) In the development phase, the manager works with the sales associate to create a Performance Management Plan (PMP). This involves determining the sales associate's major goals, defining areas of responsibility, setting performance objectives, identifying standards of performance and assigning priority and weight to each objective. The PMP is similar to a job description developed on an annual basis. The reason for creating a PMP is to provide a means of measuring a sales associate's performance against specific, mutually agreed-upon objectives.

In most real estate organizations, individuals are given a job description so they know what they are required to do. Unfortunately, most of these job descriptions are task-oriented activity lists. Sales associates are told what to do but not what results are expected. This limits their scope and inhibits their initiative.

In order to structure a position for results, we need to begin by setting forth the sales associate's major goal. This major goal is the overall result the individual is expected to produce and should be linked to the company's strategic plan. The next step is to set performance objectives. These are specific, planned potential achievements to be accomplished within a certain time frame and with consideration for minimum acceptable standards of performance. An extremely important element of performance objectives is that they are measurable.

The next step is to assign priority to the performance objectives. In real estate, income-producing activities have greater priority than support activities. Once priorities have been assigned, the manager works with the sales associate to determine strategies and develop action plans to accomplish the agreed-upon goals.

When the sales associate is not achieving the goals in the Performance Management Plan, the manager needs to schedule a confrontive coaching session for accountability. The manager should clarify what was to be accomplished that has not been, and should ask the associate what can be done to meet the stated goals. The associate should be given ownership of the problem and challenged to come up with the solutions. The manager should ask the associate to set a time frame for accomplishing the proposed solution and should schedule follow-up meetings to monitor progress or results. If no progress has been made by the second meeting, the manager should ask again when results can be expected and set another meeting. If progress still is unsatisfactory, the manager might ask the sales associate what he or she would do if their roles were reversed. In such cases, the sales associate may resign. If the sales associate is reluctant to resign, he or she may need some assistance from the manager in deciding to make a change for the better.

RETAIN, PROMOTE, TERMINATE

Coaching for accountability enables managers to make timely and objective decisions about whether to retain, promote or terminate an individual. If a sales associate is meeting or exceeding his or her objectives, it makes sense to continue coaching that individual toward even better performance. If the sales associate constantly exceeds his or her objectives, the manager should use confrontation to discuss the associate's desire to commit to additional responsibilities. For poor performers, the manager should create a developmental plan (similar to a PMP, but for a shorter time frame) for the next 90 days and use coaching techniques to review the progress toward the goals of the plan at least once a month. If the person's performance does not improve, the manager should then terminate the sales associate.

If performance objectives were developed jointly and the manager has regularly (at least monthly) reviewed the associate's performance against those objectives, both the manager and the sales associate know whether the associate is meeting the objectives. If termination is necessary, it is less of a surprise to the sales associate because of this coaching process. In many cases, termination is a mutual decision.

In performance management, a distinction should be made between terminating and firing an individual. A manager can "terminate" a sales associate if he or she fails to fulfill expectations, is incompatible with the firm or breaks the rules. By contrast, a manager should "fire" a sales associate only if he or she is stealing, sabotaging the company, providing proprietary information to competitors, guilty of gross insubordination or is engaged in illegal or immoral activities. You should be sure of the reasons you are terminating or firing a sales associate before the confrontative conversation occurs.

Rigorous recruiting and selection strategies and committed development through careful training, business planning and coaching will minimize performance problems. When sales associates create their own business plan and are responsible for carrying it out, in most cases they will resolve their own performance problems.

These are just a few ideas in the highly complex area of coaching and human communication. For individuals whose vital tool is communication, knowledge and expertise in this discipline are absolutely vital. Real estate brokers, necessarily involved with the people in the firm and dozens of individuals outside, must constantly polish their ability to communicate if they are to be successful.

ENDNOTES

1. Dennis C. Kinlaw, *Coaching for Commitment: Managerial Strategies for Obtaining Superior Performance.*
2. Norman B. Sigband, *Communication for Management,* p. 10.
3. Julius Fast, *Body Language,* p. 1 and *ff.*
4. Robert Bolton and Dorothy Bolton, *Social Style/Management Style: Developing Productive Work Relationships.*
5. Work Institute of America, *The Manager as Trainer, Coach, and Leader.*

Chapter 11

Retaining Salespeople

Real estate managers are continually aware of their need for a vital, aggressive selling staff. They are just as continually concerned with keeping their peak performers, bolstering the efforts of their average people and doing everything they can to help any of their salespeople who are not succeeding.

Before managers can deal with their need to retain salespeople, they must understand what the salespeople's needs and desires are and what the manager should do to help satisfy them.

Chapter 11 contains guidelines to help managers succeed in keeping the best salespeople through motivation and counseling. Clues for spotting salespeople in trouble and some suggestions for coping with a variety of situations will help managers help the others. When termination seems the only answer, here are guidelines for how it can best be handled.

PERFORMANCE MANAGEMENT'S THIRD PHASE

The third phase of the performance management process is retention, promotion or termination.

Retention of peak performers is a challenge for all real estate brokers and sales managers. Some managers believe it is the chief factor in whether a company will continue to grow and improve. Consequently, a detailed, workable and ongoing retention program should be an integral part of every real estate brokerage operation.

NEED FOR RETENTION PROGRAM

Recapturing company dollars invested in recruiting and training each salesperson is necessary to continue the process of building and strengthening the company. Enormous amounts of training time and money are expended on each salesperson. To have this investment walk out the door is a loss to the company and perhaps to the person.

In the first few years with a company, a good salesperson will have built a clientele that produces about 50 percent of his or her business as personal referrals. To lose this person is to lose a significant amount of company business.

To lose qualified, productive salespeople with any degree of regularity lowers company morale and inhibits growth.

McKinsey's 7-S system provides a useful framework to evaluate how well you are managing your human resources. Your recruiting systems should target individuals who have the skills to execute your company's strategies. Your company's shared values must be communicated to your sales associates so they have a clear idea of their mission. Your management style should provide sales associates with the level of direction and support appropriate to their style and experience level. Your compensation and training systems should be designed to motivate and meet your salespeople's needs. The 7-S model can also help you identify whether a nonproductive salesperson should be terminated or whether organizational factors are hampering productivity and should be corrected.

RECRUITING

Retaining salespeople who are a credit to themselves and the company begins with a solid recruiting program. If it is vigorous, comprehensive and selective, the company will attract the effective sales staff it needs. Finding out what motivates a candidate will help you hire the right people and will ultimately help you manage them and provide the appropriate incentives to retain them.

Managers should be aware that they are in keen competition for the services of good salespeople not only with other real estate firms but also with all other types of business that have a product or service to sell. You only need to read the help wanted ads to note the intense recruiting for and the attractive offers being made by business and industry to prospective salespeople. Brokers need to emphasize the unique advantages of a career in real estate sales and orient their recruiting program to specific objectives.

For example, for a good self-starter in real estate sales, there is no limit on potential earnings. While handling properties and making a good income, a sales associate can initiate and develop a personal investment program by buying attractive properties for his or her own account, using the income from sales to provide all or part of the necessary capital. When more capital is required, the salesperson knows the right financing sources and already knows the people he or she will be dealing with, another unique advantage of the wide contacts made in real estate selling. Thus, real estate sales offers two ways to reach income goals and to do it faster.

GOALS

Formal goal setting is an important part of the performance management process. First, the individual, working in private, should set down in writing his or her precise goals as they relate to real estate. Then these goals should be shared with and reviewed with the broker or manager. A person's goals should be the basis for regular coaching sessions.

The individual's goals should include more than real estate production. Work goals are only part of a whole range of personal goals: family, social, physical, mental, spiritual. All will bear on the salesperson's lifestyle as well as his or her business performance. The broker should be aware of the individual's other personal goals because they will contribute to an understanding of the salesperson and help the broker deal with the person's goals as they relate to business performance.

When salespeople participate in a goal-setting session with the broker, they are competing with no one else; they are being evaluated by themselves. They are being measured by goals they have set and that they believe are attainable.

Many salespeople are reluctant to set business goals. This feeling reflects a fear that failure to attain them will result in ridicule from their peers. When goal setting is a strictly private matter between broker and salesperson, no one but the broker need know if a salesperson doesn't attain his or her goal.

To be effective, a goal should be

- attainable,
- measurable,
- for a definite time period, and
- in writing.

Attainable Goals

Goals should be realistic. It is folly to set a goal to make $200,000 in one year if the best salesperson in the area has never made more than $100,000 in a similar period. It is just as impossible to set a goal of 50 exclusive listings a month if that figure is more than the total number of listings available in your area in a single month.

Goals should be neither too easy nor too difficult. If the best salesperson in your firm has enjoyed an income of $50,000 per year, a realistic increase to $60,000 might be the new goal.

Goals should be flexible. They should realistically anticipate changes in the market that are almost certain to occur in any 12-month period. A new subdivision may open up unexpected markets, or a downturn in the economy could result in a tight money market. Be ready to show your salespeople how to include flexibility in setting their goals.

Goals should include every phase of the business. For example, a salesperson shouldn't bypass efforts to increase listings in established neighborhoods and focus only on selling lots in a new subdivision. Demonstrate the value of increasing volume in every service your firm provides.

Measurable Goals

To be measurable, a goal must be specific. If a salesperson sets a goal of 60 exclusives in a calendar year, the goal is measurable. If on the other hand, the salesperson's goal is to do better than last year's 50 listings, a total of 52 could mean success. But the salesperson might have gotten 65 listings if that had been the established, measurable goal. Thus, the target should be definite, measurable and realistic.

Show the salesperson how to break down goals into definite time periods, taking into consideration seasonal fluctuations in real estate activity in your market, setting goals higher in the most active months and lower when business is slow. The practical exercise of working out monthly breakdowns on various business goals makes them easier to measure and also serves to remind a salesperson how much time has passed and how much more intense his or her efforts need to be. A subset of goals must be set that describes the specific tasks to be accomplished to meet the overall goal.

Time Limit on Goals

The frequency of measuring progress toward established goals rests with management. Real estate people who have used this technique for years believe reviews should be scheduled every three months for a one-year objective, every year for three-year goals and every two years for ten-year goals.

One-year goals are the most common and surely most important. They are also the most easily measured and easiest to structure. Many firms establish longer-range goals of three, five or ten years. The unpredictability of the economy, the times and the variables of today's transient society make long-range goals for individual salespeople more difficult to establish. But they are extremely important for top management.

Whatever the outcome, goals should not be put aside. It has been a tradition in too many real estate offices that when goals are missed, the program is dropped. This is an evidence of management's weakness and is not the salesperson's fault. If the sales staff is missing goals there are two likely reasons: They weren't practical in the first place, and the review should have been scheduled at more frequent intervals. Find out why goals were set too high and study the results to discover where the weaknesses are. Spend some time on your own determining how to solve the problem, then spend time with the salesperson involved, discussing what went wrong and why. Work together to find the solution. Set new goals immediately.

Written Goals

Putting goals in writing is important for two reasons: They will be more specific than in the case of conversational goals, and they avoid misunderstanding and misinterpretation common to oral communication. The speaker means one thing, the listener is hearing with his or her own and perhaps quite different needs to be fulfilled. Seldom, if ever, is oral communication on this level accurate. Unless written, goals can be forgotten or may be rationalized or postponed to a later date. Written goals are a stronger motivating factor for a salesperson and are a factual basis for management to present when it comes time to review together the salesperson's progress.

What should be put in writing? A number of progressive real estate businesses today ask their salespeople to set goals in three areas:

1. Income—dollars, sales, listings
2. Personal/Family—house, car, service to community
3. Professional—schooling, books, organizations

Income   The salesperson states how much money he or she wants to earn. Next, averaging the past performance of the office, the person determines accurately the number of listings and sales needed to reach this income goal. Figure 11.1 shows how individual salespeople set their income goals.

Personal/Family   One salesperson may have a new, larger home as a goal; another may want a dreamed-of family vacation. To a real estate person a new car could be both a personal and a business goal because it is essential equipment for the job. Service to the community might be wholly personal (or at least seem to be) like working with Girl Scouts, or being a park district or library trustee; or it could be quasi-business-related, like being active in the Chamber of Commerce or serving on an area planning commission. Realistically, any community activity can lead to improving a real estate person's business even though business had no bearing on the person's desire to participate in that organization.

Professional   Professional goals will add substance to income and personal goals. In setting professional goals, salespeople can examine the opportunities available to increase their knowledge and skills in the real estate business.

At the very least, the firm should help salespeople who want to expand their real estate knowledge and professional skill. Participation in

FIGURE 11.1 Production Targets: Setting Income Goals

Salesperson _____ Office _____

19____ Income target _____

Required target income first quarter _____

First Quarter Projections

	Target			Actual				
	Units	Leads	Appts.	Units	Leads	Appts.	Earnings
January:							
Sales	___	___	___	___	___	___	___
Exclusives	___	___	___	___	___	___	___
February:							
Sales	___	___	___	___	___	___	
Exclusives	___	___	___	___	___	___	___
March:							
Sales	___	___	___	___	___	___	
Exclusives	___	___	___	___	___	___	___

Review of First Quarter

	Projected units	Actual units	Projected leads	Actual leads	Projected appts.	Actual appts.
Sales	___	___	___	___	___	___
Exclusives			___	___	___	___

Residential Sales Council™ courses can enable salespeople to win specific professional designations and certification of professional competence that adds to their prestige in their peer group and business community as well as bringing them personal satisfaction.

It is extremely important that the broker also be motivated and set a good example. In addition, the more the top salespeople are motivated and the better they perform, the more the average salespeople will improve. Motivation can be increased and sustained through a reward and recognition system. It is also important that opportunities for advancement exist within the company. But because the goal process and self-image development program is continuous, there must always be opportunities for continuing education both within and outside the company.

MEETING SALESPEOPLE'S NEEDS

A broker's first responsibility is to create and maintain the best possible working environment for the company's salespeople and then to provide the tools for getting the job done.

The working atmosphere must be positive and invigorating. No matter what else a broker may provide for his salespeople, the best working climate is one that allows them to realize their full potential in achieving personal goals and objectives. Everyone on the company team, both individually and together corporately, needs to be happy in the business and to experience a feeling of accomplishment.

Here effective management provides leadership to meet the needs of each person in all of the following areas:

- Direction/Goals
- Training
- Policy
- Opportunity
- Recognition
- Security
- Leadership

Direction

Before a company can expect its salespeople to understand fully what it is trying to achieve, management itself must know what it is doing and where it is going. This direction needs to be specific in terms of both short-term and long-range goals and incorporated into the company's strategic plan.

According to Peter F. Drucker, renowned management consultant and author of many books on the subject, questions should be raised continuously about corporate purpose and mission. Drucker contends that few companies have any clear idea of what their mission is. He believes this lack is one of the three significant causes of major mistakes. The other two, he says, are that managers have no feeling for what the company is really good at and what it is not good at, and that they do not know how to make "people" decisions. Most of the time spent on personnel decisions, he adds, goes into selecting people at the bottom and not at the top. Drucker concludes that "the least time is spent on selecting the colonels and this is the step where you are really picking the future generals."[1]

It is neither necessary nor desirable for salespeople to know all the minute details of a company's operation or all of its plans. However, they do need to know and to be a part of some of the management objectives and what their role is in the accomplishment of those objectives so they have ownership in the company's success. This sense of participation on the part of salespeople, understanding where the company came from, where it is and where it is going gives direction to their daily work.

Training

Firms that seem to attract the most desirable salespeople are those that provide an ongoing training program. This means training for all salespeople on a regular basis. It includes in-house training during weekly sales meetings, special training seminars and outside professional courses. Basics of the real estate business cannot be covered too often. With continuous learning, the likelihood of a slump is lessened, and a sense of confidence that comes with new or renewed knowledge will be increased.

John Wooden, UCLA basketball coach for many years, is considered by many to be the best all-time coach of the game. His record of coaching teams to the national championship will be difficult to equal. He is the only man ever to be inducted into the Basketball Hall of Fame both as a player and a coach. Wooden emphasizes the value of attention to the smallest details and the repetition of the fundamentals of the game. He says, "If you keep too busy learning the tricks of the trade, you never learn the trade." In his book, *They Call Me Coach,* Wooden states:

> One of the little things I watch closely is a player's socks. No basketball player is better than his feet. If they hurt, if his socks don't fit or if he has blisters, he can't play the game. It is amazing how few players know how to put on a pair of socks properly. I don't want blisters. So each year I give in minute detail a step by step demonstration as to precisely how I want my players to put on their socks—every time. Believe it or not, there's an art to doing it right and it makes a big difference in the way a player's feet stand the pounding of practice and the game. Wrinkles which cause blisters can be eliminated by just a little attention.[2]

When was the last time every salesperson in your office recited verbatim his or her listing dialogue on discount points, basic monologue on overcoming various buyer/seller objections, or basic expired listing or for-sale-by-owner presentation?

Policy

The establishment of an official, understandable policy is absolutely essential for every office. A clear, firm, simple policy and procedures manual that covers situations that arise in the course of daily business can prevent or solve most misunderstandings and disputes. Some of the topics that should be in writing, assembled in a policy and procedures manual, include commission schedules, advertising, open houses, phone duty, arbitration, sales meetings, appropriate attire, antitrust, fair housing, agency, use of forms, and so forth; it covers any aspect of the real estate business that is basic to its success.

Opportunity

Another vital aspect of retention in terms of meeting salespeople's needs is to establish procedures whereby salespeople know they have the opportunity to grow. Specifically this means the absence of restrictive policies that could inhibit an individuals' earning capacity. It can also mean making salespeople aware of the opportunity to move into a new job such as branch manager or sales manager.

While these positions are often viewed as promotions, it should also be recognized that an outstanding salesperson frequently can out-earn an individual at the management level, and an extremely successful salesperson will not necessarily make a good sales manager. The success ingredients for each are different. However, if a salesperson's skills and desires lead toward management, he or she needs to know that opportunities exist through expansion and/or diversification.

How does a small firm accomplish this?

Managers who have a well-trained, aggressive selling staff can find more time to concentrate on developing a stronger image, a growth image. They look for good merger and acquisition opportunities with like-minded real estate firms, or they expand into new marketing areas; or plan diversification into such areas as property management or commercial-investment sales.

They communicate to the sales staff that management and other opportunities are available to persons who can demonstrate ability and who are growth and company oriented.

Recognition

Sensitive managers understand that their salespeople have a basic human need to be recognized through expressions of appreciation and praise for a job well done. When managers do this, they are taking a big step toward attracting and holding good salespeople. Aside from the professional recognition earned, each of us needs to be recognized for just being there, for being a person of intrinsic worth. How can this be accomplished in a real estate sales office?

Ring an "Action" bell every time a listing or sale is made.

Build a "Sales Column." This can be done on a corkboard. Pin a 3" × 5" card with a salesperson's name, the dollar volume of the listing or sale, the address of the property, and watch the column grow. Some months it may reach a couple feet in length. And when it doesn't, its lack of growth serves as a reminder of action needed!

Sponsor a Residential Sales Council™ course for the top lister of your employee salespeople.

Include nonconfidential data on every listing and sale as a regular feature of the office newsletter, even if it's only a one-pager.

Award a company pin to each salesperson who reaches a target listing or dollar figure.

Explore and use every kind of personal publicity acceptable in your local newspaper: Salesperson of the Month; Million Dollar Listing and Sales for the Year; news of promotions; attendance at REALTORS® National Marketing Institute® or National Association of REALTORS® courses and conferences. Publicity possibilities are limited only by your imagination and the type of news used by the local editor.

If you decide to conduct contests, set them up so there are lots of winners. The winners should preferably be teams. Contests naming individual winners tend to draw the same winners. As a result, the enthusiasm of other sales associates for contests wanes. Make any contest of short duration so enthusiasm remains at a good level and so you can schedule several contests every year.

A broker tells how the combined merit of training and recognition elicited unexpected results. In a "Salesperson of the Month" recognition award, one of the firm's top salespeople won, as expected. But the next month, a new licensee, only six months into her career, followed everything she had learned in the training sessions and topped the whole sales staff!

Formal recognition programs should include everyone. After all, it is from their ranks that future managers and superstars will emerge. The firm will benefit from recognizing and encouraging them. Just as the superstars in any field of human activity need recognition for stellar performances, average salespeople, who represent the majority in most offices, need to be recognized and encouraged for their accomplishments.

Security

For most people, security means money; and money can be earned by motivated, well-trained, knowledgeable real estate salespeople. Management provides the security by providing an adequate, competitive commission schedule that is fair and consistent for all the parties involved, as well as training opportunities. Many companies offer a variety of commission options so salespeople can choose the option that is best for their situation.

Beyond this, salespeople must feel that their opportunities to earn money are at least as good and probably better with your firm than with any other. These feelings of security result from many factors.

Reputation   The company either has or is building a good reputation in the community. Salespeople need to be constantly aware that the client's interests are being served; that misunderstandings or problems with either buyers or sellers are resolved quickly. These concerns lead to a good image for the company in any community. On the other hand, when a company's relationships with its clients are not good, it is difficult for that firm to hold good salespeople. Because it is easy for salespeople to reaffiliate with a different firm, you cannot afford for your firm's reputation to be hurt.

Sales Program   The company must have a listing and selling program that augments and supports the salesperson's individual efforts. Such a program can include a client referral service, a client follow-up service, consistent advertising programs, recruiting and training programs and a genuine concern for filling the client's needs.

Leadership   While this subject is covered in Chapter 2, certain points should be stressed again.

A crucial cause of losing good salespeople is weak management. Without strong leadership, salespeople experience a free-floating anxiety because, consciously or unconsciously, they look to their broker or manager for inspiration and guidance. The broker must be the person who knows what the company is doing, where it is going and how it is getting there. A manager sets the pace.

From the salesperson's point of view, effective leadership means that work is done properly, decisions are made when they are needed and company morale is high. When these leadership factors are operating daily, the broker will be able to give more time and attention to planning and executing both short-term and long-term company objectives; the salesperson will be able to devote full time to productive listing and selling.

MOTIVATION

Another important element of retention is motivation. It is important to the success of management and every member of the sales staff. Webster defines *motive* as "an emotion or desire operating on the will and causing it to act." That is why brokers and salespeople continually search for methods, techniques and programs to keep the staff's motivation level high.

The many factors involved in successful listing and selling are well-known and can be studied, learned and implemented. But the actual sales production of each individual is a matter of personal motivation. Motivation determines how well each individual learns required skills. And once those skills are learned, the motivation level of the person determines whether or not the acquired skills will be used. That's why asking the right questions during the selection process is so important—so the manager will know what motivates the sales associate.

If it is sustained and consistent, authentic motivation comes from within. Motivation is a logical, emotional outgrowth of a self-directed person's attitudes and experiences. External stimuli such as pep talks, sales seminars and motivational sessions can be helpful, but they do not get the day-to-day job done. There is an important place for motivational sessions, but they provide only temporary modifications in personal behavior or work performance. They do not prepare a person to work effectively and enthusiastically over the long-term. This is one reason why in the recruiting process careful screening of individuals is so important. It should separate and eliminate the easily discouraged individuals from the persistent ones who keep going despite the countless hurdles or difficulties they encounter.

Maslow's Hierarchy of Needs

A widely accepted theory of motivation is Abraham Maslow's hierarchy of needs. Maslow suggests that human beings are constantly seeking to fulfill their wants. When one level of need is satisfied, another comes into focus and determines where the individual's energy is expended. Five levels of needs can be thought of as a pyramid with the base being the lowest unmet need that has the most influence on the individual (see Figure 11.2).

Five Basic Needs   Physiological needs—food, shelter and air—are the most basic of all human needs. Fulfilling these needs is essential to keep the individual alive. They therefore take top priority until they are satisfied.

Security needs are next most important. These are the needs to protect oneself from outside danger, both present and future. They become the primary determinants of our behavior after physiological needs have been satisfied at least to some extent. A starving person may risk his or her life for food, ignoring security needs to respond to the lower, more basic physiological needs.

Social needs come into the picture after physiological and security needs have been met. Here we think of the need to be loved, to be accepted by others and to belong to a group. Think of all the things we do to make ourselves attractive to other human beings and how painful it is when we are ignored or rejected.

Ego needs for self esteem and status are next in the hierarchy. We want to think well of ourselves and be proud of who and what we are. We also

FIGURE 11.2   Hierarchy of Needs

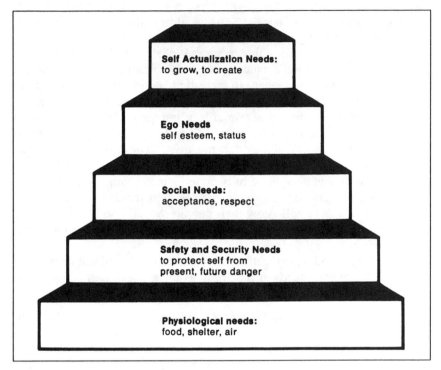

Adapted from *Motivation and Personality,* 2nd edition, 1970, by permission of Harper & Row publishers.

want others to recognize our worth by according us the respect we deserve. Ego needs become a powerful force after the physiological security and social needs are at least partially met. Think of how much it can mean to a person to have an important title, a nice office and other symbols of status that remind him or her and others of that individual's importance.

Self-actualizing needs are at the top of the pyramid. These are the needs to develop, to create and to contribute. "If an acorn could dream it would dream of becoming an oak tree." In the same way, most human beings have a desire to become more fully human, to use themselves more effectively and to fulfill their potential. There are occasions when a task is so enjoyable, interesting and challenging that we lose ourselves in it, and no external reward is necessary to keep us at it.

Their Implication   As you look over this hierarchy of needs, reflect for a few moments on the best job you ever had, a job that really "turned you on." What was so great about that job? In a typical group of managers or workers who are asked this question, the responses almost always include words and phrases like "challenging," "personal accomplishment," "demanding," "exciting," "creative," "had responsibility," "lots of freedom" or "recognition." In our best jobs we almost always have our social, ego and self-actualizing needs well met.

Where does money fit in this picture? Probably at different levels for different people. To some people money is important to put bread on the table; to others money is a means to security; to others money is important to buy the clothes, car and house that enable them to socialize with certain people; to still others money is primarily a symbol of self-worth. And to some people money is important because it makes possible the freedom to grow and develop, to do things "on my own." The implication for the manager is clear: find out what need is uppermost in an individual's mind and try to satisfy that need more fully on the job. A change in title may be as powerful an incentive to someone as a salary increase.

Skilled managers will know their people so well and be so aware of their changing needs that they can sense what the next steps in motivation should be.

Your understanding of the motivational needs of the individuals in your group and the overall needs of the group as a business-oriented team can be achieved by

- putting your own motivation in proper perspective so as not to tune out your team;
- letting everyone know the reality of any given situation; and
- providing the atmosphere of open communication necessary for each to evaluate his or her point of view in respect to those of the group as a whole and those of management (a technique that allows for a change in position in the light of feedback without a feeling of compromise or frustration) and recognizing that people can change their habits.

The basic motivational process, individual in nature, must be planned and sustained. It must be communicated so ably that it becomes something the individual discovers and internalizes. Then, motivation becomes an inner drive that causes a person to move toward a goal.

A leader knows that motivation, like growth, is inherent in people. The leader's task is not so much motivating others as it is releasing the potential that is already there and directing it to produce desired results.

Dr. Maxwell Maltz, in *Psycho-Cybernetics,*[3] discusses self-image psychology and its relationship to successful achievement. In Maltz's opinion, self-image is important because it defines the limits within which a person will work most effectively to achieve his or her objectives. If people's self-image can be improved, the number and type of their successes can be increased.

Webster defines *success* as "the satisfactory accomplishment of a goal sought for." Therefore, two factors that a person must possess can be clearly defined: realistic goals and a self-image that makes their attainment possible. Nebulous or inconsistent goals and/or a low self-image would most likely lead to failure. The power of positive thinking can work with some people but not with others. It is effective only when it is consistent with an individual's positive self-image.

Therein lies the challenge of self-image modification: changing and strengthening it with information that is experienced and absorbed. The salesperson experiences by responding actively to new information, rather than accepting it passively. Their whole person is involved. They are dynamic. They come alive.

Management has a responsibility to assist the salesperson by providing possible success experiences. When this is done, the motivational process becomes so much a part of that person that it is expressed through successful activity. But successful activity will not be viewed the same by every associate. Depending on where developing associates are in their career life cycle, they will see things quite differently.

CAREER LIFE CYCLE

Every individual goes through a life cycle in their career. When they begin their first job, they enter the introduction stage of their career. They need to invest a great deal of time in learning about their industry, company and position to pave the way for their future success. New sales associates are not yet very productive. Typically, their earnings are low, yet their expenses may be high because of the need to upgrade their wardrobe, buy a car and pay rent.

The growth stage of a sales associate's career is characterized by a spurt in productivity as individuals are able to apply what they have learned. People become more confident and more competent. They develop a reputation as a knowledgeable and successful real estate salesperson. Their income is higher than it was when they were learning the business, and increases come more often. Sales associates in the growth stage seek promotions and find themselves in intense competition with other salespeople. To combat the competition requires innovative self-promotion.

After several years of high earnings, sales associates enter the maturity stage. Their career has stabilized, maybe even plateaued. Earnings grow more slowly or may decline. Mature workers face fierce competition, both from people in the growth stage and from other mature workers. To protect their position requires continued self-promotion.

Each person's career eventually begins to decline. Productivity decreases, which may result in lower earnings. If productivity declines too much, the sales associate may be terminated for nonperformance. Because people in the declining stage of their career are no longer affected by their competition, they have less need to engage in self-promotion.

CAREER STAGES AND MASLOW'S HIERARCHY OF NEEDS

The level of needs on Maslow's hierarchy that a person seeks to satisfy is related to which career stage they are in. Individuals in the introductory stage of their career are generally motivated by survival/security needs. They seek rewards that help them to pay the bills. But to be motivational, the reward needs to be within their grasp. New sales associates are unlikely to be motivated by a $500 prize for the first person to reach a million dollar goal because this goal is out of their reach. These individuals may also be motivated by professional development opportunities, such as attending real estate classes or being mentored.

Sales associates in the competitive growth stage are motivated by rewards that satisfy their ego and self-esteem needs. Recognition could be in the form of awards, plaques, their picture on the wall or bonuses. The $500 prize mentioned above would motivate these individuals. Sales associates in this stage often make excellent mentors because they receive the credibility they seek from the newer sales associates.

Mature associates may be motivated by affection/affiliation and/or by self-actualization needs. These individuals are earning an acceptable income that gives them a feeling of self-worth. Now they may desire relationships and a feeling of belonging. Money may be less important for them than recognition. One way to provide this recognition is to empower mature sales associates by giving them more responsibility and more say in decision making. Self-actualized people want to live life to the fullest. It makes them feel good about themselves to give something back to the firm or to the community. They may satisfy these needs by becoming active in volunteer organizations or by planning social functions for the company. Encourage them to take a leadership role in board or association activities or give them an opportunity to participate in the mentoring program, training programs, and sales meetings. Other likely motivators for this group are awards and additional vacation time.

Those whose career is in decline are usually at the security or affection/affiliation state of Maslow's hierarchy. These people need to feel secure that their position with the firm is not in jeopardy. They also need to know that they are liked and respected by the sales team. Membership in a club or other social motivators are called for.

COACHING

Coaching the individual salesperson is a logical and integral part of the retention program. A former sports editor once wrote that "the coach who can get most out of his athletes, who can understand their psychological makeup and motivate them to achieve their goals, is the one who will succeed, given the proper talent."

Peak Performers

Coaching needs to be provided on a regular basis for the exceptionally talented person as well as for the average one. Productive people appreciate being told what a significant role they play in the growth of the company. Successes can be highlighted and shared with the whole staff. Management sometimes takes it for granted that these people are motivated, happy and pleased with their work and with the company. This may or may not be true. But if these assumptions are false, the great risk exists that they may leave the company with little or no notice and often for some trifling reason that could have been prevented. Understanding what motivates your peak performers will enable you to offer the incentives that meet each individual's needs. Excellent performance may warrant a promotion or added responsibilities. You can give your top sales associates additional recognition by asking them to share their knowledge by making a presentation at a sales or training meeting or by serving as a mentor to a new member of the firm. Coaching for these people should be scheduled at regular intervals, not just when there's a slump or a problem.

Coaching sessions with peak performers can and should determine if there are unique reasons for their success or if any problem areas exist in which management might be of help. Constructive evaluation should be sought. If the productive people feel some aspect of the business operation is in need of attention, be it company procedures or individual situations, their feelings are a much better guide for management action than the run-of-the-mill complaints of nonproducers. Give yourself every opportunity to re-recruit your peak performers.

Average Salespeople

A regularly scheduled method of goal review is a more appropriate coaching strategy for the average salesperson. A quarterly review is usually considered best. Frequency of reviews should be governed by the company's individual situation. While these reviews should be similar to those of peak performers, specific attention needs to be paid to performance, work habits and the production goal the salesperson has set for himself or herself. It is less important to cover company policies and objectives, except as they are influenced by the salesperson's performance. Management difficulties can be avoided if coaching takes place before a salesperson experiences a production slump.

The manager needs to determine how to help the salesperson with his or her problems (whether stated or unstated) and, more important, what steps the salesperson should be taking. The latter's current methods should be reviewed, and listing and sales procedures should be discussed. Together, manager and salesperson should review the reasons why some transactions succeeded and others failed. The salesperson probably has the answers, but they may be ill-defined or exaggerated. It is up to the manager to help the salesperson clarify his or her performance profile so the individual can arrive at the proper conclusions.

After a coaching session, the salesperson should know more clearly what he or she is trying to accomplish and just how the company is trying to help. Equally important, the salesperson will have received renewed affirmation of his or her value as an individual and importance to the firm.

Salespeople in Trouble

When salespeople run into trouble, there are a host of possible causes and some valuable clues. These may include the salesperson's

- being inflexible,
- fighting change or clinging to the status quo,
- lacking imagination/creativity,
- becoming defensive,
- having personal problems,
- lacking team spirit,
- growing lazy or possible poor health,
- being unwilling to take a risk,
- being unwilling to recognize the value of planning and goal setting,
- being disorganized, and
- passing the buck.

In the real estate business, productivity should almost always increase because it builds on an expanding base of referrals from past clients. Thus, a slump is easily spotted by a falling off or leveling off of production. Whatever the cause, obvious or hidden, the effect usually shows up fairly soon in poor performance. It is important to detect the trend and do something about it before it becomes a serious problem for both the salesperson and management. Every salesperson has a production level at which he or she is happiest, most comfortable and most productive for the company. Evidence of a change indicates a need for a coaching session.

Coaching calls for the best communications skills management can muster. A coaching session should be arranged for a time and place where the manager and the salesperson can sit down quietly, free of interruption, to converse freely. The manager should come to the session prepared with the facts and figures that indicate a problem threatens or already exists.

The manager should be prepared to deal with differences in perception of the situation. It is natural that the salesperson may enter such a discussion with an air of suspicion, a degree of resentment or a feeling of considerable discouragement regarding his or her ability to succeed in real estate sales. If it is suspicion, the manager will need to put the salesperson at ease; if resentment, the manager will be prepared with facts and perhaps employ the "mirror" technique to let the salesperson tell the story his or her own way; if it's a discouraged person who settles down for the conversation, the manager will help that salesperson focus on some of the things he or she has done right and help that person find more methods to be successful. But above all, the manager will listen with both eyes and ears. Understanding body language can be a great aid to management in coaching work. And when the nonverbal message disagrees with what is being said, ask the salesperson to explain what he or she has just told you because it's not really clear to you yet. You may find that the fault lies in the way you phrased a question; that the information you are getting may be what the salesperson thinks you asked for, but it isn't really what you wanted to learn.

Once the point has been made that a problem exists, the manager must get to the root of it. This can take time. But it usually results in the manager and the salesperson arriving at a mutually satisfying solution. It might mean some added training or a refresher course in some aspect of real estate sales the person is uncomfortable with. Occasionally it means suggesting the salesperson get away for a complete change for a few days and come back refreshed in mind and spirit. Whatever the outcome, bear in mind that the person in trouble needs reaffirmation of his or her value and potential in the firm just as much as, and perhaps more than, the top producers. For the person in trouble, it will take the form of encouragement rather than outright praise. All the while, the focus must be on performance, and the salesperson's accountability for that performance.

New Salespeople

New salespeople should receive coaching similar in some ways to those in a slump. Consideration must be given to the details of their work habits and daily activity. Wayne C. Dawson, in an article on new salespeople, wrote, "A recruit accustomed to direction will frequently fail, despite training, if firm day-to-day direction is not imposed. Business executives agree the total worth of a company can be established by the effectiveness of good management. Most aspiring salespeople want to be managed tactfully. How else can they learn successful habits?"[4]

Thus, concern for the individual, attention to detail and a positive sense of direction begin in the formative stages of the company/salesperson relationship. This is when the foundation for all further coaching is established.

RETENTION AND THE 7-S MODEL OF ORGANIZATIONAL ANALYSIS

Lack of motivation is just one possible reason for a sales associate's lack of productivity. Sometimes other factors within the organization present barriers to productivity. The 7-S model provides a framework for managers to think through all of the elements that may be causing the problem. Using this model, here are some examples of other organizational problems that could be affecting productivity.

Is the sales associates' problem due to a lack of training (systems)? Is management providing the direction and support appropriate to the sales associate's level of commitment and experience (style)? Does the sales associate know what the company believes is important (shared values)? Does the sales associate get along with the other salespeople (staff)? Does the sales associate have a clear reporting relationship (structure)? Is the entire company lacking a crucial skill, such as prospecting (skill)? Does the company have a clear strategy for where it is going that provides direction for its staff (strategy)?

If management determines that there are no organizational barriers to productivity and the company is doing everything possible to motivate and support its salespeople, it may be necessary to consider termination of a nonproductive individual.

TERMINATION

Termination occurs because of a lack of performance or a failure to follow the rules. It differs from firing which is a result of illegal or immoral activities. Terminating a salesperson is never easy. There is no rule book to follow in deciding exactly when and why this step must be taken. Nor is it easy to pinpoint the exact time a manager decides it is simply not possible to motivate a certain salesperson sufficiently to continue the relationship.

No matter how personable or how much "fun" a salesperson might be, a nonproducer takes up valuable desk space, spends company dollars, sets a bad example and lowers the morale of the entire office.

Some of the root causes of failure on the part of salespeople are the inability to acquire needed skills, lack of determination or lack of emotional resources necessary to succeed in the real estate business. When management comes to this determination, the only course of action is termination.

Even when termination is accepted as the only answer, it involves trauma for both the salesperson and the firm. No one likes to fail and start over. No one likes to admit having chosen the wrong person or the wrong firm. But once the decision is made and management has admitted its mistake, it is time to act.

Deep as the trauma may be at the time, experience has proven that termination brings a genuine sense of relief to the salesperson. In most cases the individual has been aware (even if only in a vague way) that he or she has been frustrated and has not been carrying a full share of the work. Such people will seldom leave voluntarily because they do not know what else to do or how to go about making a change for the better. By clarifying the issue and forcing the decision through coaching toward accountability, a strong manager enables the salesperson to find work to which he or she is better suited and in which this person will be happier. This resolute and sometimes face-saving process serves the best interests of the salesperson and the company.

There will also be times when the salesperson decides to terminate the relationship. It may be for what appear to be inadequate reasons. This individual may have a burning desire to see his or her name on the door, to see it in lights and on a letterhead. In short, this person thinks it's time to go into business for himself or herself.

When this happens, wise management will wish the salesperson well. Not only has this person played an important part in the success and growth of the firm but in this proposed new role, he or she will be in a position to become a valuable colleague in the business. If you try to hold the salesperson back, he or she may leave anyway to be an unhappy or difficult competitor. The maintenance of a continuing good relationship is always the wiser course. It can be mutually rewarding. And who knows, the day may come when that former salesperson will decide to return to your company or suggest a merger of two very successful operations.

UNDERSTANDING

In today's complex society, many salespeople tend to feel business relationships are temporary and that they must really go it alone. Management's challenge in meeting this personality need is to so understand its people that it conveys a feeling of security, a positive sense of direction and a favorable working climate in which everyone can grow. Leaders in management must demonstrate their concern for people by helping them work as mature, responsible adults in a self-fulfilling service industry.

Obviously such things as adequate and attractive facilities, an efficient office staff, sales training and educational programs and complete listing and sales services are essential. Important as these ingredients of the real estate business are, full cooperation and a genuine appreciation of each other's goals are also necessary. When all these are provided, each person can work in his or her own way to achieve their full potential.

ENDNOTES

1. Peter F. Drucker, "A New Compendium for Management," *Business Week,* February 9, 1974, pp. 48-58.
2. John Wooden, *They Call Me Coach.*
3. Maxwell Maltz, *Psycho-Cybernetics.*
4. Wayne C. Dawson, "New Salesman: Handle with Care," *Real Estate Today,* October 1973, p. 31.

Chapter 12

Forms of Compensation and Fringe Benefits

A well-designed compensation plan is an important key to a real estate firm's profitability. If after compensating its sales associates the firm doesn't have enough money left to pay its expenses and make a reasonable profit, it won't be in business for long. In addition, compensation plans are important elements in attracting and retaining high performance sales associates and in motivating all of the firm's agents.

No single type of plan will work for all firms, or even for all sales associates within a firm. Plans need to be tailored to meet each firm's goals and the needs of its sales associates at various levels. This chapter describes some of the major types of compensation plans used in real estate firms—from the 100 percent commission plan to straight salary. It explains the concept of the breakeven point and the importance of distinguishing between employees and independent contractors when designing a compensation plan.

A WELL-DESIGNED COMPENSATION PLAN IS ESSENTIAL

One of the important systems in a real estate firm is its compensation plan. A *compensation plan* is a statement of how a sales associate will be paid and what charges or expenses the sales associate will be responsible for. An attractive and competitive compensation plan helps you recruit and retain high performing sales associates. Because your compensation plan also affects the firm's finances as a whole, a well-designed compensation plan is an important key to the firm's profitability.

Compensation plans also involve the 7-S factors of strategy, staff and shared values. For example, commissions can be designed to support the company's business strategies by paying a higher commission for in-house sales. Staff is an important consideration when designing compensation plans, both to provide the type of incentive that will satisfy your salespeople's needs and to match the plan to the agent's capabilities so that the company does not lose money because of low producers. Finally, compensation systems can be set up to foster shared values such as teamwork or to encourage competition among the sales associates.

Compensation plans generally are based on either commission or salary, or a combination of the two. Within those categories, however, there are many variations. Two recent trends in compensation represent the opposite ends of this spectrum. One is the 100 percent commission plan. Under this plan, instead of a split, salespeople receive the entire commission on their sales, but pay the broker for support services. This type of plan appeals to independent sales associates who like to run their own businesses. The other trend is to pay salespeople a straight salary. This type of plan provides salespeople greater security and fosters teamwork because salespeople aren't competing with one another for commissions. Both of these plans will be discussed in greater detail in this chapter.

A creative and flexible compensation plan is an important element in attracting and retaining high performing sales associates. A well-designed plan will motivate and meet the needs of each individual agent. However, it's unlikely that the same plan will satisfy the needs of high producers and low producers alike. Plans should be tailored to the needs of different levels of sales associates. New sales associates often need a more secure income while they are learning the business. Experienced sales associates may be willing to assume a greater degree of risk in exchange for the potential of greater reward.

Your compensation plan is also critical in ensuring that your firm remains profitable. If after you pay your sales associates you don't have enough left to pay the firm's expenses and make a reasonable profit, you won't be in business for long. Computer programs are available that enable you to test various compensation plan options against your firm's actual production numbers to ensure that the plan you choose meets your company's needs. The Real Estate Brokerage Managers Council™ offers a course that teaches managers how to use the computer to evaluate compensation plans. Another useful source of information in designing a compensation plan is the Council's book, *Compensation Planning: The Key to Profitability*.[1] Much of the information in this chapter has been adapted from that book.

Because of the independent contractor relationship, it is important that your compensation plan be carefully structured and explained to anyone seeking to join your firm. It is strongly recommended that you have your attorney review your compensation plans for compliance with local and federal laws.

THE BREAKEVEN POINT

An important concept to keep in mind in designing your firm's compensation plan is the idea of the breakeven point. There are two kinds of breakevens—the firm's and the agent's.

The Firm's Breakeven Point

To determine the firm's breakeven point, first you need to know your Gross Commission Income, or GCI. This is the income left after the split has been paid to co-op brokers and referral companies. The GCI is the money available to run your business before you pay the sales associates. It is important to know what percentage of each dollar is distributed to each area of expense. A real estate firm's categories of expense typically are

- commissions and fees paid,
- advertising,
- office occupancy,
- office equipment,
- communication system,
- materials and supplies,
- promotion costs,
- education and travel,
- salaries for support staff,
- staff benefits,
- professional services,
- debt service,
- reserves, and
- profit before taxes.

Breakeven is the lowest amount of income required to cover the firm's total operating expenses. However, most firms don't want to just break even; they want to make a profit. For this reason, as shown above, you should budget a profit margin in calculating the breakeven point.

Commissions and fees paid directly to agents are typically the firm's largest expense item. If your compensation plan is not designed carefully, you may not have enough of the GCI left to cover the firm's expenses after paying agents. These expenses must then be paid out of the firm's profits or you must lower expenses. But lowering expenses means you may not be providing the support your agents need for optimal productivity.

The Agent's Breakeven Point

The agent's breakeven point is the point at which a sales associate has earned enough revenue for the company to cover the sales associate's share of the company expenses. When designing a compensation plan, it is important to try to match the plan to the sales associates' capabilities. Sales associates who are low producers should be recruited into plans that have low breakeven points. This means a lower split and/or higher chargeback at the beginning until the associate's production level reaches the breakeven point. It is prudent to have every sales associate's breakeven well below his or her expected revenue production so that even if the sales associate's production drops, it does not drop below the plan's breakeven point. High producers may have plans with higher breakeven points because they are more likely to achieve them. Computer technology enables you to easily tailor your compensation plans for sales associates at various levels.

COMMISSION PLANS

The payment of straight commissions is still the most popular and effective method of compensation for salespeople. Here are some things to keep in mind about commission plans.

It is important to remember when evaluating commission splits that if you do not retain enough of the commission dollars to make a profit and to provide the services salespeople need to do their jobs, you will be unable to attract or keep the caliber of salespeople you need.

Compensation should satisfy emotional as well as financial needs. Money may be a symbol to some, to others it is an absolute necessity, and to still others it offers a way to show that they are the best. In most cases, it should be remembered that a salesperson is usually interested in total income, and the commission split can be less important than the total number of dollars he or she can earn during the year.

Commission schedules should be agreed upon formally by the broker and salesperson. They should be detailed in writing. The best plan is a combination of things that work, motivate, get results, are fair and show a profit for the company. Although you want your plan to be competitive, it is not wise to meet or better a competitor's commission rate if it is unrealistic. Commission is only one part of the entire package that makes your firm a desirable place to work.

Two common features of commission plans are splits and chargebacks. Splits refer to the division of the gross income into two parts—one for the agent and one for the company. They are usually expressed as a percentage, such as a 50/50 split. Generally, as agents earn more commission, their share of the split increases to reward their higher production.

Chargebacks are expenses for facilities and services provided by the company that are deducted from the agent's share of the split, as defined in the compensation schedule. The company uses chargebacks to recover expenses while meeting a target profit. Many of the items charged back correspond directly to items in the company's expense list.

There are a variety of different types of commission plans.

Fixed Split Commission Plan

A 1993-94 survey by the Rocky Mountain Consulting and Training Group, Inc., indicated that 15 percent of the firms responding offered a fixed split commission plan with no graduations or increments.[2]

Incremental Plans

The most commonly used type of commission plan is the incremental plan. These generally consist of several "levels" or "thresholds" based on the amount of GCI. For each level there is a predetermined split of gross revenue between the agent and the company. The higher an agent's GCI, the larger percentage share he or she earns. An incremental plan might look like this:

Level 1:	to $20,000	50%
Level 2:	to $40,000	60%
Level 3:	above $40,000	70%

The sales associate's share of his or her GCI is 50 percent until $20,000 is reached. Between $20,000 and $40,000, the agent's share is 60 percent; and above $40,000 it is 70 percent. The commission schedule normally applies to one year's income. Each year the agent starts at the lower split and works back to the higher split.

In a progressive incremental plan, the agent starts each year at a split level based on his or her previous year's production. These plans are more attractive to higher producers because they do not have to return to Level 1 at the beginning of each year.

It is crucial when designing an incremental plan that the compensation plan not go to the highest split until the breakeven (including budgeted profit) has been reached. Otherwise the rest of the fixed expenses will need to come out of the firm's budgeted profit.

In addition, each sales associate should be viewed as a profit center. The compensation plan should make each individual sales associate's "company" profitable so that the company as a whole is profitable. When lower producers receive too high a split or cannot cover their expenses, the company can end up drawing funds from high producers to subsidize low producers. If, as a result, the company cannot offer sufficiently attractive plans to the high producers, they may go elsewhere. One way to ensure that low producers are covering their share of expenses is by charging back sales associates for resources or services depending upon their split.

The advantage of traditional incremental plans for sales associates is that they typically have a low level of chargebacks so the sales associates bear a relatively low degree of risk. The sales associates have definite goals to motivate them and feel rewarded for doing well. Although the company typically pays more costs for the agent upfront with an incremental commission plan, it benefits by retaining more money as sales associates earn more within each level, because they don't receive the higher share until they reach the next level and it applies only to commissions earned on that level.

Retroactive Plans

The retroactive plan is similar to the incremental plan. The major difference is that when agents reach the amount specified to move to a new level, the higher percentage split is applied retroactively to income from lower levels. In a well-designed retroactive plan, the levels are set so that the agent does not advance to the next level until he or she is producing enough GCI to cover all expenses and budgeted profit applicable to that higher split. This type of plan is a strong motivator because sales associates receive lump sum cash rewards when they reach a higher level (the percentage difference between the two levels on all GCI up to that point).

100 Percent Commission Plans

One of the newest compensation trends is the 100 percent commission plan, also called the chargeback plan. Under this plan, the sales associate receives the entire commission income he or she generates but pays the company for support services plus a set amount of monthly fees for the use of shared services such as desk space rental, telephone answering, membership fees, office space rental, institutional advertising, secretarial services and so on. The agent might also pay the company a brokerage fee (for example, 5 percent off the top of the agent's GCI), or a transaction fee (for example, $250 per transaction).

According to Ron Schmaedick, whose company has adopted this approach, the 100 percent commission plan requires a major change in a brokerage firm's traditional way of doing business.[3] The traditional firm attracts buyers and sellers to do business with the firm and employs (or contracts with) sales associates to service them. In the 100 percent commission firm, Schmaedick says, the broker acts as an intermediary who distributes essential services to the entrepreneurial sales associate. Sales associates control their own marketing strategies and their expenses. The firm "provides an environment that enables sales associates who are self-starters, self-motivated, self-directed, and personally organized to reach their maximum potential." Schmaedick believes this arrangement is attractive to many sales associates who entered the real estate business because of the independence it offers. It appeals to confident high producers who are willing to take the risks necessary to attain the 100 percent split. It is not recommended for low producing or inexperienced agents, because both the firm and the agent risk losing money.

The High Split Plan with Chargebacks

This plan is a compromise between the traditional incremental plan and the 100 percent plan. Under this plan, the sales associate receives higher splits than he or she would under an incremental plan but is responsible for more expenses. For example, a plan may pay a 50 percent split to $20,000, then a 90 percent split. The sales associate may be responsible for paying expenses for such things as advertising, signs, telephones, and office supplies and services, but fewer chargebacks than on a 100 percent commission plan. This type of plan can be attractive to sales associates because it offers a higher split than the incremental plan but more security than the 100 percent commission plan.

The Rolling Average Plan

This plan differs from the commission plans already discussed in that the agent does not start over again each year. The split is continually recalculated based on how much income a sales associate brings in over a specified period of time. With this plan, the income over the previous period determines the split to be used for the next period. If a sales associate had a large income during the last period, he or she would be at a high split for the next earning period.

The past period that determines the split level is often a year, but it can be more or less. The next period that indicates how often the rolling average is recalculated is generally shorter. Three-month periods are frequently used to recalculate rolling averages.

Rolling average plans are most advantageous for high producers because they can maintain a high split level without a period of low split at the beginning of each new year. This type of plan is a good motivator because sales associates must maintain high enough sales to maintain the high percentage split.

Combined Schedules

Under a combined schedule, an agent is given a different percentage of GCI for different types of sales activities. In other words, different split schedules are applied to various types of sales activities. But no matter which type of sales activity and which commission schedule applies to it, the GCI from all sales activities counts toward the total GCI that determines when the agent moves up to the next level in a particular schedule.

Combined commission schedules can be used in any type of compensation plan.

By using combined schedules, a company can encourage sales associates to direct their efforts toward particular types of sales activities. For example, if the company would like to encourage its sales associates to make more in-house sales in relation to co-op sales and referrals, it could give them a higher percentage of the GCI for making in-house sales.

Combined schedules can also be an effective recruiting and retention tool. If you know that only 20 percent of your sales are in-house, you could offer an attractive commission for these sales while offering an acceptable percentage for other types of sales. This could be attractive to potential sales associates or ones who are considering moving to a competitor.

Basic Plus Plan

In this type of plan, Level 1 is the basic split that applies to all levels and is expressed in terms of a percentage of the GCI. Splits at all other levels indicate how much more sales associates will be paid on top of that basic split as an incentive. For example:

Level 1: Basic split 50 percent   to $20,000
Level 2: Basic split 50 percent plus 20 percent to $40,000
Level 3: Basic split 50 percent plus 40 percent above $40,000

At Level 1, the sales associate receives the basic split of 50 percent of GCI. At Level 2, the associate receives the basic split of 50 percent plus 20 percent of the basic split on income between $20,000 and $40,000. At Level 3, the associate receives the basic split of 50 percent plus 40 percent of the basic split on income above $40,000.

Salary

Although the majority of salespeople (92 percent according to a 1993 statistic[4]) work solely on commission, a number of firms are moving to a salary system. Some brokers predict that salaried compensation is the wave of the future and will continue to increase in popularity.[5] By definition, salaried sales associates must be employees of the real estate firm; a salary form of compensation is inconsistent with the independent contractor relationship.

Some firms pay beginning sales associates a salary until they gain some experience, then put them on a commission plan. Firms often require that salespeople earn a minimum in gross commission income, such as $50,000, in order to qualify for a salaried employee program. Although there is usually a cap on salaries, a combination salary plus bonus program gives high producers an opportunity to earn far more. At one firm, for example, sales associates who earn their base salary plus an amount to cover their benefits, plus a set contribution to the company, receive any excess earnings on a generous monthly payment schedule.

A salary form of compensation can be appealing to sales associates because it provides a stable income without the peaks and valleys inherent in most commission systems. They get a regular paycheck and don't have to worry about cash flow or about paying quarterly taxes to the government. With a salary plan, sales associates feel that the company is investing in them and allowing them to focus on customer service.

A salary form of compensation benefits the broker as well. It increases the sales manager's authority over sales associates and makes it easier for management to secure their cooperation. It can be an effective tool in recruiting new staff and reducing turnover among the sales force. One of the biggest benefits of the salaried system, according to some brokers, is the team atmosphere it encourages. Sales associates are more likely to work together and to cover for one another when there is no commission at stake. As one broker who has adopted this system puts it: "[With a salary system] there is absolute trust between all members of the team. When one of my sales associates is on vacation, someone will always step in to look after the associate's business without thought of compensation."[6]

A danger in a straight salary compensation plan is that there may be a lack of incentive to achieve optimum production. In addition, it can be difficult for the company to reduce its fixed expenses, and low producers may be kept on the payroll for too long. One way to avoid these problems is to use a combination salary and commission plan. This can help attract good sales associates to join the firm. It can also motivate them to help the company meet its objectives by enabling them to increase their earnings when they beat their goals.

OTHER METHODS OF COMPENSATION

Salespeople's financial situations and the state of a firm's business sometimes cause management to look to other methods of compensation. There are several, some possible with independent contractors and some limited to salespeople employed by the firm.

The following alternative ways of compensating salespeople are discussed separately as they apply to independent contractors and to employees. This relationship is discussed in more detail in Chapter 8. Whatever form of compensation the broker chooses, he or she must be aware of the employee/independent contractor relationship.

This material is not meant to be used as a legal guideline. Laws change constantly, and legal counsel is essential for the broker's protection when planning and instituting any compensation plans. Brokers can obtain direction by contacting the legal services department of the National Association of REALTORS®. Many state associations provide legal services for their members as well.

Draws—Independent Contractors

Because the compensation of independent contractors must in no way resemble a salary, draws against commissions, whether or not earned, are extremely dangerous and should be carefully examined with legal counsel before they are initiated. If a salesperson requires compensation beyond what he or she can generate through commission income, that individual should be employed at a salary until he or she can become self-sustaining, at which time the person may become affiliated on an independent contractor basis.

While it is not generally advisable, a broker may make a loan to an independent contractor salesperson. However, such a loan should be evidenced by a note, should be at interest, and the broker should insist upon full payment and enforce payment if necessary. The broker should always be cautious about a note secured by future commissions and should only withhold payments on the note from commissions due to the salesperson with a written understanding to cover the payment.

It is critical that compensation arrangements that deviate in any respect from a straight commission basis be reviewed by legal counsel prior to implementation.

Draws—Employees

Draw systems can be used against future commissions, against earned commissions or against the possibility of earned commission. Draws are regular payments very similar to a salary.

In a draw against future commissions, there may be no commissions currently earned but the draw continues. It is a flat, even rate, and it is not increased or reduced according to current earnings. In such cases, the sales associate may be ahead of the company or behind it, changing position many times during the year. All the sales associate is concerned with is that X number of dollars will be available to him or her at a certain time each month. This is the simplest form of draw and perhaps one of the most dangerous because such a draw will probably be interpreted as being a salary in disguise.

In a draw against earned commission, payments derive from commissions that have been accumulated. They may be drawn in part or in full but the sales associate has the comfort of knowing that even if a sale does not close for several months, he or she can draw the money on that sale at any time.

The pitfall here is that in such a system the sales employee usually draws on future commissions as a matter of practice rather than emergency. A bookkeeping problem arises and trouble surfaces when sales fall through. Another difficulty of this system is that the company's cash position may be jeopardized if the draw is overused.

Another draw is against the possibility of earned commission. Under this plan, a sales associate can draw against a possible earned listing commission simply by bringing in a listing. The broker evaluates the listing. If it is a good one, the draw would be allowed. This, unfortunately, adds one more dimension to a rather complicated draw system.

In both of the above types of draw, the broker should take precautions to protect himself or herself and have a clear understanding of the agreement with the sales associate. Specifically, there should be some evidence in writing as to repayment, payment of interest and the status of each of the parties in the event of termination. Some brokers who offer draws not only charge interest but require that a note be signed covering each draw. In some cases, brokers require that the sales associate's spouse cosign the note.

A third type of draw system is the draw against the possibility of earned commissions while the associate is in a training period. In this type of draw a sales associate earns while working, perhaps part-time, through a training period. He or she may earn some commissions during this period. A typical draw of this type pays one half of the earned commission and the other half is deposited by the broker in a custodial account in the salesperson's name. At the end of the training period, a reserve is accumulated upon which the new sales associate can draw until fuller production is achieved.

A fourth variation on financing methods in draws is the minimum guarantee. In this system, the broker, either by an oral or written promise or in writing, puts a floor on the earnings of a new sales associate. The broker simply guarantees that the sales associate will earn a minimum number of dollars in a specified time and if he or she does not earn that amount, the broker will pay the difference.

One Alternative to the Draw   An alternative for getting new sales associates over a financial hump is for the broker to go with the associate to a bank, credit union or other lending institution and cosign a note. The sales associate repays the lender and at the same time establishes credit so future loans can be made without a cosigner. An advantage of this system is that the broker need not tie up his or her own funds, need not pay interest and can keep a close watch on the progress of the new sales associate. In some instances, a broker will issue two checks to a sales associate on a closed sale. The commission is paid one-half in the name of the sales associate and the other half in the name of the sales associate and the lender. When the check is endorsed to the lender, the debt that was cosigned is partially liquidated. This system demonstrates the faith the broker has in the sales associate, but it does assure repayment and the reduction of the broker's liability.

FRINGE BENEFITS

Fringe Benefits

As for providing security for salespeople in a real estate firm, the best security is within the individual. A well-trained salesperson should be able to do well selling in any market, anywhere. In addition to this personal security, which can be built up and nurtured, some fringe benefits will help provide additional measures of financial security. Some of these benefits can accrue to independent contractors and salespeople alike; some cannot.

Profit Sharing and Pension Plans—Independent Contractor   Self-employed retirement programs are quite common. Such plans may be arranged through banks, insurance companies, trust companies, mutual fund companies and other financial institutions. Under such programs, the amount contributed to the retirement program, within specified limits, is excluded from the independent contractor's taxable income. Earnings on the sums contributed are likewise not currently taxable. Brokers will find it desirable to encourage their independent contractor salespeople to set up such retirement programs in consultation with their legal counsel.

Profit Sharing and Pension Plans—Employee   Employees are entitled to participate in company or firm pension and profit sharing plans. The difference between a pension and profit sharing plan is basically a difference in the nature of the broker's commitment to contribute. A pension plan usually involves a commitment on the part of the broker to contribute to the plan each year, whereas a profit sharing plan will normally require contributions only in those years in which a profit is made by the company.

Pension and profit sharing plans must qualify under the Internal Revenue Code in order for the broker's contributions to them to be tax deductible. The requirements governing eligibility, participation and essentially every other feature of such plans are extremely comprehensive and specific, and competent legal counsel should be consulted in their development and implementation.

Pension and profit sharing plans for sales or other employees of a broker can significantly reduce labor turnover and increase employee job satisfaction. They involve continuing obligations and costs, however, and therefore should not be established without extensive prior analysis of the commitment and the wide variety of forms such commitment may legally take.

Sliding Scale Bonus Plans—Independent Contractor   Bonuses paid to independent contractors must be a bargained for, predetermined reward for achievement. They should not be discretionary payments lest they be considered salary and jeopardize the salesperson's independent contractor status. Bonus plans must be carefully designed to achieve their purpose, which is motivation of the salesperson to optimum productivity. They are usually set up on a sliding scale basis.

Bonus Plans—Employee   It is not easy for a broker with a staff accustomed to receiving commissions on a fixed schedule to initiate a bonus plan. In most cases it is necessary to adjust the commissions downward, and this is invariably a painful procedure. It is especially difficult to initiate such a plan because of its effect on the present commission schedule. Bonuses are usually most rewarding to high producers and may be resented by less productive employees.

The best bonus plans are those that do not encourage sales employees to either leave or loaf. They do not make a lump payment once a year because this might suggest a target date to leave the company or tempt a salesperson to take it easy until that sum is used up. They should be rewards and not merely a gift to an employee for having survived another year with the firm. The basic requirements of a good bonus plan are that it rewards achievement and motivates the associate to even greater productivity.

Insurance Programs—Independent Contractors   Legal counsel should advise the broker which, if any, insurance programs may be open to participation by independent contractors who pay their own premiums. When such arrangements are possible, the independent contractors enjoy the benefit of group rates and the possibility of getting better coverage than they might obtain under individual policies.

Insurance Programs—Employee   Many brokerage firms provide insurance programs for their employees. Group insurance programs for life, major medical, dental, accident and health and long-term and short-term disability coverage are available. Employed personnel are eligible for insurance benefits, whether the broker provides them as a wholly subsidized fringe benefit or on a contributory basis. However, such programs must be reviewed with legal counsel to assure that they satisfy the requirements of the Internal Revenue Code. Otherwise, payments for such benefits may not be tax deductible to the company and may be taxable to the sales employee.

Other Fringe Benefits—Employees Only   Paid vacations and sick leave are benefits confined to an employee/employer relationship.

SUMMARY OF COMPENSATION FOR SALESPEOPLE

In short, to recruit and retain the best sales associates, it is essential that you offer a diverse "menu" of compensation schedules to meet the competition. Plans should be tailor-made so that they do the following:

- Achieve your firm's profit objectives
- Attract quality sales associates
- Reward and motivate your high performers
- Offer adequate security and motivation to increase production to your inexperienced and low producers

Fortunately, today's sophisticated computer technology makes it easier for you to design and administer competitive compensation plans that are both profitable and attractive.

OFFICE PERSONNEL

Efficient, well-organized, responsible office personnel can add to your firm's profitability. They can relieve your sales associates from time-consuming paperwork and administrative duties, enabling them to focus on listings and sales and making them more productive.

COMPENSATION

Office personnel are generally salaried company employees whose salaries come out of the company's fixed costs. To ensure that you are paying your support staff a realistic, competitive wage, you need to systematically establish salary ranges for your office personnel.

Research the going rate for comparable positions in your area. Many times large companies in your area will provide data on salary ranges they pay for comparable positions. Some Chambers of Commerce conduct annual wage-salary surveys in their communities. The Small Business Administration is of help too. The Civil Service publishes guidelines on salary ranges for each job in your office. Adopt a formula for a base salary based on what you consider fair compensation for a new person starting within that position. Be fair and honest with your employees when establishing base salaries, but take care that you're not so nice that you put yourself in the red on your profit and loss statement. Some brokers think the answer to all personnel problems is giving a raise. This is usually only a temporary solution to a deeper problem.

The best way to handle staff compensation is to explain at the beginning of employment exactly what the salary will be. Most brokers do an effective job at this point. What causes problems is a lack of regularly scheduled reviews and raises. It is not likely that any raise given to an individual employee will be kept secret within the office for very long. The best way to handle compensation and avoid problems is to establish a policy on salaries. This spells out salary policy for the entire length of time of their employment. This policy should stipulate beginning salaries, when salary reviews will take place and under what circumstances raises will be given.

Once the base starting salary for each position within your organization is established, it becomes a simple matter to set the top limit. When the top limit your company is willing to pay for each position is established, it's necessary to determine how an employee reaches the top level.

Employees should understand how they can move beyond the established limits for the job they hold. This might be achieved by taking on greater responsibilities within the job held or by qualifying for promotion to a higher job.

Often when support staff are paid on an hourly basis, there is no incentive for these employees to work more efficiently because their pay is not tied to sales. However, the company's revenue is tied to their efficiency. There are incentive programs that reward office staff on the basis of performance. Profit sharing programs are probably the most common. In such programs, salaried employees share a percentage of the gross profits, split equally among all the salaried employees. Another solution might be to link their pay to salespeople's efficiency.

Many companies provide investment opportunities for salaried office employees. By providing employees a vehicle for investing in their company on an everyday basis, these opportunities encourage them to take an active interest in the firm and promise exciting opportunities for future economic growth.

In recent years, there has been a dramatic increase in the use of agents' assistants in the real estate industry. These agents' assistants may be either licensed or unlicensed. They may work for the broker, or they may be paid directly by the sales associate for whom they work. In addition to keeping track of appointments, handling paperwork and making cold calls, personal assistants who are licensed may also take on such tasks as showing homes to prospective buyers and taking listings, and should be compensated appropriately for these tasks. In addition, if they are licensed, they may earn some form of bonus or commission on personal business in addition to the income they are paid as an assistant.

FRINGE BENEFITS

The possible list of fringe benefits that a broker can offer his or her office personnel is endless. Among the most popular are health, life and disability insurance and special discounts on commissions or fees on the sale of the employee's homestead or investment properties.

Paid vacations, retirement plans, stock options, expense accounts, travel allowances, contests and prizes, free memberships in fraternal and business societies, country clubs, health clubs, counseling and psychiatric counseling are among the fringe benefits currently offered.

Many brokers are not aware of what these programs cost. It is easy for a company to "fringe itself to death." Many brokers give employees benefit upon benefit only to have the employee leave to take a position with another firm because of higher take-home pay. Many large corporations feel that if fringe benefits total more than 10 percent to 15 percent of the gross earnings of the employees, they exceed normal limitations. Many employees, despite demands for fringe benefits, prefer higher take-home pay.

Before implementing a fringe benefit program, make certain that the entire employee group is enthusiastic about it. A broker may respond to requests from a few employees only to find out after implementing a costly program that the majority of the employees actually do not want it. This is particularly true when fringe benefits are given in lieu of a salary increase.

Research has indicated that many fringe benefits do not provide the employer with the intended original objective of acting as an employee retention device. The most important concept to remember in compensating employees is this: Give them an environment in which to work where they are comfortable, have a strong sense of security and exciting possibilities for future growth with an employer who truly cares about them and their problems.

CONCLUSION

Compensation is important, but it is only one of the elements of the total "value package" that you offer your sales associates. A variety of nontangible considerations also helps to create an attractive package. These include the following:

- Access to training, information and career development programs
- A good office environment, complete with support staff, management systems, equipment and resources
- Systems that control recruiting and retention of quality agents and support staff
- A positive company image and a strong reputation in the community
- Strong management that limits potential for errors and maximizes opportunities for business
- Systems that reward and recognize successful and contributing sales associates as well as provide motivation and guidance

This value package will contribute not only to the success of individual agents but by extension to the company as a whole.

ENDNOTES

1. David Cocks and Larry Laframboise, *Compensation Planning: The Key to Profitability.*
2. In *Management Issues and Trends,* vol. 9, no. 5, p. 3.
3. Ron Schmaedick, "Switching to a 100 Percent Plan—An Inside Look at RAMS Realty, Inc.," *Management Issues and Trends,* vol. 9, no. 5, pp. 4-5
4　"A Historical Look at Salaried Compensation," *Management Issues and Trends,* vol. 8, no. 4, p. 1.
5. "A Historial Look at Salaried Compensation," p. 3
6. Jack McCafferty, "Succeed With Salaries," in *Management Issues and Trends,* vol. 9, no. 5, p. 7.

Chapter 13

Financial Systems and Records

Even the smallest real estate office needs to have a system of cost control. By establishing a budget and a matching system of cost accounting, brokers can know at a glance whether or not they are running a profitable operation.

This chapter deals with basic accounting methods, guides you through the important business of determining costs accurately, shows you how to analyze your income dollar and how to reflect these last two factors in an operating statement. Included are details on analyzing costs for any size operation and on computing the costs of running a real estate brokerage business.

Charts and other data shown here can be copied and adapted for your own use.

TWO REASONS FOR A GOOD ACCOUNTING SYSTEM

New brokers, generally having started their careers in sales, typically have a salesperson's approach to problems and are often prone to overlook their need for a good accounting system. They may operate with only a checkbook until it comes time to prepare their income tax returns. Their tax service will inform them that their increase or decrease in cash is probably not the same as their taxable income. Because they have purchased equipment, perhaps an office building, they have spent a lot of cash that is not deductible as an expense but must be capitalized and expensed out gradually (depreciated or amortized) as the assets lose their value.

Brokers soon learn they must have an accounting system for two main reasons: various income tax reports and good managerial control. Taking advantage of the different software packages designed specifically for small one-office and large multioffice real estate firms will save time and money in getting records in a timely fashion to make better decisions faster.

While their business is small, owner-managers need only a simple bookkeeping system. They make all of the decisions alone and can adjust rapidly to new conditions. Few, if any, reports are required because they can observe most variables in the making. It often suffices for small brokers to use generalized expense and income accounts, often using as few as ten accounts to trace their income and expense. However, the beginning brokers would be wise to get some help in originating their accounting system so it can expand and become more sophisticated as they grow without starting over on a new system. Aside from the extra cost involved, switching systems sometimes causes brokers to lose the direct comparative value of their past data.

As the business grows, brokers must delegate authority. Now they must be able to control expenses on which they are not making all the decisions. Each link in their chain of command represents a span of control. Having the proper accounting records gives management the tools it needs to evaluate each span of control—such as each branch office, and so forth.

Systems are one of the most important variables in the 7-S model because they determine how things actually get done. Financial systems are a key system because they support the company's business strategy. These systems and records provide the means for management to track its performance in executing its financial strategies directed at achieving the firm's long-term strategic intent.

BALANCE SHEET

The balance sheet is really a report of the financial condition of an enterprise as of a specific date. (See Figure 13.1.) Oversimplified, your financial position is made up of all your possessions (assets) offset by your debts (liabilities). The difference between your assets and your debts is your net worth or owner's equity. Since assets are generally maintained at net book value (cost less depreciation to date) instead of current market value, the statement of position is accurate for tax reporting purposes but not for an absolutely true financial position. The real value of an operating company is not its net worth but the current value of its probable future earning power (liquidation value sometimes must be considered if the company consistently produces a loss or marginal profit).

FIGURE 13.1   Balance Sheet

BK Realty, Inc.
Balance Sheet
as of December 31, 199X.

Current Assets		Current Liabilities	
Cash	$ 96,555	Deferred Commissions Payable (closed transactions)	$ 3,875
Deferred Commissions Receivable (closed transactions)	6,150	Note Payable– Short-Term	29,950
Total Current Assets	**$102,705**	Income Taxes Withheld	21,525
		Total Current Liabilities	**$ 55,350**

Fixed Assets		Long-Term Liabilities	
Furniture and Equipment	$ 86,100	Note Payable– Long-Term	$ 20,910
Less: Depreciation	19,065	**Total Long-Term Liabilities**	**$ 20,910**
Net Furniture and Equipment	$ 67,035	**Total Liabilities**	**$ 76,260**
Leasehold Improvements	32,595	**Owner's Equity**	
Less: Depreciation	13,530	Common Stock	$ 88,560
Net Leasehold Improvements	$ 19,065	Retained Earnings	23,985
Total Fixed Assets	**$ 86,100**	Owner's Equity	$112,545
Total Assets	**$188,805***	Total Liabilities and Owner's Equity	**$188,805***

*The balance sheet is called this because total assets and total liabilities plus owner's equity must balance (be equal).

Balance Sheet Relationships

When financial people look at balance sheets, they often note three common relationships.

The first common relationship is *current ratio*. This ratio measures the firm's ability to pay its bills. This is the arithmetic ratio of total current assets to total current liabilities. The formula is: CA ÷ CL. For example, if a firm's net current assets (current assets are assets readily converted to cash, such as marketable securities) are $50,000 and its short-term debts are $25,000, then it has a 2 to 1 current ratio which is considered healthy. As assets decrease and/or liabilities increase, the ratio decreases to less than 2 to 1 which increases risk to solvency. Bankers, who tend to be conservative when lending money to firms, like to see a ratio of at least 2 to 1.

The second common relationship is working capital. In this case, $50,000 less $25,000 equals $25,000, total current assets less total current liabilities. (The formula is CA – CL.) *Working capital* is additional liquid assets above the amount owed that can be used by the firm to implement its strategies.

The third common relationship is *equity ratio*. If this company had total assets of $100,000 with total liabilities of $45,000, the equity ratio is $100,000 less $45,000, equalling $55,000 equity or 55 percent equity ratio. The formula is TA – TL = Net Worth ÷ TA = Equity Ratio. As the ratio approaches 100 percent or 1, the firm has less debt, resulting in less financial risk.

INCOME STATEMENT

The income statement, sometimes called a profit and loss (P&L) statement or operating statement, portrays the ongoing operation of the company in terms of dollars for a specific period. The income statement must reflect total sales commissions and revenue by each principal division of the company.

The expenses should reflect both operating and nonoperating expenses. Operating expenses are those costs necessary for the operation of the business. Nonoperating expenses are costs that are not due to the actual operation of the company (i.e., interest and debt and/or income taxes).

NET INCOME

Net income may be defined as the earnings that management has produced during a specified period for all those who have invested capital in the enterprise. It might also be described as being made up of revenues, a positive factor, minus negatives, which are expenses, deductible losses and income taxes. Do not be confused because the word cash has not been used. Cash often has little or nothing to do with the calculation of net income, especially under accrual-based accounting systems or for any enterprise that owns nonliquid assets.

Net income is the income remaining after all expenses have been paid. The income after deducting only operational expenses (does not include interest and taxes) is called Earnings Before Interest and Taxes (EBIT).

> Example: Gross Revenue
> – Operational Expenses
> = Earnings Before Interest and Taxes (EBIT)
> – Interest
> = Earnings Before Taxes (EBT)
> – Taxes
> = Net Income

EBIT measures the business decisions and the efficiency of the company's operations. If EBIT is a negative number, the operation has produced a loss. If EBIT equals "0," the company has broken even. If EBIT is a positive number, the company has made a profit from operations.

EXPENSE VERSUS COST

It is typical for business people to misuse the term expense when they talk of the expense of buying equipment or buildings. Buying buildings or equipment is a cost for an asset. The depreciation of those assets is an expense. Costs of making or buying assets are not expenses; they are "costs of" the assets acquired. Expense means that you have given up something of value to obtain revenue.

Gross revenue or gross income is the total dollars that a firm takes in from all available sources. Gross revenue is 100 percent of the income to the company. Expenses will represent a percentage of gross revenue. If gross revenue is $1 million and commissions paid to salespeople is $530,000, then 53 percent of gross revenue is commissions paid to salespeople. If $80,000 is spent on advertising, then advertising expense is 8 percent of gross revenue.

A typical example of a properly structured income statement is shown in Figure 13.2.

Expenditures from Gross Revenue

Commissions and fees comprise the single largest category of expenditure from gross revenue. These expenses take more than one-half the gross income, regardless of the company's size or type of operation.

Owner/brokers should distribute listing and sales splits to themselves the same way they do to regular salespeople. Personal income from managerial duties should appear in summary value of the service provided.

Figure 13.3 illustrates a typical gross revenue chart.

**FIGURE 13.2   Income Statement, CRB Realty, Inc., Year End
(December 31)**

Revenue	199X	%*
In-house Transactions	$1,042,574	40%
Other Co. Sale/CRB List	533,784	25.3%
Other Co. List/CRB Sale	533,784	25.3%
Gross Revenue	$2,110,142	100%*
Operating Expenses		
Franchise Fee	105,507	5%
Sales Commissions	1,002,317	47.5%
Bonus Commissions	17,446	.83%
Advertising	168,811	8%
Selling Expenses	42,203	2%
Sales Management	105,489	5%
Salaries	167,767	8%
Communication	63,293	3%
Occupancy	126,587	6%
Other Operating Expense	142,065	6.7%
Depreciation Expense	15,800	.75%
Total Expenses	1,957,285	92.8%
Net Operating Income (EBIT)	$ 152,857	7.2%
Interest Expense	3,210	.15%
Earnings Before Taxes (EBT)	$ 149,647	7.09%
Income Taxes	49,088	2.3%
Net Income**	$ 100,559	4.8%
Common Stock Dividends	100,000	
Addition to Retained Earnings	559	

*Not all percentages are exact due to rounding.

**At the end of the year, total Net Income must be paid out in dividends, kept in the company as "retained earnings" and listed in the balance sheet under owners equity, or a combination of both as seen above.

FIGURE 13.3   Gross Revenue Chart (Definition: All Income Received by Company)

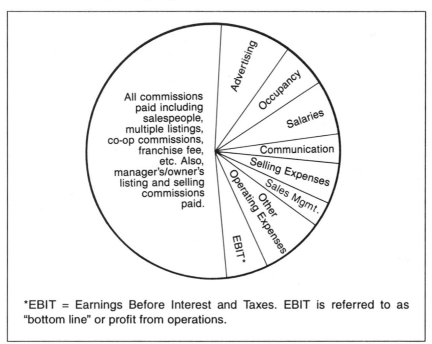

All commissions paid including salespeople, multiple listings, co-op commissions, franchise fee, etc. Also, manager's/owner's listing and selling commissions paid.

Advertising
Occupancy
Salaries
Communication
Selling Expenses
Operating Expenses
Sales Mgmt.
Other Expenses
EBIT*

*EBIT = Earnings Before Interest and Taxes. EBIT is referred to as "bottom line" or profit from operations.

Following are other major expenditures from gross revenue:

- *Advertising.* Every year brokers spend millions of dollars advertising the properties they have listed for sale. In addition, they spend a considerable number of dollars on institutional advertising to promote the services offered by their companies.
- *Selling Expenses.* In addition to advertising, there are other expenses tied directly to selling, such as "for sale" signs.
- *Sales Management.* This area is becoming an ever more important part of the real estate industry. Manager compensation can vary greatly. Some managers are paid a stringent salary; others are paid straight commission; still others are paid a combination of salary and commission.
- *Salaries.* The real estate industry is using more and more personnel who work on a salary basis. Typical employees include secretaries and bookkeepers.
- *Communication.* Sophisticated telephone equipment is having an impact on expenses in today's real estate business. Brokers should search different long distance telephone companies to find the best services and

price for their businesses. Included in communication expenses are voice mail, E-mail, mobile phones and other electronic services.

- *Occupancy*. Payment for office space includes rent, utilities, janitorial services and maintenance. Rent should reflect what the occupied space would cost on the open market. Where there is an ownership interest in the building occupied, accounting records should be separated to delete ownership applications and loan retirement items and show only what should be paid as a typical tenant. (Otherwise, profit/loss as part owners of the building would be commingled with the profit/loss of the brokerage business.)
- *Other Operating Expenses*. Other operating expenses include insurance, license, dues, legal and accounting fees, taxes (other than income), equipment, supplies, postage, bad debts, auto expenses and miscellaneous office expenses.
- *Depreciation*. Most owners account for depreciation in the income statement. It is the used-up portion of an asset that must be accounted for to guarantee proper entry for replacement.

See Figure 13.4 for a profit and loss analysis of a company operation.

ACCRUAL VERSUS CASH BASIS ACCOUNTING

The cash basis of accounting means that revenue is acknowledged when cash (or something of value) is actually received. Expenses are recognized only in amounts for which cash has been paid. The cash basis is normally used for small businesses because the accounting is simple and less costly. Current income taxes can be saved if all expenses are paid as incurred. When large receivables and payables are accumulated, the profit or loss picture can be greatly distorted through cash basis accounting.

The accrual basis of accounting dictates that one accrues revenue when the service is rendered or the sale is made. The time of collecting the cash proceeds or commission from the sale has no direct bearing on the timing or the amount of the revenue. To keep the accrual system as realistic as possible, a reserve could be established for lost sales if past experience warrants it. Expenses are recognized in the same manner, when they are incurred or become payable, and not when cash is paid out. The accrual method allows brokers to match expenses with revenues in the proper period thereby portraying a truer profit or loss position. Be careful of trying to get the best of two worlds by reporting revenue on a cash basis (when the sale is closed) but accruing expenses and charging them out at the end of the accounting period. The Internal Revenue Service will normally demand that you consistently stay on an accrual basis. All external expenses and revenues are funneled through your receivable and payable accounts when you employ pure accrual accounting. However, many firms operate as if on a cash basis until the end of the accounting period, at which time all expenses and revenue are adjusted to the accrual basis. With the proper procedures

FIGURE 13.4   Profit and Loss Analysis of Company Operation

I. Gross Revenue (from sales and listing fees)
   1. In-house transactions $_____
   2. Other company sales/your company listing $_____
   3. Other company list/your company sales $_____
   4. Total co-op transactions $_____
   5. Gross revenue (lines 1–3) $_____

Expense Analysis

Operating Expenses

II. Commissions and Fees
   6. Internal sales staff commissions (including bonuses) $_____
   7. Owner's listing fees and sales commissions $_____
   8. Cooperating broker's commissions $_____
   9. Franchise fee $_____
   10. Total commissions and fees (lines 6–9)

III. Advertising
   11. Newspaper classifieds $_____
   12. Institutional $_____
   13. Direct mail and brochures $_____
   14. Radio $_____
   15. Television $_____
   16. Yellow Pages $_____
   17. Other $_____
   18. Total advertising (lines 11–17) $_____

IV. Sales promotion:
   19. Courses, training and conferences $_____
   20. Travel and conventions $_____
   21. Entertainment $_____
   22. Contributions, service activities (including service clubs) $_____
   23. Sales awards, contests, testimonials $_____
   24. Institutional gifts to clients and prospects $_____
   25. Other $_____
   26. Total sales promotion (lines 19–25) $_____

V. Sales management:
   27. Sales managers salaries and/or fees $_____

VI. Salaries
   28. Managers (other than sales) $_____
   29. Clerical $_____
   30. Secretarial $_____
   31. Other staff $_____
   32. Payroll taxes $_____
   33. Employee benefits (include hospitalization, profit sharing, etc.) $_____

FIGURE 13.4   Profit and Loss Analysis of Company Operation
(Continued)

VII. Communications:
    35. Total telephone (including equipment and $_____
        calls—excluding Yellow Pages)
    36. Electronic answering service $_____
    37. Other $_____
    38. Total communications (lines 35–37) $_____
VIII. Occupancy:
    39. Rent $_____
    40. Utilities $_____
    41. Janitor services and maintenance $_____
    42. Total occupancy (lines 39–41) $_____
IX. Operating:
    43. Licenses (real estate, notary, etc.) $_____
    44. Dues (local, state and national real estate $_____
        associations, chamber of commerce, profes-
        sional societies)
    45. Insurance (liability, error and omission, $_____
        worker's compensation
    46. Legal and accounting $_____
    47. Taxes (except payroll, state and federal $_____
        income and company owned building)
    48. Equipment (depreciation, repair and/or $_____
        rental)
    49. Supplies, printing, maps, plats and photog- $_____
        raphy
    50. Postage $_____
    51. Interest on business loans (not that included $_____
        as economic rent on building)
    52. Bad debts (including losses on advances to $_____
        salespeople
    53. Auto expense $_____
    54. Other $_____
    55. Total operating (lines 43–54) $_____
    56. Total expenses (parts III–IX) $_____
X.   Summary:
    57. Total operating expenses (lines 18, 26, 27, $_____
        34, 38, 42, 55)
    58. EBIT (Subtract line 56 from line 5) $_____
    59. Interest expense $_____
    60. EBIT (Earnings Before Taxes) (Subtract line $_____
        58 from line 57)
    61. Taxes $_____
    62. Net Income (Subtract line 60 from line 59) $_____

established, accounting time can be saved through the adjusted accrual method without distorting the interim statements.

It is best to seek professional tax assistance before deciding which method to follow.

AVOIDING FRAUD

Brokerage owners must always presume that embezzlement could happen to them. Signing all checks can help prevent embezzlement, but the following steps are also recommended.

Full audits with interim unannounced reviews should be conducted by outside sources such as an independent CPA firm.

All bank statements and cancelled checks should be returned to the owner, not to the person in control of accounting and not to the person who balances out the checking account each month, Each statement, together with the cancelled checks, must be examined monthly when received by the owner and should at least appear as if they have been examined carefully. Occasional calls about checks to the person balancing the books each month helps support the fact that the owner is looking at every check. This simple procedure alone will probably do more than any other to prevent embezzlement.

Different people should handle the deposits and checks with a tie-in between deposits and checks. Checks should not be written to pay out salespeople's commissions unless there is evidence of a commission deposit having been made for the company on that transaction.

Two people should sign checks and two other people should handle bank deposits.

The ratio of commission payout to gross revenue should be watched. If there is a change in this ratio, the owners may have a problem.

Be sure check protection systems prevent digits being added without it being obvious. For example, leaving space behind the figures and wording on a check could make it easy to change $100.00 to $100,000.

BUDGETARY CONTROL

To run a business successfully, management must be able to plan, coordinate and control its business operation. A budget is a financial formula to operate within for a future period. Budgets are usually projected for each expense line item monthly for the next full year. To exercise the proper control, management must make continuous reviews and comparisons to the budget so that undesirable variances can be noted and corrective action taken.

Steps in Preparing a Budget

Budgeting can be done as an "incremental" process—using last year's budget as a base from which to start. Alternatively, budgeting may be a "zero-based" process—starting from scratch each year to validate every expense in the budget. Or it can be a combination of incremental and zero-based, which is probably the best option.

Assuming top management has decided what must be done to reach their objectives, they should now call in the various people responsible for attaining these objectives and have them work up their own budgets (with a minimum of direction from top management). Often top management can subtly influence middle or lower management to project a budget for both sales and expenses just about in line with what they want. It is important that the budget be set by the chain of command responsible for attaining that performance. People who set their own budgets are much more likely to stick to them than those who have budgets set by someone else.

The budget must be prepared with two considerations in mind:

1. It mast be broken down to areas of one person's authority, such as branch offices or departments.
2. It must be compiled to comply with the established accounting framework to accumulate and measure the data.

In order to control expenses for budgetary purposes, standard expenses must be determined. Therefore, management must not only know how much the actual expenses and revenue are at the present time, it must know through standards what they should be. Expense and revenue standards can provide these measures to gauge present performance. Generally we look to the past for these standards of performance and expense to obtain the desired future performance. Using these past revenue/expense/profit relationships, a realistic budget can be prepared to obtain a planned profit for the future.

FLEXIBLE BUDGET

Although a target budget will be kept in focus, a flexible budget is more meaningful. This budget will reflect expenses for each level of revenue produced. The flexible budget is far more realistic and usable than a fixed budget because it takes into account both fixed and variable expenses of the operation to be controlled.

Variable expenses are caused by production. No production, no expense. In a real estate operation, the following expenses are variable: commissions, fees, management overrides—all are a percentage of gross revenue.

Fixed expenses, on the other hand, are not caused by production and exist whether one unit has or has not been produced. The following expenses are relatively fixed: sales management salaries and fees, salaries,

FIGURE 13.5   Breakeven Budget Chart

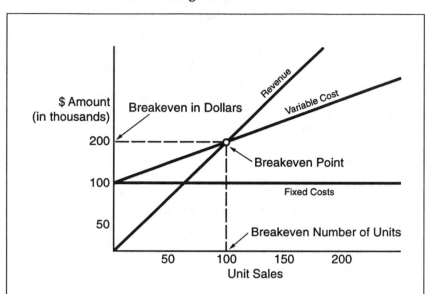

advertising, communications, occupancy and other operating expenses (property taxes, auto expense, insurance, dues, and so on.).

BREAKEVEN POINT

Knowing how much of each of these fixed and variable expenses will be incurred as a standard for the operation of each office or department, we can now measure and gauge each manager's operation. They not only can be watched to see that they meet or exceed their production quotas but they are also measured to see that they attained these quotas or positions with all costs in proper alignment. All of this data can be set up in the form of a table(s) and/or graph(s) that can also portray very conspicuously the budgeted breakeven point, the point at which revenue equals expenses, for the office or department. A simplified version of a breakeven-flexible budget chart is shown in Figure 13.5.

It must be understood that fixed costs do not always remain fixed but must at times be shown as a vertical rise, such as when your business grows to a point where another salaried person must be added. When a firm goes all out for volume and bigness at any cost, it will feel the effects of the limit of its personnel's capacity or expertise and/or the limit of the market potential. When this happens, the fixed costs such as advertising and selling expense become inefficient and skyrocket upward to the point where profit eventually diminishes rather than increases with more volume. This is the opposite result of the one hoped for.

Rules of Thumb for Breakeven

The broker should know the following by the month, quarter and year:

- Number of exclusive listings
- Number of sales and sales volume in-house (own firm selling own listings)
- Number of co-op sales and sales volume, listings and volume sold by co-op
- Average revenue per unit
- Total expenses
- Number of units produced (sale equals one unit, listing sold equals one unit)

The following example illustrates how to find out how many units per month are required to break even. Assume average revenue per unit is $455.00 and overhead per month is $10,000 (including owner's salary). Therefore $10,000 ÷ 455 = 22 units to break even.

Since there is generally a relationship between the number of exclusive listings and the number of units made the following month, assume the number of exclusive listings last quarter is 157 (a quarter gives a more reliable sample) and the number of units last quarter is 105. Since 22 units are needed to break even, the ratio, therefore, is

$$\text{Step 1:} \quad \frac{105}{157} = \frac{22}{x}$$

Step 2: $105 x = 3,454$

Step 3: $x = 33$ listings a month needed to break even

With the proper records on the number of contacts needed on average to get an exclusive listing or make a sale, calculate how many contacts per day are needed by your office to break even per month and how many contacts it would take per day on average to make your budgeted profit.

TYPES OF BUDGETS

As many budgets can be prepared as there are departments or lines of authority to fix responsibility within the framework of a firm's accounting capability. They include budgets for sales, listings, advertising, selling and administrative expense, cash, new office development and overhead. Segmented budgets only involve management people who have responsibility and control for a given area.

Chapter 14

Marketing and Statistical Controls

Marketing and statistical controls are essential tools of real estate management. Effective records tell a broker where his or her business is coming from. They are basic to setting sales and service goals and planning the budget that will undergird the operation. Salespeople can be trained, guided and coached more effectively when management has records of their individual performance. Furthermore salespeople who understand how good recordkeeping improves their effectiveness in selling and thus has a positive effect on their income are much more willing to keep necessary records.

Management needs good records as a basis for money planning. Accurate and frequent detail on how performance is meeting goals and budget standards enables management to make short-term decisions on where more money needs to be spent as well as where cutbacks will help adjust to temporary situations.

Finally, marketing and statistical records show growth patterns as they evolve, strengths and weaknesses of people or departments, and they suggest changes that should be made all along the line. This week's records become next week's guide to management action.

CONTROLS ARE NOT RESTRAINTS

When management talks to salespeople about controls, the staff often has the impression it means restraints, confinement or rigidity. In this context the word controls implies a certain loss of freedom of movement. Yet everyone is aware that controls are an essential part of the operation of a business. In the present context, controls relate to the data necessary for planning and guiding a successful real estate marketing business. Generally, sales and marketing oriented people will acknowledge that controls over financial aspects of the real estate business are essential but are reluctant to acknowledge the need for controls over its marketing aspects.

The marketing of real estate is concerned with several factors. It obviously requires listings in sufficient quantity to meet sales and income goals. Furthermore, if they are to sell, listings must be priced realistically and be in the price range of prospects the firm services. In addition, the broker must develop the ability to sell these listings in a reasonable period of time. Just as clothing retailers' inventories must be in sizes, styles and colors appropriate for the market a store serves, so must brokers maintain a listing inventory that fits their market. It is necessary to establish controls over the quantity so the company always has listings. Control of the quality of the listing inventory is also necessary.

Several of McKinsey's 7-S of Organization Analysis are taken into consideration here. What is the company's strategy for obtaining listing inventory? What systems are in place to price properties realistically? What skills do the associates exhibit as a whole to obtain quantity and quality of listings? What shared values exist as to what in fact is considered a quality listing? Structure and style in the control of the inventory also may be considered.

Another factor essential to marketing real estate is inquiries or buyers or customer traffic. Does the firm have enough to enable it to achieve its sales and financial goals? Brokers cannot leave to chance the fact that they will eventually have enough interested or qualified buyers.

Like the financial systems discussed in the last chapter, marketing and statistical controls are key systems that support the company's business strategies. By keeping close track of sales, inventory and other statistics, management can determine whether its marketing strategies are working. Marketing systems that track advertising results can help the company determine where advertising dollars will be most effectively spent.

Controls can be provided over the marketing aspects of the real estate business without confining the salesperson and sales manager. Furthermore, proper controls should help them carry out their responsibilities and achieve their goals.

LISTING SOURCES AND CONTROLS

Since all listings start by obtaining a listing lead or information on somebody thinking of selling, brokers should keep accurate records of their listing leads. With this knowledge, listing leads and potential listings can be expanded.

If the information has not been obtained in the initial interview, a staff person can phone the seller a short time after the listing has been taken.

FIGURE 14.1 Listing Worksheet

Listing office	Date		Renewal	Code
By				

Owner's name	Town
Owner's address	Phone
Occupied Tenant's name	Phone
Title Taxes	Legal
Special assessments	Incorporated
Living rm.	Fireplaces
Dining rm. Den	Porches
Kitchen	
Breakfast rm. Family rm.	
Bedrooms ( )	
Baths ( )	Powder rm.
Basement Crawl Slab	Recreation rm.
Utility rm.	Inclusion, remarks, interior finish:
Heat Cost	T
Wtr. htr.	B
Storms - screens	S
Sq. ft. liv. area	GS
Builder	HS
Motive	PAR
Possession Key:	Mtg. info. Price
Age Lot Style	Garage
Rooms Brs. Baths Construction	Owner's name & property address:

Sample ad

Check list

___Taxes	___Listing complete
___Square feet	___Sign put up
___Inclusions	___Referral service
___Special assessment	___Discussed and arranged
___Distance to facilities	___Picture taken
___Comments	___Brochure left
___Triggering features	___Market value appraisal made and presented

During the same interview, the caller can determine if the seller is pleased with the firm's service to date and solicit suggestions as to how the service might be improved.

Listing Worksheet

Watching some real estate salespeople gather information on a listing makes one wonder if they think they are following in the steps of Abraham Lincoln, jotting all the information on the back of an envelope as Lincoln reportedly did when writing his Gettysburg Address. There is general agreement that a listing must be complete (data on room sizes, taxes, utilities, location, lot size and seller's telephone number) and accurate if it is to serve as a base for a selling package, enabling salespeople to show the property effectively. To most cooperating salespeople, the listing sheet will be their first exposure to a new listing. It therefore behooves the listing salesperson to provide complete and reliable data. This is best accomplished by using a form that includes every item that needs to be recorded. See Figures 14.1 and 14.2. The office secretary or whoever processes the listing can be instructed not to process it until all blanks are filled in and every item in the checklist is complete. If the listing worksheet is incomplete, the secretary can advise the manager who then carries out whatever follow-up is necessary with the listing salesperson. With computer technology and rules and regulations of MLS Systems, this task is made easier.

Comparative/Competitive Market Analysis

Any time the subject of listing properties is discussed, the importance of obtaining them at the proper price is emphasized. A responsible broker will recommend a listing price that is likely to assure a sale in a reasonable amount of time and bring the seller the highest price the market will bear.

Using a competitive market analysis (CMA) or similar system, the salesperson establishes the listing price for discussion with the seller. This gives the office a listing price based on comparables and enhances the firm's professional image. See Figure 14.3.

In many firms, before a presentation is made to the seller, the salesperson submits the competitive market analysis to his or her manager for approval. In this way management is sure that all listings taken will be priced at such a level that they will sell readily. Thus tomorrow's potential problems of overpriced listings can be avoided by providing controls today.

The very same competitive market analysis form can be used to show the seller not only the price the salesperson recommends but both why and how he or she arrived at the figure. Many software programs are available that will calculate the CMA easily and efficiently adding accuracy and speed for the agent.

FIGURE 14.2   Listing Work Sheet To Be Entered into MLS Computer System

Residential Data Form

Indicate type of Property (R,C,W,N,F or H): ☐ **REQUIRED**

R=Residential   C=Condominium   W=Waterfront
N=New Construction   F=Farm (over 5 acres)
    H=Hobby Farm (5 or less acres)

DIRECTIONS: *Requireds are marked by an R*
    # = Numeric only answer
    * = Code set answer

BOARD USE ONLY:

MLS #   ☐☐☐☐☐☐☐ (1)

Received: _____

Entered: _____
_____
_____

SECTION I

R Firm/Off ID #: ☐☐☐☐ – ☐☐   **R** Agent ID #: ☐☐☐☐☐

R LIST PRICE ☐☐☐☐☐☐☐ # (2)

R LIST DATE ☐☐/☐☐/☐☐ # (3)

R EXPIRATION DATE ☐☐/☐☐/☐☐ # (4)

R COMM SUB/AG BKR ☐☐☐☐☐ (5)

R COMM BUYER BKR ☐☐☐☐☐ (6)

R VAR. RATE COMM. ☐ (Y/N) (7)

R NAMED EXCEPTIONS ☐ (Y/N) (8)

R LICENSEE INTEREST ☐ (Y/N) (9)

R AREA ☐☐☐☐ (*) (11)

R SCHOOL DISTRICT LEA # ☐☐☐ (*) (12)

STREET NUMBER ☐☐☐☐☐☐☐ (13)

R STREET NAME ☐ (DIRECTION) (14)
☐☐☐☐
☐☐☐☐

R MUNICIPALITY ☐☐☐☐ (*) (15)

R COUNTY ☐☐☐☐ (*) (16)

SECTION II

R TAX KEY NO. ☐☐☐☐☐☐☐☐☐☐☐☐☐☐ (17)

ELEM./MIDDLE/HIGH ☐☐☐☐ ☐☐☐ ☐☐☐ (*) (18)

ZONING - (SPELL OUT) ☐☐☐☐☐☐☐☐ (19)

AD CODE ☐☐☐☐ (20)

R # OF BEDROOMS ☐☐ #. (22)

R # OF FULL BATHS ☐☐ # (23)

R # OF HALF BATHS ☐☐ # (24)

R APPX. TFA SQ FT ☐☐☐☐☐ # (26)

UPPER LVL SQ FT ☐☐☐☐☐ # (27)

MAIN LVL SQ FT ☐☐☐☐☐ # (28)

LOWER LVL SQ FT ☐☐☐☐☐ # (29)

BASEMENT SQ FT ☐☐☐☐☐ # (30)

R APPX. ACREAGE ☐☐☐☐☐☐☐ # (31)

NOTE: Required appx. acreage or lot size - See Lot
    Size in Section 3

SECTION III

NOTE: ACREAGE OR LOT SIZE REQUIRED.

R LOT SIZE OR FRONTAGE & SQ FT ☐☐☐☐☐☐☐☐☐☐ (32)

R STYLE ☐☐☐☐ (*) (33)

ASSOCIATION FEE ☐☐☐☐☐ # (35)

R TAXES ☐☐☐☐☐☐ (36)

R TAX YEAR ☐☐ (37)

R WARRANTY ☐ (Y/N) (39)

R BATH OFF M-BED ☐ (Y/N) (40)

SPECIAL ASSESS. ☐ (Y/N) (41)

FLOOD PLAIN YEAR
(100 or 500 Year)
☐ N = NO (42)

R FRML DINING RM ☐ (Y/N)

R 1ST FLR LAUNDRY ☐ (Y/N)

R FIREPLACE ☐ (Y/N)

R CENTRAL AIR ☐ (Y/N)

GARAGE EXTERIOR ☐☐☐ (*) (44)

GARAGE- # CARS ☐☐ # (45)

GARAGE DIM ☐☐X☐☐ (WxD) (46)

R GARAGE ATT/DET (A/D) or N= None (47)

SECTION IV

DIRECTIONS: Required if there is a room. Please round all dimensions to
the nearest lowest foot

LEVELS: B = Basement, L = Lower, M = Main, U = Upper
BATHS: Full = Full Bath, Half = Half Bath

	LENGTH – WIDTH APPRX. DIM	LEVEL
BEDROOM 1	☐X☐	☐ (51)
BEDROOM 2	☐X☐	☐ (52)
BEDROOM 3	☐X☐	☐ (53)
BEDROOM 4	☐X☐	☐ (54)
BEDROOM 5	☐X☐	☐ (55)
BATHROOM 1	☐	☐ (56)
BATHROOM 2	☐	☐ (57)
BATHROOM 3	☐	☐ (58)
BATHROOM 4	☐	☐ (59)
LIVING ROOM	☐X☐	☐
DINING ROOM-FML	☐X☐	☐
KITCHEN/DINETTE	☐X☐	☐
FAMILY ROOM	☐X☐	☐
UTILITY ROOM	☐X☐	☐
OTHER ROOM	☐X☐	☐

R NAME/PHONE ☐☐☐☐☐☐☐☐☐☐☐☐☐☐☐☐☐☐ ☐☐☐–☐☐☐ (61)

SECTION: V

R DIRECTIONS ☐☐☐☐☐☐☐☐☐☐☐☐☐☐☐☐☐☐☐☐☐
☐☐☐☐☐☐☐☐☐☐☐☐☐☐☐☐☐☐☐☐☐ (62)

REVISED   7/95

(over)

FIGURE 14.2   Listing Work Sheet To Be Entered into MLS Computer System *(Continued)*

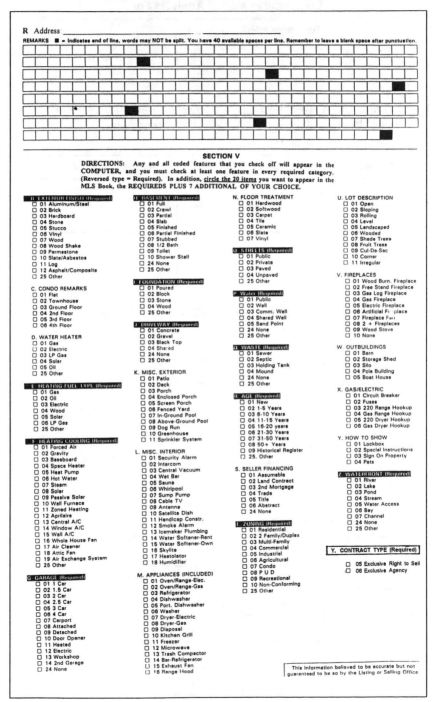

R Address

REMARKS ■ = Indicates end of line, words may NOT be split. You have 40 available spaces per line. Remember to leave a blank space after punctuation.

SECTION V

DIRECTIONS: Any and all coded features that you check off will appear in the COMPUTER, and you must check at least one feature in every required category. (Reversed type = Required). In addition, circle the 20 items you want to appear in the MLS Book, the REQUIRES PLUS 7 ADDITIONAL OF YOUR CHOICE.

B. EXTERIOR FINISH (Required)
- ☐ 01 Aluminum/Steel
- ☐ 02 Brick
- ☐ 03 Hardboard
- ☐ 04 Stone
- ☐ 05 Stucco
- ☐ 06 Vinyl
- ☐ 07 Wood
- ☐ 08 Wood Shake
- ☐ 09 Permastone
- ☐ 10 Slate/Asbestos
- ☐ 11 Log
- ☐ 12 Asphalt/Composite
- ☐ 25 Other

C. CONDO REMARKS
- ☐ 01 Flat
- ☐ 02 Townhouse
- ☐ 03 Ground Floor
- ☐ 04 2nd Floor
- ☐ 05 3rd Floor
- ☐ 06 4th Floor

D. WATER HEATER
- ☐ 01 Gas
- ☐ 02 Electric
- ☐ 03 LP Gas
- ☐ 04 Solar
- ☐ 05 Oil
- ☐ 25 Other

E. HEATING FUEL TYPE (Required)
- ☐ 01 Gas
- ☐ 02 Oil
- ☐ 03 Electric
- ☐ 04 Wood
- ☐ 05 Solar
- ☐ 06 LP Gas
- ☐ 25 Other

F. HEATING COOLING (Required)
- ☐ 01 Forced Air
- ☐ 02 Gravity
- ☐ 03 Baseboard
- ☐ 04 Space Heater
- ☐ 05 Heat Pump
- ☐ 06 Hot Water
- ☐ 07 Steam
- ☐ 08 Solar
- ☐ 09 Passive Solar
- ☐ 10 Wall Furnace
- ☐ 11 Zoned Heating
- ☐ 12 Aprilaire
- ☐ 13 Central A/C
- ☐ 14 Window A/C
- ☐ 15 Wall A/C
- ☐ 16 Whole House Fan
- ☐ 17 Air Cleaner
- ☐ 18 Attic Fan
- ☐ 19 Air Exchange System
- ☐ 25 Other

G. GARAGE (Required)
- ☐ 01 1 Car
- ☐ 02 1.5 Car
- ☐ 03 2 Car
- ☐ 04 2.5 Car
- ☐ 05 3 Car
- ☐ 06 4 Car
- ☐ 07 Carport
- ☐ 08 Attached
- ☐ 09 Detached
- ☐ 10 Door Opener
- ☐ 11 Heated
- ☐ 12 Electric
- ☐ 13 Workshop
- ☐ 14 2nd Garage
- ☐ 24 None

H. BASEMENT (Required)
- ☐ 01 Full
- ☐ 02 Crawl
- ☐ 03 Partial
- ☐ 04 Slab
- ☐ 05 Finished
- ☐ 06 Partial Finished
- ☐ 07 Stubbed
- ☐ 08 1/2 Bath
- ☐ 09 Toilet
- ☐ 10 Shower Stall
- ☐ 24 None
- ☐ 25 Other

I. FOUNDATION (Required)
- ☐ 01 Poured
- ☐ 02 Block
- ☐ 03 Stone
- ☐ 04 Wood
- ☐ 25 Other

J. DRIVEWAY (Required)
- ☐ 01 Concrete
- ☐ 02 Gravel
- ☐ 03 Black Top
- ☐ 04 Shared
- ☐ 24 None
- ☐ 25 Other

K. MISC. EXTERIOR
- ☐ 01 Patio
- ☐ 02 Deck
- ☐ 03 Porch
- ☐ 04 Enclosed Porch
- ☐ 05 Screen Porch
- ☐ 06 Fenced Yard
- ☐ 07 In-Ground Pool
- ☐ 08 Above-Ground Pool
- ☐ 09 Dog Run
- ☐ 10 Greenhouse
- ☐ 11 Sprinkler System

L. MISC. INTERIOR
- ☐ 01 Security Alarm
- ☐ 02 Intercom
- ☐ 03 Central Vacuum
- ☐ 04 Wet Bar
- ☐ 05 Sauna
- ☐ 06 Whirlpool
- ☐ 07 Sump Pump
- ☐ 08 Cable TV
- ☐ 09 Antenna
- ☐ 10 Satellite Dish
- ☐ 11 Handicap Constr.
- ☐ 12 Smoke Alarm
- ☐ 13 Icemaker Plumbing
- ☐ 14 Water Softener-Rent
- ☐ 15 Water Softener-Own
- ☐ 16 Skylite
- ☐ 17 Heatolator
- ☐ 18 Humidifier

M. APPLIANCES (INCLUDED)
- ☐ 01 Oven/Range-Elec.
- ☐ 02 Oven/Range-Gas
- ☐ 03 Refrigerator
- ☐ 04 Dishwasher
- ☐ 05 Port. Dishwasher
- ☐ 06 Washer
- ☐ 07 Dryer-Electric
- ☐ 08 Dryer-Gas
- ☐ 09 Disposal
- ☐ 10 Kitchen Grill
- ☐ 11 Freezer
- ☐ 12 Microwave
- ☐ 13 Trash Compactor
- ☐ 14 Bar-Refrigerator
- ☐ 15 Exhaust Fan
- ☐ 16 Range Hood

N. FLOOR TREATMENT
- ☐ 01 Hardwood
- ☐ 02 Softwood
- ☐ 03 Carpet
- ☐ 04 Tile
- ☐ 05 Ceramic
- ☐ 06 Slate
- ☐ 07 Vinyl

O. STREETS (Required)
- ☐ 01 Public
- ☐ 02 Private
- ☐ 03 Paved
- ☐ 04 Unpaved
- ☐ 25 Other

P. Water (Required)
- ☐ 01 Public
- ☐ 02 Well
- ☐ 03 Comm. Well
- ☐ 04 Shared Well
- ☐ 05 Sand Point
- ☐ 24 None
- ☐ 25 Other

Q. WASTE (Required)
- ☐ 01 Sewer
- ☐ 02 Septic
- ☐ 03 Holding Tank
- ☐ 04 Mound
- ☐ 24 None
- ☐ 25 Other

R. AGE (Required)
- ☐ 01 New
- ☐ 02 1-5 Years
- ☐ 03 6-10 Years
- ☐ 04 11-15 Years
- ☐ 05 16-20 years
- ☐ 06 21-30 Years
- ☐ 07 31-50 Years
- ☐ 08 50+ Years
- ☐ 09 Historical Register
- ☐ 25. Other

S. SELLER FINANCING
- ☐ 01 Assumable
- ☐ 02 Land Contract
- ☐ 03 2nd Mortgage
- ☐ 04 Trade
- ☐ 05 Title
- ☐ 06 Abstract
- ☐ 24 None

T. ZONING (Required)
- ☐ 01 Residential
- ☐ 02 2 Family/Duplex
- ☐ 03 Multi-Family
- ☐ 04 Commercial
- ☐ 05 Industrial
- ☐ 06 Agricultural
- ☐ 07 Condo
- ☐ 08 P U D
- ☐ 09 Recreational
- ☐ 10 Non-Conforming
- ☐ 25 Other

U. LOT DESCRIPTION
- ☐ 01 Open
- ☐ 02 Sloping
- ☐ 03 Rolling
- ☐ 04 Level
- ☐ 05 Landscaped
- ☐ 06 Wooded
- ☐ 07 Shade Trees
- ☐ 08 Fruit Trees
- ☐ 09 Cul-De-Sac
- ☐ 10 Corner
- ☐ 11 Irregular

V. FIREPLACES
- ☐ 01 Wood Burn. Fireplace
- ☐ 02 Free Stand Fireplace
- ☐ 03 Gas Log Fireplace
- ☐ 04 Gas Fireplace
- ☐ 05 Electric Fireplace
- ☐ 06 Artificial Fireplace
- ☐ 07 Fireplace Fan
- ☐ 08 2 + Fireplaces
- ☐ 09 Wood Stove
- ☐ 10 None

W. OUTBUILDINGS
- ☐ 01 Barn
- ☐ 02 Storage Shed
- ☐ 03 Silo
- ☐ 04 Pole Building
- ☐ 05 Boat House

X. GAS/ELECTRIC
- ☐ 01 Circuit Breaker
- ☐ 02 Fuses
- ☐ 03 220 Range Hookup
- ☐ 04 Gas Range Hookup
- ☐ 05 220 Dryer Hookup
- ☐ 06 Gas Dryer Hookup

Y. HOW TO SHOW
- ☐ 01 Lockbox
- ☐ 02 Special Instructions
- ☐ 03 Sign On Property
- ☐ 04 Pets

Z. WATERFRONT (Required)
- ☐ 01 River
- ☐ 02 Lake
- ☐ 03 Pond
- ☐ 04 Stream
- ☐ 05 Water Access
- ☐ 06 Bay
- ☐ 07 Channel
- ☐ 24 None
- ☐ 25 Other

Y. CONTRACT TYPE (Required)
- ☐ 05 Exclusive Right to Sell
- ☐ 06 Exclusive Agency

This information believed to be accurate but not guaranteed to be so by the Listing or Selling Office

FIGURE 14.3 **Comparative Market Analysis Form**

Comparative Market Analysis For				
Address	**Recommended Price**	**Bedrooms**	**Lot Size**	**Extras**

1. SIMILAR HOMES RECENTLY SOLD. These tell us what people are willing to pay . . . for this kind of home . . . in this area . . . at this time.

Address	**Price**	**Bedrooms**	**Lot Size**	**Extras**
1.				
2.				
3.				
4.				

2. SIMILAR HOMES FOR SALE NOW. These tell us what we are competing against. Buyers will compare your home against these homes.

Address	**Price**	**Bedrooms**	**Lot Size**	**Extras**
1.				
2.				
3.				
4.				

3. EXPIRED LISTINGS—SIMILAR HOMES UNSOLD FOR 90 DAYS OR MORE. These illustrate the problems of overpricing.

Address	**Price**	**Bedrooms**	**Lot Size**	**Extras**
1.				
2.				
3.				
4.				

Listing Activity Control

When making the presentation, the salesperson describes the sales activities the firm will provide the seller so the property will be sold for the highest price in the shortest time, with minimum effort, inconvenience and worry to the seller.

All too often, however, salespeople tend to act as if their goal has been achieved when they get the listing. They do not follow through with the same perseverance they mustered to obtain the listing to see that the seller does, in fact, receive the three benefits mentioned.

Activity controls or progress controls should be maintained to enable the salesperson and the firm to be aware of the activity on the listing. Such controls, used effectively, remind the sales department to expand or alter marketing activities as required. Again, computer technology can be used to enhance the efficiency of this operation.

Figure 14.4 is a listing progress control form that can be kept by either the salesperson or the office secretary. In most cases it is best kept by the salesperson or the salesperson's personal assistant on computer records.

The form provides a record of facts for future reference. This form first provides for the recording of data that will be essential when offers are obtained and presented. The salesperson will have a record of his or her recommended listing price as well as the estimated sale price so that these can be shown to the seller if an offer other than full price, terms, and so on is presented. Furthermore, at the time the listing is taken, the salesperson determines the precise dates he or she will counsel with the seller as to activity data, customer reaction, progress toward a sale and what changes and/or adjustment, if any, need to be made. Unless this is done, the salesperson often procrastinates about contacting the seller until the listing is close to expiration. This causes a bad relationship between seller and salesperson. Here, if the seller insists the property be listed slightly above the recommended price, the salesperson might then inform the seller that if the property remains unsold for, say, 30 days, the salesperson will request a price adjustment. The date for the adjustment being recorded, the salesperson has committed himself or herself and the seller to bring the price in line.

An advertising record is provided as part of this system. The person responsible for placing advertising can reflect on what advertising has been done and determine whether further ads will be run and in what paper.

Estimated showings per week provides the salesperson data to determine whether or not the home has been shown enough to expose it to the market. Estimated number of showings is figured by querying both fellow salespeople and cooperating brokers. If keys are kept in the office, a key book can be checked to see how often the key has been taken out. Or the salesperson may choose to ask the seller how many cards have been left by salespeople or ask the seller to keep a record of how many times the property

FIGURE 14.4   Exclusive Action Progress Control

Salesperson: _____

Seller: _____Address: _____

Date Taken: _____Expiration Date: _____List Price: _____

Salesperson's Recommended List Price: _____

Caravan/Office Tour Fig. Est. Value:_____

Salesperson's Estimated Sale Price: _____

Target Date for Price Reduction: _____

Advertising Record

Paper A	B	C	D	E			

Estimated Showings Per Week

Week 1	2	3	4	5	6	7	8
9	10	11	12	13	14	15	16

Salesperson's Contact Record

Date	Remarks	Date of Next Contact

is shown. Records can also be kept on computer using one of several desk manager software programs.

Some brokers provide the seller a record sheet for jotting down the name of each salesperson and firm that shows the property. The listing salesperson collects this data periodically and contacts the showing sales-people to obtain feedback providing the prospective purchasers' opinion of the property.

Real estate salespeople are often reluctant to discuss the number of showings with the seller. It almost seems they think if they don't discuss the subject, the seller will not be aware of a lack of showings. On the contrary, a salesperson has the responsibility of knowing whether the property is being shown frequently enough to result in a sale; and if it is not, to determine why. The cause can only be corrected if it is brought to the surface.

Listing Effectiveness

By studying the deviation between listing price and selling price and comparing it to the local market, brokers can measure their efficiency. For example, a broker might note that his or her sales prices for the past year were 10 percent below listing price. The broker can compare this to the record of other brokers. Such records are obtainable through the Multiple Listing Service or by simple observation. If the competition seems to sell homes at 5 to 7 percent below the listing price, the broker should review his methods of estimating value. Such a high deviation between the listing and sale price means a too-high listing price is probably increasing the length of time required to sell a property.

On the other hand, the broker might find his or her listings are selling at 1 to 2 percent below listing price while typically, in the market, homes sell at 5 to 7 percent lower. This might indicate the broker is being too conservative in estimating value. Possibly the broker is losing some listings because his or her estimates of value have been below other brokers' recommendations and less than what the seller realistically expected to receive.

Similarly, the length of time a broker's listings remain on the market should be compared to how long the properties listed with others take to sell. If the homes a broker lists remain unsold for 15 days on average, while homes in the market are generally unsold for 45 days, this can provide an excellent sales tool when the broker makes presentations to sellers. Con-versely, the broker might find the average length of time his or her homes are on the market exceeds that of competitors. In this case, steps must be taken to change the broker's marketing and sales techniques.

The percentage of listings that expire is also a measure of the effec-tiveness or ineffectiveness of the marketing activities. Since percentages of expirations vary with the strength or weakness of the market from one part of the country to another, the broker can compare his or her percentage of listings that expire with other brokers' as well as with his or her own expirations from year to year.

CUSTOMER CONTROLS: SUPPLY AND DEMAND

As the level of demand (prospects or inquiries) for real estate fluctuates, brokers must change their prospecting practices. Similarly, as the level of supply (sellers) increases or decreases, brokers must alter their activities in securing and servicing listings. Thus far in this chapter we have discussed methods of staying on top of listing sources and marketing practices regarding sellers. Let us now look at the other half of the supply-demand relationship, the buyers, also referred to as inquiries.

The listing controls mentioned have caused no additional work or burden on the salesperson. In fact they were designed to make life easier. They require no additional recordkeeping but provide the salesperson with easy-to-use forms for data he or she is already collecting, probably in a haphazard fashion. Now the salesperson is able to keep the same data in a time saving fashion. The same can be true of customer or inquiry control.

Figure 14.5 is an inquiry form which becomes the salesperson's permanent record for each prospect. Each salesperson is supplied with a pad of no-carbon-required forms in two colors. The prepunched original becomes his or her permanent record, kept in a three-ring binder. The colored copy is given to the office secretary and weekly tabulations are made as shown in Figure 14.6. Alternatively, a variety of computer programs can be used keep these records more efficiently and accurately.

The information on the inquiry form has numerous uses. It enables the salesperson to record names, addresses and telephone numbers of prospects during the first contact. The salesperson is not encouraged to obtain total information on the inquiry sheet at the time the call comes in. The first objective in receiving a call is to make an appointment, not to qualify on the telephone. The salesperson will continue using the inquiry form when face to face with a prospect. Several good customer/client-based software programs are available where the salesperson enters information on the customer during their initial telephone conversation.

If the need for coaching a salesperson arises because of poor production, the sales manager asks the individual to bring his or her inquiry book or computer program so the manager can review the progress on each inquiry in an organized way.

The inquiry data as shown in the weekly summary also measures the effectiveness of each advertising medium and the price range of the inquiries the office is obtaining. Are they higher or lower than is typical in the marketplace and has this been by design or by accident?

FIGURE 14.5   Customer Data Sheet

Salesperson's Name

Date_____Name_____

Address_____Phone_____

City_____Zip_____

Company_____

Position_____Transportation_____

Address_____Phone_____

City_____Zip_____

Source:
Advertising:_____

Sign   Referral   Walk-in   Rent   Open house   Letter

Property_____Price_____

Has Worked With_____

Requirements

Style_____Const_____When Needed_____

Bsmt_____Gar_____FmRm_____Frpl_____Bdrms_____

Baths_____Family Size_____Boys_____Girls_____

Lot Size_____School_____Church_____

Choice of Towns_____

Present Housing Situation_____

_____Price Range_____

Income_____Down Pay_____Pres. Mtg._____

Other_____

_____

_____

_____

FIGURE 14.6 Customer Response Worksheet

Sources

A study of homebuyers indicates that all buyers fall into three categories from the standpoint of their place of origin: The upgraders are people already living in the community and possibly looking for a larger or smaller place. Maybe it is a new family formation, a young couple just getting married or a couple tired of renting and looking for a home of their own.

The second category is the metropolitan movement. This is a family moving from one section where, unlike the upgrader, the prospect is not familiar with neighborhoods or prices and therefore has different buying habits demanding different servicing.

Generally upgraders are rather specific on the neighborhood in which they want to live. But metropolitan movement prospects can be shown numerous other neighborhoods since they will be more open. Look for local studies that report on how long these two types are in the market before they buy.

The third buyer is the transferee. This prospect is moving from one geographical area to a totally different one. Transferees are generally in the market for a shorter time. Some studies indicate they will make a decision on the fourth day of their house-hunting trip.

Brokers may elect to cater to any one or more segments of the market. By observing the characteristics of customer inquiries, they can determine how effectively their advertising and promotional program is reaching the segments of the market they have chosen.

Another benefit of reviewing characteristics of inquiries is that it enables brokers to establish sales training programs, sales contests and sales management techniques tailored to their market.

As levels of customer inquiries or traffic change, salespeople must sharpen their ability to execute the steps of the sales and listing process.

As an example, when customer traffic is at a high level, there is no reason for salespeople to work on inquiries. Canvassing will not be needed when traffic is high enough to supply a constant stream of people with whom to work. On the other hand, during this period, possibly the salespeople should be more concerned with their ability to qualify, making sure they are showing or working with the right people.

By studying levels of customer traffic, the sales manager can plan a better sales program on listings, since increased customer traffic or demand will eventually mean pressure on available merchandise or supply. Management can forecast when tight listing markets will evolve and then place greater emphasis on training in the listing process.

CUSTOMER PROFILE

Equally as important as understanding the characteristics and buying habits of the inquiries is understanding the profile of the people who eventually buy from the firm. Customer profiles can be maintained in several ways. The two most popular involve the salesperson completing a brief customer profile report. For firms that prefer the sales staff not to be involved in reports, profiles can be developed by telephone or mail surveys conducted by office staff directly with the buyer.

Figure 14.7 shows data typical in a customer profile. By comparing customer profile data with inquiry data, you can see the real effectiveness of advertising media. In one study, while all newspapers accounted for 33 percent of the total traffic, they accounted for 19 percent of the total sales. Referrals accounted for only 14 percent of the total traffic and they resulted in 52 percent of total sales. One out of every two and one-half referrals were sold in this study, while only one out of fourteen advertising prospects were sold.

Such a study gives direction for budgeting expenditures in newspaper advertising. It also influences the money a firm will spend on public relations programs that encourage referrals.

The time lapse between the date of first contact and the eventual date of the sale enables management to plan sales programs. As an example, as Figure 14.7 shows, sales follow inquiries in this study by about four weeks. Therefore, when inquiries drop, the sales manager can anticipate that sales will tend to drop if everything remains equal.

The manager, therefore, can institute certain changes to respond to a drop in inquiries, such as greater concentration on converting each inquiry into an appointment, programs of improved advertising and improved referral programs. On the other hand, when inquiries rise, the manager can anticipate sales reacting accordingly. Therefore, adjustments (as indicated earlier) such as a step up in listing performance are called for and advertising can be cut back.

Also if this study indicates the broker is working primarily with upgraders and metropolitan movement prospects, he or she is obviously doing a mediocre job of follow-up. In other words, because upgrader and metropolitan movement prospects shop for nine to eleven months, sales-people tend to lose contact with the prospects after 30 days. One way to increase sales would be to improve follow-up rather than promote additional inquiries.

Customer profile data regarding the average age of the buyer can influence selection practices, office decor and themes of advertising.

SALES AND LISTING REPORTS

In previous chapters we touched on goal setting. Goals generally focus on incomes. The goal setting method may involve the breaking down of incomes into income from sales and income from listings, the number of appointments required in order to obtain the projected sales and listings as well as the leads or inquiries required in order to achieve a needed number of appointments. The use of sales reports is essential to visually illustrate

FIGURE 14.7   Customer Profile

Salesperson_____

Buyer's name_____

Address of property_____

Town_____

Source:	Paper A	Paper D	Walk in
	Paper B	Sign	Open House
	Paper C	Referral	Brochure Ad

Date of first contact_____

Date of sale_____

Buyer's motive_____

First home purchase?   Yes___   No___

How many homes owned previously?_____

Buyer's previous town, state_____Buyer's age_____

Family size (Include all adults and children) planning to occupy house_____

What did customer ask for?

Price	Style	No. Bedrms.	Town	Other

What did customer buy?

Price	Style	No. Bedrms.	Town	Other

how effective individual salespeople and the sales team are in achieving sales and listing goals.

Sales reports might arrange salespeople not only in order of dollar volume produced but also in order of number of units sold. The latter method recognizes that the effort to sell a $90,000 piece of property is often the same, in fact often greater, than the effort to sell a $200,000 parcel.

Therefore, in the latter method, the salesperson who has sold the greatest number of properties receives the greatest recognition. Separate recognition might also be given for top selling salespeople and listing salespeople.

The frequency with which sales reports are published varies greatly. Some progressive companies use a form of daily reporting as a pacing device to illustrate the constant strength of the market. Computers and fax machines are two means of informing salespeople at all times that there is fast action in the marketplace.

It is equally important for management and staff to know how the company as a whole is doing in relation to its goals, its performance last year and its competitors. Too often a firm will take great pride in its own sales records or disappointment in its performance without comparing its record to that of its competitors. For example, the broker might be pleased with a 15 percent increase in sales when a review of the activity in his or her market (obtainable through the Multiple Listing Service or local government records) might show that sales in the market had risen 25 percent. This would obviously indicate that potentials had not been achieved. Similarly, in a down market the broker might be concerned at having an increase of only 5 percent in sales; but when compared to the market's decrease of 25 percent due to tight money conditions, this 5 percent increase might be more palatable from the standpoint of protecting the firm's position in the market.

Figure 14.8, Competitive Activity Report, shows data that might be accumulated by a staff person and reviewed either monthly or semimonthly or even several times a week. Computer technology can be used to accumulate this data automatically using MLS records.

RECORDKEEPING

In establishing marketing and statistical controls, management should be sure that a great deal of recordkeeping is not required on the part of salespeople. If the suggestions made here are carried out, the salespeople only keep data they need to service their buyers and sellers.

When you ask people to provide data for marketing and statistical controls, such as inquiry sources, it is easier to get their cooperation if they understand that it will benefit them. When they know controls can increase their income, they will do their part in making them work.

FIGURE 14.8   Competitive Activity Report

Office _____   Month Ending _____

	Office Sales Salesperson-Price	All Company Sales In M.L.S. Area Salesperson-Price	Competition Sales Company & No. Sold	Office X's Salesperson-Price	All New Company X's In M.L.S. Area Salesperson-Price	New Competition X's Company & No. Listed
Total for mo.						
Total yr. to date						
Total for same mo. last year						
% increase this mo. to corresponding last yr.						

For example, comparing records of the company's listings with what is currently selling best in the market can help salespeople direct their energies to the most productive areas. If the records show that the company is listing moderately priced properties but higher priced properties are what is selling, the salespeople could begin prospecting for higher priced inventory. Similarly, if the company has 15 listings around a lake but no lakeside property has sold in nine months, the sales associates should instead begin prospecting in areas where properties are selling.

The accumulation and coordination of the data can be handled by staff people in relatively little time, especially if the company has a computer system.

ADVERTISING

Many companies have prospered and expanded with good marketing and advertising methods; while many more have gone out of business because of overspending on improper advertising. Similarly, thousands of real estate firms fail to grow because they do not realize what good advertising and promotion can do for them and how important it is to get the right message to the right public.

Brokers can no longer put up a sign, advertise in the local paper and feel content that they are doing a good job of advertising. They need to expose their listings and services to every possible buyer and seller.

The speed with which all businesses have changed in the last quarter century is mind boggling. Change promises to be even more accelerated in the years ahead. Brokers who fail to realize this will be in for an ever-decreasing share of their market. The question today is not can we afford to advertise? It is can we afford not to?

How does a firm begin to develop an advertising program? The best way is to first understand what advertising is and does; have a clear picture of the firm's advertising objectives and the image it wants to convey to the public; and finally, make a thorough analysis of the marketplace and the people it needs to reach.

Once these facets are mastered, management sets the ad budget, studies the media available and decides which it will use. Implementing the program is the next step. It is a continuous task, requiring people with special talents to perform a variety of jobs. Just as important as the implementation of an advertising program is the follow-up, measuring the effectiveness of the media chosen and being prepared to make quickly whatever changes media response or market changes dictate.

Understand Advertising

All advertising falls into two categories: merchandise, or product, and institutional.

Merchandise advertising is aimed at stimulating immediate action for the goods or services the firm wants to market. These ads are written to tell the public about specific properties or developments and are aimed at persuading people to call the broker and get full information. Merchandise advertising is aimed at making the phone ring immediately.

Institutional ads focus on creating a favorable image of or attitude toward a broker's goods or services. Ads of this type focus on long-term results. Unlike merchandise ads, they do not generate immediate action. They aim to keep the firm's name before the public, hoping that when a broker's services are needed at some future date people who have seen the ads will contact the firm.

Understanding the Firm's Image

Know what the people in your marketplace think of your firm. Do they really know you? Have they used your firm? Do they avoid doing business with brokerage firms? Do they rely on real estate services?

The public is seldom interested in the real estate business and the services brokers provide. They have to be told. A broker's marketing program should educate people about the things you can do better for them than they can do for themselves.

Search out data, chart it and learn to sense trends as they begin to develop. Surveys made by banks, title companies, industry and schools of business administration are often available for the asking. The first three sources are as interested in a strong local economy as any broker is. Cooperative effort along these lines strengthens the relationship between these groups.

Advertising Budget

Advertising expenditures in the average brokerage run approximately 6 percent of gross commission income. For current national averages contact the Economics and Resources Division of the National Association of REALTORS®. Budgeting a higher or lower percentage may be dictated by circumstance. The important thing is to establish a dollar figure. It will be needed before any media choices can be made.

ADVERTISING MEDIA

A practical guidebook, *The Manager's Guide to Real Estate Marketing,* by Hal Kahn, CRB, CRS and published by the Real Estate Brokerage Managers Council™, is a valuable source of information on all advertising and promotion media. Kahn's book contains information on methods of research, the development of the marketing plan and some good examples.

This book cannot cover the subject in detail as Kahn's does but will list the media available and what each can do to serve brokers' needs.

Signs

Dollar for dollar, For Sale and Sold signs give brokers the best return on their advertising expenditure. Signs not only generate calls on properties for sale; they also help get new listings. Many firms fall to recognize the value of Sold signs. Potential sellers have a way of mentally transferring a Sold sign from another house to their own.

Make sure the company sign has good eye appeal, is colorful and easy to read. Keep copy at a minimum. The firm's logo should be on all signs.

Logos

A logo is the graphic arts trade name for a logotype or identification mark. In recent years logo designs have tended to become very simple. Major industries have eliminated complex art work, choosing simple forms that can convey an image in a matter of seconds. The amount of lettering is also reduced drastically for the same reason.

Logos should be consistent throughout a firm's advertising and promotion campaign and on all its business printing.

Newspapers

Newspapers take the biggest share of brokers' advertising dollars. In order to measure newspaper advertising results adequately, they should be separated into three parts: display, open house and classified.

Display advertising is more costly than classified but offers certain advantages that may well pay for the added cost. Display advertising captures reader attention by its greater visibility. A well laid out display ad projects a marketing image that can pay off months or even years later when an owner who has seen it decides to list his or her property.

There are several keys to good display ads. Have the ad laid out professionally. Use a minimum of copy, leaving a good amount of white space around it. Be sure to use the company logo. Write the ad to appeal to clients who can afford the type of property advertised and place the ad in a publication they read regularly.

Open house advertising is similar to classified advertising only in that records should be kept on the business it generates, measured against what regular classified ads bring in. Records should also be kept of both the sales and listings such ads bring in. Such records will help a broker decide whether more of the firm's ad dollars and the salespeople's time should be channeled toward open house activities. In some areas of the country open houses are not commonly used.

Classified advertising has been described as the marketplace of the people. Brokers spend the largest percentage of their advertising dollars in this medium. Flexible in cost and size, classified ads offer a unique advantage to all, from the largest multioffice operation to the newest, smallest firm.

How much classified advertising should a firm run? Company size controls this to a large degree. A small office would have a hard time playing a dominant role in classified; a large corporation has little trouble taking command. Small offices can counter this in several ways. They may decide to put all their advertising eggs into this one basket and forget other media. If they do not do this, they will have to put tremendous effort into writing prize-winning, telephone-ringing ad copy. They can determine which day's ads pull best and advertise more on those days. A word of caution is needed here: Don't record just the day the respondent calls; be sure to record which day's ad is being checked out. Many brokers find it pays to run double or triple column ads on good response days. Then on days when ads do not pull as heavily, ad dollars are put to work elsewhere.

Television

Big company or small, large city or small, a key question today is should brokers use television? Much thought must be given to the key objectives of the advertising master plan when a firm considers this medium. Most brokers dismiss television because it is too expensive. But there might be a place in a company's growth plan for this high exposure medium, especially with the advent of the more competitively priced cable television. If the prospect will not get the message from newspapers, the broker can take it to him or her via television. It is a medium that should be considered mainly by growth-oriented companies. Its main plus is that it is a tremendous image builder. Results are hard to measure, but over the long pull listings will be easier to get for companies who use television than for those who do not.

Television cost is based on the number of families reached and varies with the size of the city. Buyers usually have the choice of sponsoring a whole program, 60, 30 or 10-second commercials or 5-second station cut-away ads, the latter at a lower cost. This wide price range puts television within the budget of many brokers.

When considering television, ask the following questions:

- Do we have an adequate sales staff?
- Do we cover the major areas where ads will be seen?
- Are we growth oriented?
- Are we willing to spend more money today in order to have market penetration for future business?
- Will a television campaign enable us to show properties, or will it just build the company image?

If your television campaign results in showing properties, potential sellers will be more willing to list with the firm.

Give television a lot of thought before you sign a contract to use it. Used judiciously, it can be an excellent growth tool.

Radio

Almost every one of the plus features that apply to television fit radio but at a much lower cost. This makes radio advertising practical for companies of all sizes. The question becomes do brokers use AM, FM or a combination of the two? The answer to this depends on the type of market the firm is in. A telephone survey of clients, asking what stations they listen to, can be a guide to making a final selection.

Billboards

Outdoor advertising is one of the oldest advertising forms and is certainly an effective one. Most billboards are rented by outdoor advertising companies. The key advantage to billboards is that locations can be contracted at key intersections within a firm's marketing area. Billboards provide advertising 24 hours a day for as long as the space is under contract.

Billboard messages and layout should be prepared by professionals. Most amateurs tend to use too much text. The message should be short and catchy and should carry the company logo. Motorists should be able to read it in five seconds maximum. Therefore it must be kept to seven words or less.

Yellow Pages

Advertising in the Yellow Pages is often overlooked as an effective medium for brokers. The oversight is difficult to explain because real estate advertising is aimed at getting the telephone to ring! Yet many brokers question the need for this form of advertising.

People seldom bother to write down phone numbers when they drive by a For Sale or Sold sign, listen to the radio or watch television. When buyers and sellers want to call a broker they reach for the phone book. Brokers who make it easy for potential clients to find them in the phone book say this relatively modest investment pays off. As one broker puts it, "Let their fingers do the walking, let your salespeople do the showing."

Direct Mail

All advertising to be good must repeatedly contact and target the desired audience. Direct mail makes this possible. It is also a medium few brokers use properly. Once a direct mail list is developed, it should be used over and over again, getting the firm name and word of its services and successes into the homes and offices of everyone with whom it does business or wants to.

Much direct mail can be a cross between institutional and merchandise advertising and company public relations. Company brochures illustrate this point. A well-designed, carefully written brochure can tell your company's story and can be used in many ways. It is most effective when a self-addressed return card asking for more information is enclosed.

A sales brochure prepared specifically to promote a new company development or to interest industry in building a factory, warehouse or office building in the broker's market area requires a lot of preliminary work on the part of the broker and the services of professionals in the graphic arts to put it into an attractive package. Brochures prepared for professionals should be prepared by professionals.

Direct mall pieces can also be used to announce a series of institutional or service ads. Backing up direct mail with other kinds of advertising makes sense and provides continuity and variety to a campaign.

WHO SHOULD WRITE THE ADVERTISING?

The following guidelines will help determine who should write the advertising and provide tips for writing ads.

Sales Manager

Does this person have time to write ads in addition to managing the salespeople? Does he or she have the skills to write phone-ringing ads?

Broker

To the questions above, add this: What other directions of company growth will take the broker away from consistent attention to this important task?

Advertising Agency

Large companies with big budgets find this the best answer. The agency fee may be offset by better results. Ad agencies may also be the answer for smaller firms that cannot produce successful copy.

Part-Time Ad Writer

Brokers and sales managers should ask themselves how much their time is worth. Part-time ad writers can be engaged at an hourly rate, freeing the staff for higher paying, more productive work.

Salespeople

Before deciding on this method, ask if the salespeople have the ability, time, inclination and creativity needed to write good ads. Can they write copy that represents the firm in the manner and at the price you will be paying?

Computer Software

There are software programs that create classified ads for real estate. Some brokers give these much acclaim.

Whoever writes the ad copy must keep several points in mind. If a firm's ads are to control the market they must gain the buyers' attention, hold their interest and induce them to call for more information. All this action starts with attention-getting leads. To write good leads requires an understanding of the basic motives of people. The four most important to ad writers are

1. self-preservation and safety—the desire to stay alive and well;
2. money—the desire to make it, the bargain instinct to save it;
3. prestige—the need to feel important, the matter of pride; and
4. family—love.

People who read classified ads want to know the property's location, number of rooms (or bedrooms), price and terms, and design.

Ad copy should have a minimum of abbreviations and it should not tell the whole story. If an ad tells everything, there is little reason to call except to buy the property, and the broker misses countless buyers for all the other properties he or she has to sell.

MEASURING THE RESULTS

The importance of measuring the results of all advertising was stressed earlier in this chapter. It is important that records be kept regularly so management has an up-to-date picture of the effectiveness of the program. The same data will prove valuable later when decisions must be made to continue certain media or make some changes. Figure 14.9 and Figure 14.10 are two forms that can be used to collect data on ad response. The figures shown previously also collect useful data on classified ads as well as other client sources.

Institutional campaigns are more difficult to assess quickly but their effectiveness is proven over the long-term. Good institutional campaigns help a company to grow and they play a strongly supportive role for the sales staff. When a firm has a good reputation, salespeople's jobs are made a lot easier. And when salespeople are content, staff turnover is lower and management's task is also easier, allowing more time to focus on long-term growth and other creative work.

FIGURE 14.9 Weekly Report

Name_____ Date_____

Calls for the Week

Address	Date	Paper A	Paper B	Referral	Other Paper	Other

Results from Open House

Address_____ No. Through_____

No. Names_____ Good Prospects._____

FIGURE 14.10 Advertising and Call-In Sheet

Date	Address	Paper A	Paper B	Referral	Sign	Area Paper	Phone Book	Other	Other Agent-Office	Time & Appointment Date

Everyone involved in planning, preparing and responding to advertising should be kept informed of the results of everything the company does to reach its public. Salespeople should know which ads pull strongest, which days of the week are best for classifieds and how the company measures the campaign's effectiveness. When everyone is kept informed, records tend to be kept more accurately, and there is a continuing interest in the whole advertising effort. Computer technology can be used to make record-keeping even more efficient.

PUBLIC RELATIONS

The image a firm projects through its advertising should be integrated with good public relations, for the two are closely interrelated. Public relations is as diverse as management's involvement in community affairs and organizations, conducting a good publicity campaign with newspaper editors and news directors of radio and television stations, sponsoring sports and cultural teams and events and providing giveaways that are of good quality, useful and remind the public of your company.

Every person who gets a good living from a community ought to give back a share of it in personal service and the promotion of good local causes. When people join a service club, country club, PTA or fill an elected or appointive office in local government affairs, they represent not only themselves but the firm with which they are affiliated. Every time a salesperson takes a training course that will upgrade him or her professionally, wins the company's monthly sales contest or handles an important transaction is a reason for the company to send out a publicity release. New salespeople joining a firm and promotions within the firm should be announced to the public. Talk shows need participants with experience in a wide variety of fields. Management should let program directors know that people on their staff have expertise in real estate and are available for appearances on radio or television. It's all grist for the firm's publicity and public relations mills.

Be willing to speak up about the special concerns of the marketplace. Subjects like home warranty programs or planned unit developments are of interest to the public. Brokers should be willing to discuss them with newspaper editors and radio and television people. Environmentalists and conservationists are always looking for support for their projects. Brokers should look for ways to tell the public they favor the concepts that make the community a better place to live. After all, they are on the front lines every day, selling that community as a fine place to live!

Junior colleges and high school adult education classes are asking for brokers to teach real estate subjects. High school career seminars offer opportunities to tell young people how exciting a career in real estate can be. Their students are, after all, the source of tomorrow's brokers. And while brokers are engaged in some of these public relations activities on their own behalf, they are also being paid for their time, which is an interesting twist.

Non-Cash Contributions

What do you do when the budget is spent and there is simply not enough cash to cover further requests for support by community groups? You might offer the front window for a promotional display, if the request is for an antique or hobby show, 4-H or Scouts. Then tell the public about it in your weekly ad, inviting them to come by and enjoy it. That promotes both the project and the firm.

Promotional giveaways can often be used instead of cash outlays. If the PTA is having a book sale, the church a rummage sale, the garden club a plant sale or the school band a bake sale, they all will need tote bags. Offer to supply these (with your logo on them, of course) and watch your firm's name appear all around town, gathering goodwill for both the project and the company.

More traditional forms of promotion and good public relations involve sponsoring sports teams, providing signs and flags for pet parades and other community outings, underwriting award banquets, placing display ads in amateur theater programs and cultural and civic benefit programs. Calendars are among the oldest promotional items in American business. They are still a good way to get the firm name into a great many homes and offices at very low per item costs.

If the firm has a large conference room or training center, make it available for community and nonprofit organization functions when it is not needed for business. Garden clubs, voter groups or study clubs will sign up for it. If you have enough extra money in your print budget, provide small memo pads to these groups. They will be carried home, getting the firm name into still more households. Be sure the telephone number is also imprinted.

If space in your office is suitable for the precinct polling place, you could offer it for use on election days. Voting creates high-volume traffic of citizens concerned about what is going on in the marketplace. Serve them coffee and send them away with a token giveaway with the firm imprint— a pencil, rainhat, memo pad, tote bag or a packet of paper coasters.

Communication Pieces

Annual reports are another form of advertising that crosses over into public relations and promotion. Just as industrial firms prepare annual reports that tell their story to shareholders and the financial community, so real estate brokers can develop annual reports that do a special job for them. Such a report could include details of the firm's growth over the past year, a summary of its listings and sales in both numbers and dollar volume, mention of a few of the most important transactions handled, the services the firm offers, the qualifications of the management and staff and whatever projections can safely be made for the coming year.

Such reports can be mailed to all active clients, bankers, attorneys, local government officials, leaders in business and commerce and the civic leaders in the community. It should be a highly professional product.

Newsletters serve in-house as well as external communication and promotion needs. They can be as simple as a one-page sheet written exclusively for staff, telling of goals achieved, new objectives, new staff or salespeople added and promotions within the firm. External newsletters usually avoid the chattiness acceptable for internal publications. They tell in a more formal way what the firm achieved, sales and staff additions and accomplishments, plans for growth or expansion, mention of recent publicity the firm has received and perhaps some promotional copy relating to the marketplace the firm serves. Here again the broker is the person out front selling the marketplace to newcomers. Why not remind others now and then how a broker does that?

Newsletters can be an expensive public relations tool. When well-done they perform a useful service. They should be prepared in a format that makes them easy to keep on file. Banks have discovered that their newsletters are shared by a great many people in the firms that receive them and are kept for further reference. A broker's newsletter could be just as effective a public relations tool and well worth its cost.

TELEPHONE CONTROLS

The use of company telephones for personal and long distance calls should be covered in the policy and procedure manual. How it is answered is covered in orientation training and continual training programs. The importance of answering the telephone promptly and well also relates to the success of the firm's advertising and promotion program.

The dollars spent on advertising are supposed to make the telephone ring. When it is not answered promptly and properly, the result is a loss of advertising money and effort as well as the buyers and sellers it is meant to attract. Everyone in the firm should appreciate the role they play in using the phone to help reach individual and company goals.

Be sure anyone answering the phone knows enough about the properties advertised to be able to talk about them intelligently. Be sure they answer the phone in a friendly tone. Be sure they keep a checklist of the information they need to get from that first call right by the phone. *Make the telephone a sales instrument.* It can be an instrument of both control and growth.

Effective use of the marketing and statistical controls suggested here have resulted in the strong growth of real estate organizations all over the country.

Chapter 15

Appraising and Analyzing the Patterns of Growth

When a real estate firm has a well-established staff working under good management, it eventually reaches a point where the firm appears to be serving its immediate market as completely as is possible. Then the likelihood is that management begins to think of growth, either in terms of opening another office, expanding its services or enlarging the operation at its present site.

Whatever the reason or the course being considered, it is important that management understand the external environment in which the real estate firm operates. As markets become increasingly sophisticated and the pace of change accelerates, brokers need to understand where their firms can fit most profitably, both now and in the future.

When contemplating growth, brokers should also understand the stages of development that real estate firms go through. Larry E. Greiner, formerly on the faculty at the Harvard Business School, wrote an analysis for the July/August 1972 issue of the *Harvard Business Review* in which he showed how a company's past provides clues for management that are critical to its future success. This chapter presents a condensation and adaptation of Greiner's article, "Evolution and Revolution as Organizations Grow." Greiner argues that management, with a sense of its organization's history, can turn organizational crises into opportunities for further growth.

GROWTH COMES IN MANY VARIETIES

During the 1960s, the economy was growing so quickly that companies did not have to worry about their competitors. Real estate firms of all sizes thrived in the flourishing economy. But in the 1970s and 1980s, this economic growth began to slow down due to a variety of factors, including scarce resources, increasing energy costs, trade barriers, political tensions, economic slowdowns and a leveling off of population growth. Companies could no longer depend on growing along with the economy; the only way to increase their profitability was to increase their share of the existing market. The only way to get that share was by grabbing it from the competition.

As a result, the real estate business became highly competitive and by the 1990s the number of firms shrank. Hardest hit were the middle-size firms, many of which were forced out of the market. Large national firms such as CENTURY 21® and ReMax®, with their many franchisees, became the dominant firms in the marketplace because they were able to offer a broad menu of services, a national scope and economies of scale. Small, specialized niche firms serving segments of the market that the leaders overlook have also done well.

It is in this environment that managers need to analyze their firm's patterns of growth. While the reasons for undertaking growth are as varied as the people responsible for the undertaking, one basic measure influencing the decision must be profit: "If we expand and if this growth takes place, what will the increase in profit be, measured against the risk involved?"

Before appraising and analyzing the patterns of growth, it is necessary to establish a base from which growth takes place. There is a definite operational philosophy in every type and size of real estate organization. This tends to break down into a small office or a large office approach.

THE SMALL OFFICE

The five-person to ten-person residential office represents the majority of the real estate brokerage operations in the United States. The owner is most often the manager as well as a selling broker. These small firms tend to be identified in one area of the market. They may become experts in a selected neighborhood or in a particular product or service, and they represent themselves as such. This is known as niche marketing. For example, a firm may specialize in the high end of the market or in selling new homes. The ideal market niche is big enough to be profitable, has growth potential and is of little interest to major competitors. These small firms develop a core competency in order to sustain a competitive advantage.

Potential Pitfalls

Owner-managers of these firms may neglect basic management functions because they continue to do what they like to do best—selling. Their close ties with salespeople may also result in loose management.

There may be a lack of line command and a delay in decision making if the only decision maker is out selling.

There may be a lack of planning, of setting goals and objectives: Where are we going and how are we going to get there?

Instead of specializing, a firm may take a generalist approach, taking any business that comes its way. Everyone in the office may handle some commercial or some industrial or appraisal in addition to residential.

Objectives

Determine who should be the manager. This should not automatically be the owner. Entrepreneurs frequently make poor managers. Wise brokers know whether selling is their forte and desire. If it is, they should be smart and objective enough to find someone else to manage the firm.

Keep a professional image and stay within the framework of the organization's competence. When an opportunity presents itself to do work outside of the firm's area of competence, it can be a wise decision to refer this work to a specialist and not risk tarnishing the firm's image. This affords much closer control and gives a better opportunity to train people effectively. It also establishes proper delegation of authority and definite job responsibilities.

THE LARGE OR MULTIOFFICE OPERATION

There is a trend toward having more salespeople per office. This has evolved for several reasons. For one thing, the increased revenue needed to reach the breakeven point and generate a profit requires a higher volume of transactions. Also, covering a broader area from one location can keep overhead proportionately lower than it would be with ten people in two offices. Management philosophy stresses a high degree of specialization, the organization is departmentalized and each department stays within its own sphere of influence and specialization, or has its own management team.

Potential Pitfalls

Frequently there is not a solid base from which expansion can develop. Ego may cause the broker to expand the firm too quickly rather than taking a phase-in approach.

A loosely controlled budget results in the profits of successful offices being used to subsidize a new operation for an excessive period of time.

If the firm expands vertically into related fields, such as real estate management or mortgage financing, without experienced personnel, there is a tendency to continue to concentrate on brokerage while the other operations suffer.

There can be a lack of effective communication systems. The larger an organization becomes and the faster it expands, the greater the danger of a breakdown of communication. As the number of levels of management grows, managers who are not in direct contact with the operational people are not as sensitive to communication as they should be. Too often they make decisions affecting operational people without consulting with them beforehand.

There is a tendency to make decisions through committees, believing that when the committees are informed, everyone else will be informed.

As an operation grows, there is a tendency to fill up desks just to fill in space. This creates a morale problem with productive salespeople and generates resentment.

Constant competition with other big offices can lead to the big office syndrome: seeking bigness for its own sake. Attempts to create an image for the public of being the biggest firm in the market are frequently the outgrowth of emotional decisions.

While a selling sales manager is an acceptable method of operation, unless this individual's job is specifically organized in this manner and delineated in his or her job description, there tends to be a conflict as to where the sales manager's management duties begin and end.

Objectives

The 7-S model of organizational effectiveness is a useful tool to examine the large or multioffice firm's objectives. These objectives should include

- a very strong company philosophy served by organization-oriented management. The company philosophy represents its shared values, the firm's fundamental beliefs that help determine its direction and goals.
- a clearly defined organization chart and a detailed policy and procedures manual with job descriptions that support the organization chart. This provides structure that delineates responsibilities and reporting relationships within the firm.
- close communication at all levels of management, particularly between each office sales manager and his or her supervisor (generally the general manager or broker/owner). Both formal and informal communication are part of the systems that facilitate day to day operations. Management's style will influence the type of communication systems it puts in place.
- reports measuring production against goals communicated to all of the individuals responsible for contributing to sales. Measuring results helps

the company determine how well its strategies are working to achieve its goals. By communicating those results to its sales associates, management sends a message about what it considers to be important.

- cost controls. A system of budgeting for expenses with checks and balances to assure careful observance of budget limitations or necessary adjustments by top management.
- systems and procedures. A belief on the part of management that there is a need for definite systems and procedures.
- carefully programmed advertising and public relations professionally done, creative and goal-oriented. The image the company projects should reflect its market strategy and the firm's skills, or core competencies.

CONSIDER YOUR REASONS FOR WANTING TO GROW

In any appraisal or analysis of the patterns of growth, the reasons for the desired growth should be considered as objectively as possible at the very outset by those who are responsible for the final decision. Productivity and profitability are critical reasons for growth, but there may be other motives and reasons that will have a substantial effect on whether the outcome is successful.

In the next section, we'll look at the stages of development in real estate firms and how these stages affect a firm's decisions regarding growth.

RELATION TO REAL ESTATE BUSINESS

One primary goal real estate firms share with other businesses is the desire to achieve joint and personal financial success. No matter what the business, good managers realize that success is not a pinnacle upon which their company will sit for many years. Success is only a temporary level in the continuing growth of an organization. It is this very growth and the change it brings that lead it to become more successful.

When an organization has hit a level of success and stays there for a long time, it could well be that the operation has stagnated; or management may have decided this is where they really want to stay.

If in stagnation, the owners may think they have a successful operation, but they have really stopped growing, having failed to keep up with the market trends and with what the competition is doing. Eventually such a firm will find itself in a very difficult position.

But if the owners really like the company's present size and pace, they can retain many of the same management practices over a long period of time. Companies that decide they do not want to grow may have top managers who prefer the informal style of a small company. Should they choose to grow, these people could well do themselves out of a job and lose the way of life they enjoy.

Brokers who are interested in growth are constantly striving to keep their organization in tune with the marketplace and the changes going on around them. They realize that success, being a temporary state, will almost always lead to developmental changes, that change is an inevitable part of growth.

Therefore, it is safe to say that when a real estate firm finds success and has built on a strong economic base, the manager will generally start the organization into a new growth cycle. Such a growth cycle might include opening a new office or recruiting several new salespeople for the sales staff; or adding a backup clerical staff; or initiating a new department such as building or commercial/industrial.

Such growth and expansion usually cause change within an organization. People who have been with the firm for a long time generally resent change. They are secure in the framework of their old job description. They are often jealous of new departments because a great deal of attention is paid to that part of the organization; or they are envious of new salespeople because the broker seems to devote more attention and time to new people and their training than to the old. Thus, change often brings with it a sense of uneasiness in the organization. Such uneasiness often leads to a crisis. The crisis can be manifested in a variety of ways.

Several fairly common crises include older salespeople demanding they be given more attention or they will leave the organization; or a money crisis caused by the start-up costs of expansion into a new homes department; or a new commercial-investment division or other type of vertical expansion drains cash reserves, leading to a real financial crisis.

Whether the crisis is in people or finances, the manager must find a solution. This solution can take many forms (as discussed in earlier chapters of this book) but a solution must be found if the firm is to survive. Good managers anticipate the crisis and manage by objective; they foresee problems that are likely to arise as the firm enters a period of change and are ready with a solution.

STAGES OF DEVELOPMENT IN REAL ESTATE FIRMS

"Management, in its haste to grow, frequently overlooks such critical development questions as: Where has our organization been? Where is it now? And what do the answers to these questions mean for where we are going?" according to Larry E. Greiner, writing in the *Harvard Business Review*. "Instead, its gaze is fixed outward toward the environment and the future—as if more precise market projections will provide a new organizational identity.

"Companies fail to see that many clues to their future success lie within their own organizations and their evolving stages of development. Moreover, the inability of management to understand its organization development problems can result in a company becoming 'frozen' in its present stage of evolution or, ultimately, in failure, regardless of market opportunities."

As a company moves through its developmental phases, it goes through periods of evolution and revolution. Greiner defines these terms as follows:

- The term *evolution* is used to describe prolonged periods of growth where no major upheaval occurs in organizational practices.
- The term *revolution* is used to describe those periods of substantial turmoil in organization life.
- Evolution equates to periods of growth, while revolution equates to periods of change.

Each developmental phase, Greiner says, "is both an effect of the previous phase and a cause of the next phase." For example, the owner's management practices in the formative stage of the firm eventually lead to demands for decentralization as the business grows. How management solves its problems in each revolutionary period determines whether the firm will move forward into its next stage of evolutionary growth. According to Greiner, there are at least five phases of organization development, each phase characterized by both an evolution and a revolution.

KEY DIMENSIONS OF DEVELOPMENT

Greiner's model suggests that a firm's structure plays a critical role in influencing corporate strategy. He regards the following five key dimensions as essential for building a model of organizational development:

1. Age of the organization
2. Size of the organization
3. Stages of evolution
4. Stages of revolution
5. Growth rate of the industry

We will deal with each element separately but Figure 15.1 illustrates their *combined* effect. Each dimension influences the next over a period of time. As all five elements begin to interact, a realistic picture of organizational growth emerges.

It is well to note here that low-growth industries spend longer periods of time in each evolution stage and encounter revolution stages at a much slower rate than is true in medium and high-growth industries. The reverse is true of high-growth industries where companies have to build staff and expand facilities and services rapidly. Such firms find both evolution and revolution phases accelerated. Variations in real estate market conditions can also affect the growth pattern of individual firms. Real estate brokerage firms that once were high-growth companies may temporarily encounter slower growth periods. Thus, you are cautioned to keep your thinking flexible in using the charts contained in this chapter.

FIGURE 15.1   Model of Organization Development

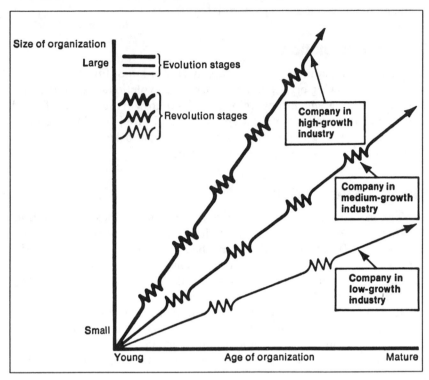

Reprinted by permission of *Harvard Business Review.*

Age of the Organization

The horizontal axis of Figure 15.1 shows the age of the organization. This is the base from which an organization grows. A company's age not only determines how much history and data a manager has available to study, it also contributes greatly to the attitudes of management. Thus, management strategy and structure are subject to strong influences because both are strongly rooted in time. The important thing here is that good management does not permit its attitudes to become frozen. When attitudes are watched carefully, staff behavior becomes predictable and is easier to change.

Size of the Organization

The vertical axis of Figure 15.1 represents the size of the organization and shows the difference in the time span in which both evolution and revolution occur in companies of different size. What a chart cannot illustrate is the fact that as a company increases in size, new challenges and problems are presented, the size of the management team increases and every job becomes more fully interrelated.

Stages of Evolution

Starting with a small, young company (lower left of Figure 15.1), you can see how growing organizations experience evolutionary periods. This is the time during which they enjoy sustained growth and remain free of major economic setbacks or disruptive internal problems. During these periods only modest adjustments seem necessary to keep the company growing under the original management structure.

Stages of Revolution

The jagged lines on the chart mark inevitable periods of revolution. Whether it comes sooner or later, revolution certainly comes. Study case histories of real estate firms or examine the changes on *Fortune's* "500" list and you find that periods of turbulence and change come to every company. It is these periods of revolution that call for greatest examination and bring the challenge of adjusting to changing needs.

It is in the stages of revolution that so many companies fail because management is unwilling or unable to make necessary changes. Companies that adjust their management practices to respond to changing needs and market conditions are the ones that move into the next, strong period of evolution.

Growth Rate of the Industry

The speed with which a real estate firm experiences phases of evolution and revolution is affected not only by the strength of its structure but by exterior market fluctuations as well. Upturns and downturns in the general economy bring strong pressures on the real estate business. In a rapidly expanding market, real estate managers must be ready to add to their sales staff rapidly. When general market reverses occur, managers who are prepared to find their way around adverse conditions can still make a profit. Companies less well-prepared will encounter major difficulties.

In Figure 15.2, "The Five Phases of Growth," each evolutionary period is characterized by the dominant management style used to achieve growth; each revolutionary period is characterized by the dominant management problem that must be solved before growth can continue.

It is suggested that you follow the chart and refer back to it frequently while reading the balance of this chapter.

One important thing to keep in mind is that each phase not only results from the previous phase but is also a cause of the next phase. You should also be cautioned that in the real estate business Greiner's five stages of

FIGURE 15.2   The Five Phases of Growth

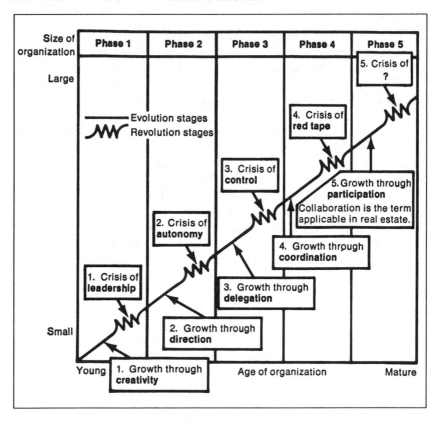

Reprinted by permission of *Harvard Business Review.*

growth do not necessarily occur sequentially. Different departments in your firm may be partially in crisis number two and partially in crisis number three at the same time. In addition, a department may "drop back" to an earlier stage when a new manager is introduced or a new market opens up. It is important that top management recognize the various problems that confront your organization so you can anticipate them and find solutions for them.

PHASE ONE: GROWTH THROUGH CREATIVITY

This first growth period represents the birth stage of a real estate firm. Four characteristics of this period are

1. an almost total lack of formal management;
2. frequent but informal communication;
3. long hours, modest income; and

4. the company responds to the marketplace and hasn't yet learned to control it.

Organizations in this stage have several characteristics. One is that the founders/owners are technically oriented—that is, they spend almost all of their time listing and selling real estate. They are most concerned with creating real estate services and working to market them. Even if they are anxious to hire qualified salespeople, their main effort is devoted to their own market activities.

A second characteristic of firms in this stage is that there is little emphasis on management. The owners feel they don't have enough time for it. Their energies are channeled into producing more business for the company and selling their services to the community.

Communication is infrequent and informal, often consisting of a few words telling of a new listing or sale as people pass one another in the hallway. Formal communications and sales meetings are considered a waste of time that take away from efforts to list and sell properties. If other salespeople work for the organization, they are likely to be independent contractors who receive little or no direction from the owners.

Broker/owners of these firms work long hours and are rewarded by a very modest income. Their strength lies in the future and in their ability to build an organization.

Their activities are controlled by the immediate marketplace. As they begin their merchandising program and follow up on listings and sales, they react to the marketplace. But they never take time to sit down and decide what they are going to do to control it. If the public says it wants one type of service this week, they will run in that direction to provide it; if next week the public asks for a different type of service, the owner will respond to that.

Certainly all good management responds to the public. But good managers also attempt to plan in advance in order to have some control over the marketplace through their merchandising impact. In the creativity stage, beginning brokers do not do this but respond either to what the market offers them or asks of them.

Growth through creativity may continue for many years, depending on the seriousness of these brokers and their desire to see the organization grow. A great many real estate firms with two, three or five salespeople tend to stay at this level and never rise above it. There are two reasons.

First, the caliber of their salespeople is not such as to help the company grow in size and win a larger share of the market. Second, the owners are simply not management-oriented and therefore refuse to acknowledge the fact that problems may be developing in their growing organization.

This eventually results in a leadership crisis.

Crisis of Leadership

The leadership crisis is probably the most critical crisis that a firm faces in the five stages of evolution and revolution. If it does not survive this first crisis, the organization will never grow. If the owners do not recognize this crisis of leadership, the firm may fail after only a short time in business.

Essential as all of the foregoing "start-up" activities are, they pose a problem. As the owners continue to sell and do a better job, and as they add salespeople, the company starts to have some impact on the community. At this point, the owners discover that they must begin to really manage the business.

What are some of the signs that a firm is facing a crisis of leadership?

One of the easiest signs to spot is that salespeople need assistance. They may be running in several directions at once. There seems to be a tremendous waste of effort. Sales may be missed because the salesperson wasn't properly trained to close the transaction; or listings may be lost because the salesperson didn't know how to prepare a competitive market analysis and use it to make a forceful presentation to the prospective seller. Perhaps the owners have had complaints filed with the Real Estate Board or the Real Estate Commission because a salesperson was ignorant of a state law—something he or she should have been made aware of through proper training and management control.

Another leadership crisis sign is that the owners become aware of the need for better accounting methods and more complete statistics. They don't understand why the number of sales made is rising but their bank balance is declining. They have only a general sense of whether salespeople are productive based on the total number of sales and listings made. They probably are unaware of the concepts of revenue per unit or breakeven point. As a result, owners feel a lack of control over their organization.

Another major cause of a leadership crisis is uncontrolled growth of the sales staff. In their efforts to promote the growth of their business, brokers may allow almost any salesperson to join their organization. The sales staff may grow from 3 or 4 qualified people to 25 or 30 people working either full-time or part-time. Such fast, uncontrolled growth may result in continuing financial losses even as the firm grows in size and sales. Incapable or inadequately trained salespeople can cause the advertising budget to get out of hand, with a lower and lower return for ad dollars spent.

At this point, knowledgeable owners realize it is time for them to find a strong business manager, someone who has the necessary knowledge and skills to introduce new business techniques and to solve the company's managerial problems. This decision may be critical for the continued success of the company. But this is easier said than done. The founders often hate to step aside, even though their skills are entrepreneurial rather than managerial. The challenge is to locate a strong business manager who is acceptable to the founders.

Good salespeople don't always make good managers. Thus, the broker may be best suited to continue as one of the firm's top salespeople, do a strong job of public relations and strengthen the organization by finding someone else to handle the business management tasks.

For example, if the broker is a strong listing and selling agent and brings in commissions of $100,000 to $200,000 a year, his or her value to the firm is almost certain to be greater in sales than it will be in management. It makes sense then to hire a manager to run the business, one who uses management skills and techniques the broker may never have acquired.

Whether management work is done by the owner or by someone hired as the business manager, let us assume that the firm has solved its leadership crisis. The company is now poised to move into a new period: growth through direction.

PHASE TWO: GROWTH THROUGH DIRECTION

This new evolutionary period in real estate firms has certain character-istics:

- A policy and procedure manual is developed, outlining rules and regu-lations of the firm.
- Specific job description are written for each person in the firm that enable sales staff and office personnel to know exactly what is expected of them.
- Communications become more formal, more frequent.
- Accounting systems are established.
- Budgets are developed.

In this new growth period, management frequently develops incentive programs for the salespeople, outlining minimum quotas necessary to achieve their sales goals. Everyone in the organization is aware of estab-lished work standards and accepts personal responsibility to sustain them.

Formal accounting systems are introduced. They not only provide exact cost figures for the day-to-day operation but also enable the owners to keep track of the cash flow of the business and what obligations it will sustain and incur. Along with this, budgeting is introduced, and the practical direction of the company's overall economic policies is begun.

Communications between management and the sales staff become more formal as the hierarchy of titles and positions is initiated. The owner or manager still makes all the decisions of the firm and establishes tighter control over the sales staff.

One of the dangers of the more formal communication system is that people no longer just sit down and talk about problems. Management may overreact to the new formality by becoming too directive in its style, telling people what it wants done without bothering to consult them on the best way of doing it.

Another possible danger is that budgets set up under a control system may not be truly goal-oriented. They may be simply figures on a piece of paper. When this happens, growth continues but has little direction except on an annual basis because that is the time span of the budget itself.

On the positive side, the new management is making firm decisions, and this is certainly an improvement over the lack of direction the company suffered in its previous phrase. So, although there are still problems, the firm enjoys a period of growth through direction. And management's compensation is basically a salary that generally fluctuates with the increase or decrease in business and the resulting profitability.

As time passes, however, some cracks develop in this solid foundation, and the company faces a crisis of autonomy.

Crisis of Autonomy

While the new management is more efficient, it eventually becomes inappropriate for controlling a larger, more diverse and more complex organization. There is too much centralization of authority, and the company seems to stagnate because everything must go through the key manager or the owner before action can be taken. Creativity is often stifled. Salespeople find themselves torn between following formal procedures and taking initiative. It is in this stage that salespeople often become unhappy and leave the firm.

As the manager becomes more involved in everyday management problems and setting up budgets and controls for the organization, he or she begins to know less and less about the actual business of listing and selling real estate. The manager becomes increasingly out of touch with the marketplace and cannot be of much assistance when salespeople seek help in solving their marketing problems. The result is that salespeople lose their enthusiasm for following the manager's direction.

The crisis of autonomy can be serious when the manager or owner does not want to give up control. In a smaller organization, the manager may be the broker who has discontinued selling in favor of management. These individuals may believe they are doing a good job of managing, and they don't realize that their lack of delegation has resulted in lower level managers or salespeople who are not accustomed to making decisions. When these managers move up to a different type of position, delegating some of their authority to others, they are frustrated to find that others don't do things as well as (or the way) they did. At this point, they may step back to resume control because of what they see as the inadequacies of their subordinates. Had they delegated and prepared others to take over their position, they would have found the transition much smoother.

The autonomy crisis is often difficult to identify, and the company simply flounders. Either there is a lack of creativity under this overly directive management or things go badly when authority is delegated.

Because these situations are difficult to recognize, managers must be on the watch constantly. If they are getting good feedback from their salespeople, the problem will be brought to the manager's attention. If the managers are getting neither feedback nor satisfactory results, they must look to themselves and the preparation they have given those to whom they have delegated authority.

PHASE THREE: GROWTH THROUGH DELEGATION

Wise real estate managers recognize that their firm's new growth calls for new management skills, and they begin to delegate authority and to decentralize their organization. This decentralization or delegation of authority moves the company into the phase of growth through delegation.

Characteristics of this phase of growth are

- beginning delegation of authority;
- beginning decentralization;
- introduction of control systems;
- management focus on problems; and
- communication becomes less frequent and more formal.

If during this evolutionary period the firm looks to increase its share of the market, through either acquisition or expansion of its present facilities, managers may actually have more authority than during prior phases. With the opening of branch offices, the organization may be decentralized, with each office given authority to run its own operation. The company may in effect become three, four or five different companies (depending on the number of branches) under one general name, each branch having autonomy.

Whenever possible, duties are delegated to branch office managers or to the persons in charge of specific duties. Rather than directing people as they did in Phase Two, management now delegates authority to those on the firing line and allows them to work for the best results they can attain.

Control systems are set up, and top management keeps abreast of what branch offices are doing through regular reports. At this stage of growth, real estate firms are likely to offer bonuses to stimulate the branches to do their best.

Now top management manages by exception, focusing its attention on troubled areas. As long as a branch office runs smoothly, top management pays it little attention beyond the regular review of its operations and how its results relate to goals and budgets. However, management pays great attention to offices that are new or having trouble getting off the ground. They work to solve people problems wherever they occur. This is described by some as management by crisis.

During this period, communication from top management becomes more infrequent and very informal. About the only time lower level managers hear from top management is when there is a problem. A call from the boss is not welcomed.

What are some of the dangers in Phase Three that move a company from growth through delegation into the crisis of control?

One of the results of successful growth of an organization is that top management loses touch with lower management. When this happens, top management also loses its empathy for the outlook and problems of lower management. When communication is at its worst, top management loses all real contact with what is happening in the marketplace and devotes all its attention and energies to being business managers.

Top management runs the risk of losing its empathy if it becomes more interested in production quotas than in the people who meet them. It may then try to push expansion by offering incentives and bonuses as the sole motivator with no regard for individuals' personal motives and goals.

Finally, in this decentralized environment, the reward system focuses on the individual. Each manager who is responsible for a particular area is compensated with individual bonuses or salary increases.

The period of growth through delegation can be a difficult one for managers because they can never be sure what authority to release, what to retain. Confusion about releasing authority and who the appropriate person is to release authority to is the root of emerging problems. Though the firm can enjoy great growth through delegation and, it is hoped, an increase in profits, management is creating future problems that eventually result in a crisis of control.

Crisis of Control

Now top management discovers that they are losing control over their operations. They have given so much authority to the branch offices that they have created little kingdoms within their own larger kingdom. This has two results.

Branch managers leave to start their own companies. They've been educated so well in how to run a real estate business that they believe they can run their own business.

Or top management discovers that the branch managers are no longer responsive to the needs of the whole company. They run their autonomous operations without bothering to coordinate plans, training and other essential facets of the business with top management or with the managers of the firm's other branches.

During this crisis, top management moves to regain control of the situation. Sometimes they try to turn back the clock and return to growth through direction. But the firm has grown in size and scope to the point where this form of management no longer works. What does succeed in solving this crisis is careful planning to coordinate controls. Rather than returning controls to top management, a compromise is worked out. People and practices are coordinated in such a way that top management and branch offices begin to move together as a force. The company gradually works its way out of the crisis of control.

PHASE FOUR: GROWTH THROUGH COORDINATION

During this evolutionary period, top management establishes new, more formal systems to achieve greater coordination. Note that the characteristics of this phase correspond to elements of the 7-S model.

The five characteristics to watch for are

1. a real consolidation of the operation as systems and people are coordinated (systems, staff);
2. organizational structure changes (structure);
3. management entering a "watchdog" phase (style);
4. control systems and profit centers emerging (systems); and
5. establishment of formal planning procedures (strategy).

The organization actually begins to consolidate and bring leadership back into focus. This is rarely, if ever, an announced action; it can seem to evolve almost by accident but is actually the result of careful planning. Top management develops new, more formal systems, works with lower level managers to coordinate them and makes certain everyone is in agreement before any new system is introduced. Ideas are sought from lower management, but they may not be forthcoming because these individuals harbor uncertainties caused by the lack of communication in the growth through delegation phase.

The consolidation of this phase may involve closing branch offices; or it may be achieved by consolidating management itself, weeding out deadwood. "Growth for growth's sake" is put aside. The focus of the firm's efforts is to create a well-functioning management team.

The firm's organizational structure becomes departmentalized by service or function. Groups such as residential, commercial-investment and property management are established, and management authority becomes diversified vertically for the first time. For example, the managers in the residential group or in the commercial-investment group work together as a team, where once they worked as individuals in their separate offices.

Profit centers are now set up by product groups rather than by branch offices. For example, the profit centers would become residential, commercial-industrial, investment, property management and so on. If there are ten residential branch offices, each would be considered a subgroup within the residential profit center. If the business is purely residential, the profit centers may be made up of geographic groupings such as the northern office, main office, southern office and so on.

Each department group now stands and falls on its own—almost as a separate company. If, for example, the commercial division is not doing well, top management spends time finding out what the problem is and how it can be solved. The commercial division may be revamped completely or dropped for a time.

Top management assumes a watchdog role over the various departments, keeping a close eye on reports. If they see a lack of coordination beginning to develop between departments, it is their job to bring them back together.

In this phase, the reward emphasis may change to profit sharing and stock options. Because there is true coordination of ideas, everyone shares in the success of the entire operation.

Probably the most significant trait of the growth through coordination phase is that formal planning procedures are established and reviewed before being implemented. At this stage the management staff may also be enlarged to initiate new programs and assure smooth coordination between upper and lower management. Capital expenditures are now budgeted carefully—not only on a yearly basis but on a two-year to five-year basis for long-term goals.

In this phase of evolution, bookkeeping and accounting procedures become more sophisticated because a greater number of departments must be coordinated. A centralized accounting system is almost a necessity.

In short, management coordinates every idea and system throughout the organization, making sure everything is checked and counterchecked before it is acted on. The company begins to become ultrasophisticated, with everyone making sure they know what everyone else is doing, and the firm is likely to move into the crisis of red tape.

Red Tape Crisis

Lower managers begin to criticize the higher managers for not knowing what is going on in the various departments or branches. In focusing on the paperwork and making sure the system is working properly, top management seems to have forgotten what the business of brokerage is: selling real estate.

In its effort to coordinate everything, top management has become more concerned that the proper forms are filled out and that the proper reports are given to the right individuals than they are about actual production. Procedure has become more important than the problem. Red tape has taken over to the point that when the company goes out of business, the managers can tell you exactly why it failed. They are so engrossed in paperwork that they neglect to correct the problems that could cause the business to fail.

Although new ideas are well-coordinated before they are put to use, they almost all originate with top management because the lower level managers have never been encouraged to come up with new ideas. And because these lower level managers are concerned only with the production of their individual profit centers and their survival, they spend little time in creative thinking.

Management is now challenged to use the crisis of red tape as the reason for entering a new phase of evolutionary growth through participation.

PHASE FIVE: GROWTH THROUGH PARTICIPATION

This phase of growth builds around a more flexible and behavioral approach to management. Here are its five characteristics:

1. Greater spontaneity in management
2. Focus on problem solving and innovation through team effort
3. Coordination of all those involved in management decisions
4. Rewarding the whole team for successes
5. Management education programs

Management now enters a phase of less formal control and self-discipline. At this point the organization begins to work truly as a team with interaction and creative ideas coming from all areas. For teams to function well, management must be 100 percent committed to the team concept. Similarly, team members must be strongly committed and loyal to the organization. Finally, the organization must be flexible and adapt well to change.

In a team environment, management's focus is on problem solving and innovation. All managers are involved with planning for the future and anticipating problems that may result from their plans. They truly have learned from experience as they moved through the five phases of growth. They understand that for each solution they have come up with, a new crisis has been created. Now when they plan, they anticipate the crisis and consider how they might overcome it.

The organization develops a structure that facilitates the coordination of department teams. Top management includes all the department heads in management decisions (Depending on the size of the company, this could be from two to twenty people.) and encourages them to come up with creative ways to handle the problems at hand. Management supports collaboration, not competition, and there is a high level of trust.

Top management's style, instead of being delegative or watchdog, becomes participative. They join hands with lower managers and salespeople in making joint decisions, discussing each one thoroughly before they move ahead. The organization has clear goals and objectives that managers communicate openly and honestly to everyone in the organization.

The makeup of the team is important. There must be contributors, collaborators, communicators and challengers in order for the team to function effectively.

- *Contributors* are task-oriented individuals who like to provide information and data and push for high performance standards.
- *Collaborators* are goal-oriented. They see the vision, mission or goal as all-important, and they are flexible and open to new ideas.
- *Communicators* are process-oriented. They are effective listeners who facilitate involvement by others, conflict resolution and consensus building.
- *Challengers* question the goals, methods and ethics of the team. They are willing to disagree with the team leader, and they encourage the group to take risks.

A good team contains all of these types of people to help balance one another's strengths and weaknesses. For example, if the communicator focuses too exclusively on process, the collaborator will bring the group's focus back to its goal. Similarly, if the challenger alienates the other team members by pushing too hard, the communicator will help to de-escalate the tension and resolve the conflict. Another way of putting the same thing is: "A team doesn't only employ hotdogs or superstars. In sports the most valuable players are not necessarily the highest scorers. They're often players who help create a situation in which their team scores." (*Canadian Manager,* Fall 1988)

The organization's control system is that of mutual goal setting. Goals are set with all management department heads. Each department head understands the goals of every other department and how all are interwoven with the problems of the entire company.

The company's reward system is linked to the productivity of the team, not of individuals. If the team as a whole does well, all of its members are rewarded with bonuses. If a particular department within the team does well, its members may receive an additional bonus.

In short, the focus is to solve problems with team action, to use more minds to come up with better solutions to problems. In some cases, teams may even cross departmental boundaries. For example, the commercial-investment group may help the residential group solve a problem that the commercial-investment group had encountered and resolved successfully in the past. Formal systems are simplified. Communication becomes easier from top to bottom and red tape disappears, allowing people to spend more of their time in creative, productive pursuits.

Frequent conferences are called to solve problems. These are not formal meetings. Rather they are informal gatherings of two or three key individuals to exchange their thoughts on any problems that may be threatening to develop. This increase in spontaneous communication helps everyone in the organization to realize that they are part of the decision-making process.

For the first time, the firm provides training for managers so they understand their responsibilities and what is expected of them. Finally, top management constantly encourages each department and each manager to come up with new ideas that might increase the productivity of the whole company. In this way, the company begins to enjoy growth through participation or team effort.

See Figure 15.3 for a graphic summary of the five phases and the organizational responses required in each phase.

GUIDELINES

Know where you are in the developmental sequence. Get to know the various phases so you become aware of just where your firm is and so that you are alert to the need to change. Work through the phases in their natural flow. Don't try to skip any phase or to work against it. Each has its strengths and learning experiences that will contribute to the ensuing phase. Don't try to avoid the periods of revolution. They have the positive element of contributing stimulation, pressure, awareness and the challenge to come up with new ideas that will carry you into the next growth period.

Recognize the limited range of solutions. You will learn that each crisis stage and your solutions for getting out of it differ from any preceding crisis. If you try to use solutions that worked for prior crises you will find it impossible to move into the next phase of growth.

Look ahead. Be prepared to dismantle troublesome organizational structures before a situation gets out of hand. In order to move ahead you may have to move people (yourself or others) around, either within the company or to a new outside affiliation.

Your ability to sell your ideas will be essential to your success. Your awareness and understanding of the current problem and your foresight in seeing how your solution will fit into the next phase of growth are among your most important management skills.

Realize that solutions breed new problems. The 7-S model is based on the concept that all of the elements of an organization are interrelated. Make a change in one element and all of the organization's other elements are affected. It follows that solutions for today's problem in a growing organization will eventually cause a new problem. Thus, the ability to solve a current problem through greater understanding of the company's long-term goals (rather than "pinning the blame" on a particular person or factor) will prove a positive determinant of what happens to the firm in the future.

Real estate managers should develop the knowledge and skills that will enable them to predict future problems and so prepare solutions and coping strategies before things get out of hand. Management should be sure they want the company to grow. They may decide their present size suits them well, both in the income it produces and the way of life it offers. If they decide they want to grow, it should be based on a genuine desire and not just because there's more money there to be made.

FIGURE 15.3   Organization Practices during Evolution in the Five Phases of Growth

Category	Phase 1	Phase 2	Phase 3	Phase 4	Phase 5
Management Focus	List and Sell	Efficiency of Operations	Expansion of Markets	Consolidation of Organization	Problem Solving and Innovation
Organization Structure	Informal	Centralized and Functional	Decentralized and Geographical	Line-Staff and Product Groups	Coordination of Department Teams
Top Management Style	Individualistic and Entrepreneurial	Directive	Delegative	Watchdog	Participative
Control System	Market Results	Standards and Cost Centers	Reports and Profit Centers	Profit Centers	Mutual Goal Setting
Management Reward Emphasis	Ownership	Salary and Merit Increases	Individual Bonuses	Profit Sharing and Stock Options	Team Bonus

This chart has been changed only slightly to relate it more closely to the real estate business.

Changing market and economic conditions demand growing skills. Studying detailed phases in this chapter offers today's real estate leaders one way to meet and overcome whatever new challenges lie ahead.

Chapter 16

Market Analysis

Real estate organizations need to stay on top of a changing market in order to maintain their competitive edge. Well-planned and well-implemented market research should be the basis for all of a firm's strategic and market planning. Whether the firm needs to adjust its marketing and financial plans to take advantage of new opportunities or to decide whether to expand or add services, the firm's plan of action is more likely to be successful if it is based on a thorough evaluation of the competitive environment in which the firm operates. This chapter discusses how to conduct effective market research. It examines how to determine what competitive information a company needs and how to go about finding that data.

MARKET RESEARCH ESSENTIAL TO SUCCESSFUL SELLING

We know that regardless of economic conditions, as long as there are properties that need to be sold, there is a real estate market. The market collapses entirely when no one wishes to sell, when a concern with external events causes people to stay put, or when they have no rational need to make a real estate move. Otherwise, whether in a falling or a rising market, as long as people feel a need to move, there is an opportunity for real estate sales. The question then becomes: What is happening in the market that will affect your firm, whether for better or worse, and how will you adjust to the situation?

Well-planned and well-implemented research should be the basis for all strategic and market planning within a company. Strategic and marketing plans that take into account all of the potential forces that affect your company will be more successful than plans created in a vacuum. For example, based on listing availability, one broker believed there was sufficient business to justify expanding to a second location across town. But he was dissuaded from doing so after learning that the total listings in the community were running under 100 a month, and he was already the exclusive broker for 30 to 40 of them. Statistical evaluation of the market proved there was turnover, not expansion. By doing some basic research, the broker saved the considerable expense of opening an additional office that would not have increased his share of the market substantially.

Research is the first step in an effective planning process. The firm must determine what it needs to know about itself, its local market and its external environment. The following research process framework is a tool to make sure your research methods are effective. The framework consists of these steps:

- Choose the environment you want to study.
- Decide what information you need to know.
- Identify what you already know.
- Determine what information is missing.
- Develop a plan to obtain the missing information.
- Evaluate the data as you collect it.
- Analyze the raw data in context.
- Apply the information to the strategic planning process.
- Control the research plan by measuring its effectiveness.

In this chapter, we will focus on the three environments you can study: (1) your firm, your local market, and the external environment; (2) the information you need to know and where to find it; and (3) evaluating and analyzing the data you collect.

EVALUATE AND ANALYZE THE DATA

There are two kinds of data you can collect: primary and secondary. Primary data is collected by a researcher from an original source. An example of primary data is interviews you conduct with existing customers. Secondary data is information gathered from references, such as newspaper studies. It is important to know whether your data is primary or secondary so you can determine its reliability and accuracy.

Evaluation and analysis of the data you collect are important in order to test the reliability of the information, to make sure you aren't using the same source to confirm one fact and to confirm that you have an accurate understanding of the data. *Evaluation* is the process of studying the raw data as you collect it in order to determine how valid it is. *Analysis* is the study of the raw data in context in order to turn it into information you can use.

The three steps in evaluating raw data are

1. identifying the source and its reliability,
2. estimating the accuracy of the information, and
3. eliminating false confirmations.

It is important to determine the source of your data because all data was produced for a specific reason. You need to know who collected your data and why. When you know the source of the data, you can decide how much you can believe that source. One way to judge is: If the source has been correct in the past, it is probably reliable.

Accuracy, on the other hand, is the correctness of the data. Ask whether that source could have obtained accurate information despite time, access and financial limitations. One way to determine that accuracy of data is by confirming it with another source. But before believing the confirmation, be sure you evaluate the accuracy and reliability of that source to avoid false confirmations. Here is an example of a false confirmation: To confirm data about a company that she found in Standard & Poor's, a sales associate looked at TRW's business profiles. Looking more closely, she found that TRW's major data source for its information is S&P. Therefore, TRW cannot be used to confirm S&P's validity.

Similarly, articles in two trade magazines that support one another's story may be a false confirmation if both magazines printed their story from the same press release. This illustrates why it is so important to determine the source of both the original data and the confirmation of that data.

THE THREE ENVIRONMENTS

The three environments that should be studied are the company, the local market and the external environment ("the big picture"). The logical place to begin is with the company environment because it is easier to gather information on the company, and it makes sense to look at the company's own capabilities before comparing it to its competitors or looking at the big picture.

The Company

The 7-S framework can help a company evaluate the internal impact of a strategic decision. For example, if a company is considering expansion, here are some of the questions that could be asked using this framework.

- *Shared Values:* What are the company's fundamental beliefs? How will expansion affect those beliefs?
- *Systems:* Are the firm's systems (e.g., recruiting, training, financial) efficient?

- *Staff:* Does the company have the right combination of people? Is their productivity increasing or decreasing? If sales associates' productivity is declining, what is the cause and how will it affect the proposed expansion?
- *Structure:* Will the organizational hierarchy help the company expand successfully?
- *Strategy:* Does the company have a long-term or short-term strategy? Does the proposed expansion support that strategy?
- *Skills:* What special capabilities give this company its competitive advantage? Will the proposed expansion build on those capabilities?

The Local Market

Factors that influence the strength and growth potential of a given market area include population, labor demand, housing demand, geographic factors, the area's economic base, restrictive codes and ordinances, tax loads, the existence of vacant land and the need for utilities.

Population   Overall increase or decrease in population as recorded by the Census Bureau, Village Hall or city authorities can provide some interesting data on the growth potential of a real estate company. Any decrease should be cause for concern about what the long-term trend might be.

It is essential that each broker have some concept of the total number of available units for sale during any given period.

The first step in the analysis is to determine the number of properties that represent the inventory in the trading area. If statistics indicate there are 3.4 individuals per family unit, the area population total divided by 3.4 gives the approximate number of living units. Taking out of this number rental apartments or other units that would not serve as a part of the real estate marketplace results in a net housing inventory available. This inventory should then be converted into the number of possible units that could be sold each year. The result will indicate whether the market is sufficiently strong to support entry into the market or expansion.

Turnover statistics can best be obtained by checking figures in such easily identified areas as water meter turn-ons, phone company hook-ups, club membership turnover, church transfers and country club changes. In one residential area, a swimming club of 350 members indicated a consistent turnover of between 40 and 50 each year. When analyzed, these figures represented 8 to 10 who dropped membership because their children no longer needed the swimming facilities. The balance were transferred out of the area, indicating some 10 to 12 percent of the available housing units were changing hands every year. These turnover figures when applied to the total housing inventory will give some indication of the total market. After applying a factor on the percentage a broker might reasonably expect to obtain, a definite decision can be reached as to whether there is enough potential in that marketplace to support expansion or the entry of a new company.

Labor Demand   Demand for skilled, semiskilled and unskilled labor creates a marketplace for real estate that either requires expansion to take care of the inquiries or indicates a need for a larger housing inventory.

The most obvious source of labor demand is the entry into the community of new manufacturing or service facilities that will create a demand for labor. For example, a 2,000-room hotel was erected in Las Vegas, which by its very construction and operation required labor to build, run and maintain. The rule of thumb in the hotel industry of 1.5 employees per room indicates a need for approximately 3,000 employees in this hotel operation. Such a demand creates a real estate market.

New manufacturing facilities, the establishment of shopping centers or a discussion with personnel directors of already established local businesses about their labor requirement forecasts can verify the strength of the local economy and the demand for people.

The expansion of recreational facilities of all types also develops a sizeable labor market that results in increased need for real estate services.

Public relations calls on local industries by the key person in a real estate business can elicit information on their expansion plans and provide an excellent guide to growth potential which would not otherwise be evident. A good example of this is an automotive assembly plant employing approximately 10,000 people. An increase of 10 percent in orders can be felt directly in terms of new hires that result in a substantial upswing in the demand for residential housing. Under normal conditions, the increase or decrease of 1,000 people in an operation of that size could not be measured without obtaining the information directly from company officials.

Housing Demand   One of the factors that not only affects volume in a real estate market but also influences timing for expansion is the fluctuation in demand. One statistic that ought to be examined is the length of time the average home is on the market.

A homebuying company from Elizabeth, New Jersey, has measured the length-of-time-of-ownership for the properties purchased on behalf of corporations from their employees. A gauge of the marketplace was obtained by keeping track of the number of days the property was owned by the home buying corporation. Since it materially affected the company's investment in the property, it was important. However, for brokers doing strategic planning, a market that indicates a change either way could be valuable information.

For instance, if the number of days required to sell a property is increasing, it could mean that a substantial increase in exclusive listings obtained from "by owners" would result. Also, a shortening in the time required to sell properties might indicate a demand of such proportion that buyers would be attracted to do business with brokers so they would hear about new listings the moment they come on the market. An analysis of this demand as evidenced by the fluctuation of classified ads in the paper, an increase in signs and a study of Multiple Listing Service records could give statistical valuation to the housing demand.

Geographic Potential   Geographic factors also influence the strength of a given real estate market. The historic strength of a community based on accessibility to transportation by waterways or rail has now been amplified by accessibility to raw material resources, power supplies, water for industrial cooling, airports, interstate highways and finally strategic location in surrounding markets. One of the interesting developments in the United States has been the growth of regional centers like Atlanta, whose geographic location has given them a material advantage in the expansion of the community. Add another factor of living desirability in communities like Phoenix where the year round climate has attracted a wealth of manpower. Factors like these make the expansion of all kinds of industry and services a natural sequence of cause and effect.

Conversely, environmental restrictions, especially in areas that are smog prone, can put a damper on expansion. Some areas like the New York metropolitan area are restricted by natural barriers of ocean and water and mountains, conditions that tend to fragment the growth of areas in peculiar ways.

Restrictive Codes and Ordinances   Many areas of the country today are being adversely affected by stringent building codes, zoning ordinances and "no-growth" policies. Such political interference can seriously obstruct a marketplace.

A typical example is a village deciding against permitting the erection of higher than three-story buildings within its boundaries, delaying much desirable construction that would convert low tax revenue properties into higher tax revenue properties. The resultant increase in tax load on individual residences causes a reaction against the price structure and deteriorating market values in this area. These restrictive zoning ordinances can have considerable impact on the desirability of real estate expansion.

On the other hand, if there are some reasonable, sensible master plans or flexible codes that will permit easy construction and maximum use of land, they could be a positive indication that expansion is timely.

Tax Loads   One factor that has a direct bearing on the potential of an area is its tax load. Buyers can easily translate a light tax burden into mortgage payments that permit them to raise their sights on their house economics. Conversely, relatively high tax burdens discourage buyers from purchasing property in such areas. Brokers planning expansion will want to study the tax load potential that might be placed on the community they are considering currently or in the future. Such a study will take into account the projected demand for school services that account for a major portion of the tax load. Ask whether additional facilities will be built, whether there is any demand for improved educational facilities on the part of the taxpayers and even how the school system compares with those in surrounding communities. Consider, in addition to this, the type of village or city government in existence and the kinds and types of people involved in the local administration.

A low tax rate can be a mixed blessing. A do-nothing city administration can have a stifling effect on the growth of the community. Change in administration can promise progressive, aggressive action which will stimulate the area, even though taxes are sure to increase. The point here is that low taxes are not necessarily desirable if adequate services and good administration are not being provided.

Vacant Land   Just as a lack of geographic restrictions makes expansion possible, so does a lack of expansion within a town cause problem. When a town sees itself as a small individual unit and fails to expand its boundaries as it grows, vacant property soon fills up with construction. Large estates are broken down to provide additional land for a very few buildable parcels. When this happens, a standoff in the increase in deed transfers takes place and the market becomes highly restricted and competitive.

If an area is landlocked by mountains or other geographic restrictions, this can become an acute problem. The question then arises: Will the town deteriorate or will its desirable features provide for movement in and out, keeping the inventory of real estate in good condition and highly desirable? At this stage, good schools, strong and active churches, up-to-date shopping centers, viable transportation and strong community, civic and cultural interests will make for a strong marketplace. In the absence of good community services and land for expansion, the result could well be a deteriorating market that should be judged critically.

Need for Utilities   The inordinate and insatiable demands of the American public today make a good supply of energy and water crucial to an expanding real estate market. Knowledgeable brokers will evaluate the availability of these two resources and the effect the supply may have, either good or bad, on their market area. Obviously, good water and energy supplies will be a positive contribution to the growth potential of an area, stimulating interest in that marketplace by both people and industry.

Along with the availability of utilities is the consideration of waste disposal. Under current Environmental Protection Agency philosophy, the establishment of proper facilities for waste treatment and garbage disposal become important considerations. The expansion potential of whole areas has been reduced drastically by building permit refusals based on inadequate sewage handling facilities. A thorough investigation of these services is of prime importance.

The External Environment

The external environment consists of everything outside of the company or the local market. This encompasses political, economic, ecological, social and technological factors, and industry trends. This environment provides industries, markets and companies with opportunities, but it can also constrict their activities. Furthermore, companies and local markets have no control over these external factors. However, if you can think ahead and anticipate possible changes, you can plan your strategies accordingly.

Economic factors may include such things as the national unemployment rate, the general availability of credit, interest rates, inflation rates, the level of disposable income and which areas of the country are growing.

Social factors include the influence of women in the job market, the aging of the U.S. population and changing tastes in homes.

Examples of political factors would be a possible increase in taxes and a proposed limit on mortgage deductions.

A technological factor might be that customers have greater access to information about real estate listings through on-line services, reducing their dependence on REALTORS®.

Ecological factors would include environmental concerns such as radon, hazardous waste, asbestos, lead-based paint and high tension wire regulations.

Sources for information on the external environment include newspapers, such as the *Wall Street Journal,* Congressional reports and industry associations.

THE PORTER MODEL

A Harvard professor, Michael Porter, has developed a tool that can be used to conduct a competitive market analysis. According to Porter, five major forces determine the nature and degree of competitiveness in the local market. These are the bargaining power of suppliers, the bargaining power of customers, the threat of substitute products or services, the rivalry among existing competitors and the threat of new competitors. The last three forces all relate to the competition and will be discussed together.

Suppliers

Suppliers to the real estate industry provide customers, services, money and inventory. Examples of suppliers include lenders, title companies, newspapers and other suppliers of advertising space, cobrokers who supply sellers, and builders who supply inventory. Because a firm needs its suppliers in order to do business, this gives suppliers some power in the market. It is important to know who your suppliers are and how their businesses are growing or declining in order to know whether there is any real estate to be sold or money to buy it with.

Information you will need to gather on suppliers includes the turnover rate, how quickly the inventory is growing, how many new homes are planned or being built (total number of building permits issued), the mortgage rates and how much mortgage money is available at local lenders, the price of advertising and so on. A study of the volume of new buildings being developed will give an indication of future potential not only in terms of numbers but also in terms of physical direction and use. Records of deed transfers will indicate the turnover rate and whether it is increasing or decreasing. This information can be gathered from town hall records of building starts, title companies' or county recorders' records of deed transfers, the National Association of REALTORS® library, brochures, meetings with local builders and other sources.

Customers

Customers are defined as sellers and others who pay for the services of a real estate firm. This includes both past and potential customers. Customers have many real estate firms to choose from. Your firm has a better chance of getting their business if you know what your customers want or need.

One common method for talking about customers is to create a customer profile. This is a composite picture of your firm's typical customer and should include both existing and potential customers. A customer profile should contain information about your customers' geographic distribution, demographic characteristics, psychographic characteristics and behavioral tendencies.

Geographic data about customers is needed to help you determine what geographic areas your company currently services and can service in the future. You can obtain geographic data by looking in the company's files for past customer addresses. A customer survey can help you determine what areas need real estate services.

Demographic data includes the age, sex, family size, family life cycle (single or married, whether they have children and their ages, etc.) income, occupation, education and so on of your firm's prospective and current clients. Demographics will help you predict how many people in an area might sell their house (e.g., because of retirement). It will also help you determine how much individuals might be able to spend on a house (income and occupation). Demographic data can be obtained from your local library, the U.S. Census Bureau, on-line computer databases, Donnelley Demographics and other sources.

Psychographic information refers to the personality and lifestyle of customers. It can include such information as whether they are introverts or extroverts; conservative, liberal or radical; leaders or followers; high achievers or low achievers. This information is often used to help shape advertising. For example, soft drink producers design their advertising campaigns to attract physically active, group-oriented nonprofessionals because their psychographic studies show that the majority of their customers have these characteristics. It can also provide a guide to what topics customers might enjoy discussing.

Sources for psychographic information include advertising companies and The Lifestyle ZIP Code Analyst. The Lifestyle ZIP Code Analyst is a consumer market analysis reference guide published by Standard Rate and Data Service. It lists the number of people within a particular ZIP code area who are interested in such things as cultural activities, career-oriented activities, foreign travel, sports, home computers, gourmet cooking and so on.

Buyer behavior is used to explain or predict how a customer will behave regarding a specific product or service. It may tell you how often people in a specific geographic area buy new houses; what benefits they seek, such as economy, status or dependability; and what marketing factors they are most likely to respond to, such as price, quality, service, advertising and so on. Information on buyer behavior can be obtained through customer surveys, open houses and industry statistics.

Once you know what you need to find out about your customers, you could also hire a market research firm to obtain the data for you.

Competitors

In the fast growing economy of the 1960s, companies could increase their profitability through growth. During the 1980s, the economy's growth slowed, forcing business to begin vying with their competitors for a piece of the pie. To be effective today, a company's marketing strategy must be cognizant of, and focus on, the competition.

Competitors are other firms that sell real estate now or could sell real estate in the future. The more firms there are in a marketplace, the greater the competition for business. Because it is fairly easy for new real estate firms to enter the market compared with manufacturing or other types of companies, your firm must compete not only with other existing firms but with the ongoing threat of new firms as well. Another type of competitor is the "substitute" for the services of a traditional real estate firm. Substitutes could include for sale by owners, lawyers, or even unbundled services. It's a safe bet that other substitutes will evolve in the future. Customers have a great deal of bargaining power. They don't have to do business with your firm. If you don't know what firms you are competing with or what they offer, you may lose customers to those firms.

Information about competitors might include who they are and the market share of each competitor, which sell the most units and earn the highest revenue, what are the advertising strategies of each, what kind of people they have and hire and what is their image. The McKinsey 7-S model can help you analyze the effectiveness of your competitors' organizations. Another tool that can help you understand how your firm measures up to its competition is a Customer Perception Survey (see Figure 16.1). This survey tells you what is important to your customers and how they perceive your firm in relation to other firms.

In addition to existing competitors, you need to know how many nonbroker sales there are (e.g., for sale by owners, by builders, by attorneys), whether any franchises are moving in, and whether there are any companies not currently in the real estate industry that are likely to start selling real estate.

Potential sources of competitive information include the following:

- Ad agencies
- Trade journal articles
- Newspaper ads
- Competitor's promotional literature
- Comparable sales figures
- Zoning and building permits
- REALTOR's listing statistics
- Consultant's reports
- Dun & Bradstreet rating
- TRW report
- Chamber of Commerce literature
- Competitor's personnel want ads
- Former employees
- Customers

MARKET ANALYSIS CHECKLIST

What must you know about a new market area? You cannot know too much, but these points are essential.

What is the population today and what is it projected to be in five years, ten years, fifteen years?

What are the zoning laws, land restrictions, land improvement costs for sewer, water and other municipal services?

What is the type of municipal government? What has been its attitude toward growth? What is its projection for expansion and development of both land and government services?

Is the school system adequate? What is the teacher/pupil ratio? Can present facilities accommodate expansion? What is the current and projected tax structure? What is the total dollar volume of business done in the area each year?

FIGURE 16.1 Customer Perception Survey Results

Company Characteristics	How important is this to you?	Carriage Trade Realty	CRB Realty	Green Coat Realty	Realty 100
Size and Geographic Territory					
Firm is national	2	1	1	5	5
Firm is local	4	5	5	1	1
Firm is networked and well established in area	5	5	3	5	5
Firm has more than 10 sales agents in the office	3	1	4	5	4
Characteristics of Sales Agents					
Agent sells over $1,000,000/year	3	3	1	1	3
Agent is friendly	5	5	4	4	5
Agent has more than 5 years' experience	4	3	4	4	4
Agent looks professional	5	5	4	4	4
Agent drives an expensive car	4	5	3	4	4
Agent has been referred to me by others	4	5	3	3	4
Agent is certified by CRB	2	3	4	4	4
Agent listens to and understands my needs	5	5	3	3	4
Agent is responsive	5	5	3	3	4
Type of Services					
Firm is multiservice	1	1	3	5	3
Firm offers low-cost financing (e.g., low closing rates)	5	1	2	5	2
Firm specializes in your market	5	5	3	2	5
Firm offers a variety of warranties and guarantees	4	3	2	5	2
Firm has a relocation service	1	1	1	5	5
Operations					
Firm handles paperwork smoothly	4	5	3	3	4
Firm closes deals on or before schedule	5	5	3	3	4
Firm develops long-term relationships with its buyers	5	5	2	2	3
Sales agents are well managed and highly productive	1	5	2	3	4
Firm is computer networked	1	5	4	4	4
Firm gets listings off the books quickly		5	3	3	4
Firm is financially stable	4	5	2	3	4
Firm has low turnover rate	1	5	1	3	4

Rankings (1=low, 5=high) How well does each company do this?

Source: Real Estate Brokerage Managers Council Course, Evaluating Competition.

FIGURE 16.1   Customer Perception Survey Results *(Continued)*

Marketing/Image					
Firm's name is well recognized by the public	2	5	2	5	5
Firm has a high-class image	3	5	2	2	3
Firm has a down-home friendly image	5	2	3	3	4
Firm is active in the community	4	5	2	2	3
Firm has a reputation for pricing homes accurately and effectively (to sell)	5	4	3	3	4
Firm spends money advertising homes for sale	5	5	3	5	5
Firm has a reputation for hiring at least 50% women and minorities	2	1	2	3	2

What is the trend over the last five years?

How many new telephones were installed last year? What is the telephone company's projection for the future?

What are the plans of the principal builders in the area? Is land for development readily available?

How many real estate offices exist in the area? How many salespeople work the area? How much of the total market does each firm enjoy?

Who are the leaders? What types of offices do they have? Are their techniques modern? Get acquainted with most of the brokers in the area.

What do the opinion makers say about the area and its future? You should talk with local bankers, municipal officers, hospital administrators, ministers, Chamber of Commerce officials, school officials, builders, attorneys and other key business and professional people

Spend some time with a local REALTOR® board executive. He or she can supply you with valuable statistics and vital information about the area.

Determine what the typical home is in the area. What is its selling price? What are the most expensive and the least expensive homes selling for this year? Are homes appreciating in value?

Who is the typical buyer? Determine age, place of employment, income, occupation, family size and so on.

Determine what advertising media services the area best. What will it cost to use?

CONCLUSION

For any changes that occur in the industry or in the market, you need to ask yourself five questions:

1. What competitive factors are affected?
2. What is the specific effect of each factor?
3. Does the change make life easier or tougher for the affected group?

4. Does competitive pressure on my firm increase or decrease—and why?
5. How will we adjust to the situation—regardless of whether it is positive or negative?

Conducting ongoing market research and competitive analyses will help your firm stay on top of a changing market. This will enable you to

- maintain a competitive edge,
- adjust marketing and financial plans,
- take advantage of new opportunities, and
- adjust staffing according to changes in the market.

Chapter 17

Growth of a Firm:

Horizontal and Vertical Expansion

Real estate firms can grow in a variety of ways: by hiring more salespeople, by branching into neighboring locales, by adding new services, or by merging with or acquiring another firm. This chapter will examine how firms can grow through vertical and horizontal expansion. Growth through mergers and acquisitions will be discussed in Chapter 18.

Horizontal expansion occurs when a residential brokerage opens another residential brokerage office. The firm stays close to the business it knows best but broadens its geographic coverage.

When a firm uses the reputation it has built and the contacts it has developed to expand into related services or real estate disciplines, it is engaged in vertical expansion. Every added service or discipline spreads the promotion of the company name over more units, reduces the cost load on individual profit centers and increases the profitability of the whole business.

Expansion of any sort can be complex and risky. Before pursuing any expansion opportunity management has to decide whether it really wants to expand. Brokers should not plunge into expansion without asking themselves the following questions:

- What are my objectives?
- What are the risks?
- Do the potential rewards outweigh those risks?

WHY FIRMS RISK EXPANSION

Common reasons for expanding a real estate business include: to take advantage of a good opportunity, to increase profitability, to enter a new market or increase market share, to enhance the firm's image or reputation or to establish a name in the community.

Expansion should never be undertaken lightly. Major business moves are always risky. Financial risk is caused by the presence of debt while business risk exists because of fixed costs. However, there are four factors that can mitigate the risk involved in making business decisions:

1. Leading economic indicators are positive.
2. The move fits with the company's strategic intent.
3. It provides a sustainable competitive advantage.
4. It capitalizes on organizational capabilities.

Let's look at each of these factors.

Economic Indicators

Everyone knows that it is easier to take a risk during an up market. The trick is to know when an up market is going to go bad and when a bad market is about to start an upward cycle again. A manager does this by evaluating the lead indicators. These are factors that help you predict the potential impact that a change in the external business environment can have on your business. This allows you to be proactive versus reactive. Some examples of lead indicators are inflation rates, interest rates, changing demographics, technological advances, additional self-employment services businesses and layoffs to name a few. By picking the necessary indicators and assessing the information thoroughly, an owner/manager can significantly reduce the risk involved in making business decisions.

Strategic Intent

Another important consideration is whether the proposed move fits in with the firm's strategic intent, or its vision. Using strategic intent to make decisions helps to ensure that the firm allocates its resources in ways that are likely to have long-term benefits. Thus, the owner/manager knows the firm is using its money and energy in productive ways. If a proposed change does not fit with a firm's strategic intent, it may not be a wise use of resources, even in good economic times.

For example, a firm's strategic intent may be to become the leading provider of high-end real estate services in its marketplace. The firm has an opportunity to purchase another firm that specializes in midrange condominiums. In evaluating this opportunity, the firm should consider whether making this acquisition would be a wise use of its limited resources given its strategic intent. A proposal to open a branch office, add personnel, offer a new service, or whatever, should be evaluated to determine whether the move will help move the organization toward the achievement of its strategic intent.

Sustainable Competitive Advantage

Sustainable competitive advantage is what gives a firm an edge over its competitors. A firm's competitive advantage might be its customer service, its well-established name in an area, its image and reputation or its friendly salespeople. Will a proposed business decision advance an existing competitive advantage or give the firm a new competitive advantage?

Organizational Capabilities

Another name for organizational capabilities is core competencies. In McKinsey's model, these are the skills an organization develops and exploits to maintain sustainable competitive advantages. Building a business on core competencies builds a competitive advantage. Core competencies are

- what the company does well,
- the glue that binds existing businesses, and
- the engine for new business development.

Business decisions are less risky when they allow the firm to draw on what it knows best, that is, when the firm has the necessary organizational capability. One criterion for expanding a business is whether the expansion helps the firm develop or acquire core competencies that will help the firm achieve its strategic intent.

HORIZONTAL EXPANSION

Horizonal expansion occurs when a firm offers the same services but offers them in additional offices in the same market or in a new geographic location with the intent of increasing its market share and therefore its profitability. Dramatically increasing the size of an existing office is another form of horizontal expansion.

An important factor in the success or failure of a horizontal expansion program is the performance of top management. The manager of the original office will no longer be the chief, handling minute details to make sure that everything is done right. This person's ability to motivate, train and delegate becomes critical to the success of the new branch. This transition to management often is filled with frustration and personal turmoil for sales-oriented people. It often results in company production dropping drastically. But given a six-month period for both the selling broker and the broker's old clients to adapt to his or her new role as manager, company production usually turns around, more than making up for the broker's lost selling production.

There are some hard facts to keep in mind in reaching a decision to expand horizontally:

- It will take longer than you think to organize and start up.
- It will cost more than you plan.
- It will not operate exactly the way you want it to.
- It will take longer to make a profit than you expect.

Moreover, it is a mistake to assume that two offices will eventually double your profit. Keeping these facts in mind can help you avoid costly mistakes.

COMPETITION STUDY

Expansion within an area or to another area can be greatly affected by the type of competition you may encounter. An in-depth study of who is operating in the area, the kinds of services they offer and the success they are experiencing can be a strong indication of whether or not this would be a desirable area to move into. How to conduct a market analysis is discussed in Chapter 16.

Because some areas are completely dominated by one or more very strong brokers, expansion into these areas would be difficult and costly. Where markets are tightly controlled and the competition is firmly entrenched, you would need to plan a large expenditure for advertising and promotion in order to make any kind of impact. However, a careful market analysis might show that your firm's core competencies would fill a void in the services offered in that particular marketplace, making the effort worthwhile. Or the competition might be set in its ways and not flexible. In a time when real estate marketing is undergoing a great many changes, its inflexibility could provide an excellent opportunity to make an expansion move.

In other cases, the market may be divided among many poorly trained, unaggressive brokers. Under these circumstances, the lure is an apparent lack of tough competition, but the costs, time and fortitude required to invade and build up this market must be calculated carefully.

By contrast, if the area you are considering for expansion has little or no competition, or the competition is primarily in "by owner" sales, expansion can be accomplished relatively quickly, effectively and inexpensively, resulting in great progress in a short time.

Serious consideration should be given to engaging the services of a reputable professional marketing survey firm that can test the quality of the competitors' service, the impact of their name on the community and the strength of their hold on the market. In one case study, it was assumed that a particular broker was exceptionally strong. But research revealed that the name was unknown to almost 80 percent of the community. This fact largely negated the first impression of a strong organization. The competitor had obviously not penetrated the market as deeply as the outsider had assumed.

ECONOMIC BASE FOR EXPANSION

The economic base of an area is also an important factor in its expansion potential. A highly diversified economic base or a single-unit natural resource base make good economic sense for expansion.

A study of both the geographic and the economic base of a community and a recording of its cyclical nature or its rise or decline should be of definite interest to a broker planning expansion. Expanding in a declining market could bring on economic disaster. Equally important is filling an expansionary vacuum in services timed to be made on the upswing rather than at the peak.

TIMING OF EXPANSION

One of the crucial factors in expanding an office so that it shows maximum profit in the shortest time is the timing of the expansion.

In one area of the midwest, the historic down market is in the late fall and early winter period from November through December. In addition, the strong market is between May and the end of August. Knowing these two factors, timing expansion to coincide with the strong May market would eliminate several months of poor business before meeting the upswing. A prospective facility might be rented or purchased but not actually put into production until the time was as favorable as possible. It might also mean a delay based on timing if the best period of the year had passed.

If in studying the market potential of an area there seems to be a downtrend as a neighborhood changes, the decision to move from that location to another might better be made as soon as practicable. There is little doubt that serious consideration of timing an expansionary move is particularly important.

FINANCIAL REQUIREMENTS

The first thing a broker who is thinking of expanding horizontally must deal with is the money needed to start up a new office. Financial requirements for a new branch office will vary greatly depending on the purpose of the branch. If it is to be merely a small field or branch extension of other offices that will contain only two or three salespeople, the start-up cost will probably be minimal. The branch office may be located in a construction trailer or in a new home in a subdivision or a similar structure that will have minimum initial requirements.

However, for a full-grown branch office that is fully staffed by sales-people, startup costs can range from $60,000 to more than $100,000. These figures include capital and carrying costs needed to start the office and to run it until it generates enough income to carry itself.

Unfortunately, too many brokers consider only the actual physical outlay of cash for the structure, its improvement or remodeling and the furniture that will go into it. Then, when there is still no positive cash flow after three or four months, they run out of money and find they must close the new branch because of poor planning. When this happens, the salespeo-ple lose all faith in the leadership of the company.

In addition to the startup costs, the broker should estimate how long it will take for the office to break even or generate a positive cash flow. For a new office in a new area, this could take six to nine months. On the other hand, if the broker has a well-established sales force in the area and is simply moving their physical position to a new location, a positive cash flow could be expected almost immediately.

If the hard costs of opening the new office plus the funds that will be needed to carry the office until it achieves a positive cash flow add up to more cash than is available, it may be necessary to postpone opening the branch or to obtain additional funding. But don't scrimp on pennies that will eventually cost you thousands of dollars.

Detailed checklists of the requirements that should be considered in estimating the startup costs for a real estate office are provided at the end of Chapter 19.

CENTRALIZED VERSUS DECENTRALIZED

Management's decision whether to operate the business in a central-ized fashion or to decentralize and give each branch considerable autonomy can find arguments favoring both methods.

Advantages of a centralized operation include management's closer control and more direct supervision of accounting, purchasing, training, closing and advertising. Centralized accounting enables management to control expenses more closely. Each profit center is set up with budget and expense records of its own and can be checked regularly by both the branch manager and the main office. Banking that is done centrally often enables the firm to develop leverage factors that prove helpful in expansion. Centralized purchasing and advertising also enable top management to keep closer control of important expense items. When you are centralized, training can be part of an overall recruitment-selection-training-retention program for the entire firm.

Centralized closing is debatable. The positive factors for keeping this part of a brokerage business centralized include financing. Here again, leverage with the local bank can sometimes sustain a transaction that might otherwise fail. If you decide to decentralize that part of your operation only, a closing coordinator from the main office might represent management.

Decentralization has its distinct advantages too. If a manager has the ability to delegate responsibility and authority and get psychological commitments, you can have a branch manager who is not only a sales manager but an office manager and perhaps even a vice-president in charge. This person may be literally an independent working under the firm's name, perhaps having a share of the operation or some stock in it. Such a branch operation can even be capitalized as a separate corporation.

Decentralized branches not only permit the manager greater freedom to operate according to local market conditions, they also challenge that manager's flexibility, efficiency and ability to develop the branch business according to his or her own concepts as they fit the firm's general policy and goals. The manager in a decentralized operation also enjoys a stronger image in his or her local community. Top management in these situations report that such branch operations are easier to measure in matters of efficiency and that this style of operation definitely cuts overhead.

Whichever style is chosen, each branch operation should be assigned its fair share of main office administrative costs. Accounting, training, travel and entertainment expenses of top management all relate to basic company operations and should be shared by every office. This is best solved by computing the percentage of time spent by each of these individuals for the benefit of the branch office directly and for the benefit of the company as a whole. Then the appropriate percentages are allocated back to the branch office.

THE BRANCH MANAGER

Once it has been decided what type of branch office will be added and the type of management it will require, the next step is to find a manager. Brokers who have expanded horizontally recommend hiring the manager for the new location as early as possible in the expansion process and involving that individual in the planning and decision making for the new operation.

It is generally wise to hire a branch manager who is familiar with the new market area. But it is the manager's leadership skills that are the most important factor in the success of a new office. Many promising operations start in good locations and in attractive offices with all of the background services that could be provided, then fail because of inadequate management. Conversely, there have been many examples in which both the facilities and marketplace were not especially strong, but a skilled manager was able to pull together all of the elements to make the operation successful.

Hiring the branch manager from within your existing operation can give you an edge because this person is familiar with your operation and supports your company's goals and objectives. As you recruit staff, you should give some thought to the management potential of the people being considered. Testing, training and development should be a regular part of any organization that is considering expansion. One way to develop management is through an assistant manager program where a qualified sales associate is given a job description that includes management tasks and is allowed to perform them under the guidance of the broker. As these skills are developed and encouraged, the whole expansion program becomes possible.

The branch office manager may not need the entire spectrum of qualifications and characteristics needed to run a full office. If that person is not involved in such activities as cost analysis, budget control, statistics and advertising, skills in those areas will not be needed.

It is important that a complete job description be prepared so the new branch manager knows exactly what is expected of him or her. After the initial outline of the job description is drawn up by the owner, it is a good idea to hold an in-depth meeting with the branch office manager to develop a final job description that is mutually agreeable. Certainly, the branch office manager should understand how the expenses are allocated if he or she is to be compensated on any type of percentage of the office's net or gross.

To develop a management rather than a salesperson's perspective, the branch office manager should be encouraged to attend courses offered by the Real Estate Brokerage Managers Council. In addition, joining the Sales Marketing Executives or the American Management Association will expose the manager to other executives in the local community.

COMPENSATION PACKAGE

Compensation for branch managers will vary greatly depending on the duties the manager is expected to perform.* The size of the manager's salary is also related to the availability of qualified managers in your marketplace, the competition for their services and what is needed to retain them. Compensation packages for managers can vary from straightforward, simple plans to ones that are very complex. All management compensation plans must take into account the impact of the manager on the company's revenue.

A number of firms pay their branch office manager no salary. In these cases, the managers are selling managers who have the opportunity to increase their sales volume because they hold the title of office manager. Though this arrangement has the advantage of not increasing the company's

---

* Part of the information in this section is abstracted from the book, *Compensation Planning: The Key to Profitability,* by David Cocks and Larry Laframboise, published in 1995 by the Real Estate Brokerage Managers Council.

overhead for salaries and compensation, it puts the branch manager in the position of competing with his or her sales personnel. It can also make it difficult to motivate managers to perform their managerial duties because they feel they are not being paid for these activities. A nonselling manager is more likely to focus on controlling and guiding the efforts of the sales personnel to meet the sales goal of the branch.

Another type of compensation plan gives the manager no salary but pays a percentage override of the gross sales of his or her office. This is most appropriate for managers who have no control over the expenses of their office and therefore should not be penalized for improper cost accounting. When their main task is to increase sales volume, it makes sense that managers be compensated on a percentage of either the gross or company dollar.

Some firms pay nonselling managers a base salary plus an agreed upon incentive such as an override. *Overrides* are a specified percentage of a specified revenue. Generally, the higher the revenue that the override is to be calculated from, the lower the percentage the override should be. Some revenue groups commonly used for overrides include:

- *Gross revenue:* This is the total income of the office, including residential sales and all related commissions, rentals, referrals, appraisal fees, insurance revenues, property management fees and so forth.
- *Total gross commission income:* This is the total amount of commission income, including referral fees, rentals and the manager's personal production.
- *Net operating income:* This is what is left of the gross revenue once compensation payments and all off-the-top deductions have been made. It represents the amount of money available for paying the cost of office operations and profit.
- *Earnings of agents:* This is the amount of money paid to agents through commissions, bonuses and anything else specified in their compensation plans.

Overrides are usually specified as a percentage rate, such as 3.5 percent of Gross Commission Income (GCI) to be paid quarterly. The fairness of this rate as well as the impact it has on the company should be reviewed regularly and, if necessary, renegotiated annually.

A base salary plus override plan is most appropriate for managers who are directly involved in the control of costs and overhead for their offices. The total of salary plus the override should reflect the manager's marketplace value.

Overrides calculated on fluctuating factors such as agent productivity may create a good incentive for the manager to encourage and help agents close as many sales as possible. It should also provide the manager with some incentive to recruit and retain good agents. However, there is a danger that managers could grow complacent and invest their energy in the retention and motivation of a few select agents, possibly to the detriment of the company as a whole. Systems should be in place to ensure that the manager's actions are accountable beyond the mere scope of a paycheck. If a manager is receiving a high base salary with overrides, the manager's performance should be judged against recruiting, retention and the company dollar so the focus on profit for the company is not overlooked.

In addition to the manager's base salary plus overrides, other components of the compensation package could include perquisites (perks), task completion incentives, bonuses and similar benefits.

Perks have a tangible value and should be included as part of any compensation package offered to a branch manager. These can take many forms. Some common examples are as follows:

- Receiving company commissions for personal sales
- Possibilities to sell certain services (for example, training) or products to agents at a profit
- Business expenses related to attendance at conventions and other business functions
- Use of a company car

Task completion incentives reward the manager for the completion of specific tasks. For example, in addition to the daily duties of managing an office, financial rewards might be made for successfully recruiting agents, offering training or coaching and increasing the percentage of productive agents.

Bonuses are another effective way to provide managers with the incentive to complete specific goals. Some situations where it might be appropriate to reward a manager with a bonus include the following:

- Reaching a targeted production level set by the company
- When the company as a whole or when individual agents reach specified goals

Another option to be considered when putting together a compensation package for a manager is profit sharing. This is usually paid in regular monthly or quarterly periods. Such a plan may state that a set percentage of any profits retained by the branch office or by the company over a specified period of time is to be paid out to a manager in regular payments. A manager who has the latitude to control all factors affecting the office is more appropriately rewarded by profit sharing than by other compensation plans. Care must be taken to ensure that profit sharing is contingent upon meeting objectives that are intended to maintain long-term profitability.

Compensation should be adapted to the specifics of the situation. It should not only be attractive to the manager but should also be tailored to meet the needs of the company. In short, the compensation package should be designed to reward results and to create the best relationship between the branch manager and the owner in order to generate the best results.

Compensation must be fair and equitable to encourage new managers and retain other managers. The owner who tries to skimp on management's compensation is shortsighted because skimping can have a negative effect on the whole operation.

COST COMPUTATIONS

One tool to assist managers in evaluating the risk of opening a branch office is the breakeven point analysis. The purpose of a breakeven analysis is to determine the minimum production requirements needed to cover the new branch's fixed costs.

To determine the breakeven point, you need to calculate the average revenue you anticipate earning per sale. Once you've determined your fixed costs and the projected average income per sale, you can determine the number of sales that need to be made in order for the branch to break even. For example, if you will have $30,000 in anticipated overhead and you expect to make $1,200 in revenue per sale, it means 25 sales are necessary just to break even.

A second formula is used to estimate the unknown projected income.

$$\begin{array}{l}
 \text{Anticipated average listing price} \\
\times \text{ Commission rate} \\
\times \text{ Number of listings projected to be obtained} \\
\times \text{ Percentage of listings that should be sold} \\
\div \text{ Office commission splits} \\
= \text{ Projected income}
\end{array}$$

For example:

$$\begin{array}{l}
 \$70{,}000 \text{ average listing price} \\
\times \text{ .07 (7\% commission)} = \$4{,}900 \\
\times \text{ 20 listings (10 salespeople averaging} \\
 \text{ 2 listings per month)} = \$98{,}000 \\
\times \text{ 70\% of the listings sold} = \$68{,}600 \\
\div \text{ 2 (representing a 50/50 company split)} \\
= \$34{,}300 \text{ projected income}
\end{array}$$

When you can estimate the projected income or the projected number of sales needed, you can also convert it to the number of salespeople needed.

DETERMINING NUMBER OF SALESPEOPLE REQUIRED

There are two basic theories to use in determining the number of salespeople needed in a real estate firm. One is the quantity theory, and the other is the quality theory.

The quantity theory suggests that real estate companies should hire as many salespeople as possible, hoping that each will bring in enough sales for their large numbers to show a generous cash flow.

The opposite is the quality theory in which a broker has fewer salespeople and trains them thoroughly so that each is able to generate a handsome individual income as well as a profitable company dollar. Another possibility is to use a combination of the two theories.

One determining factor in calculating the number of salespeople you will need is the economics of the proposed office. If the proposed office economics indicate that $30,000 per month is needed to cover overhead, and the average sales commission generates approximately $1,200 to your salespeople, on a 50/50 split, 25 sales per month are needed to cover basic expenses. If the rule of thumb in your area is approximately two sales per month per sales agent, you will need 12 salespeople just to break even.

Relationship to Developed inquiries

Another rule of thumb used is the relationship to developed inquiries. The company should be keeping statistics on how many inquiries come in in relationship to appointments made, a ratio that relates finally to sales themselves. Enough salespeople must be available for opportunity time and/or floor time to be able to handle the inquiries and make appointments in order to have final sales; and the final sales should directly relate back to the inquiries so the salesperson is assured of making a reasonable income.

Relationship to Population Turnover

At one time many companies thought in terms of mileage circles—that a branch office should service X number of square miles per salesperson. However, it is generally recognized now that this is not a useful rule of thumb. It is more important that the number of salespeople in the branch office be in relationship to the population turnover in the area. Obviously this turnover does not include people moving into or out of apartments because they do not require sales assistance. However, the population turnover of people in the sales market itself and the anticipated percentage of their share of the market can give a good indication of the number of salespeople needed to serve them.

If population turnover in the area is low, fewer salespeople are needed. Keep this in mind in arranging the initial square footage at the branch office to avoid allocating more space than is needed.

NEED FOR EXPERIENCED STAFF

Finally, you should pay attention to the experienced people who will form the core of the operation. The success of the office often depends on starting with some experienced people who produce sales immediately. This is preferred to starting an office with a completely new staff who need 3 to 6 months to become familiar with the market and start generating income. You should also consider the number of experienced salespeople who may want to join the firm in their area.

Further information about opening a branch office, from selecting a location to setting up control systems, can be found in Chapter 19.

VERTICAL EXPANSION

Vertical expansion (also referred to as diversification, vertical integration and ancillary services) occurs when a company offers services other than residential real estate. A company can open departments that offer services in specialized real estate disciplines such as appraisal or commercial-investment brokerage. Or they could offer services related to the residential real estate discipline such as insurance, relocation or finance. Figure 17.1 could be an organization chart for a diversified firm. It highlights the various disciplines or branches of knowledge involved in the real estate business.

Vertical integration can provide economies of scale when you use the same customer base to offer services that complement each other. It can provide new profit centers for the company. It can also provide a value-added service for customers, for example, by enabling them to obtain a mortgage through the same company through which they buy their home. It is likely that present and potential users of specialized services are already customers of your more traditional services. Your objective is to keep your customers by satisfying as many of their needs as possible.

There are a variety of strategies a firm can choose from to accomplish vertical expansion. It can offer the desired service itself as a captive operation; it can enter into a joint venture with an entity that provides the service; or it can refer customers to a service provider with which it has developed an affiliate relationship.

RESIDENTIAL BROKERAGE

Residential brokerage is the base on which most real estate firms are built. Brokers who achieve success in residential work and are interested in expansion may move into another subdiscipline of brokerage or perhaps into one of the other major real estate disciplines, or both.

New Homes

Though the new homes subdiscipline in residential brokerage is a fairly recent development, it has become a large part of many brokerage

FIGURE 17.1 Organizational Chart for a Diversified Real Estate Firm

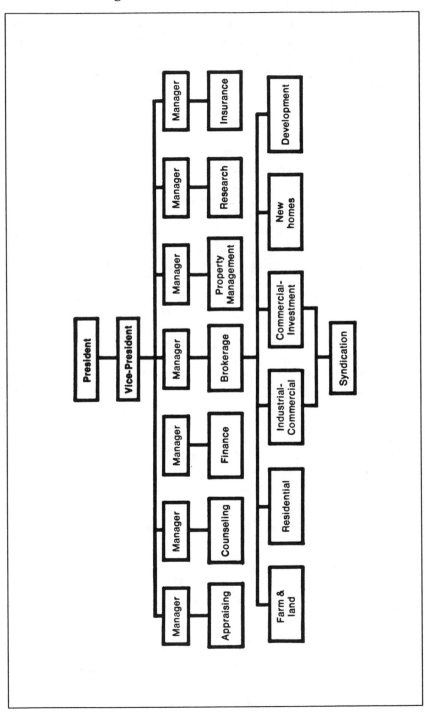

operations. Some firms sell only new homes while others may even further specialize in selling in one subdivision or developed area.

A further subdivision of new home sales is destination properties, that is, properties people retire to. These destination properties generally offer an attraction such as a lake, a golf course, skiing and so on. Today's retirees are more vigorous than ever before and seek recreational activities in their retirement locale.

Selling new homes differs from selling resale homes and requires a different type of salesperson. It more closely resembles selling a product such as a car or an appliance and generally involves a great many visits by customers to the property before they make up their minds to buy. Compensation is also handled differently; often salespeople are paid on a unit instead of a percentage basis.

Traditionally, brokers have been discouraged or prevented from listing or selling new homes by builders who prefer to handle their own sales when the market is good, and many builders have their own sales operations. However, builders are more likely to turn to brokers for sales help in a difficult market.

Selling new homes can provide a useful source of buyers for existing homes. In one major metropolitan market, 13 percent of the potential buyers who go into a broker's office buy new homes. But many people who come in to look at new homes actually buy preowned properties because a builder cannot provide financing and cost flow. Without a new homes department, a broker in that market would lose all or a portion of those potential buyers.

Another benefit for brokers in new homes is that as they sell them they get to know the buyers and are in on the ground floor for resale listings. Also, the buyer acquiring a new house probably has one to sell, creating another chance for a listing and sales commission.

New homes are excellent field offices. A desk, phone, heat and light are all it costs the broker. Local home furnishings merchants usually will furnish models in exchange for promotion of their names and services. Salespeople who work in model homes free up desk space in the main office.

There are several ways a broker can add a new homes department. The most common is to sell the homes for a builder. Another option is for the broker to joint venture with a builder in acquiring and developing land and constructing the houses. Joint venturing in development can be risky, however, depending on local market conditions, land availability and construction costs.

Relocation

Another subdivision of residential real estate is relocation. This consists of handling corporate properties and working with executives who are being transferred. A relocation service can be operated within the real estate firm as a profit center. However, the relocation business is staff intensive, requiring people to call on corporations, find homes, make referrals and handle corporate properties. To offer this service, many firms that are not large enough to have their own relocation operation will affiliate with other companies who do not compete in their marketplace. A relocation business helps firms be full-service, can be a profit center and will generate business for a real estate company.

FINANCE

Finance is an allied discipline of real estate. However, many brokerage firms are profitably integrating finance into their operations as part of their total real estate services.

Brokers can enter the mortgage finance business on a variety of levels. On the simplest level, they might have a computer terminal in their office that is used to qualify people and give them rates; they would receive a fee from the lender who provided the terminal. Alternatively, they might have a mortgage officer on site, either in a joint venture relationship or in a rented space. Finally, they might have a full-fledged mortgage banking operation in which they process and own the loan, and either sell or keep it.

One REALTOR® created a mortgage business in order to provide better service for customers after a bad experience with a mortgage company that decided to raise its points without warning, upsetting buyers who were scheduled to close. Having its own mortgage business helps the firm because it knows that the mortgage process will be handled well. By working with more than 20 lenders, it provides customers a valuable service by being able to offer many mortgage choices. It also offers buyers conveniences they would not be able to get at a bank, such as enabling them to write a mortgage application in the evening or on weekends.

The mortgage business had the dual benefits of offering customers a valuable service while increasing profits for the company. When interest rates came down, the company contacted its customers about refinancing its loans, and almost 100 percent refinanced with them. The company is also there when customers need money for college tuition or a bridge loan. This creates tremendous goodwill and loyal customers.[1]

Affiliate relationships can help you when you decide to offer ancillary services. For example, the company that would buy the real estate firm's mortgages helped them get started by setting up a computerized system within the company to process the mortgages and by offering training classes for the people who would handle the loans. This important vendor relationship enabled the company to get up to speed quickly to capitalize on current market demand.[2]

INSURANCE

Like finance, insurance is one element of a full line of services many firms want to offer. However, many firms have discontinued insurance departments in recent years, citing problems in servicing accounts and a decrease in the commissions paid by insurance companies. REALTORS® say a critical mass of business is needed in order to obtain good rates from insurers. However, because the big insurance companies have grown so large, it is difficult for even the largest real estate firms to attain that critical mass of customers. Working with a joint venture partner is one way for a real estate firm to successfully enter the insurance business.

Insurance is a natural tie-in with real estate. Everyone who contacts a broker is a potential client for some type of insurance policy. And everyone who buys real estate will need insurance, ranging from liability, mortgage protection, fire and theft, to all manner of special policies that require the broker to find special underwriting. Providing insurance services to customers adds to the broker's potential value to clients.

Another benefit is that an insurance department keeps the broker's name before the public through the simple, routine steps essential to year-round service. Reminders of approaching renewal dates and suggestions for updating coverage are among the best public relations tools an insurance department has. The friendly birthday or anniversary card is the kind of gesture recipients appreciate, and it gives brokers an opportunity to get their name into people's homes on happy occasions.

Selling insurance adds to a firm's total profitability because it lays off overhead and contributes to cash flow. No matter what size the department, the insurance premiums keep coming in. On the other hand, claims can run ruinously high, and there is a low profit ratio per policy. The broker needs to concentrate the writing of policies within the office, keeping salespeople's attention and effort on the much more productive activities of listing and selling properties.

Insurance must be a high dollar operation to be profitable. Some brokers estimate that a firm should have a quarter million dollars in premiums before an insurance department is worthwhile. Others argue that this service should be continued on a narrow profit margin because of its public relations value to the firm.

TITLE INSURANCE

Another affiliated service brokers can offer customers is title insurance. Depending on the state the broker operates in, the title business could be a captive or affiliated company, a joint venture, or the broker could simply receive a fee for referring the customer to a specific title company that provides a sound policy with good rates and service. In addition to being a useful customer service, an advantage of this business is that a new title insurance policy is needed each time a property changes hands.

STRATEGIC ALLIANCES

A creative new form of vertical integration involves strategic alliances. Strategic alliances enable a real estate company to use its company's infrastructure to support other companies and, at the same time, use the strength of those other companies to support its presence in other markets without having to open real estate offices there. For example, Kahn REALTORS®, a New York firm with 3 offices and 65 sales associates, created strategic alliances with real estate firms with similar philosophies in geographic areas the firm wanted to penetrate. Through the alliance, those companies can choose to buy training, advertising, marketing and consulting services from Kahn REALTORS® on a menu basis, paying only for the services they use. The companies also are required to add "Better Homes & Gardens" to their names.

This program has been very profitable for Kahn REALTORS®. Alliances have created more referrals and the company has increased its presence in the markets it identified. Having more people come to its training programs has also increased the firm's profitability. Because it runs the training programs anyway, additional students from other companies increase the firm's bottom line. Similarly, if the firm prints 10,000 homes magazines for its own use, it can print them more economically if it prints 30,000 and the allied companies pay for the other 20,000 copies.[3]

OTHER REAL ESTATE DISCIPLINES

In addition to offering ancillary services such as those just described, a firm may decide to add other, specialized real estate disciplines to its residential practice. The following are brief descriptions of the major real estate specialties.

FARM AND LAND BROKERAGE

A farm and land brokerage office specializes in the sale of producing and nonproducing farms and ranches as well as raw land. This subdiscipline of brokerage has become increasingly profitable as investors buy land for future use and appreciation. Brokers who understand the tax laws involved in buying and holding raw land, the value of producing farms and ranches, and can also envision future uses of the land will find this a lucrative department. This discipline also requires a knowledge of appraisal, research and finance. The REALTORS® Land Institute of the National Association of REALTORS® offers education in this area.

INDUSTRIAL

Industrial real estate includes all land and buildings either utilized or suited for industrial activities. In addition to manufacturing and directly related activities, industrial real estate includes distribution and warehousing of the manufactured product, wholesaling, research and development or laboratory activities, and office space related to industrial activities. The facilities of transportation companies that provide terminal space and maintenance as services to industrial firms also fall within this category, including public warehousing facilities and airport terminal services. In addition, business services such as publishing and printing, vehicle and equipment repair are regarded as industrial activities.

Although residential brokers may sell some industrial property, brokerage of this type is usually found in separate firms that specialize in it. Larger companies often have separate industrial offices.

Industrial brokers must be knowledgeable in appraisal for valuation, finance for arranging loans, research for understanding present value and calculating future value of proposed income streams or special purpose properties, and in some instances, property management to counsel the client on the operation of a proposed purchase. The Society of Industrial and Office REALTORS® of the National Association of REALTORS® provides information in this area.

COMMERCIAL-INVESTMENT TRANSACTIONS

Like industrial transactions, commercial-investment transactions are very complex, requiring knowledge of all of the major real estate disciplines. The increasing sophistication of investors as well as the need to have a solid understanding of complicated and ever-changing tax laws (tax expertise has become a discipline in itself) make it necessary for brokers to obtain specialized training in this field.

Commercial and investment sales generally require more time and effort per sale than residential sales. They require a lot of paperwork, as work-up data on properties must be packaged for prospective clients. They also require more planning and cooperation with state and local authorities as well as extensive interaction with specialists to complete transactions. Despite the additional work, however, commercial and investment sales provide a high company dollar return. While desk costs are higher than in residential sales, profitability on these transactions is excellent.

One reason to consider adding this discipline to an existing brokerage operation is that potential clients are already at hand. A company executive who has bought a home may also need office or plant facilities. Or a broker's present clients may have investment property they wish to sell. This could be anything from a corporation's outgrown factory or office building to property acquired through inheritance. Frequently a residential broker can find a big opportunity in supplying commercial facilities to an expanding residential community. A series of institutional ads that focus on basic real estate investment principles have been known to elicit responses from wholly unexpected sources. Some of them could come from people you have been doing residential business with for years.

Finding the right salespeople is key. Many commercial-investment sales require intense creativity and determination to put all the pieces together and lots of perseverance and patience to see transactions through. Salespeople have to be numbers-oriented and able to effectively communicate the sophisticated terms of the discipline to people who have money to invest. Buyers may turn away rather than admit they don't understand the technicalities of a transaction. Salespeople going into commercial-investment need lots of lead time—sometimes as much as two years. And they require management dedicated to giving them sound advice and continuing encouragement.

A broker establishing a commercial-investment or industrial division must determine whether residential salespeople will be permitted to handle these types of properties. What effect will excluding residential salespeople from this area have on sales volume and morale? What will be the effect on the firm's reputation if residential salespeople try to compete with industrial or investment salespeople for the same client? What effect would any proposed restrictions have on salespeople's independent contractor status? These questions must be dealt with carefully as you consider expansion plans.

The benefits of adding a commercial-investment division to your operation include spreading the cost of institutional advertising and other overhead over more profit centers, interdepartmental referrals and opportunities for equity investment by the brokers. In addition, the firm's image and prestige are enhanced when major buildings are sold.

There are some cautions, however. It can be difficult to get exclusives in this area; owners of this type of property are reluctant to be tied up. There are also public relations hazards that could affect the firm's image adversely. For example, if a broker's commercial department is putting together a transaction that is opposed by a segment of the public and emotions at a zoning meeting run high, the result could be bad public relations that affect every division of the company negatively. In addition, a broker could spend a lot of time and money on a transaction that falls through. For this reason, more and more brokers are now charging consulting fees for commercial-investment work.

The Commercial Investment Real Estate Institute provides information and excellent courses in the commercial-investment field, leading to the Certified Commercial Investment Member designation.

SYNDICATION

In many states, securities departments are ruling that many syndications, historically considered real estate sales, are now classified as security transactions. More and more people are becoming involved in the ownership of real estate through multiple group ownership, syndication or limited partnerships. This method of real estate investment can involve hundreds of millions of dollars.

Most firms doing a substantial amount of partnership and syndication transactions find it desirable, if not in fact necessary, to obtain a securities license permitting them to go in whichever direction is dictated by the final disposition of their clients' holdings. Syndications are becoming more attractive than single client transactions. As long as syndications show a good profit, they continually generate the capital needed for more investing, and these clients come back over and over again. Syndications appeal to people who historically invested in mutual funds, stocks and bonds.

The Real Estate Securities and Syndication Section of the National Association of REALTORS® provides training and publications in this area.

APPRAISAL

Appraisal services are often sought when present and future property values must be measured with accuracy. Appraisers estimate the value of residential, commercial and industrial properties, and most appraisers have strong backgrounds in finance, property management and research.

An *appraisal* is a well-supported estimate of value usually based on one or more of three accepted approaches to value: the cost approach, the sales comparison approach and the income capitalization approach.

A competent appraiser usually has a background in real estate and related disciplines gained through training and experience in analyzing various types of property. For example, an appraiser who specializes in residential valuation needs a background in residential brokerage and a knowledge of current and past markets. He or she must also have knowledge of new homes and their construction costs to utilize the cost approach to value. Familiarity with investment properties is also needed to calculate the income to be derived from income-producing properties.

Recordkeeping is of prime importance in appraisal work. An efficient filing system for organizing records, maps, data, statistics and correspondence is essential. Appraisers need to gather and analyze assessments, taxes, zoning regulations, deed and property descriptions as well as information on comparable properties, current construction costs and any other facts used in arriving at a value conclusion.

All relevant information is applied to the valuation problem and reconciled to arrive at a final value conclusion. The conclusion is developed in a formal report and presented to the client along with supporting photographs, maps or plats.

Appraisal assignments vary in content and cost depending on their simplicity or sophistication. Appraisal fees may be hourly, per diem or set on a job-plus-cost basis. A broker contemplating expanding into appraisal work must know all the costs involved, including the value of the appraiser's time, secretarial costs, a share of general office cost, automobile and/or travel expenses and other miscellaneous costs. The latter might include the fees of professional photographers, surveyors and other professionals whose work is essential to the estimation of property value.

What are some of the advantages of adding an appraisal department? It is a low-overhead operation, requiring little clerical help to type reports, many of which are standardized. Every time a highway is built or a structure is enlarged, appraisals are needed. In some cases, whole towns are being assessed, reestablishing values for tax purposes. Corporations are fine prospects, especially when an entire company is moving, building, buying or planning to transfer a number of employees.

On the negative side, starting up an appraisal business is time-consuming. It requires a lot of development before it produces a good income. Anyone going into appraisal work should plan a long lead time.

Conflict of interest is another potential problem that should be monitored carefully. When a conflict occurs, the broker may find himself appraising a property only to lose the listing to another broker.

It is growing more difficult to get appraisal credentials. All 50 states require the licensing or certification of appraisers who perform certain types of assignments.

Information on the appraisal field can be obtained from the Appraisal Section of the National Association of REALTORS®.

PROPERTY MANAGEMENT

Property management refers to financial and operations management of properties for an owner for a fee. Property managers may also be consultants who advise owners on methods of increasing the value of a property.

The property manager performs the administrative tasks necessary to achieve the owner's specified objectives. Duties may include marketing and leasing, managing the operation and maintenance of the property, collecting rents and keeping records, long-range planning for the property, budgeting and supervising staff. Types of properties that require the services of a manager include: apartments, office buildings, condominiums, shopping and retail centers, mixed-use buildings, industrial parks, mobile home parks and single-family residences.

Opportunities for property management abound in large metropolitan areas because of the high concentration of income-producing properties there. However, other opportunities exist in smaller communities and resort areas located throughout the United States.

Property management is a natural outgrowth of residential and commercial listings. It is almost a necessity for firms that have an investment department. Because many investment properties are absentee-owned, it is to the broker's advantage to be able to offer management services along with the investment itself. Property management is a logical tie-in to relocation, which often requires the firm to manage the property. The firm already has incurred the overhead for maintenance personnel; property management then spreads this expense while providing another source of income.

A residential brokerage can engage in property management on a number of levels from simply renting properties to full-fledged management of the property.

Property management interacts with appraisal in evaluating a client's property; with finance, to assure the best type of mortgaging; with brokerage, to advise whether to sell or hold the property; and with research, to indicate when rentals should be raised and to inform the owner on general market trends.

As in residential sales, marketing and leasing activities must comply with applicable fair housing laws.

One of the advantages of starting a property management department is that it has an even cash flow. A broker with a substantial property management operation need not care as much about market fluctuations because this profit helps offset some of the losses incurred when residential sales are slow. A long-term management contract is another form of security. And a company that does a good job in management is in a prime position to lock in an exclusive when the time comes to sell the property.

People from the residential staff can help rent management's properties, adding to their income too. This increases the total service aspect of real estate brokerage.

The prestige of having the firm name on large buildings is a plus. It is another way of keeping in the public eye and informing people that the firm helps in a variety of ways.

Property management also has some disadvantages. For one thing, fixed salaries are involved for all the people essential to the operation. These include the individuals responsible for rent collections, repairs and record-keeping for the owner. There also is a smaller percentage of profit than in brokerage. A company has to handle a great many properties before it realizes a sizeable return.

Inadequate repairs and unsatisfactory maintenance can lead to tenant problems and resultant poor relations with the owner. Certainly anything connected with a negative consumer relationship that results in bad publicity will have an immediate adverse effect on the whole company.

There is higher liability in management, which can bring some problems of contract cancellation, and it is absolutely essential to carry good insurance. A great deal of bookkeeping is required in property management, and the department or its representatives must be on 24-hour call.

The Institute of Real Estate Management of the National Association of REALTORS® offers courses and publications in this area as well as the designations Certified Property Manager, Accredited Management Organization and Accredited Residential Manager.

COUNSELING

Unlike management, appraisal or brokerage, real estate counseling is not a discipline but a process. While objective in analysis, the Counselor directs his or her efforts toward the client's best interest through evaluation of options, advocacy of the client's best interests and development and execution of appropriate strategies.

Those designated a Counselor of Real Estate (CRE) are members of The Counselors of Real Estate, the professional consulting affiliate of the National Association of REALTORS®. A Counselor of Real Estate is a seasoned real estate practitioner who provides advisory services to clients.

The Counselor brings to each assignment a broad range of experience in the real estate field combined with technical competency in more than one real estate specialty. CREs are recognized by their peers as having consistently demonstrated the highest levels of knowledge, experience, integrity and judgment in the practice of real estate.

CONCLUSION

All the foregoing disciplines in real estate can be operated as separate businesses rather than being under a single roof.

When brokers regard real estate disciplines in the same way they are thought of in the field of education—where special fields of knowledge are grouped under that one word, education—it may be easier for them to focus on the thrust of their particular discipline, aware that the other fields of specialization will contribute to their needs as they arise.

ENDNOTES

1. Harold Kahn, "Seizing the Opportunities of Vertical Integration," in *Management Issues and Trends,* vol. 10, no. 1, 1995, p. 6.
2. "Seizing the Opportunities of Vertical Integration," p. 6.
3. "Case Study: Strategic Alliances at Kahn, REALTORS®, Inc," in *Management Issues & Trends,* vol. 10, no. 1, 1995, p. 7.

Chapter 18

Growth of a Firm:

Mergers and Acquisitions

Companies can also grow through mergers and acquisitions. Combining the complementary strengths of companies can increase their total market impact. A merger may be the salvation of companies struggling to survive. The material in this chapter applies whether management is looking for another company to acquire or is being acquired.

GROWTH WITHOUT BIG CAPITAL OUTLAY

In evaluating the operation of their companies, management frequently cites the following difficulties:

- Inadequate advertising and promotional budget
- Little free time for the broker
- Lack of financial security for the broker
- Small impact made on the market
- Lack of continuity
- Harder to make more money
- Difficult to broaden base of operation
- Difficult to attract experienced people
- Inability to penetrate new markets

What can the broker do to improve one or more of these categories in order to have a more profitable operation? If there is limited capital available, the answer lies in one of two directions: Either attempt to merge into a larger firm that offers all or more of the services as outlined above or find other small companies of similar size, merge them into a single operation and effect needed economies yet provide more complete broker-age service to the consumer.

A case history shows how eight small brokers merged into one major operation with minimum cash and capitalization. This merger occurred in a large metropolitan area where the brokers had offices separated geograph-ically by basic markets. They closed nonproductive offices and concen-trated on the best ones. Each broker was assigned specific duties, from the president of the merged operation to the training manager. They were able to attract a number of new salespeople as a result of the merger. They were also able to broaden their services to the public and develop programs such as trade-in and guaranteed sales plans that they had been unable to provide as individual offices. Since the merger, there have been a number of changes. Only five of the original eight brokers remain. However, their overall success has justified the merger. They were able to do it by a very simple formula dividing the cash and capitalization requirement based on the number of salespeople each broker brought into the merged operation. The most important feature of this merger was that the brokers all willingly accepted an assignment in the merged operation in the area in which they excelled.

It is admittedly a frightening experience to consider merging with another company or to face the acquisition of your firm by another firm. But with an honest, fair appraisal and long-range planning a merger can enable the following to occur:

- A stronger company image
- Sufficient size to assure adequate advertising and promotional budgets
- An effective training program
- Improved ability to compete for listings
- The physical size to offer adequate consumer services
- More free time or the opportunity for a vacation for the managers
- Shared responsibilities

Owners of a real estate firm should honestly evaluate where they expect to be in their operation one year and five years hence, list all the firm's attributes and deficiencies and then decide on objectives and goals. A successful merger or acquisition will bring the owners and agents closer to those objectives and goals. If it will not, then there is no good reason for the transaction.

DISADVANTAGES

Licensed brokers and real estate salespeople are independent thinking businesspeople. The majority are independent contractors. There are no time clocks. Their opportunity to achieve is unlimited. It has always been interesting to observe their broad spectrum of productivity and the fact that there is really no typical salesperson. Some real estate salespeople are satisfied with $15,000 or $20,000 a year in earnings. Yet many top producers consistently earn $100,000 to $200,000 per year. What does this have to do with mergers or acquisitions? It has a great deal to do with them because the typical broker may see justification in a merger or acquisition, but when it comes to deciding to do it, the psychological impact of that decision is overwhelming. No real estate broker, small or large, wants to lose his or her identity. Thousands of real estate salespeople who were making an excellent income associated with a good active broker have left to open their own company, not just because they thought they could make more money but because they wanted that personal identity, additional independence and freedom of action. It is hard to convince this type of individual that his or her ultimate goals could be achieved by merging with another office or offices.

The major disadvantage of any merger or acquisition is the loss of identity and the need to adhere to someone else's direction and policy. Franchise operations try to overcome these disadvantages by preserving local management identity and responsibility, while providing the advantages offered through the successful operation of a larger firm without complete takeover.

Another disadvantage could be the basis of compensation in the acquisition or merger. If it is not a straight cash transaction and stock is given in lieu of cash, the broker must consider the market risk involved in holding stock and its fluctuating value based on economic conditions.

Once the broker gets past the psychological impact and decides the logical direction of expansion is through acquisition or merger, he or she must approach the decision-making process on as scientific a basis as possible.

WHAT TO LOOK FOR

A firm can expand through acquisition and merger within its current market, into new markets, and even into different cities or states. One New Jersey firm, over a period of five or six years, made ten acquisitions that developed into 98 real estate offices in five states and four mortgage banking operations.

Once the broker determines the direction the expansion will take, what is the procedure? Before the broker can determine the method of acquisition and the price, it is necessary to get a clear picture of the assets (both physical and productive) that will be acquired and how they will affect the continuing operation. The firm being acquired must have at least one of four advantages:

1. A location in a highly productive market area
2. Recognized productivity by the existing sales organization
3. Good internal management
4. Good reputation and image

The first things to look for are: current production, built-in expenses, management continuity, image, identity and status, and differences in operation.

Current Production of Sales Staff

Determine the number of licensed salespeople presently with the firm, what each has earned for a period of at least two years and what goals each has set for current production. If adequate records are not available, sit down with the management and list all licensed staff, examine their earnings for the previous year, if possible, and then analyze their production month by month. Discuss with management the productive ability of each salesperson, whether they have the ability to produce more business if greater advantages are offered through the merged firm. The ultimate price of the purchase of a real estate firm is going to be directly proportionate to the productivity of its sales staff.

Built-In Expenses

Acquisition of a firm includes assuming many of its obligations. Therefore, it is critical to analyze the operating expenses of the firm in detail, listing all the obligations that cannot be eliminated by virtue of the merger or acquisition. As an example, in most cases a real estate company will have a lease for a period of years. The merged operation may not plan to operate out of that location once the transaction is complete. But the lease will be the obligation of the new firm.

In addition, there can be other obligations: health benefits for employees or obligatory bonus arrangements. A policy on division of commissions that differs from that of the other company can present an immediate problem. Other obligations may include the leasing of various types of equipment. These are some of the obligations for which the succeeding firm will be responsible. This is why it is absolutely essential that the operating statements be carefully analyzed.

Management Continuity

Management is often one of the essential things being bought. This determination must be made in the acquisition of any firm. Will the licensed salespeople remain with the merged firm if present management is eliminated? It is very difficult to merge or acquire a firm and put new management in charge immediately. To so do disrupts the operation and has a tendency to hurt morale and affect production. Therefore, it is essential to approach existing management with the idea that they remain for a reasonable period of time until the transition is complete. Most merger or acquisition agreements generally insist on some sort of contract with existing management for a period of at least one year, preferably longer.

Image and Corporate Culture

Is the firm to be acquired a recognized, viable operation that shares a major portion of a market? If the corporate culture of the firm is changed, how will it affect the overall status of the operation and its productivity? The corporate culture affects how the agents, staff and management interact with one another and with the public. For example, a firm doing business with the country club set may have difficulty merging with a firm that is focused on low down payment, first-time buyers.

What is the market penetration of the firm being acquired? These questions must be answered by in-depth study. In many cases the firm being acquired has a stronger reputation than the one doing the acquiring, but due to ownership status or retirement the older and more reputable firm is absorbed. In one case, the company to be acquired had an outstanding reputation, had been in existence for almost 100 years and had represented thousands of clients over that period of time. Because of the advancing age of the broker and the lack of continuing management, the company was acquired by a relatively new broker. Rather than lose valued identity, the new broker incorporated the major portion of the name of the former company in the new firm name in order to take advantage of its identity and image. No acquiring firm should take an arbitrary position that its name must dominate in the merged operation. There are many things the other company may have to its advantage after the merger is complete.

Differences in Operation

Companies vary as much as individuals in their operation. These may range from divisions of commissions, floor time and use of long distance telephone calls to advertising requirements or listing procedures. Before making a final judgment in the acquisition of a firm, a broker must decide whether the differences in the operation are so severe that it would be impossible to incorporate the surviving salespeople and employees into the new operation. For example, no two firms have identical commission schedules. Can the acquiring firm offer attractive commission options to agents of both firms?

Operations may be so loose that by the time the staff of the acquired firm adheres to the acquiring company's policies and procedures, most of the staff is gone and the acquisition proves to be unprofitable. If the firm being acquired has an operations manual, compare it carefully with that of the acquiring firm. If the firm has no written documentation, the only way a broker can determine the differences is by interview. If this is the method by which the differences have to be determined, interview the management to find out the functions of their operation, the salaried employees to find out if they understand what their duties are and the salespeople to find out if they understand what management expects of them. In some cases, after all of the other areas have checked out and the transaction looks reasonable, mergers have failed because of vast differences in the types of operation. Part of the cost of a merger or acquisition is the expense of making it attractive for the agents to stay. Smart buyers and sellers recognize this in advance and generally budget funds to help the agents through the transition.

A major portion of the firm's value is in the general operation of the business. Unless those areas can be accurately evaluated, there is no reason to go on into the detailed operation to pursue the acquisition.

EVALUATING ASSETS

The nuts and bolts of an acquisition are the fixed assets of the firm. The base by which the purchase price is decided starts with an analysis of assets and liabilities. From this data the evaluation is made about productivity and goodwill. In evaluating the assets of a real estate firm, consider the following items: physical assets, listings, staff, name and reputation, management staff, lease, current commissions receivable and personnel.

Physical Assets

In the majority of cases, a real estate firm leases its space. In addition to space, it generally has desks, files, mechanical and other equipment. In many cases the equipment has been depreciated, and its current market value is greater than its depreciated value. The value of physical assets is determined by taking inventory with assigned values. All physical assets should be inspected visually. If there is any question about the assets, an office supplier can generally assist in setting current market values. In some cases the real estate company owns the building from which it operates. It could possibly be an office building where there are other tenants. In this event, a current market appraisal is necessary in order to determine the valuation for acquisition.

Listings

When purchasing a business, the buyer pays for inventory. When a broker buys another real estate company, part of the value of the company is its inventory of listings. What those listings will produce in income over a period of time can be determined mathematically with a reasonable degree of accuracy. Take the listings the firm has had over a period of a year or two. Check the number sold against those actually listed and the percentage sold by cooperative brokers to determine what the firm could expect to earn in gross income from the sale of existing listings. It is the listings presently available that will produce the income to carry the office after acquisition. Remember that there must be continuity in business and that in order for a business to have value, there must be a source of future income under new management. Listings and their marketability are therefore essential in determining the value of a real estate operation.

Management Staff

Does the firm being acquired have a young aggressive management team but just lack capital or training? Can that management staff be productive in the merged operation? Is it willing to stick with the merged operation to give it the opportunity to survive and succeed? Generally, relatively little value is assigned to the management staff because the acquiring firm normally has the management expertise to be applied to the firm being acquired.

Lease

There is a good possibility that the space leased by the real estate company was negotiated over a period of years and that there is an existing lease value that should be considered in acquisition. It is essential that the lease be examined to determine the remaining term, the rent and any obligations for increased rent, renewal options, division of cost, who furnishes gas and electricity, janitorial service, snow removal, parking lot maintenance, and so on.

Current Commissions Receivable

Determine whether the company is on a cash or accrual basis. An accrual basis provides a more accurate accounting of both the income and expenses of the operation. Most small real estate companies are on a cash basis. Therefore, most of the deferred income is not reflected in current statements. On that basis, two things have to be determined. First, get current status of all pending contracts of sale including whether they have been financed, whether commitments were issued, when settlements are expected and what commission the sales will produce. Second, get a listing of obligations that have been incurred but have not accrued. Current commissions receivable are an asset of a firm that will help defer continuing expenses. These current commissions would of course be offset by expense obligations.

Personnel

In many cases in a merged operation, one of the effective savings is the consolidation of personnel. For example, there may be an administrative broker who is the owner, a sales manager and possibly bookkeeping and secretarial personnel. In a merged operation the bookkeeping may be taken over by the parent company, eliminating the need for a bookkeeper; instead of having two individuals in management positions, one would be sufficient. The payment of personnel and their benefits are all expenses that must be considered in acquiring a firm. Be certain there are no long-term commitments or employment contracts with existing personnel that cannot be changed after the merger.

In some transactions, all salaried persons are technically terminated by the outgoing firm. All benefits are paid by the outgoing firm. The surviving firm then rehires the salaried employees with a clean slate and on terms negotiated by the surviving firm.

METHODS OF ACQUISITION AND RISK SHARING

There is no precise formula for the acquisition of a real estate company, and the price can vary substantially based on the method of acquisition. For example, a broker who plans to acquire a real estate firm and pay cash out of pocket for it with no deferred payments will look at the cost of acquisition with a very conservative and calculating eye, because once the cash is paid there is no recovery. If all of the facts and figures do not shape up as anticipated, the broker is out of luck once the settlement is made because there are no incentives to continue management of that firm for the repayment of the purchase price. Most real estate firms do not want to pay cash. They prefer to arrange payment on a deferred basis, so that part of the value is paid out of the continuing assets of the firm being acquired—the ability of the new firm to produce continuing income out of which the purchase price is repaid.

Often the balance is paid based on the success of the new firm. The outgoing owners may receive a percentage of gross revenue, company dollars or net profits over a period of three to seven years. This places some of the risk of the transaction with the outgoing (selling) owners. Buyers can pay more for a firm if they do not assume all the risk.

Exchange of Stock

Another method of acquisition is the exchange of stock. For example, a real estate company that has a major impact on a large market area, is strongly capitalized, and is publicly owned, has created an established value for its stock. When such a firm wants to acquire other real estate companies, instead of paying them either cash or deferred payments for the value of the company, it exchanges stock of its company for the ownership of the company to be acquired. The advantages for the seller are that it is generally a tax free exchange, and no tax consequences occur until the sale of the acquired stock. The other advantage is that if stock appreciates, the increased value comes without the management headaches. The risk factor is that if the bottom drops out of the real estate market, the stock is also devaluated dramatically. The advantage for the acquiring company is that it doesn't have to use any cash for its acquisitions. By buying a publicly owned company, it has sources of financing not generally available to a small, privately held company.

The exchange of stock can be attractive where there are two major corporations that understand each other's operations and feel there is a strict advantage through marriage, recognize the management of each company and are willing to exchange stock even though their respective stocks are not publicly held and there is a limited market. For example, X Company is in negotiation with Y Company that has a good market penetration where X Company is weak. In locations where X already has excellent market penetration Y is weak. X and Y have similar operations in mortgage banking and property management. A merger would provide substantial savings and efficiencies in operation. Neither stock is publicly held. Therefore, there is little or no market for the stock, but both recognize the market potential and advantages in a merger. The logical direction would be a tax-free merger so that both could reserve their cash and assets for a more efficient operation. Therefore, it is to their advantage to negotiate under these terms for a tax-free exchange of stock rather than a buyout by one or the other.

New Corporation

The last method of acquisition is to create a new corporation. Brokers may find it to their advantage to have a merged operation, create a new corporation, divide their responsibilities and develop a successful operation. In a number of cases where firms have been acquired due to management, the purchase price has been established by a guaranteed fixed price in cash with additional funds available based on the ability of management to increase the business. In other words, there would be an established kicker or percentage available out of earnings as an additional purchase price. Options may also be given to acquire additional stock based on increased earnings. This stock option could be quite valuable in the event the market value of the stock increases.

Determining Value

There are several major steps to ascertaining the value of a real estate brokerage company.* These follow.

Step 1: Determine Conditions and Assumptions   Estimating the value of a firm is no different than appraising real property. The purpose for the valuation determines the appraisal process and focus. Your first step, then, is to consider the purpose of the appraisal as well as your strategic vision or "conditions and assumptions" regarding the future of the firm. For example, the value of a firm continuing in its current operating mode can be quite different than the value to a purchaser planning to merge it into a multioffice operation.

Step 2: Reconstruct Income Statements   Reconstruct an income statement (based on the criteria established in step one) for the future operation of the business, considering the following:

- Exclude direct income and expenses from nonbrokerage activity (such as investment income and nonbusiness expenses).
- Allocate or exclude indirect expenses for nonbrokerage activity, including bookkeeping, telephone and rent.
- Impute a fair market value for all owner's services and support (e.g., wages, rent, auto and loans).
- Eliminate excess owner fringe benefits (club dues, travel and entertainment, for example).
- Project income and expenses based on the predetermined strategic vision for operations.

Continually ask yourself: "If I were to hire someone to do the job the owners are now doing, what would I pay that person?" After you review

---

*This section on Determining Value was extracted from an article by Ron Schmaedick, CRB CPM, President of Schmaedick & Associates, Inc. Consulting Services, in Eugene, OR. The article initially appeared in Vol. 2, No. 4, of *Management Issues & Trends* newsletter; published by the Real Estate Brokerage Managers Council™. Additional resources by Ron Schmaedick on this topic include:

- "What to Consider When You Sell Your Firm," *Management Issues & Trends,* June 1995, Vol. 10, No. 3.
- "Get Book Value for Your Company. Wait a Minute, What's Book Value?" *Real Estate Today,* October 1995, Vol. 28, No. 9.
- "A Win/Win Work Sheet for Merging or Buying a Real Estate Brokerage," *Management Issues & Trends,* Spring 1992, Vol. 6, No. 4, pp. 6-8.
- "So You Want to Buy a Real Estate Company?" *Real Estate Today,* April 1992, Vol. 25, No. 3, pp. 26-28.

and revise the above points as appropriate, calculate an estimate of Earnings or loss Before Interest and Taxes (EBIT).

Step 3: Reconstruct Balance Sheet   Next, reconstruct the balance sheet (again considering the criteria defined in step one), making the following adjustments:

- Include only the assets that support the brokerage activity as defined in the reconstructed operating statement and strategic plan.
- Exclude office building(s), other property held for investment, cash beyond what is necessary for the prudent operation of the firm, and vehicles and equipment not critical to the success of the firm.
- Adjust the value of the remaining assets (e.g., phone systems, computers and receivables) to current resale value.
- If the firm is on a cash basis accounting system, consider the current inventory of transactions signed on both sides and progressing toward closing. That portion due to the firm (after co-op splits and sales associate commissions less a percentage for fallout and administration cost) is an asset.
- Consider the listing inventory as another asset based on the gross potential fees adjusted for an expiration factor, co-op splits, sales associate commissions and administration cost.

Step 4: Evaluate Goodwill   Next, calculate a preliminary current owner's net worth (or stockholder's equity) based on the hard assets in Step 3.

Associate Value. Most commonly, the value of the sales associates is included in the goodwill of the firm. If the firm does not have measurable goodwill, there is no value to the sales force as a group.

Return on owner equity. Next, compute the return (yield) on the reconstructed owner's equity of the firm.

More than 15-30 percent. If the EBIT on the reconstructed income statement is in excess of 15 percent to 30 percent of the owner's equity, the firm has goodwill. Fifteen percent to 30 percent is an appropriate range considering before-tax returns on alternate investment opportunities with similar risk and liquidity. In choosing a capitalization rate from this broad range, consider the risk factors, that is, market share and market position, long-term potential of current management, sales staff and the local economy, and whether the firm is broad-based or niche and how long that position can be maintained. A change in ownership almost always causes a change in future outcomes. The selection of a capitalization rate is a subjective decision. It should be made by someone who is capable of an objective opinion of the current dynamics of the firm and its potential future profitability. Choosing a specific number within that range is a subjective decision.

Less than 15 percent. If the income is less than 15 percent of the owner's equity, there is no goodwill. With no goodwill, the upper value of the firm is the same as owner's equity on the reconstructed balance sheet. This is also known as the "current net worth of tangible assets."

If the EBIT exceeds the designated minimum return on owner's equity, then there is a value to the goodwill of the firm.

> *Example:* If the reconstructed income statement shows the EBIT is $100,000 and in the reconstructed balance sheet the owner's equity (tangible net worth) is $300,000, that is a 33 percent (before tax) return on equity. If investors require a minimum 20 percent return on equity, then 10 percent (20 percent – 30 percent) is the intangible asset called goodwill.

In recent years, it has been acceptable to calculate goodwill in a manner that allows for some goodwill even in a firm that is losing money. First, the amount of company dollar that each agent contributes to the firm in a year is calculated. Then the *desk cost,* the total annual fixed expenses divided by the number of agents, is calculated. The *margin,* company dollars minus desk cost, of only the agents contributing more than desk cost is totaled to obtain an indicated value of goodwill. This method in effect says the goodwill of a real estate brokerage is equal to the profit the firm could expect to make in one year if the firm only retained the profitable agents.

Step 5: Value the Firm   There are two recognized processes for determining the value of a firm with goodwill: (1) Value is based on current income using a multiplier or capitalization rate, or (2) Value is based on the present value of the projected income stream over the next three to five years. The method used will depend on the purpose, conditions and assumptions of the valuation.

Capitalization Method. Capitalization, or the earnings multiplier method, works as follows:

- Multiply profits (EBIT) from a reconstructed annual operating statement by a factor (multiplier) or divide by a capitalization rate.
- Calculate the multiplier or the capitalization rates, arbitrary numbers to calculate. They are established after careful study of many factors (including the business and financial risks involved, the investor's alternate investment opportunities and the cost of borrowing long-term operating capital).
- Compare capitalization rates and profit multipliers:

Multiplier	Capitalization Rate
1	100%
2	50%
3	33.3%
4	25%
5	20%

Example: If EBIT for the year is $150,000 and the multiplier chosen is two, then the value would be $300,000. If EBIT for the year is $150,000 and the capitalization rate is 50 percent, then the value would also be $300,000 (150,000 ÷ .50).

In this example, it would take two years of profits to recover the purchase price of the business. This is a common method for determining the sales price for small business opportunities including real estate firms.

The capitalization rate approach assumes the owners will earn a 50 percent return on their investment and no recovery of their capital until time of sale. Or, in other words, the 50 percent represents 30 percent return *on* investment and a 20 percent return *of* investment.

Present Value Method. The "present value" method states the value in terms of what an investor would pay today for a predictable future cash flow. These calculations can easily be made on most hand-held calculators.

This process is promoted by many academics and some accountants, but it is seldom used because of the high degree of uncertainty as to future profits to be derived from assets contributed by the outgoing owner.

To establish the value of a real estate firm using this method, project the annual EBIT on reconstructed operating statements monthly or annually for three to five years. A yield or "risk adjusted discount rate" is selected, considering the owner's other investment alternatives, the risk involved, and the cost and availability of borrowed capital. The present value of the projected income is then calculated in the same way the present value is calculated on other real estate investments. Here is an example of imputing the diminishing residual value of the tangible and intangible assets provided by the former owners when a change of ownership is anticipated. Note the reduced annual EBIT from the second through the fifth year.

Example: Risk adjusted discount rate of 33.3 percent

	Project EBIT:
Year:	*(at year end)*
1	$200,000
2	160,000
3	120,000
4	80,000
5	40,000

The present value is $325,587.

Step 6: Make Adjustments   After you complete the calculations, you may need to make adjustments depending on the nature of the reasons for valuation.

Example: In calculating the value of a firm by the cash flow method *only,* the assets critical to the operation of the business would be included in the calculated value. If cash reserves and/or investment property are to be included in an ownership change, appropriate additions would be expected.

The valuation of a multifacet firm can be simplified by "spinning off" assets or separate profit centers. For example, if the firm owns its offices, it may put them under separate ownership and lease them to the brokerage company. This should be done with the counsel of your tax accountant or attorney.

Step 7: Consider the Limitations   As you determine the value of the firm, note the following difficulties involved:

- Collection of applicable data on internal and external factors
- Imputing value of owner's services, market rent and office space
- Agreement about capitalization rates and risk-adjusted discount rates
- Uncertainty of future revenue and expense projections
- Limited comparable data
- Subjectivity of buyer (People may pay more for a business than its estimated value because they are buying a market share or location critical to their expansion plan, or they are simply "buying a job.")

VALUING THE 100 PERCENT CONCEPT FIRM

The valuation of furniture, fixtures and equipment is the same in all firms. However, in the 100 percent commission firm the listings and pending sales have no direct measurable value. Beyond the furniture, fixtures and equipment, the value of the firm is wholly dependent on the profits derived from fees for services paid mostly by the agents. Another difference in 100 percent firms is the capitalization rate. There is growing evidence that the 100 percent concept appeals more to established experienced agents who are less affected by small, short-term downturns in the market. This, together with the fact that the main revenue source is from the agents, reduces the owner's risk. The valuation steps outlined previously are otherwise generally the same for a 100 percent concept firm.

Conclusion to Business Valuation   The reader might ask at this point, why would a person be willing to receive repayment of their fixed assets? To answer that question, go back to the reason why a person will sell, whether the motivation is the desire to retire, the fact that a broker cannot progress any further individually or perhaps wants capitalization to continue. All these are motivating reasons why a person will sell other than just to make a profit.

Appraisals of business opportunities are very subjective. Considerable judgment is required. It is also important that you begin the process with a vision of what you intend to accomplish and a strategic operating plan. All determinations and conclusions must be relevant to that vision and plan.

RETAINING QUALITY PEOPLE

In most mergers and acquisitions of real estate brokerage firms, the primary benefit is the retention of quality people. Before any final decision can be made regarding a merger or acquisition, the strategies, tactics, timetable and resources needed to tell these people how important they are to the new organization must be detailed. The method of informing them, welcoming and informational events, printing of business cards and so on must all be planned and carried out in a way that will have a positive impact on the people the new firm wants to retain. The outgoing owners can have a profound impact on the success of the transaction at this point. If possible, they should be very involved in this process.

Suppose the advantages a firm had to offer were quality of management, capitalization and liquidity, expertise, market impact, physical size, effective training programs, broadened advertising base and management know-how. The most essential part of the plan before closing and after closing the deal is the realignment of staff operation of the new firm. Perhaps the advantage of purchasing another firm was to acquire its outstanding management. The individual running the other business would make an ideal sales manager for your business, or there might be other staff people who would fit into property management, mortgage financing or other staff assignments. The importance of analyzing the personnel of the firm to be acquired cannot be overemphasized. Find out how many people will stay and what their potential is. It is very important to look at the whole picture of the continuing operation.

Will a new sales manager be assigned? Will salespeople be reassigned? If the firm was acquired because of its location in the market, will salespeople from other offices be assigned there, or will salespeople from the acquired firm be moved to other locations? How many salespeople will be needed in that operation for market penetration? What staff will be needed to service those salespeople—secretaries, bookkeeper, settlement officer, sales manager?

The following general realignments are common: First, a sales manager is assigned who is familiar with the policy and procedures of the firm, knows and agrees with the sales philosophy of the firm and is prepared to implement those policies immediately. Next, personnel not needed are generally either reassigned or dismissed (such as a bookkeeper and/or secretaries, depending on central service functions; also settlement officers, depending on what type of closing department is organized). Third, salespeople are reassigned. In many cases salespeople are reluctant to move into a new sales office because they fear losing the security they have developed operating under certain management personnel. The advantages of moving must be established before they will agree to it. The variance in operation and benefits for salespeople can result in animosity between existing staff and new salespeople. Many of these situations can be avoided through the assignment of a capable training officer who can explain the advantages of the merged operation. It must be remembered that one of the original criteria in the acquisition or merger of a real estate firm was to develop a more efficient operation for greater productivity and higher profits. This cannot be achieved unless there is a properly motivated, trained staff to implement the policies promulgated by the parent firm. The sales agents and other staff generally are not ready for change. The owners initiate the change. The quality people must know the answer to the question: "What's in it for me?"

FRANCHISES

The reluctance of brokers to give up their individual identification often can be overcome by use of franchise agreements.

Advantages

One advantage is using a standardized sign that emphasizes the franchise company but also features the identity of the local broker. Because the size, color and logo of the sign are standardized, people driving around the market area see the impact of a tremendous number of listings.

Second, advertising can be merged into a major program, maintaining individual identity in the ads through phone numbers. Again, the impression conveyed to the public is that one organization has a massive volume of listings. In like manner, a heavy institutional advertising campaign promotes the service provided by the affiliated brokerage houses functioning under this one title. This can have a great impact on the market and result in increased production. Small firms can put themselves in a stronger competitive position. When a broker tries to analyze the advantages of franchising, the first thing to study is its market impact.

Third, some franchises provide standard office procedures, standardized forms, operations manuals, training and other educational tools.

Disadvantages

The disadvantages of a franchise, first, are financial. A franchise fee generally consists of so many dollars up front in order to set up the system and buy the initial franchise plus some percentage of gross commissions on a continuing basis. This comes directly out of the company dollar and affects the profits of the operation. If in the long term the franchise brings greater net profits, then it is not a disadvantage.

Another disadvantage is that certain procedures, guidelines and criteria have been set up by the franchisor, and unless the firm adheres to them it may lose the franchise. This removes some of the independence and freedom real estate brokers traditionally cherish.

One other disadvantage is the territorial limitation under a franchise. Some franchises will not give any territorial protection. As a consequence, a broker can end up with the same franchise company overlapping in his or her market area. Franchises that provide territorial protection may add to the value of the firm. When someone wants a franchise territory, they have been known to pay very well to buy out the broker who owns that territory.

Franchise operations have enjoyed rapid growth in the last several years. For the broker, franchises can be their answer to meeting competition. Unless there are other motivations such as retirement or capitalization, franchises may cut down the need for merger and acquisition.

SUMMARY

When brokers consider buying a firm, they must determine whether they can absorb the new operation without undue strain on present management and accounting personnel. They must be sure they can comfortably finance or obtain financing and working capital for the merged operation.

The many areas to be considered, such as purchase price, method of payment, employment contracts, stock options and fringe benefits cannot be taken lightly. They will create long-term direct commitments on the continuing operation. With the expansion of franchising, the industry will also see an aggressive market in the acquisition and merging of real estate firms in order to remain competitive.

Chapter 19

Opening a Real Estate Office

Here are guidelines to follow in preparing to open a real estate office—everything from how to make the very important choice of a general location, how to find the best site available, and points to consider in deciding whether to rent, buy or build. Several workable floor plans are outlined, and the advantages and disadvantages of each are explored. We also discuss practical styles of decoration and furnishings and provide a shopping list of furnishings, equipment and services you'll need to get started in real estate brokerage.

You will find ways to establish your firm's identity in the new market and ideas for introducing your staff and services to the neighborhood. We examine concepts for effective management supervision of branch offices. The control systems—financial, business and physical—necessary to operating a well-run real estate office are also covered.

The information in this chapter applies to opening an office for a new firm as well as opening a new branch office for an existing firm.

THE 7-S MODEL AND THE NEW OFFICE

Whether you are opening your first real estate office or are adding a branch to an existing operation, McKinsey's 7-S model can aid you in making the many complex decisions required, from selecting a site, to setting up systems and hiring staff, to marketing your services to the community.

All of the decisions you make should be driven by your strategic intent. The types of services you plan to offer and the market you want to serve will be key factors in selecting a site for the new office. Your strategy will also affect how you market your services to the community, the image you want to project and the media you select to send your message.

How will you staff the new office? What skills should your sales associates have to enable them to accomplish the firm's strategies? A key hiring decision is the choice of a manager for the office. This individual's management style will set the tone for the operation.

How will you structure the office? What will the organization chart look like? What will the informal reporting relationships be?

The decisions you make send your staff a message about the firm's shared values. For example, an open layout tells salespeople that communication and interrelationships are important to the company.

You will need to set up systems for the office's day-to-day workflows. Among these are financial systems, compensation systems, recruiting and training systems, and marketing systems. Budgeting and financial systems establish controls over the office's operations. Compensation systems can be designed to motivate the staff as well as to focus their efforts in the strategic areas the firm considers most important.

As we pointed out in Chapter 1, the most brilliant strategies are of little use if the organization does not support or cannot execute them. Keeping the seven interdependent variables of McKinsey's model in mind as you plan can help ensure that all of the elements of the new office are aligned behind the firm's key strategies.

SITE POSSIBILITIES

The site of a real estate office is of prime importance to its success. Finding the best place available at a price you can afford will take a great deal of your time but will be well worth every minute you devote to it. Unfortunately, many brokers don't give enough thought to finding the best location and then getting the best site there, whether you are opening a main office or a new branch operation. Instead, they take what's available in a general area and try to begin a profitable operation from there.

Let's first look at the general areas you may consider as you begin your search:

- Downtown
- Access highway or highway to an expressway
- Shopping center
- Small branch or field office ("waterhole")
- Mobile office

Downtown

A downtown location is generally best for the small residential town or suburb in which the downtown area is the business core of the community. Generally in such a town there is adequate parking, the location is easy to get in and out of, there is little or no traffic congestion, and it promises your firm strong identity in the community.

Downtown locations in large cities are usually favored by commercial-investment firms as well as property management companies.

Commercial-investment real estate firms like to be downtown, close to the financial hub of the city and near attorneys and tax accountants who are involved in many of their transactions. Whenever possible, a downtown location should be near the courthouse, where statistical records essential to commercial-investment transactions are available. However, many residential, multifamily oriented property management companies and investment offices have moved into the suburban areas to be closer to the properties they sell and/or manage.

On the other hand, large residential companies who have established a successful identity in the suburbs may decide to open a central office or a flagship office downtown. They look to the downtown area for identification and to prove to the community that their firm has arrived.

Residential firms usually use their downtown offices for administrative purposes, and fewer salespeople work out of those locations.

Downtown space is usually the most expensive available, and it may lock the firm into a very high overhead at a time when sales are not too prosperous. The high rental costs for a prime first-floor location can seldom be justified in return for the location itself. An alternative to this is prime downtown space on the second or third floor with good identification on the first floor or outside on a busy street. This still gives good identification and yet keeps cost down somewhat.

The firm fortunate enough to find adequate space at a reasonable rate on a first floor is bound to have good walk-in traffic as well as good community identification. There is much less walk-in traffic on upper floors unless good identity is established at ground floor level.

The decision whether to choose a downtown site or one in a suburban area depends greatly on the forces and direction of the community itself. If the downtown area is decaying and most of the businesses have moved to the suburbs, management would not plan to move to the city. But if the downtown area has been renewed or is maintained in a way that makes it an action center for the entire metropolitan community, there are obvious advantages to being there.

Access Highway or Highway to an Expressway

The access highway location affords good traffic flow patterns for real estate offices. Such a location also usually provides easy access for salespeople, who will use it most frequently. The location may also attract buyers and sellers because of its convenience.

The access highway office should have an easy-in, easy-out location. Traffic speed will be brisk, and you must allow adequate room for drivers to turn into and get out of the parking area. Avoid an access highway where a barrier in the middle of the road prevents drivers from turning from the opposite side of the road into the office.

Check with state police or local police departments to get their traffic count for the area and the average traffic speed. Fast food franchises (who choose their sites with great care and research) have found that if the speed is about 35 mph, people will slow down and turn into their restaurant. The same would apply to real estate offices. Thus it is well to know the *average actual speed* on the road. Simply looking at the speed limit is not enough. An access road may have a posted speed limit of 45 mph but an actual average speed of only 25 mph or 30 mph because of congestion. This could help the broker's location because cars are moving at a slower than posted speed. If the average speed is not too high, the access highway may produce stop-in traffic similar to walk-in traffic in other locations.

Access highways give excellent sign locations that can be utilized to the fullest. Most fast food franchises feel their sign should be seen for a minimum of one-quarter of a mile and preferably one-third of a mile before arriving at the site. This gives the driver adequate time to think about turning into their property. A similar rule of thumb could apply to a real estate office.

Another advantage of the access highway is that it is a well-known address. When the address is given to people coming to your office, they'll know immediately where it is and perhaps even be able to visualize the building itself.

One further advantage of an access highway site is that because it is on a main thoroughfare in the city, salespeople can cover more territory in less time.

Shopping Center

A shopping center has the advantage of high walk-in traffic. The real estate firm in a shopping center with attractive window displays will draw people into its office for inquiries.

However, on the minus side, some brokers have found that they had so much walk-in traffic it forced them to put extra salespeople on duty. This restricts salespeople's time in the field where they could be doing other work that might lead to sales or be more productive in other ways. Many times the walk-in traffic in shopping centers is similar to window shopping in retail stores. That is, people simply look at the pictures and want a little more information, but they are not serious buyers. Brokers are cautioned to choose a location that will not tie up too much effective labor for a minimum return.

Generally, the people who walk into a shopping center office are less qualified and less likely to buy property than those who walk into a freestanding building at a less convenient location.

Major shopping center space can be expensive in relation to the business it generates. Strip shopping malls tend to cost less per square foot and also give a little better sign identification.

Most shopping centers have adequate parking. Be sure to check whether parking spaces can be reserved near the office. Some brokers have moved into shopping centers believing they had ample parking only to discover the parking lot jammed with cars every day. Their customers had to walk a quarter-mile to a half-mile to get to their office because closer spaces were all taken early in the day. This also proved to be an inconvenience for salespeople and discouraged them from using that office as an operating base.

Another thing to check carefully is the identity allowed in the shopping center itself. Many shopping centers limit exterior or interior sign identification to a stipulated size that is governed by the shopping center management. If sign identification is so restricted that people will have trouble finding you, the firm has lost the whole intent of strong identification, and the only people who will know you're there are those who come into the shopping center itself.

Small Branch or Field Office

The small branch or field office (often known as a "waterhole") is the type of office sometimes installed in a new shopping center or a new area of town in which the broker feels a full-size branch office is not yet justified. Such an office would not have a full-time secretary or any assistants but perhaps would employ a part-time secretary several afternoons a week. Generally the salespeople on duty will answer the telephones and type whatever limited correspondence originates there; or all correspondence might be sent to the central office to be typed and mailed.

The small branch or field office is not only suited to new areas and subdivisions but is also a possibility for small satellite towns. For example, a broker's main office may be in a major metropolitan area 10 or 15 miles away, but the broker believes there is sufficient promise to justify a limited operation in the satellite town on a trial basis.

Brokers are cautioned to check state regulations and requirements for management of these offices. Many states view them as full branch offices and require that the manager be a licensed broker.

Mobile Office

Another alternative to the small branch or field office is the mobile office such as a trailer bus or travel bus like those made for commercial camp vehicles. The mobile office can serve temporarily as a "waterhole" office at a new location, a new subdivision or a new town. It is also ideal for brokers who have several subdivisions and want to move their office from place to place.

Generally, a trailer bus interior is customized, so there is adequate room for a personal computer and desk, and space for consultation with clients. The outside of the bus can be painted with the company name and logo. This provides institutional advertising while the bus is being moved from one location to another.

Another use for the mobile office is by brokers who sell resort properties outside a metropolitan area. In this case, they can transport several prospects at one time right in the mobile office to the location of the resort properties. Once there, the driver converts the bus into an office while agents show the properties. Thus it is ready for whatever negotiations may ensue.

Finally, novelty vehicles such as old double-deck British buses or luxuriously outfitted mobile offices may be used for philanthropic activities from time to time. These not only provide strong community identification but also offer good public relations for the firm when donated or rented at cost to philanthropic organizations for special events, parades and the like.

Branch Location in Relation to Present Office

There are several rules of thumb on how to locate a branch office in relation to a present or main office.

One long-accepted rule of thumb is that a single residential office can satisfactorily service a population of 25,000 people. This does not take into consideration the turnover rate of the population. So how do you go about establishing your own rule of thumb? Brokers can develop their own checklist for gathering necessary information. Such a checklist should answer the following questions:

- What are the physical boundaries of the community this office will serve, and do they overlap areas served by our present offices?
- What is the population of the area?
- What is the turnover rate of housing there?
- What percentage of the sales or the total business in the designated community can we realistically expect to command in three to four years?
- What barriers exist within the area to be served?

Once you have computed the percentage of business you hope to be able to control in three to four years, you can apply that percentage to the population turnover to get an indication of how many sales per year this new office should make. This figure also is a guide to the number of salespeople needed to service those sales.

Certainly when you consider branch office locations, you must look at the city's expressway system. Cities that have good expressway systems both north and south, east and west need fewer branch offices than those with a limited expressway system or none at all. Merely to open another office so you can say you have more offices is an ego trip a broker can ill afford, particularly in a difficult market.

BARRIERS IN THE COMMUNITY

There are three kinds of barriers to be aware of: constructed, natural and psychological.

Expressway systems are a plus in one sense. But they may be a constructed barrier when it comes to determining the area an office will service. Other constructed barriers are major highway systems, railroads, sports complexes, airports, industrial parks, campuses and the like.

Natural barriers are things that break up an area and make it difficult for real estate firms to transact business across or around them. They include such obstacles as rivers, mountains, hills, or ravines in a city.

One of the best examples of a psychological barrier is the refusal of individuals in one metropolitan or suburban area to list their property with a firm in an adjoining area. They may think that because the office is located in an area of $85,000 homes the office has no one qualified to sell $150,000 homes in the adjoining community. This one barrier has forced hundreds of real estate firms to string out their offices, placing them tandem style in a series of residential communities.

MILEAGE CIRCLES

To make a mileage circle study, get a detailed map of your area. Mark your office location (or proposed location) with a map tack. Determine the mileage scale of the map. Using a piece of string tied to the map tack at one end and a pencil at the other, circle the area limits you think your office might service. It might be as little as a half-mile in a densely populated area, or as much as five, ten or more miles in sparsely settled places.

Now determine what the population is within each of the circles you've drawn and the turnover rate for housing in each. Likely sources for this information include city hall, mortgage companies, utility companies, planning commissions and the like. Be sure to note whatever barriers exist within each circle.

Once you've established the circle area around the office your sales-people can service, draw mileage circles around your proposed office. Ideally, the boundary of one circle will touch the circumference of another but will not overlap. Thus you avoid the waste of duplicated sales power or office facilities in overlapping territories.

Finally, the office would ideally be located where outbound traffic moves from the metropolitan area to the suburbs. An ideal site is at a four-way intersection on the far right corner. This is considered best because a stop light or stop sign at the intersection gives drivers adequate time to look across the street, see your sign and pull in.

If the office were on the near right corner, the outbound driver would be sitting parallel at the stop light or sign and might not be able to maneuver his car into the traffic lane nearest your driveway. The near left corner has similar drawbacks and the added difficulty that the driver has to cross oncoming traffic. Finally, the far left corner, though giving better visibility, still presents the driver a problem of having to cross traffic.

Unfortunately, real estate firms are not the only ones smart enough to know that the far right corner of an intersection is an ideal one, so square footage costs there are prohibitive in many cases. But when available and affordable the far right corner is ideal.

BUILDING VERSUS REMODELING

Obviously, brokers would prefer to build a facility to their own specifications. Building allows buyers to establish their company identity, to project to the community who they are and what they are trying to accomplish.

The relative cost of building versus remodeling is a primary concern. If one costs substantially less than the other, you may be forced to opt for it even if this second choice doesn't offer the amenities you want.

Next, consider capital availability. Do you have enough capital available to tie up cash in a down payment on land and also to finance the building contract for an office? The obvious alternative is to lease space, have the owner remodel it and then amortize the remodeling costs over the period of the lease. This gives you modernized offices at a lower cost because the expense is spread over a period of years.

Vacated gas stations offer interesting remodeling possibilities—albeit more costly than some other type structures. They usually have a prime corner location and good on-site parking. Beware of the danger of hazardous waste/site cleanup costs, however.

Older homes are a natural for residential firms if they are located in a zoned business area and can be remodeled for real estate use. Another excellent building type is the outdated supermarket. Most of them have clear span ceilings that permit a variety of interior floor layouts. The exteriors can also be made attractive by using facing materials that complement the "flavor" of the neighborhood.

Finally, historic homes and buildings offer both usable office space and the community's gratitude for having saved an historic landmark—fine public relations! This is especially true when the character and important architectural elements are not changed by the broker who converts it into a sales office.

OFFICE LAYOUT

Most real estate office floor plans have several elements in common. They usually have a conference room to provide privacy for consultations with prospective purchasers and listers of property and closings. Most also have a manager's office that may be completely glassed in to allow a view of salespeople while keeping out office noise. Draw draperies may be installed to provide privacy when needed.

But real estate offices vary greatly in the arrangement of working space for salespeople and ancillary staff. Some of the most common plans are the following:

- Separate offices or cubicles and dividers
- Standing counter
- Minimum number of desks and
- Open area or bull pen

Separate Offices or Cubicles and Dividers

Separate offices can be completely closed spaces that give total privacy to the individual salesperson, or they can be cubicles, created by using dividers that may be floor-to-ceiling or perhaps only high enough to provide a salesperson some degree of privacy. Thus salespeople enjoy the security of their own desk and a private area to which they may retreat if they wish. This arrangement is used more in commercial-investment departments than in residential real estate sales offices.

The drawback to the separate office plan is that it can reduce communication within the office. Salespeople go into their offices, shut the door and immediately close out their interrelationships with other salespeople. This loss of communication can cause them to lose touch with what is going on. And a customer walking into an office of this type has no sense of the excitement or activity that may really exist there. It is much more apparent in an open sales office.

Standing Counter

One floor plan concept is the use of a long counter, at desk height, extending along one wall or around the perimeter of a room. Salespeople are assigned "desk" space (about three feet), a chair, a telephone and perhaps a cork bulletin board above each assigned space. It is restricted to salespeople's use; customers are not admitted to this area but are seen in a conference room or a private office.

What are the advantages of the standing counter plan? It's one of the least expensive ways to set up a working area. In such a plan, communications are open, information is exchanged quickly, and the sales staff is up and on its way. These simple working conditions and the closeness of staff can foster a sense of camaraderie among congenial people.

There are disadvantages, however. Such a floor plan provides no privacy and no storage space unless under-the-counter two-drawer file cabinets are placed between working spaces. It's an arrangement that gives little sense of belonging. When all they have is a counter space, a chair and a telephone, salespeople don't feel there's much prestige about what they're doing.

But the plan works well with some firms that have centralized computers. The computers occupy space in the middle of the room and are used for research in compiling information for later client interviews.

Minimum Number of Desks

Although outdated, this floor plan is still seen in some real estate offices. Four or five desks are used by as many as ten salespeople with no one assigned to any specific desk. This plan was originally conceived to discourage salespeople from staying in the office so they would be out in active pursuit of business. This arrangement gives no sense of belonging. Salespeople have no place to keep materials and records. Consequently they either work out of their homes or have no base at all for their work. Management has very little contact with salespeople in this type of office.

Communications are lost when only a few salespeople can be in the office at any one time to interrelate their efforts and ideas. Although this plan does keep salespeople on the move, the manager doesn't know where they are moving to. Unfortunately in some cases they are soon moving to another firm.

Open Area or Bull Pen

The plan probably in most prevalent use today is the open area or bull pen for salespeople.

The open area or bull pen offers a sense of belonging. Each salesperson has an individual desk in this open area and can use the conference room or perhaps a private office off the bull pen to work with clients when necessary.

There is, however, a lack of privacy and a high noise level that can be distracting when a number of salespeople are in the office at the same time. On the other hand, this plan increases communication. Salespeople tend to keep up with what is going on. A client walking into such an office may respond favorably to the air of great activity and the excitement it generates among salespeople.

Finally, such an arrangement provides open space for sales meetings, eliminating the need for the firm to rent a meeting place.

IDENTITY

The image your new office projects to the public is very important as you introduce your firm in a new location.

Some older firms choose a colonial building to maintain their image as an old, well-established firm. Other long-established firms choose a contemporary identity to convey the feeling that though they are an older firm, they have modern ideas.

Whatever type of architecture or surroundings a firm chooses, it should conform to or complement the immediately surrounding properties so the real estate office is not an eyesore in the community.

Consideration should be given to lighting the office sign at night so it can be seen for advertising purposes after office hours.

The office setting is part of the image a real estate firm presents to the community. Landscaping should be tasteful, lawns well-tended and parking lots kept clean at all times. Winter snow removal is important in regions where this is a problem.

Graphics

Sign design and colors should be uniform throughout the company. Whatever company design and colors the firm has chosen should be used in highway signs, office signs, car signs and yard signs. The identity should be carried through all print materials—letterheads, business cards, advertising brochures and other print materials.

FURNISHINGS

Furnishings should convey a pleasant atmosphere. Color coordination is critical in the design of a real estate office. Skilled color coordinators can discuss with you the theories behind selecting certain colors. For example, in sales office spaces you might use bright orange and bright yellows in the open and bull pen areas. They are "active" colors and will contribute to keeping salespeople active. Soft greens, soft blues and soft yellows in conference rooms will help clients feel relaxed at closing sessions.

Low maintenance costs are important in choosing paint and wall coverings. The use of washable wall coverings and washable paints is practical in an office. High gloss paints and wallpapers and fabrics can be distracting to the eye.

Draperies and carpets are important for noise control. They lend a warm feeling to an office and have the advantage of lower maintenance costs.

If possible and practical, identical furniture, carpets and drapery fabrics should be used throughout a firm's offices. Thus when staffs expand or an office is phased out, furnishings may be exchanged between locations.

Whatever the plan adopted, a broker must ask if the improvement cost per person can be covered in a reasonable length of time by the expected sales volume. Per unit desk costs are an important aspect of the total planning for a proposed office.

INTRODUCTION TO THE NEIGHBORHOOD

Introducing your firm in a new neighborhood requires a lot of planning. It's a major undertaking that calls for using the market research you've already done as the basis for deciding how to promote your company in imaginative and acceptable ways, and doing it within your budget.

Use your market research as the beginning point. It will provide the information you need about the kinds of businesses and people in the new neighborhood and what their interests, tastes and needs are. With this information, you can explore all the promotional possibilities open to you: person-to-person contacts, direct mail, newspaper advertising and publicity, radio and television advertising and publicity, and open house functions.

Investigate costs before you commit yourself to any form of promotion. Determine whether your staff can handle the kind of promotion you'd like to stage. Do as much as you can but don't attempt to do more than you can do reasonably well. Better to underplay your hand as you get started in a new location than to have your efforts end in confusion. Remember, you are presenting a new image in the neighborhood. A good beginning will convey to the public the standard they can expect from your firm in the future.

Person to Person Contacts

First consideration and effort is given to getting acquainted with the leaders in the area. Meet the people who run the local government, both paid employees and citizens who serve on governing boards. Business and industry leaders are also high on the list of people who should be told of your new location and the services you offer. Churches and service and civic organizations offer opportunities to meet people in groups, the kind who are likely to be "movers and shakers" in the area. Tell them how enthusiastic you are about being part of their town.

Always have a supply of business cards with you. A lot of them will be put in wallets or desk drawers and pulled out later when the person is in need of your real estate services.

Encourage your salespeople to make door-to-door visits in the new neighborhood, taking along their business cards or whatever other print promotion material you have prepared. Salespeople can simply introduce themselves and invite the residents to stop in at your new office and get acquainted. If you've planned some kind of open house, an invitation to it can be extended orally.

Direct Mail

Direct mail covers everything from the simplest postcard announcements and personal letters from your salespeople to their friends and acquaintances to formal announcement folders and invitations to an open house.

The postcards can be a simple announcement of the time and date of the official opening, inviting the addressee to come and get acquainted. This is perhaps the least expensive form of direct mail promotion you can use. Done in good taste with important details included, postcards can be very effective.

It is perfectly acceptable for personal letters to be form letters. They are more effective if they are personalized by a handwritten salutation or signed individually by the new manager or one of the salespeople. If you cannot give a form promotion letter any sort of personal touch, perhaps you should bypass using them and consider a more formal announcement card or folder or a printed invitation to an open house.

Formal announcement cards or folders can give the pertinent information regarding your new operation. For example, you can include the firm name, new address, name of the manager, office phone number and hours on one side of a printed card announcement. If you go to a folder, there's more space for your message. You could add a list of the real estate services your firm proposes to supply. Many people do not realize the broad range of services available from most real estate firms. Keep in mind that what you take for granted as general knowledge is often understood only by those involved in the real estate business.

If you plan to conduct one office open house or a continuing open house for a week or so, printed invitations will help draw a crowd. Build a mailing list of the influential people in the area, and ask salespeople to assemble their own list of buyers and sellers and other friends in the community. Use this collection of names for your open house invitations.

Whatever form your direct mail promotion takes, be sure your mailing list has the correct spelling and address for everyone on it. People like to see their names spelled correctly. Incorrect addresses mean money is wasted twice, first on printing, then on postage.

Set up your mailing lists so they can be kept up to date. Delete names promptly when people leave the area. Add names as new people move in. Computerized databases make this task easier.

Newspaper Advertising and Publicity

A series of eye-catching display ads in your local paper can be used to make your announcement to the general public. Unless you have someone on your staff who is experienced in writing and laying out display ads, ask the newspaper's space salesperson if the publisher provides such a service, or go to an established advertising agency to have the job done. However it is handled, the information in the ad is your responsibility.

Such a series of ads can tell the location of the new office, date of opening and who will manage it. One of the series might give a brief history of your firm; another might list all the real estate services you will provide. If you need salespeople to work at the new location, one of the ads might focus on this.

Another in the series might picture the best-looking properties you have listed in the area. In addition to describing the property, always include information about the new operation. If you are wholly new to the area, consider running a picture of your new office, identifying its location in relation to some local landmark if that is possible—"one block east of the library on State Street," or "on the west side of the new shopping center."

Invite the local editor for a preview visit of your new operation. Be prepared to provide the facts about your firm, the reasons why you chose to locate in the area and how you believe your firm can contribute to the growth of the community. This is a job for the manager and a valuable form of publicity. If the editor or a reporter cannot visit in person, send them a news release and/or an information packet containing this information.

Radio and Television

Spot announcements on radio and television can be one of your best advertising buys. Listen to radio and watch television shows that offer the audience you want at the time of day those buyers and sellers are most likely to listen. Off-peak hours are available at bargain rates. Are these the hours of the day when the people you want to reach are listening? Make note of the program and the time, and check to find out what a 30-second or 60-second spot announcement costs.

A well-written 30-second commercial can include all the important facts about your new location. Expanded to 60 seconds, you can include some sales talk about your services, tell about attractively priced listings and inform the public about how you can help them solve their housing problems.

Think of publicity possibilities in radio and television. Talk shows are very popular. Many of them accept telephone questions from the listening audience. If you can interest the host in a show devoted to real estate, you may handle some very interesting questions related to your business and the appearance could very well result in future business. Don't walk in cold and expect to be put on the air. Talk shows are often planned months in advance. Make an appointment to see the show's producer. Go equipped with a couple of ideas for a program that could delve into the real estate business in a way that will interest the show's audience, explain how the host can approach the topic and how you can contribute to it. Then be prepared to accept the producer's way of handling the interview, should you be scheduled.

Open House

An office open house can be kept small and simple or expanded to as large and elaborate as your budget will allow. Its size and simplicity need not limit its effectiveness.

A series of daily coffees the first week or two in your new location can give a feeling of warm hospitality to your official opening. But even the most informal event needs careful planning and continuing attention to details. Who will be in charge of floor duty so there's always someone on hand to welcome people as they come in? Will there be a guest registry; who will be responsible for it? Will you want to have some candid pictures made? Who will take them?

A more elaborate open house can be staged for afternoon or evening hours. Invitations to an open house of this kind should be more formal than you'd need for a coffee. Your local job printer can show you paper and type samples and quote prices for such invitations. You can also find user-friendly desktop publishing software to create announcements and other promotional materials.

Souvenirs

The premium business today offers a large selection of items in an equally wide price range. Choose whatever premium you think will help tell the new community about your company and will be useful to the recipient. Investigate ideas and prices from several firms.

Follow-Up

What happens after that first burst of hospitality and enthusiasm? How do you use it as a springboard to a successful everyday operation?

Your guest list makes a fine nucleus for a permanent promotion/ mailing list. These are the people who either thought enough of you or were curious enough about you to come get acquainted. They could be future buyers, sellers or people who perform banking, building or government services essential to your success. Keep these people aware of what you're accomplishing.

If your office operates on a listing "farm" system whereby salespeople are assigned specific areas to canvass in order to create spheres of influence, be sure they get names of guests from their assigned areas. It's important for them to know exactly who came to the official opening functions. These names can come in handy in casual conversation, provide a clue to a potential friend in their territory or be a source of valuable guidance in the area.

OPERATION

If you are opening a branch operation, you will want to make sure that your schedule is planned to include lots of time at the new location. New branches require the kind of management that almost becomes overmanagement. Why? For one thing, you are identified closely as the leader of the organization. It is important to both staff and customers that you be seen there frequently. Otherwise, the staff can quickly develop the feeling that "the main office is somewhere else, and we really don't matter much."

If possible, the new office should be staffed with salespeople who have been successful in other offices. They may stay in the new location only during the start-up period, a number of weeks or months, or they may move there permanently. Some firms use a temporary incentive program to get a new operation under way. A contest to promote listings or an offer of a small break in the commission split on the first ten or twenty listings taken at a new location are some ways to motivate the staff.

One successful firm with a number of branch offices schedules a luncheon session with each branch every 60 days. The broker and his general sales manager attend these luncheons together. The two of them communicate the fact that they agree on goals and progress and recognize problems. Conversation is directed to encourage staff people to discuss their problems, objectives and goals. These staff members look forward to this time spent with top management so much that when a regular date is missed the question immediately is: "Where have you been?"

A comprehensive policy and procedures manual is essential in a branch operation. Problems that come up in a branch may be different from those that occur in the main office. You should have regular reviews of this manual with branch office staff. You should provide them with a standard method of making suggestions for revising the manual, and this work should be done on a regular basis.

The effectiveness of the branch office management is especially important to the firm's top management whose supervision is likely to be intermittent at best. Experience has proved to many firms that a branch manager who has been with the firm for some time may find the job easier than an outsider who is brought in. The person who has been associated with the firm understands and supports its goals and objectives.

Goals and projections of future company development should fit those of the main office or other branch offices. They should be checked with the same regularity scheduled in the company's other offices. Both the standards of checking and the reporting forms should be identical throughout the whole company.

Staff training should be consistent throughout the company. Where possible, training sessions should be combined to serve as many offices as possible. This not only assures identical teaching of concepts, objectives and goals; it also reduces the total cost of staff training. Other facets of staff education can be individualized by offices or combined to serve everyone. Local education opportunities like adult evening classes and lectures by local people at staff sales meetings (bankers, municipal officials) may serve only a limited area. Sales specialists, psychologists, attorneys and others may speak on topics germane to the total company area. The firm's library may be located in the main office and its materials available to everyone; public libraries may serve a restricted area. Whatever your educational pursuits, be sure everyone in the firm knows what is scheduled and feels free to avail themselves of every opportunity.

When you determine how much training and education you can afford in both time and dollars, be sure everyone knows you are in favor of it. If staff people think they don't have to be trained because you really are not in favor of it, they won't attend training sessions. Here is another place management should maintain a high profile.

IMPACT

Of course it's always hard to get a new operation started. The best answer to this challenge is to get in there and make it go. If you are thinking of opening a new branch, don't sneak in. Let people know what your plans are. Develop some programs for getting listings and some programs for securing buyers. Have your office as fully staffed as you can afford. Employ the publicity and promotion techniques suited to your budget and compatible to the style of the local market.

If you have done your research and market analysis well and have chosen a strong manager and a competent sales staff, the new operation will get off to a better, stronger start and realize a profit much sooner than is possible if you try to put it together one step at a time. Get the whole package ready, then sell it with enthusiasm.

CONTROL SYSTEMS

Control systems in a new office usually depend on the firm's size. For a large firm, most control systems originate in the main office. Daily deliveries to all branches provide each with new listing and sales data and all other information relevant to the branch operations. Whether communication is by computer or fax machine, by a daily telephone call from the main office, or by a daily delivery service, it's important that everyone be kept informed.

FINANCIAL CONTROLS

Financial controls are critical because an amazingly wide range of activity can be brought into managerial focus by translating diverse plans and objectives into the common language of money. In a real estate sales operation prime attention is given to cash, expenses, income as reflected in sales, escrow requirements and the major noncash assets of the firm.

The tools available to the manager in exerting control are likewise diverse. Budgets, financial statements, petty cash funds, check authorizations and purchase orders are the hardware. Clearly assigned responsibilities are the knots that bind the control system together.

An operation where the main office retains primary control over the operations of a branch office presents few unusual problems. Office space is leased, necessary office equipment is installed and salespeople operate from what amounts to a satellite of the main office. All administration continues at the main office as if the branch were located in an adjoining room. Questions of improved management therefore relate to operation of the business as a whole and are independent of the geographical location of the branch office.

In contrast, however, when the branch office takes on the character of a small subsidiary company, a major concern of management is that "the left hand knows what the right hand is doing." When the owner-manager decided upon an independently operated branch, a major psychological hindrance to success had to be overcome. There had to be conscious recognition of a willingness to rely on someone else to operate a major segment of the business. Having made that decision, the next logical concern is: "How can I be sure that I know what is going on in the branch office?" To answer this question and to ease the pangs of anxiety, reliable tools necessary to measure performance and safeguard assets must be put to use. Almost every management book written has included detailed discussions about authority and responsibility. To reiterate, however, the key to a successful operation is to actually give the branch manager the authority necessary to do his or her job. A major pitfall lies in what is implied versus what is actual. Brokers who imply that a branch manager has the requisite authority and responsibility but continue to impose their own authority in routine operations are doomed. Only by setting objectives, measuring progress and working with the manager to both highlight and establish plans for correcting problems can success be achieved.

The day the ship's captain leaves the bridge to run the engine room, one of two things can happen: The ship will founder, or there will be a new captain on the bridge. Exercising control and meddling are two entirely different techniques.

Once the decision to establish an independent branch office has been made, the techniques for main office control of the operation must not only be established but explained and implemented. The following guidelines are the basic tools for the job. Their interdependence must be kept in mind if a reliable system of control is to exist.

Dollar Limits on Major Expenditures   A valuable control is to establish a dollar ceiling on selected or significant items of operating expense. For example, it might be feasible to establish a maximum dollar value for classified advertising during a fixed period of time. The means by which this is done is a budget. The annual plan of operation is clarified by translating it into dollar terms. To establish the budget, list the items of fixed expense such as rent, taxes and depreciation over which the branch manager has no control. Control or not, the branch is stuck with these costs and must cover them from gross income before any thought can be given to the quest for profit. The branch manager now lists his or her sales objective for the year in terms of dollars that translates to budgeted gross income. Subtracting the budgeted fixed expense from the budgeted gross income highlights the budgeted dollars available to cover the branch's variable expense and to produce net income.

The categories of variable expense over which the manager does have control are those on which he or she must focus attention. Monthly comparisons with actual operating results and their differences from equivalent budgetary amounts produce the variances that are another prime control tool. Using the "management by exception" technique, the main office can require the manager to explain significant variances from the budgetary benchmarks. A word of caution is appropriate at this point. Far too often only variances over the budget are examined. Quite as crucial to successful control are explanations of significant variances under the budget. If nothing else, such an examination can often prove the validity of the budgetary benchmark. It is also essential that managers be given monthly financial data in a format that is both meaningful and useful to them in evaluating their operation. Far too often a company will fall into the trap of giving managers data that is convenient to produce rather than what is necessary for effective operation.

Separation of Financial Responsibility   In using the various tools of control, the proper assignment of each is vital to success. The records on which the statement data is based must be valid if the statements themselves are to be reliable. The source data for these records is the same as in most accounting operations. Significant items were previously cited but because of their importance bear repeating. In turn, brief commentary will be made concerning a petty cash fund, check authorizations and purchase orders. These items, as they represent a separation of responsibility, constitute a method of control. While the examples are necessarily limited, the underlying principles apply to a large spectrum in the area of financial operations.

Each branch office should be authorized a petty cash fund of sufficient size to meet ordinary operational needs. A large dollar fund is not advisable as this is self-defeating. More frequent fund replenishment can meet most of the needs for petty cash.

Check authorizations and purchase orders are valuable tools of control. The forms themselves should be designed to meet the specific needs of a particular company. But equally important, they must be designed to assure that the necessary information is entered on the form. Both the check authorization and purchase order can be prepared in the branch office, thus aiding the branch manager in controlling expenses. The branch manager alone is now responsible for expenditures for he or she must approve each check authorization and purchase order. The manager's file copy serves as his or her record of the details of these transactions. In addition, authority to incur charges against the branch office accounts is restricted to the person directly responsible for the success or failure of the branch operation. Actual issuance of checks is handled by the main office accounting department.

Escrow funds and sales files can be controlled in a similar manner. Deposits on sales are physically made by branch office personnel with duplicate deposit slips forwarded to the main office accounting department. Withdrawals from the escrow account are authorized using a check authorization by the branch manager and physically made by the main office accounting department. Sales cases are controlled by the branch manager, who authorizes the indicated disbursements. Actual payment of sales associates and other parties is handled by the main office accounting department.

Responsibility for control of major noncash assets such as office furniture is again split. The branch manager purchases the equipment after such purchases have been approved by the main office. Payment is made by the main office accounting department after the branch manager acknowledges receipt of the equipment and authorizes payment. Annual depreciation is the responsibility of the main office and is a fixed charge of the branch. The branch manager, in turn, submits an annual inventory list to the main office for comparison with the fixed asset listing used as the basis for depreciation.

In summary, the specifics of operations vary by company, and the basic principles of control must be implemented within this existing framework if they are to be effective. This operating framework serves as a harness that gives the manager the necessary authority to perform and at the same time holds him or her accountable for that performance. Definitive measurements of performance are indicated by variations from budgeted activity. When the manager's performance is measured by means of a budget, an incentive arrangement produces a direct correlation between manager performance and manager compensation.

The main office must tailor its tools of control to properly fit its method of operation. As is true for any system, periodic review and adjustment are mandatory to keep control tools both sensitive and responsive if they are to serve as reliable sensors of business activity.

HOUSEKEEPING CHECKLIST

Whether you have a single office or supervise a multioffice operation, it's wise to establish a routine of checking the housekeeping. Tell each person responsible that this is routine and important to ensure a uniformly good impression of the firm everywhere it does business. But don't tell them when the housekeeping checks will be made.

It is only fair to share the checklist items with responsible people in each office. They can use it for their own housekeeping checks and as a reminder to the whole staff of which things are important in the general impression given people who enter your place of business.

One firm's rating sheet is illustrated in Figure 19.1. After these sheets are filled in, the person responsible is given a photocopy. Commendations and suggestions for improvements are made in a separate memo, shown in Figure 19.2. The memo then becomes a part of management's next check to make sure recommendations for correction and improvement were carried out.

GOAL SETTING

Management techniques for helping salespeople establish goals that fit their own and company needs were suggested in Chapter 4. The key point to remember is that once the company goals are established and salespeople are found who understand and concur with those company goals, individual salespeople's goals must originate with them. They are then reviewed with the manager, totaled and projected for an agreed-upon time period.

DATA FLOW

All reporting should be organized so that it becomes second nature for both management and staff to provide the main office with data essential to good recordkeeping. Reports are valuable only to the extent they provide an accurate measure of how a business is doing. Management should review all reports at least once each year to make a judgment on their value. Any statistics not being used to increase sales or control costs or evaluate growth should be discontinued; and the people who have been gathering this data should be told why such reports are no longer useful to the firm.

Whether branch operations are centralized or decentralized, staff review of listing and sales goals should be handled with regularity. This starts on a one-to-one basis between the salesperson and the local manager and moves upward until top management reviews company goals with the heads of its sales staff.

When organized well, such reporting provides top management with data to handle the entire sales department realistically, to determine whether a branch is contributing its assigned share toward company goals, to change

FIGURE 19.1   ABC Realty Housekeeping Checklist

Office: **Canada Park** Date: _____, 19_____	Rating	E — **Excellent** S — **Satisfactory** U — **Unsatisfactory** Remarks
Employment question	S	Questioned all independent contractors
Checking accounts		
General	E	Currently posted
Escrow	E	Currently posted
Petty cash	U	$50.00 fund; $18.75 in bills, $16.75 cash, $14.50 short
Files, general		
Arrangement	E	
Condition	U	Many needed new jackets
Files, exclusive	U	Advertising not used
Form letters	E	Being used regularly
Jackets	E	
Progress report	E	Advertising record used and up to date
No. inspected	U	Not kept up
X-taker worksheet	U	5 out of 14 w/out worksheet
Visual aid	E	Checked 3. Well kept and used.
Comp books	E	
Street files	E	
Files, unclosed	S to U	Some loose paper & notes. Judgment note. See comments.
Jackets	E	
Information	S to E	Good information on most files
Use of sales tools by staff	S	Most are being used
Closed files	S	Many w/loose notes & unnecessary paper 8 x 10 photos in many

FIGURE 19.1   ABC Realty Housekeeping Checklist *(Continued)*

Office: **Canada Park** Date: _____, 19____	E — Excellent S — Satisfactory U — Unsatisfactory	
	Rating	**Remarks**
Office exterior	S	
Lawn	E	Had just been mowed. Parkway needs trim
Parking lot	U	High weeds, trash and papers. Tools & signs piled behind incomplete shed. Messy!
Windows	S	Clean and shiny
Sign	U	Front sign has old REALTOR® logo
Office interior		
General housekeeping	S	Needs good cleaning. Has just fired janitorial service
Desks	E	Clean and clear
Carpeting	S	Will need replacing soon
Bulletin board	E	Well placed and current
Sign-out sheet	U	Not being used regularly
Arrangement	E	For size
Staff size and potential size	10 12	
Staff	S	1 in 8:30; 1 & Manager 8:45; 6 by 10 A.M.
Appearance	E	
Automobiles	E	
Secretary	E	Summer part-time, very knowledgeable
Supplies		
Adequate supply	E	Small but adequate
Area	E	Small but adequate
Arrangement	S	Needs straightening
Signs	S	Stored in shed. Clean
Key arrangement	E	Kept at secretary's desk, well controlled
Sign out	E	Appears to be used regularly
Equal opportunity poster	S	Posted but book covering

FIGURE 19.2   Office Inspection Memo

To: President, ABC Realty

From: Sales Manager

Subject: Inspection of Canada Park Office

The attached report is the composite finding of the team inspection made _____.

Points of deficiency were discussed with the manager and suggestions made for correction and improvement.

The janitorial service agreement had just been terminated. The office needs a good general cleaning. Carpeting is showing wear and should be replaced in the near future.

Closed and unclosed files were examined. Smith-Jones note three days overdue. Dates of Earnest Money deposits not shown on many files.

direction when necessary and occasionally to decide that a branch is not making it at present and is not likely to succeed in the future.

GETTING IT ALL TOGETHER

There is so much to plan, to supervise and to follow through on in opening a real estate office that most top management people find it practical to prepare a procedural check-off list so all details are covered. The adapted list here shows how one successful firm makes sure every item from procedures in choosing a location to purchasing pencils and paper clips becomes part of the total plan. Whether you follow the detailed checklist found in Figure 19.3 or plan one of your own, the time spent on it will be well invested.

FIGURE 19.3   **Opening an Office Checklist**

Financial Plausibility

☐ Determine that corporate funds are available
☐ Determine that proper business and market conditions prevail
   ☐ Check company growth statistics
   ☐ Check all Multilist statistics
   ☐ Check national and local financial conditions
   ☐ Check national and local mortgage money availability

Area Determination

☐ Check coverage by existing company offices
☐ Pick two or three most likely areas
☐ Check all Multilist sales statistics in key areas
☐ Check company sales statistics in key areas
☐ Check business and industrial expansion in key areas
☐ Check highway and sewer and water expansion in key areas
☐ Check school, police and fire facilities in key areas

Manager Selection

☐ Determine qualities to look for
☐ Check company personnel
☐ Check other REALTOR® personnel

Manager Letter of Intent and Contact

☐ Upon selection of manager, give letter of intent
   ☐ State salary and terms
   ☐ State approximate starting time within 60 days
   ☐ Sign the contract 30 days before opening of office

Selection of Office Site

☐ Separate store building
☐ Shopping center
☐ Other
☐ Miscellaneous
   ☐ Check outdoor sign problems re: municipality and landlord
   ☐ Check quality of surrounding commercial area
   ☐ Check trash pickup
   ☐ Check street and parking lot lighting
   ☐ Check sewer and water

FIGURE 19.3   Opening an Office Checklist *(Continued)*

❏ Check municipal licensing fees
❏ Check proximity to good subdivisions

Office Layout Planning

❏ Prepare two-dimension layout of entire building space (four-month lead)
❏ Allow five-year growth pattern re: various work and storage areas
  ❏ Waiting area
  ❏ Sales desk area
  ❏ Manager area
  ❏ Clerical area
  ❏ Conference room
  ❏ Storage area
  ❏ Coffee and coat area
❏ Check proper traffic patterns
❏ Check for proper natural and artificial lighting

Standard Leasehold Improvements and Contracting for Same

❏ Two or more bids unless dealing with known contractor
❏ Carpentry (two-month lead)
❏ Electrical (three-week lead)
❏ Painting (one-month lead)
❏ Heating
❏ Air conditioning
❏ Ceiling tile
❏ Floor tile
❏ Outdoor sign (three-month lead)
❏ Outer doors and windows
❏ Parking lot

Furnishings (four-month lead)

❏ Determination of whether to purchase or lease
❏ Determination of suppliers
❏ Order floor furnishings
❏ Arrival of floor furnishings
❏ Order decor furnishings
❏ Arrival of decor furnishings

FIGURE 19.3   Opening an Office Checklist *(Continued)*

Insurance
- ☐ Order package policy
  - ☐ Fire
  - ☐ Liability
  - ☐ Property damage
  - ☐ Product liability
  - ☐ Check of lease by insurance company for "hold harm-less" clauses

Ordering and Installation of Utilities

Municipal Permits

Janitorial Service and Original Cleanup
- ☐ Contract in place

Advertising and Promotion Planning and Execution
- ☐ Tie-in with company recruiting seminars
- ☐ Kickoff ads-classified
- ☐ Agency advertising
- ☐ Agency promotion
- ☐ Yellow Pages ad
- ☐ Residential phone book listing
- ☐ Announcement sign in display window 60–90 days prior to opening

Financial Arrangements
- ☐ Choose bank
- ☐ Open escrow account, if necessary
- ☐ Arrival of check ledgers
- ☐ Arrival of deposit books
- ☐ Arrival of deposit slips
- ☐ Arrival of rubber stamps
- ☐ Enter account resolutions
- ☐ Set up accounting ledgers

Manager Instructions Re: Financial and Closing Procedures
- ☐ Bank deposits
- ☐ Bringing deals to closing department
- ☐ Closing deals

Manager Instructions Re: Office Equipment

FIGURE 19.3   Opening an Office Checklist *(Continued)*

Office Supplies, Equipment and Stationery

❑ Order supplies

Business Forms

❑ Listing forms
❑ Purchase agreement forms
❑ Lease forms—residential and commercial
❑ Addendum to purchase agreement forms
❑ Listing kits
❑ Receipt books
❑ Title folders

Manager Instructions Re: Sales Records and Procedures

❑ Conference with manager and statistical department
❑ Manager starts collection of records one month in advance
❑ Complete review of entire procedure one month prior to opening—statistical department and new manager

Selection of Sales Staff

❑ Check all current company staff
❑ Have salespeople pass word
❑ Recruiting seminar
❑ Newspaper, TV and radio advertising
❑ New manager totally responsible

Training of Sales Staff

❑ Thoroughly indoctrinate manager with training department
❑ Attendance at current company program by manager
❑ Attendance at any current recruiting seminars by manager
❑ Register all salespeople in proper REALTOR® Board
❑ Complete policy manual review
❑ Visit other company offices
❑ Spend day in each service department

Notification of REALTOR® Boards and Department of Licensing and Regulations

❑ Notify Department of Licensing and Regulations within 30 days of opening
❑ Notify all REALTOR® Boards concerned within 30 days of opening
❑ Notify all Multilist associations

FIGURE 19.3   **Opening an Office Checklist** *(Continued)*

Miscellaneous
- ❏ Order decorative trash can (six-week lead)
- ❏ Decals—front door
- ❏ Lettering on front door and windows—logo, notary public, street number (two-week lead)
- ❏ Mail slot—front door (two-week lead)
- ❏ Order proper newspapers and periodicals
- ❏ Manager application for notary certificate—with seal
- ❏ Clean-up supplies
- ❏ Coffee equipment

Chapter 20

Technology:

The Office of the 21st Century

How they incorporate new technology into their operations is an important consideration for brokers, whether they've been in business for a long time or are opening their first office. From cellular telephones to computers to the Internet, technology is changing, and will continue to change, the way the real estate business is conducted. The creative use of technology can give brokers a competitive edge.

This chapter explores how to make good business decisions about technology and how to effectively integrate it into a brokerage operation. It also looks at some of the different types of technology in increasingly common use. But keep in mind that the technology field is in constant and rapid flux. The key is to understand how to evaluate technology rather than to know what is currently available, because that is guaranteed to soon be out of date.

THE CYBERWORLD OF REAL ESTATE

A large real estate firm in a major city has introduced a telephone listing hotline system that gives consumers access to all of the firm's real estate listings, 24 hours a day, simply by using a touchtone phone. The system also features a fax-on-demand option that allows customers to receive preliminary home information through the fax.[1]

An international real estate firm has developed its own satellite network for providing its sales force with information and education through taped presentations and lectures by top industry experts. Interactive videoconferences enable audiences in linked offices to ask questions and hold discussions with presenters and expert panels.[2]

Real estate firms are placing electronic kiosks in shopping malls to display their listings and offering a direct telephone connection to their local office.[3]

High-tech homebuyers can view color photos and detailed descriptions of homes listed by a large national real estate firm on the Internet. The file of more than 19,000 listings is updated every other week.[4]

A New Jersey firm has unveiled a new service for homebuyers that uses computers to pinpoint the geographic areas from which their buyers are most likely to come. This enables the firm's salespeople to identify where buyers for an individual home or subdivision are likely to come from and target their marketing accordingly.[5]

The digital age has arrived. Cellular telephones, beepers, voice mail, e-mail, fax machines and fax modems, as well as computers, have all become part of the broker's business. John Selleck, CRB, in the Winter 1995 issue of *Real Estate Business* ("Technology and the Broker/Agent Relationship") says, "Perhaps more than any other single development, the personal computer has changed the way real estate is done—both inside the office and out. PCs have helped streamline the flow of information and made its manipulation more accurate, timely and efficient." According to Brad Hanks, CRS, "Instantaneous communication, access to larger amounts of data, and integration of services are just a few of technology's influences on the industry. Technology will become a competitive edge with both sales associates and the public."[6]

This chapter is designed to aid brokers in making good business decisions about purchasing technology and integrating it into their operations. No formulas or simple answers exist to tell you what to do. It's necessary for you to make a thorough examination of both your internal and external environment. What you need will depend on your competitive marketplace, the size of your firm, how you presently do business and which elements of the technology available will best maximize the time and efforts of yourself, your staff and your sales associates.

McKINSEY'S 7-S MODEL AND NEW TECHNOLOGY

As with any good business decision, you need to evaluate how introducing new technology into your office will affect the other elements of your business. In particular, a new computer system will affect the firm's other systems, strategies and staff. For example, a compensation software package that enables you to calculate sales associates' commissions easier will let you set up an individualized compensation system that will more effectively motivate salespeople. On the other hand, if your new system initially produces errors in commission checks, you may experience motivation and morale problems.

New technology must support the firm's strategies, particularly its marketing and financial strategies. For example, if the firm's strategy is to maintain close contact with its clients in order to encourage referral business, it can purchase contact management software that helps sales associates accomplish this. Accounting software can help management evaluate and adjust its strategies by making it easier to generate reports that enable it to evaluate the strengths and weaknesses of the business.

In adopting new technology, management needs to keep the needs of its staff uppermost. It is critical that the system chosen be user-friendly, so people can learn to use it easily. In addition, the benefits of using the new technology should be sold to staff in a way they can respond to. They need to understand how these new tools will make it easier for them to do their jobs and will increase their productivity.

Management style is an important factor in successfully integrating technology into the firm's operations. If management's attitude is "I don't know a thing about computers and I don't want to know," the salespeople are likely to adopt the same attitude and will never use the technology to its full capacity. In the worst case, it may sit and gather dust. Or salespeople may decide to leave the firm because learning to use the computer is too much work. But if managers are enthusiastic, if they view the computer as a useful tool that will help increase productivity, and if they make practical training for themselves as well as for the salespeople a priority, the salespeople will get the message.

Technology will affect the firm's training systems. A firm that has always handled its training internally may need to bring in an outsider to teach the staff how to use its new computers. It may be necessary to designate someone in the office to answer questions and troubleshoot problems on an ongoing basis. The firm's recruiting strategies may also need to be changed, because it looks to hire sales associates who will be comfortable working in a computerized environment.

More than almost any other innovation, technology will affect every aspect of how the firm operates. If the firm effectively integrates technology into the way it traditionally has done business, it can make being a technology leader one of the competitive skills of the firm.

PLANNING FOR TECHNOLOGY

If you are considering computerizing your brokerage office, planning is critical. The place to begin is with a needs assessment. If you don't feel you have the internal capability to do this, hire a consultant to help.

Be sure to involve all levels of users in gathering information. Hold focus groups or establish an in-house task force to study the company's overall needs. Include the entire management team, as well as the agents who will use the new technology. Your agents are closest to the marketplace and know what capabilities customers expect. They're also likely to know what your competitors offer. Salespeople attend seminars and meetings and are likely to be informed about what types of hardware and software are available that would help them do their jobs better. If people are involved in the assessment process, they are more likely to support the decisions that are made.

ASSESS YOUR NEEDS

Here are some of the factors you need to assess when determining whether—and how—to proceed in adopting new technology in your firm.

First, examine your external market. What items are critical to stay competitive? Is your market moving so quickly that instantaneous data is crucial? Do buyers and sellers make decisions based on the technological level of firms?[7]

Next, examine your competition. What technology do they have? Are they technology rich or poor? Sharp managers can exploit the latter condition in recruiting sales associates or in sending a message to the buying and selling public.[8]

Then look at your internal needs. You need to determine what types of programs and systems you require to keep track of the level of business coming into your office, the profitability of that business and the productivity of your sales associates.

Assess your sales associates' needs. Your staff may not need the new technology today, but what about next year, or even six months from now?[9] Develop a shared future with sales associates. Technology will provide new markets, new customers, more information and more control at the sales associate level. Make sure the technology chosen is the technology your sales associates want and need.[10] They will accept change when the benefit is relevant to them and positively affects their bottom line.

DEVELOP AN IMPLEMENTATION STRATEGY

Once you've completed your needs assessment, you must develop an overall strategy for your information systems. Avoid the temptation to install technology on an as-needed basis, which may solve isolated problems but frequently will not enable you to expand your system or add advancements. Implement technology gradually but continually. Don't wait for a "final" solution to implement all at once. This is a period of rapid change.[11]

Finally, before purchasing new technology, schedule time for technology research. Check industry rating reports, hire a technology consultant or talk with people who use that technology in their business.

Brokers who use technology successfully treat it like any other resource, says one expert.[12] Here are the key points:

1. Computers and software are not different; they are just a better way of doing things, like a fax machine or a microwave oven. Software is a tool, and brokers need to learn how it can be used.
2. Technology is managed just like other resources. Objectives are defined and strategies are worked out that include technology. Implementation is done in phases.
3. The real estate business is still a people business. If this is not kept in mind, technology can make things worse.

You don't need to be a technology expert in order to benefit from technology. You just need to know what exists and how to apply it creatively. Spend an hour a week looking into the future and identifying the skills and knowledge you will need in order to thrive, recommends Daniel Burrus, author of *Technotrends: How To Use Technology To Go Beyond the Competition*. All brokerage managers need is an open mind and a willingness to learn to use new tools.[13]

CHOOSE SOFTWARE DISCRIMINATELY

Once you've decided to computerize your office, the first step is to determine what software you want. This will determine the type of hardware you will need to run it.

Before they make any kind of purchase—a car, a home, an air-conditioner—most people do a considerable amount of research in order to make a good decision. The same is true of software. If you don't have the time or knowledge to do the necessary research yourself, assign the task to someone else in the office who has an interest in technology. However, you need to stay involved to make sure that the software your firm purchases meets your business needs.

Real estate associations such as the Real Estate Brokerage Managers Council™ are useful sources of information about software specific to real estate brokerage offices. Another option is to hire a technology consultant. Budget the time and money needed to attend state and national real estate conventions. These are excellent forums to learn about the software available to help you and your sales associates run your business more efficiently.

In selecting software, it is critical to take an organized approach. Have a thorough understanding of how your business currently operates and identify functions that need improvement or could be made more efficient. Look for operations presently done manually that could be done more quickly and easily if they were computerized. Ask yourself what sort of reports would enable you to make better management decisions faster. Once you determine what types of reports you want, you can investigate which software programs will produce these reports.

There are many different types of software to choose from to make your business more efficient and effective. Listed below are just a few of the types of software presently available. New programs and capabilities are constantly becoming available.

- *Competitive Market Analysis* programs enable sales associates to prepare listing presentation reports using data obtained from the MLS.
- *Contact Management* software can help sales associates keep track of and follow-up on clients.
- *Sales and Management Tracking* software can provide up-to-date management reports such as listing rosters, commission summary reports and advertising effectiveness summaries.
- *Accounting* software can do all of a firm's accounting and produce general ledgers that make it easier to produce income statements, balance sheets and budget comparisons.
- *Compensation* programs enable brokers to analyze and compare commission schedules to determine bottom-line profitability.
- *Agent Information* software can provide detailed activity tracking including gross commissions, agent commissions and total sales dollars.
- *Desktop Publishing and Graphics* programs enable firms to produce professional looking invitations, announcement cards, brochures, flyers, newsletters and ads.
- *Presentation* software enables agents to produce professional looking market presentations.

Look for programs that are or can be linked so that all sales associate and managerial data can be integrated with a single data entry. Or information from a contact management program can be used to create buyer presentations without having to reenter the data.

When you evaluate software, you must determine if it is user friendly. Software that is too difficult to learn or operate won't be used to its maximum capabilities. Look for intuitive menu structures and uncluttered screens. Can you select from a list of data base items? Is it easy to correct errors? Are there useful help screens and on-screen displays of reports?

Talk to other current users of the software you are considering. Find out how the software has benefited their business and what its strong and weak points are. Also ask about their experience with the software vendor. Has the vendor been responsive? Have they gotten good vendor service?

Before you purchase any software, make sure the vendor has an 800 number so you can contact them to resolve questions. They should also have a help line for questions and maintenance after the purchase. Upgrades are another important factor. Ask the vendor how often upgrades are released and whether you can obtain them at no or low cost.

The Real Estate Brokerage Managers Council™ recommends a number of software programs, but brokers should be aware that software can quickly become outdated. It is your responsibility to investigate thoroughly before making a purchase. You should also keep in mind that whatever you purchase, another program will soon be released that does the job faster and better.

BUY HARDWARE WITH THE FUTURE IN MIND

Once you've determined what software you need, the next step is to research the hardware. Make sure the hardware you pick is capable of running the software you have selected. In addition, always decide on all the components before you make any purchases. This will prevent you from making costly mistakes. The hardware vendor you select should have a help line for questions and maintenance after the purchase.

If your computers are going to be tied into an MLS system, consider what capacity you will need in the future as the MLS data base continues to grow. One of the biggest mistakes people make when purchasing a computer is to select something that is adequate only for their present needs. But new releases of software require more and more memory. Select hardware that gives you the ability to add memory as your needs grow.

Even so, the rapid pace of technological change guarantees that the hardware you buy today will be obsolete in just a few years. Be sure to budget a line item reserve for replacing computer equipment so you have cash available to acquire tomorrow's technology. Whether or not you depreciate it in your income statement, it will be an out-of-pocket expense somewhere down the line.

Hanks advises also taking a look at the additional tools that can be added to your computer system. Scanners, digital cameras, CD-ROM players, color printers and so on can add to the benefits a computer system brings to your office. Don't overlook multimedia. Computer systems in some offices are showing videos of listing inventory, accompanied by music and a narrative of the homes' features.[14]

Online services are another area you should investigate. In real estate, online vendors provide tax information, demographic data, and foreclosure information, as well as general information about a community, its schools and its businesses. Some lenders are using online bulletin boards to post rates and programs.[15]

SYSTEMS FOR MULTIPLE OFFICES/NETWORKING

For large firms with multiple offices, you may want to consider networking, that is, tying all of the computers together so information can be exchanged electronically between the main office and branch offices. You can also network your computers within a single office. Things to think about with networking include the layout of the office, the location of the equipment and the cost to network them together.

At the time you purchase your computers, you should consider whether you may want to network them within your office or with branch offices in the future. Then set them up so you can do this without a lot of unnecessary additional expense.

Some brokers create a resource center—an area in the office that is dedicated to all of the firm's technology: computers, fax machines, copiers and the like. Grouping this equipment eliminates the often considerable expense of running cables from one end of the office to the other.

DOING REAL ESTATE BUSINESS IN CYBERSPACE

Many experts predict that computer networks and the growth of online services will eventually change the nature of the real estate profession. A growing number of real estate firms, from small offices to major franchises, are doing business via the Internet, a global network of computer networks. According to a 1995 estimate, there were more than 3,000 sites devoted to real estate, with dozens of new real estate sites being added each week. Firms use these sites to advertise properties and provide homebuyers and homesellers with basic information about a real estate transaction. Called "home pages," these sites can be, in essence, a firm's "storefront."

One New Jersey REALTOR® uses his firm's home page to feature general information about his resort market area, including local weather reports and ads of properties for sale and for rent by the firm. The firm sells expensive beachfront property, and the Internet is an ideal way to reach people with above-average incomes.

Another REALTOR® who owns a mortgage brokerage firm set up a home page on the Internet that functions as a kind of multiple listing service of loans in search of funding. For a fee, mortgage brokers, lenders and real estate salespeople can use her home page as a central location to expose a hard-to-fund loan to a broad group of funding sources.

According to one sales associate, "More than anything else, we're in the information business. And that's why the Internet is such a powerful business tool for real estate. The Internet isn't about technology; it's about the effective, efficient delivery of lots of information."[16]

These computer networks give consumers access to a great deal of information formerly controlled by real estate agents. In the future, reports National Association of REALTORS® economist John Tuccillo, real estate professionals will need to refocus their business from one based on an information monopoly to one based on a high level of professional services.

WIRELESS TECHNOLOGIES

Another area that is likely to change the face of real estate is wireless technologies. The most popular wireless tools are pagers and cellular phones. These allow real estate professionals to stay connected with their clients and staffs. There are also wireless PCs—usually in notebook or laptop form—and smaller handheld devices such as palmtop computers and

Personal Device Assistants (PDAs). In general, wireless communications require a minimum of technical expertise on the part of the user.[17]

Wireless technologies fit the needs of the mobile real estate work force perfectly. Wireless tools can help busy real estate professionals work in the field with clients yet remain accessible to their support staffs as well as other clients. Agents working on the road can access critical data, send data to their offices for distribution by support staff and receive data from clients, other agents, the office or other real estate professionals such as mortgage officers or title search agents.[18] One broker has found that because agents work on home computers or laptops, he needs less office space.

Wireless technology also gives sales associates a competitive edge by enabling them to respond to sellers in a more timely manner. They can take measurements of a property, identify comparables, call up recent sales through the MLS and target a selling price in minutes, in the seller's dining room.

SMALL FIRMS CAN ALSO BENEFIT FROM TECHNOLOGY

Not all brokers need to go high-tech today. Small brokers—those with fewer than ten sales associates and one office—may not need to computerize yet. But they should investigate what's available in the marketplace, so they are prepared when their business grows or changes.

However, a small firm may find that with an investment in technology, tasks that are currently being done manually can be accomplished more efficiently and at lower cost. For example, a firm may have a full-time administrative employee who does the firm's income and expense accounts on a ledger sheet. This person may be paid a salary of $15,000 to $20,000 a year, plus benefits. A software program might enable the firm to input the same information in 25 percent of the time. If it costs $5,000 to buy the hardware and software and another $5,000 for someone to produce the income and expense data, the firm may save $10,000 to $15,000 a year on that operation.

Although large firms are in the forefront in adopting the new technologies, for smaller firms, technology can help to level the playing field. Hanks offers some ideas for small firms to consider in maximizing their hardware and software dollars.[19]

- Make sure your equipment is fully upgradeable and compatible with your intended uses.
- Offer a balance of software to your sales associates and staff: access to the MLS computer, word processing, databases, and spreadsheet programs; even consider desktop publishing to market and advertise properties and sales associates.
- Make sure the software is easy to use. You want sales associates to market, not to spend days learning how to use programs.

- Compare products that are designed specifically for your industry with those sold over the counter. It's easier than you think to customize "off the shelf" programs to your needs. While larger firms can hire programmers, you can hire college students majoring in computer science to customize the application to your needs. This may not require much money, because the students can often use the experience as credit toward an internship or independent study program.
- Look for software that can be linked to other programs, allowing you more flexibility in creating the modules you need. For example, if you are tracking your listing inventory in a data base, you can link expenses charged to that listing to a spreadsheet. Additional costs to that listing are automatically updated in the spreadsheet.
- Make sure your software provider has adequate support for your needs. Find out if the support is at an additional cost, how many technical support people are staffing the lines and what hours support is available.
- Look at networking computers, even if you only have three or four computers. Networking can allow sales associates and staff to keep up to date on all changes in listings and escrows. Electronic mail can make communications quicker and easier. It's not very expensive to network a small office.
- It's not necessary to have the fastest, feature-rich computer system. For firms operating on a tight budget, fast with fewer features may be the way to go. Some features can always be added at a later time.

TRAINING

Without adequate training, your new computer equipment is just an expensive paperweight. When you are buying your computer equipment, ask the vendors what kind of training they offer. Computers are becoming more user-friendly, but training is still the only way to ensure that your staff is taking full advantage of the capabilities of this new tool.

You could hire a training consultant or send your staff to a computer course at a local college. Another option is to ask the computer teacher at your local high school to recommend a student who is computer literate. Bring that student into your office for a few hours after school several days a week and let him or her do your training at a level that is comprehensible to a sales associate. It's a win-win situation: The student will be paid for putting his or her knowledge to use, and the sales associates will have a friendly trainer who speaks their language.

Keep in mind that sales associates are bottom-line oriented, even when it comes to computer training. Show them how the program will benefit them. Don't throw around terms like "contact management program." Instead, ask them: "How would you like to let your buyers and sellers know monthly what you and the office are doing for them, at the push of a button?" Similarly, sales associates may have no idea what desktop publishing is.

Explain to them that these programs will enable them to make personal brochures and flyers quickly and easily, so they can do all sorts of marketing that they couldn't do before. Let them know the benefit to them, how this technology can be used to make them more successful.

Remember, many people are afraid of technology. Most people can't even program their VCR. Sales associates need to know that technology is just another tool they can use to become more productive. A good approach to overcome their fear is to ask your sales associates what they could be doing right now that would make them more productive in contacting or in making presentations to buyers and sellers. Then show them how the computer can help them do these things.

Be sure to set up a consistent day and time to conduct your computer training. This not only makes it easier for your sales associates to plan their time, it also sends the message that you consider the training to be an important use of their time.

Before you begin training, try to obtain the commitment of your sales associates. If they don't want to learn how to do mail merges or desktop publishing, no matter how good your training program is, you will have an uphill battle. In addition, make sure all the managers and leaders in your company know how to use computers, recommends Ron Solberg. "When the company's leaders aren't using the office electronic mail system, it's difficult to encourage use among others."[20]

Training is most effective when done in small groups, with no more than two people to a computer, one hands-on and the other observing. Try to pair a sales associate who is comfortable with computer technology with one who is not. The technologically oriented individual will like the recognition of helping the other partner. Centralizing your computers in a resource center makes it easier to train your sales associates in small groups. In a resource center with three computers, you can easily train a group of up to six people. One-on-one instruction may be a good idea for those who are sensitive about learning computer basics in a group environment.

When your sales associates have completed their computer training, make sure they have lots of opportunities to use what they've learned. If people don't put their computer training to use immediately, they tend to forget what they've learned.

Once you've introduced computers into your firm, any new sales associates you recruit should know how to use a computer. In the job description, require sales associates, managers and staff to receive a minimum number of hours of computer training annually.

Finally, designate a willing and knowledgeable person inside or outside the office to answer computer-related questions about hardware and software. Some larger offices have designated specific staff members as resident experts who can keep the office current on the most recent software versions and applications and make sure all hardware and software manuals and support materials are readily available.[21]

MEETING TOMORROW'S TECHNOLOGICAL CHALLENGES

Owners and managers need to expect technological change and have a plan to incorporate technological advances as they occur. But it's important to be sure that technology is not just an expense but an asset that actually improves the productivity of your business, according to Hanks. Keep in mind that computers are tools, a means to an end: selling real estate.

In many cases, customers drive the need for technology. For example, customers are demanding a more professional competitive market analysis (CMA) report. At one time a competitive market analysis—a list of the properties currently on the market, those sold in the last six months, and those that had expired—was obtained manually from the MLS and typed on a one-page form. Now, you can pull CMA programs directly from your system that can include a cover page addressed to the individual seller, a biography of the sales associate and a history of the company. In addition to listing all the properties now on the market plus the ones that sold and expired, the CMA also can list all the properties the sales associate or the company has sold in the last one or five years, and the company's market share.

These marketing strategies impress sellers, who are more likely to give you their listing. In addition, you used to have to produce this information in your office. But with wireless technology, now you can take your laptop computer into the seller's home and update your marketing information on the spot. The sales associate who offers the seller the most knowledge and professionalism is the one who is most likely to walk away with the listing.

Technology can also give your firm an advantage over competitors in recruiting and retaining sales associates. Once sales associates become used to a computerized environment, they are more likely to stay in that type of environment.

HIGH TECH, HIGH TOUCH

It's important not to lose sight of the fact that real estate is a people business. Awareness and empathy with the consumer are very important. Technology brings with it the danger of becoming high tech, low touch. But it is important when going high tech to remain high touch. If you lose touch with your consumers, if you lose the empathy that is necessary in your business transactions, technology will do your business more harm than good.

The personal involvement of the buyer and seller cannot be computerized. However, used properly, technology enables sales associates to touch their customers—both buyers and sellers—daily, letting them know what they can do to service their needs.

CONCLUSION

Technology will not solve all your firm's problems. It will not make a bad salesperson better. But it will allow good salespeople to use their time more effectively and to close more transactions. As a result, the best agents will be able to earn much more.

In the 1980s, many managers resisted technology. But in the 1990s and beyond, real estate managers will need to effectively integrate technology into their business operations. In the information age, only those companies and individuals who keep pace with technology will be able to compete successfully.

ENDNOTES

1. *MarkeTrends, Real Estate Business,* vol. 14, no. 2, Spring 1995, p. 10.
2. Ibid.
3. Farnsworth, "Navigate the Information Super Highway," *Real Estate Business,* Spring 1994.
4. "Home Shopping in Cyberspace," *MarkeTrends, Real Estate Business,* vol. 14, no. 2, Spring 1995, p. 14.
5. "Computers Map Out Buyer Sources," *MarkeTrends, Real Estate Business,* vol. 14, no. 2, Spring 1995, p. 14.
6. Brad Hanks, "How the Small Firm Can Join the Technology Revolution," *Management Issues and Trends,* vol. 9, no. 6, Dec. 1994, p.4.
7. Hanks, "How the Small Firm . . . ," p.4.
8. Hanks, "How the Small Firm . . . ," p.4.
9. Hanks, "How the Small Firm . . . ," p.4.
10. Tom Koenig, CRB, "Increasing Productivity Through Technology," in *Management Issues and Trends*, vol. 9, no. 6, December 1994.
11. Koenig, "Increasing Productivity . . . ," p.6.
12. Stan Chmielewski, "Technology for Broker Owners," a presentation at the Management EXCELebration 1995 of the Real Estate Brokerage Managers Council™.
13. Interview with Daniel Burrus in *Management Issues and Trends,* vol. 9, no. 6, Dec. 1994, p. 2.
14. Hanks, "How the Small Firm . . . ," p. 5.
15. Hanks, "How the Small Firm . . . ," p. 5.
16. Pamela Geurds Kabati, "Working, Winning on the Web." REALTOR® News, week of Nov. 6, 1995, pp. 13-15.
17. Kabati, "Working, Winning on the Web," p. 13-15.
18. Roald Marth, CRS, "Wireless Technologies Move into Real Estate," in *Real Estate Business,* Spring 1995, pp. 36-44.
19. Hanks, "How the Small Firm . . . ," p. 4-5.
20. Ron Solberg, "People: The First Step in Computerizing Your Firm," in *Management Issues and Trends,* vol. 9, no. 6, Dec. 1994, p. 3.
21. Solberg, "People," p. 3.

Chapter 21

Shared Values and Ethical Business Practices

This book has examined the elements of managing a real estate business using the 7-S model of organizational management. In the final chapter we look at the 7-S variable of shared values, and specifically the value of ethical behavior.

Ethical behavior is the hallmark of a professional. Real estate practitioners are part of a group that is obligated to protect and promote the best interests of the public. Those who act unethically reflect negatively not only on themselves, but on the reputation of all real estate professionals.

Furthermore, good ethics is good business. Owners and buyers who believe they are treated with integrity and professionalism will refer others to you and your firm.

This chapter defines what is meant by ethical behavior. It describes the rules governing agency and real estate agent's fiduciary responsibilities. It also examines the ethical responsibilities of real estate professionals to buyers and sellers, to other licensees, and to the community in which it does business.

ETHICS INVOLVE MORE THAN THE LAW

The most critical task facing today's real estate managers is that of providing leadership for their organizations to build the capabilities that will enable them to respond to the threats and opportunities of the rapidly changing business environment. McKinsey's 7-S model can assist them in this process by providing a framework for understanding the complexity of

384

organizations and how the seven interdependent variables of structure, strategy, systems, style, skills, staff and shared values interact to influence an organization's ability to change.

This book concludes with a discussion of shared values. These are the fundamental values around which a business is built and which help shape its behaviors and attitudes, goals and objectives. One important shared value that managers impart to their firms is the value of ethical behavior.

ETHICS

Ethics is concerned with right and wrong.* It's important to recognize that right and wrong are not the same as legal and illegal. The law is a set of minimum standards that society will tolerate, while ethics is right for right's sake. Political figures frequently defend their actions by saying they didn't do anything illegal. However, most people expect those in positions of public trust not just to meet the minimum acceptable standards of the law but to act in an ethical manner as well.

Ethical behavior is subjective and is defined differently by different people. In addition, an act can be ethical or unethical depending on the motive of the person performing the act. For example, attempting to persuade the state licensing agency to tighten the requirements for real estate licensing by requiring more education would be ethical if it were based on the belief that this action is necessary in order to protect the public. However, the same action done for the self-serving purpose of keeping down the number of new competitors would be unethical.

One way to test whether behavior is ethical or not is to apply the Golden Rule: "Do unto others as you would have others do unto you." Ask yourself: "Would I want someone else to act in this manner toward me?"

Albert Schweitzer defined ethics as follows:

> Ethics is the name we give to our concern for good behavior. We feel an obligation to consider not only our own personal well-being but also that of others and of human society as a whole.

In Dr. Schweitzer's philosophy, ethical behavior is based on regard for others. It is concerned with the well-being of society as a whole. Ideally, real estate practitioners should feel that they are part of a group and that they are mutually obligated to protect and promote the best interests of the public.

Many real estate firms give recognition to top producers of sales and listings. But an overemphasis on financial rewards could lead some brokers and sales associates to regard customers and clients solely as means to an

---

* This section is excerpted from William H. Pivar & Donald L. Harlan, *Real Estate Ethics: Good Ethics = Good Business,* Real Estate Education Company, 1995.

end. Although real estate professionals expect to be adequately rewarded for their efforts, the first concern of a professional is to meet the needs of the client and the public in a proper and ethical manner.

There is a practical benefit in ethical behavior. Referrals are important in the real estate business. Owners who believe you've worked for them honestly and professionally will refer others to you or your firm. Owners who are referred to specific brokers or sales associates are presold on their integrity and professionalism. Buyers who come to them because of referrals know that they will work hard to find a property that best meets their needs and will do so in an open and honest manner. So good ethics is good business. In fact, many companies are beginning to present "Superior Customer Service Awards" specifically awarded for customer/client satisfaction based in part on ethical behavior and integrity.

Much of the American public has a negative perception of real estate agents' ethics. In a 1994 Gallup poll asking people to rate the honesty and ethical standards of people in 26 different fields, real estate agents came in 19th place, below lawyers and U.S. Senators. According to an article in the *Wall Street Journal,* a Florida real estate agent and educator who administered a test measuring ethical reasoning to a class of real estate agents she taught found that the agents ranked just above high school students in their ability to make ethical judgments. Moreover, she found that more experienced agents scored lower than less experienced ones.[1]

A poll conducted by the Opinion Research Corporation of America for the American Association of Retired Persons (AARP) and the Consumer Federation of America (CFA) in 1995 reflected a similar distrust of real estate agents. The survey found that many consumers want more active regulation of real estate agents by state regulatory agencies. A majority of those surveyed believe that state real estate commission boards should be more independent of the industry. Nearly half said agents should comprise a minority of board membership, while 15 percent believe agents should not be permitted to serve on real estate boards at all. A large majority of those surveyed (86 percent) said regulators should develop an information pamphlet that real estate agents should be required to give to their customers. Significantly, recent homebuyers and homesellers were the biggest supporters of more active and independent real estate regulation.[2]

This is not the ethical reputation that the real estate industry wants.

The National Association of REALTORS® has done a great deal to promote professionalism and to instill in licensees the concern that ethics must play a part in their daily lives. The National Association of REALTORS® has published a code of ethics that is a pertinent guide to professional dealing with others. This Code of Ethics is important to every real estate licensee, whether or not he or she is a member of the National Association of REALTORS®. If brokers fail behave ethically and to police themselves, consumer groups and the government will assume that responsibility.

According to the National Association of REALTORS® Code of Ethics:
The term REALTOR® has come to connote competency, fairness, and high integrity resulting from adherence to a lofty ideal of moral conduct in business relations. No inducement of profit and no instruction from clients can ever justify departure from this ideal.

REALTORS® have a duty to uphold professional standards in their dealings with the public. This duty includes compliance with all applicable fair housing laws and regulations.

In fulfilling their duties to clients and customers, brokers and sales associates must understand and adhere to the rules governing agency.

AGENCY[3]

Real estate brokers represent a principal and have a fiduciary duty to their principal that includes loyalty, obedience, full disclosure, confidentiality, due diligence, care and the duty to account for all funds received. A real estate agent can represent the seller; can represent the buyer; or can be a dual agent, representing both buyer and seller.

Seller's Agents

Traditionally, most real estate agents have represented the seller. They receive their agency authority through a formal right-to-sell agreement, i.e., a listing. The firm that lists the property is known as the listing broker. Other brokerage firms working with the listing broker are called selling agents and usually are subagents of the listing broker, although they could elect instead to represent the buyer.

Buyers may be unaware or may lose sight of the fact that the selling agent is working for the best interests of the seller. Seller's agents must be careful to caution buyers not to reveal information to them that the buyer would not want the agent's principal to know.

Even though an agent may intend to be a seller's agent, statements to a buyer such as "I will get you the best deal possible," have led buyers to believe that a seller's agent represented them. Courts have sometimes ruled that the seller's agent had agency duties to the buyer when the agent's words or actions led the buyer to believe that the agent was serving him or her.

Buyer's Agents

Buyer agency is a rapidly growing area in real estate. The buyer's agent has a fiduciary duty to the buyer, not the seller, and uses his or her knowledge to further the buyer's interests. Information that the buyer confides in the buyer's agent would not be given to the seller.

Buyer's agents agree to use their best efforts to locate a property that best meets the buyer's needs and assist the buyer in making the purchase.

The buyer-agency agreement customarily provides that the buyer will pay a fee if a purchase is made. However, the buyer generally does not have to pay any fee if the buyer's agent receives a designated share of the listing agent's commission.

Dual Agents

When one agent represents both the buyer and seller in a transaction, this is known as dual agency. If an agent were a buyer's agent and the buyer wished to purchase a property listed for sale with his or her buyer's agent, there would be a dual agency situation. In a dual agency situation, both buyer and seller should be fully informed of and consent to the dual agency. In addition, buyer and seller should agree that the agent may not disclose confidential information received from either party, so as not to give one party an advantage over the other. For example, the agent could not tell the buyer that the seller would accept less or tell the seller that the buyer would pay more.

DISCLOSURE

Most states require a formal written disclosure of agency to both buyer and seller. Even if a disclosure is not mandated, agents have an ethical duty to make certain that buyers and sellers fully understand the agent's agency role. To make certain that there is no misunderstanding as to agency status and duties, the agent should prepare a written declaration of agency, and this should be signed by buyers as well as sellers. A copy should then be given to all of the parties involved.

OFFICE POLICY ON AGENCY*

Two main areas of law give direction on how a real estate licensee should proceed in dealing with agency relationships. These are (1) the common law of agency, and (2) state statute.

The common law of agency is created through case law. Because it is constantly being developed and refined through new litigation, case law can be ambiguous and inconsistent and may leave many gray areas. State statutes on agency tend to be clearer and more definitive, and may supersede case law.

Brokers should have an office policy manual that gives direction on how to create an agency relationship with consumers. However, office policies on agency are only effective if they accurately reflect the

---

* This information was abstracted from *Loss Prevention Bulletin No. 11,* a Supplement to *Real Estate Today* prepared jointly by the National Association of REALTORS® and Victor O. Schinnerer & Co., November 1994.

requirements of state law. Brokers should always keep current on legislative changes taking place in their state and update their office policy manual accordingly.

OTHER ETHICAL RESPONSIBILITIES

In addition to behaving ethically toward buyers and sellers, real estate agents also have a responsibility to treat other licensees and the agents and staff in their own offices with integrity and decency. Their ethical responsibilities to these groups include the following.

Responsibilities to Other Licensees

- Cooperate with other brokers wherever possible.
- Avoid interfering with another licensee's client.
- Refuse to cooperate with unethical brokers.
- Uphold professional standards.
- Avoid unfair competitive practices.
- Apply the Golden Rule in determining procuring cause and sharing of commissions.

Responsibilities to Other Licensees in Your Office

- Employ ethical hiring practices; avoid false or misleading statements and discriminatory practices.
- Properly supervise employees and/or sales associates.
- Handle salesperson commissions equitably.
- Report unethical acts to the proper authorities.
- Provide a positive working environment.

The real estate brokerage manager sets the tone for the office. When managers behave ethically in all of their interactions with the public, with other brokers and with the salespeople in their own office, they increase the likelihood that their salespeople will also act in an ethical manner. The manager should set forth clearly defined office policies governing ethical behavior and ensure that they are strictly enforced. But actions speak louder than words. Sales associates will adopt the values the manager acts on, rather than those the manager states. If the manager acts ethically, ethical behavior will become a shared value in the organization. And this is a goal worth striving for.

SOCIAL COMMITMENT

In today's business environment, companies' responsibilities extend beyond making a profit. The public increasingly expects companies to stand for certain social principles.

Spiegel's Hank Johnson asserts:

To ignore civic responsibility is to ignore the mutually beneficial relationship between you and the market.[4]

According to Frank Feather, author of *The Future Consumer,* the ways through which mutually beneficial relations can be achieved include core values and socioeconomic responsibility.

Core values, another term for shared values, reflect the company's commitment to excel and to be socially responsible within its community. For example, Northern Telecom's core values are:

- *Customers:* Create superior value for customers.
- *People:* Our people are our strength.
- *Teamwork:* Share one vision; we are one team.
- *Innovation:* Embrace change, reward innovation.
- *Excellence:* Our only standard.
- *Commitment:* We do what we say we will do.[5]

Northern Telecom's core values are similar to those in other successful firms. Such companies emphasize respect for staff, a focus on quality, value and customer service, uncompromising integrity in all of the firm's dealings, and the importance of flexibility and continuing innovation. Hewlett-Packard's core values are almost identical to Northern Telecom's but add the core value of making solid contributions to the communities in which it operates.

Although business alone cannot solve society's social and economic problems, socioeconomic responsibility means that companies ought to give something back to the community. The Vermont ice cream maker Ben & Jerry's is the only firm in the world with a Director of Social Mission Development. Part of the firm's mission is "to improve the quality of life of a broad community—local and global."[6] To that end, the firm has a variety of community initiatives that support projects promoting social change. Feather calls such firms socialistic entrepreneurs.

Another socialistic entrepreneur is Magna, the auto parts maker. The firm's culture is based on fair enterprise, worker participation and community orientation. Its aims are spelled out in a corporate constitution. This document stipulates percentages of the firm's pretax profits that must go to employee shareholders; to "charitable, cultural, educational, and political institutions *to support the basic fabric of society*"; and to foster "*long-term entrepreneurialism* across the company."[7]

Companies that take their socioeconomic responsibilities seriously do well, as well as do good. Companies that have an inspiring vision and a culture truly committed to social values augment the company's image in the eyes of its customers and are more competitive in the marketplace.

ENDNOTES

1. "Teacher Gives Real-Estate Agents Below-Average Grades on Ethics," in *The Wall Street Journal*, Marketplace, B1, July 26, 1994.
2. "Consumers Want States To Put More Resources Behind Real Estate Regulators," *Real Estate Insider,* Dec. 15, 1995, pp. 6-7.
3. "Consumers Want States . . . ," p. 6-7.
4. Frank Feather, *The Future Consumer,* p. 139.
5. Feather, *The Future Consumer,* p.141.
6. Feather, *The Future Consumer,* p.142.
7. Feather, *The Future Consumer,* p.144.
8. Feather, *The Future Consumer,* p.139.

Bibliography

Chapter 1

Peters, Tom, and Robert Waterman. *In Search of Excellence.* New York: Harper & Row Publishers, 1982.

Peters, Tom, Julien Phillips and Robert Waterman. "Structure is Not Organization." *Business Horizons.* June 1980.

Chapter 2

Batten, J.D. *Tough-Minded Management.* New York: American Management Association, 1963.

Buchanan, Paul C. *The Leader and Individual Motivation.* New York: Association Press, 1962.

Chinelly, John V. Sr. *The Meaning of Management.* Miramar, Fla.: Chinelly Real Estate, Inc.

"Crazy Times Call For Crazy Organizations." *The Tom Peters Seminar.* In *Working Woman* (August 1994).

Katz, Robert L. "Skills of an Effective Administrator." *Harvard Business Review* (Sept.-Oct. 1974).

Knowles, Malcolm and Hilda. *How to Develop Better Leaders.* New York: Association Press, 1956.

Peters, Tom, Julien Phillips and Robert Waterman. "Structure is Not Organization." In *Business Horizons* (June 1980).

Schultz, Dr. Whitt N. *Bits and Pieces.* Fairfield, N.J.: Economics Press, 1973.

Tannenbaum, Robert, Irving Wechsler and Fred Massarik. *Leadership and Organization.* New York: McGraw-Hill, 1961.

Townsend, Robert. *Up the Organization.* New York: Alfred A. Knopf, 1970.

Chapter 3

Tannehill, Robert E. *Job Enrichment: The Modern, Proven Method to Motivate Your Employees.* Chicago: The Dartnell Corp., 1974.

Chapter 5

French, Wendell L. *The Personnel Management Process.* Boston: Houghton-Mifflin, 1970.

Reyhons, Ken. *Recruiting Sales Associates.* 2d ed. Chicago: Real Estate Brokerage Managers Council, 1990.

Sweet, Donald H. *The Modern Employment Function.* Reading, Mass.: Addison-Wesley, 1973.

Yorks, Lyle. "Let's Change the Job—Not the Man." In *Real Estate Today* (Jan. 1974).

Chapter 6

Batten, J.D. *Tough-Minded Management*. New York: American Management Association, 1963.

Blanchard, Kenneth, and Patricia and Drea Zigarmi. *Leadership and the One-Minute Manager*. New York: Morrow, 1985.

Career Proficiency Evaluation Program, The. El Paso, Tex.: Vocational Research Data Complex, Inc., 1975.

Ellis, Steven K. *How To Survive a Training Assignment: A Practical Guide for New Part-Time or Temporary Trainers*. New York: Addison-Wesley, 1988.

Fear, Richard A. *The Evaluation Interview*. New York: McGraw-Hill, 1973.

Fear, Richard A., and Byron Jordan. *Employee Evaluation Manual for Interviewers*. New York: The Psychological Corporation, 1943.

"Guidelines on Employee Selection Procedures." Equal Employee Opportunity Commission, Federal Register. Aug.1, 1970.

Hall, Ed. *It's Showtime*. Winfield, Ill.: Benchmarks for Success, Ltd., 1991.

Lyman, Howard B. *Test Scores and What They Mean*. Englewood Cliffs, N.J.: Prentice Hall, 1971.

McGregor, Douglas. *The Human Side of Enterprise*. New York: McGraw-Hill, 1960.

Maltz, Maxwell. *Psycho-Cybernetics*. Englewood Cliffs, N.J.: Prentice Hall, 1960.

Mayer, David G., and Herbert M. Greenberg. "How to Choose a Good Salesman." In *Real Estate Today* (Jan. 1970).

Multiple Personal Inventory. Princeton, N.J.: Marketing Survey and Research Corp., 1956.

Porter, Arthur. *Cybernetics Simplified*. New York: Barnes & Noble, 1970.

Porter, Henry. "Manage Your Sales Force as a System." In *Harvard Business Review* (Mar./Apr. 1975.).

Roberts, Don C. "Testing for Real Estate Sales Ability." In *The Texas REALTOR*® (May 1973).

Screening and Selecting Successful Real Estate Salespeople. El Paso, Tex.: Vocational Research Data Complex, Inc., 1974.

Tatsuoka, Maurice M. *What is Job Relevance?* Champaign, Ill.: Institute for Personality and Ability Testing, 1973.

Chapter 7

North, William D. "How to Choose What's Right for You." In *Real Estate Today* (Aug. 1974).

Chapter 8

Behavioral Sciences Newsletter (Sept. 23, 1974).

Stone, David. *Training Manual for Real Estate Salesmen*. Englewood Cliffs, N.J.: Prentice Hall, 1965.

REALTORS National Marketing Institute®. Training films, 1968–1975.

Chapter 9

Maltz, Maxwell. *Creative Living for Today*. New York: Simon & Schuster, 1967.

Chapter 10

Bolton, Robert, and Dorothy Grover Bolton. *Social Style/Management Style.* New York: American Management Association, 1984.

Boorman, Howells, Nichols and Shapiro. "Interpersonal Communications in Modern Organizations." In *Behavioral Sciences Newsletter.* Glen Rock, N.J.

Chase, Stuart. *The Tyranny of Words.* New York: Harcourt, Brace and World, 1938.

Fast, Julius. *Body Language.* New York: Pocket Books, 1971.

Flesch, Rudolph. *How To Write, Speak and Think More Effectively.* New York: New American Library, 1963.

Giffon and Patton. *Fundamentals of Interpersonal Communication.* New York: Harper & Row, 1971.

Goldhaber, F.M. *Organizational Communications.* Dubuque, Iowa: Wm. C. Brown, 1974.

Harriman, Bruce. "Up and Down the Communications Ladder." In *Harvard Business Review* (Sept./Oct. 1974).

Hayakawa, S.I. *Language in Thought and Action.* New York: Harcourt Brace & Co., 1972.

Keltner, J.W. *Elements of Interpersonal Communication.* Belmont, Calif.: Wadsworth, 1973.

Lee, Irving J. *Language Habits in Human Affairs.* New York: Harper and Co., 1941.

Nichols and Stevens. *Are You Listening?* New York: McGraw-Hill, 1957.

Sigband, Norman B. *Communication for Management.* Glenview, Ill.: Scott, Foresman, 1969.

Sigband, Norman B. *Management Communications for Decision Making.* Los Angeles: School-Industrial Press, 1973.

Work Institute of America. *The Manager as Trainer, Coach and Leader.* Scarsdale, N.Y.: Work Institute of America, 1991.

Chapter 11

Brown, Stanley M., ed. *Business Executive Handbook.* Englewood Cliffs, N.J.: Prentice Hall, 1953.

Burns, Bill. "Psychologist in the Lineup." In *Human Behavior.* Los Angeles: Manson Western Corp., June 1973.

Cyr, John E. *Training and Supervising Real Estate Salesmen.* Englewood Cliffs, N.J.: Prentice Hall, 1973.

Dawson, Peter F. *Managing for Results.* New York: Harper & Row, 1964.

Maltz, Maxwell. *Psycho-Cybernetics.* Englewood Cliffs, N.J.: Prentice Hall, 1960.

May, Rollo. *Existential Psychology.* New York: Random House, 1961.

Meyer, Paul. "Dynamics of Motivational Development." Waco, Tex.: Sales Motivation Institute.

"Probing Opinion." *Harvard Business Review* (Mar./Apr. 1974).

Saint Laurent, Henri. "What It Takes to Star in Selling." *Salesman's Opportunity Magazine* (Mar. 1974).

Smith, Charles M. "Goal Setting, the Attainable Dream." In *Real Estate Today* (Mar. 1974).

Wooden, John. *They Call Me Coach.* New York: Bantam, 1973.

Chapter 12

"A Historical Look at Salaried Compensation." In *Management Issues and Trends* 8, no. 4.

Cocks, David, and Larry Laframboise. *Compensation Planning: The Key to Profitability.* Chicago: Real Estate Brokerage Managers Council, 1995.

Management Issues and Trends 9, no. 5.

McCafferty, Jack. "Succeed with Salaries." In *Management Issues and Trends* 9, no. 5.

Schmaedick, Ron. "Switching to a 100 Percent Plan—An Inside Look at RAMS Realty, Inc." In *Management Issues and Trends* 9, no. 5.

Chapter 13

An Accounting System for Real Estate Brokers. Chicago: National Association of REALTORS®, 1972.

Backer, Morton. *Modern Accounting Theory.* Englewood Cliffs, N.J.: Prentice Hall, 1966.

Bierman and Dyckman. *Managerial Accounting.* New York: Macmillan, 1971.

Cost of a Salesman's Desk. Chicago: National Association of REALTORS®, 1972.

Dixon, R. *Essentials of Accounting.* New York: Macmillan, 1966.

Dixon, Robert L. *The Executive's Accounting Primer.* New York: McGraw-Hill, 1971.

Heckert, Josiah B. *Accounting Systems.* New York: Ronald Press, 1967.

Steffey, John W. "Creating a Budget That Works." In *Real Estate Today* (Aug. 1974).

Wixon, Rufus. *Principles of Accounting.* New York: Ronald Press, 1969.

Chapter 14

Case, Fred E. "Real Estate Economics: Market Analysis." In *California Real Estate Magazine* (Nov. 1974).

Drucker, Peter. *Management: Tasks—Responsibilities—Practices.* New York: Harper & Row.

Peckham, Jack M. III. "Real Estate Investment Newsletter." In *Real Estate Today* (Sept. 1974).

Real Estate Advertising Ideas. Chicago: REALTORS National Marketing Institute®, 1973.

Chapter 17

Boyce, Byrl N., and Stephen D. Messner. *Management of an Appraisal Firm.* Chicago: Society of Real Estate Appraisers, 1972.

Harrison, Henry S. *Houses: The Illustrated Guide to Construction, Design & Systems.* 2d ed. Chicago: Real Estate Education Company, 1992.

Managing an Appraisal Office. Chicago: American Institute of Real Estate Appraisers, 1971.

The Real Estate Management Department—How to Establish and Operate It. Chicago: Institute of Real Estate Management, 1967.

Chapter 21

"Consumers Want States To Put More Resources Behind Real Estate Regulators." In *Real Estate Insider* (Dec. 15, 1995).

Feather, Frank. *The Future Consumer.* Los Angeles: Warwick Publishing, Inc., 1994.

Pivar, William H., and Donald L. Harlan. *Real Estate Ethics: Good Ethics = Good Business.* 3d ed. Chicago: Real Estate Education Company, 1995.

"Teacher Gives Real Estate Agents Below-Average Grades on Ethics." In *The Wall Street Journal* (July 26, 1994).

Index